"This comprehensive and fascinating journey through the unique landscape of the Weird West analyzes texts from a fresh perspective that resonate with social issues of the present day. From Native American and African American representation to sexual and racial identity, this book will inspire further research and discussion."
—PAUL GREEN, author of *Encyclopedia of Weird Westerns*

"This wide-ranging interdisciplinary collection stretches the genre boundaries of the Western into the speculative and the weird and in so doing enables us to think differently and better—uncannily—about its deep history and its often unquestioned ideological assumptions."
—NEIL CAMPBELL, author of *The Rhizomatic West: Representing the American West in a Transnational, Global, Media Age*

"*Weird Westerns* is brave, original, and timely. The editors have compiled an assortment of rich, insightful, and daring scholarship that applies multiple theoretical approaches to the shifting landscapes of the (Weird) Western."
—MONICA MONTELONGO FLORES, assistant professor of English at California State University, Stanislaus

"This exciting volume showed me how 'weird' the complex Western genre has always been: thankfully never living up to what so many pretend it is. With essays by established scholars and illuminating newcomers to the field, we see how the Western has always played, indeed depended, upon questions of race and gender to make sense of itself and of the cultures we live in. It will be a go-to book in the thriving field of western U.S. literary and cultural studies."
—WILLIAM R. HANDLEY, coeditor of *True West: Authenticity and the American West*

WEIRD WESTERNS

POSTWESTERN HORIZONS

General Editor
William R. Handley
University of Southern California

Series Editors
José Aranda
Rice University

Melody Graulich
Utah State University

Thomas King
University of Guelph

Rachel Lee
University of California, Los Angeles

Nathaniel Lewis
Saint Michael's College

Stephen Tatum
University of Utah

WEIRD WESTERNS

RACE, GENDER, GENRE

Edited by KERRY FINE, MICHAEL K. JOHNSON,
REBECCA M. LUSH, and SARA L. SPURGEON

University of Nebraska Press | Lincoln

© 2020 by the Board of Regents of
the University of Nebraska

All rights reserved. ∞

Library of Congress
Cataloging-in-Publication Data
Names: Fine, Kerry, 1974–, editor. | Johnson,
Michael K. (Michael Kyle), 1963–, editor. | Lush,
Rebecca M., editor. | Spurgeon, Sara L., editor.
Title: Weird Westerns: race, gender, genre
/ edited by Kerry Fine, Michael K. Johnson,
Rebecca M. Lush, and Sara L. Spurgeon.
Description: Lincoln: University of Nebraska
Press, [2020] | Series: Postwestern horizons |
Includes bibliographical references and index.
Identifiers: LCCN 2019035378
ISBN 9781496221162 (hardback)
ISBN 9781496221780 (paperback)
ISBN 9781496221742 (epub)
ISBN 9781496221759 (mobi)
ISBN 9781496221766 (pdf)
Subjects: LCSH: Western stories—History and
criticism. | Western television programs—
United States—History and criticism. | Western
films—United States—History and criticism. |
Race in literature. | Women in literature. | Race
on television. | Women on television. | Race in
motion pictures. | Women in motion pictures. |
West (U.S.)—In literature.
Classification: LCC PS374.W4 W37 2020 |
DDC 809.3/874—dc23
LC record available at
https://lccn.loc.gov/2019035378

Set in Scala OT by Laura Buis.
Designed by L. Auten.

CONTENTS

Introduction: Westworld(s): Race, Gender, Genre in the Weird Western 1
MICHAEL K. JOHNSON, REBECCA M. LUSH, AND SARA L. SPURGEON

Part 1. The Weird West, Past and Present

1. Attack of the Monstrous Vegetable: Bret Harte's Pioneer Nightmare and "Miscegenation" Dream 39
TARA PENRY

2. Strange Country: Sexuality and the Feminine in Robert Coover's *Ghost Town* 67
ERIC MELJAC AND ALEX HUNT

3. A Selective History: Identity and Identification in "Deadlands" 92
NICHOLAS WILLIAM MOLL

Part 2. Native Reclamations and Representations

4. Mongrel Transmotion: The Werewolf and the Were/Wear/Where-West in Stephen Graham Jones's *Mongrels* 119
JOSHUA T. ANDERSON

5. Indianizing the Western: Semiotic Tricksterism
   in William Sanders's *Journey to Fusang* 150
   SARA L. SPURGEON

6. Magnificence and Metas in
   Professional Westerns 174
   DOMINO RENEE PEREZ

Part 3. Surrogate *indians* and Other Indigenous Metaphors

7. Defamiliarizing the Western on
   the Extraterrestrial Frontier: Jonathan
   Lethem's *Girl in Landscape*. 199
   JOHANNES FEHRLE

8. Shining the Light of Civilization: The Savage
   Other of the Frontier in *Firefly* and *Serenity* 231
   MEREDITH HARVEY

9. Racial Metaphors and Vanishing *indians* in
   Wynonna Earp, *Buffy the Vampire Slayer*,
   and Emma Bull's *Territory* 255
   REBECCA M. LUSH

Part 4. The African American Presence in the Weird Western

10. The Mad Black Woman in
    Stephen King's *The Dark Tower*. 289
    JACOB BURG

11. *Uncle Tom's Cabin* Showdown: Stowe, Tarantino,
    and the Minstrelsy of the Weird West. 313
    JOSHUA D. SMITH

12. Race and Gender in the
    Time Travel Western 348
    MICHAEL K. JOHNSON

Part 5. The Undead in the Weird Western

13. Go West, Old Man: Or, Buffalo Bill and
    the "Yellow Peril" in *Zeppelins West* 375
    CYNTHIA J. MILLER AND A. BOWDOIN VAN RIPER

14. AMC's *The Walking Dead* and the Restructuring
    of Gender and Race on the Neofrontier 397
    SCOTT PEARCE

    Afterword: This Is (Not) the End. 433
    STEPHEN GRAHAM JONES

    Contributors 437
    Index 443

WEIRD WESTERNS

Introduction

Westworld(s): Race, Gender, Genre in the Weird Western

MICHAEL K. JOHNSON, REBECCA M. LUSH,
AND SARA L. SPURGEON

> These violent delights have violent ends.
> —William Shakespeare, *Romeo and Juliet*,
> quoted in HBO's *Westworld*

The western may call up images of Monument Valley, tumbling tumbleweeds, high-noon shoot-outs, and romanticized "cowboys and Indians" versions of the attempted genocide of indigenous peoples. The genre has also been used by a wide range of authors and filmmakers to communicate myriad contradictory, sometimes even decolonizing, visions. While the classic western has largely been associated with a mythic view of the violent colonization of the nineteenth-century American West, its powerful, evocative, and surprisingly flexible tropes have resulted in infinite revisions and critiques. More than a hundred years after the official close of the last frontier in the American West, and despite being ostensibly anchored to a particular geographic location and a fairly precise point in history, the genre continues to be reinvented and hybridized.

In one of the genre's most recent reincarnations, the science fiction and horror western thriller series *Westworld* (2016–present), which HBO describes as being "set at the intersection of the near future and the reimagined past," the wealthy guests that visit the high-tech amusement park pay for the chance to "live without limits in a world where every human appetite can be indulged."[1] It seems telling that the American West and the western genre feature squarely as theme-park experiences where people (mainly wealthy, white, and male) can live out their fantasy lives in an imaginary past with the aid of futuristic technology. The western genre, even when it purports "realism," is often deeply rooted in fantasy and has always shared many elements with its historical sibling, science fiction. And, as Cynthia Miller and Bowdoin Van Riper demonstrate in the two volumes of the critical anthology series *Undead in the West* (2012), "the undead have put the 'wild' back in the Wild West in ways never envisioned in traditional Western tales yet oddly resonant with them."[2] Perhaps one of the distinctive features of the western, as important as the showdown or the desert landscape, is its ability to form unexpected combinations with other genres, and the odd resonance those combinations create between the different genres.

This volume, which analyzes texts as wide-ranging as nineteenth-century literary westerns, supernatural horror westerns, space westerns, alt-history westerns, steampunk westerns, and westerns from the field of Indigenous Futurism, examines the ways authors, filmmakers, and game makers have reimagined the western in tandem with speculative literary traditions. Sometimes these texts function to reinforce the traditional depiction of race and gender in the American West and at other times challenge how race and gender have been operationalized in portrayals of this region (both as it exists in our real world and as it gets imagined in speculative texts) and within the genre of the western. Our collection is attentive especially to how issues of power and privilege are portrayed in "weird westerns," which we define as texts that utilize a hybrid genre format, blending canonical elements of the western with either science fiction, fantasy, horror, or some other component of speculative literature.

We occasionally use the word "Indian" in this introduction in full awareness that Gerald Vizenor (Anishinaabe) has argued repeatedly and convincingly that it is a strictly European term intended to erase the varied cultures of native inhabitants of the Americas. Nomenclature has been historically defined and confined by colonialist structures, and word choice, grammar, and capitalization can inform colonial versus decolonizing approaches.[3] Because many of the texts studied by us and the contributors to this collection pre-date other usages, and since there is no universally agreed-upon term to refer to the indigenous peoples of the Americas within native communities today, depending on the context of our discussion we will utilize the terms "Native American," "American Indian," "native," and "Indigenous." Academic discourses will frequently vacillate between Native American or American Indian, particularly depending on the publication date of a work or in-house press style rules. Some scholars, writers, and community members prefer "American Indian" because this is the language used in government-to-government treaties between the United States and tribal nations and thus aligns with discussions of sovereignty. The term "American Indian" also carries with it the political legacy and activism of the American Indian Movement. When possible, we and the contributors to this volume provide tribal affiliation in lieu of more generic nomenclature in order to counter the pan-Indianism endemic to the western genre.

Paul Green writes in *The Encyclopedia of Weird Westerns* (2009) that the weird west or the weird western is "a comparatively recent label of a genre that incorporates supernatural, fantasy and sci-fi elements in a Western frontier theme."[4] The weirdness of westerns is multifold, particularly as it relates to issues of race and gender. However, to best understand how science fiction, fantasy, and the supernatural "weird" the western, a general overview of more traditional westerns and their relationship to race and gender is in order.

Western Expansion: The Western Genre Past and Present

In highlighting the potent contradictions at the heart of the western and the geography and history from which it springs, Jane Tompkins argues that the genre utilizes the invasion and conquest of what we now call the American West in such a way that the region itself paradoxically "functions as a symbol of freedom, and of the opportunity for conquest."[5] In its glorification of acts of white male violence and frequent denigration of the feminine, she continues, "the Western *answers* the domestic novel," shaping popular notions about what acceptable femininity and masculinity look like in the United States from the nineteenth through the twentieth centuries.[6] John Wayne, Tompkins points out, "the actor whose name is synonymous with Western films, became *the* symbol of American masculinity from World War II to Vietnam," whether Wayne played a gun-slinging outlaw (as in the most popular movie of 1939, *Stagecoach*), a gun-slinging lawman (as in 1959's *Rio Bravo*), or a gun-slinging outlaw who becomes a gun-slinging lawman (as in 1969's *True Grit*).[7] The western, in other words, is a genre obsessed with the violence necessary to police the borders of white American masculinity as those borders grind against gender and racial identities, cultural and social identities, Native American frontiers and national borderlands, and imaginary lines between civilization and savagery, freedom and conquest.

The exact origins of the western are a matter of some debate. Lee Clark Mitchell, like many scholars, credits James Fenimore Cooper with having "cleared the ground for the genre in his celebration of frontier landscapes, feats of violence, and masculine self-construction" arguing that Cooper's Leatherstocking Tales, which begin in 1823 with *The Pioneers* and include his most popular work, *The Last of the Mohicans* (1826), provide "the model on which all other attempts. . . . will be practiced."[8] This model, like many westerns that follow it, includes a beautiful but hostile wilderness, Indians as noble savages, Indians as savage savages, captive white women, tragic mixed-race women, and brave white male rescuers with very large guns.

Importantly, however, Mitchell also maintains that the fact that none of the Leatherstocking Tales were actually set in the geographical Far West of North America is irrelevant to their classification as westerns.[9] *The Last of the Mohicans*, like Charlotte Lennox's 1750 novel *The Life of Harriot Stuart*, which Marta Kvande and Sara Spurgeon argue is actually the first published western, takes place in colonial-era upstate New York.[10] What is important about landscape in a western, according to Mitchell, is that it consistently presents "the opportunity for renewal, for self-transformation, for release from constraints associated with an urbanized East" frequently representative of a supposedly emasculating, effeminate civilization the white male hero is both escaping and defending.[11] As *Star Trek* creator Gene Roddenberry (among many other writers of science fiction) understood, however, the transformational western landscape with its all-important frontier between civilization and savagery can easily be projected beyond North America—into outer space, for example, still carrying with it the classic western's images, ideas, and values into a far future setting—or, conversely, moved right back to the dusty confines of nineteenth-century Arizona for a battle between *Cowboys & Aliens* (2011).

In its most traditional format, the western is a mythic blend that romanticizes settler colonialism. Whether it's Cooper's Leatherstocking Tales or revisionist takes such as *Little Big Man* (1970), a core issue in many westerns is the paradox of championing white characters that perform stereotypical "*indian*-ness" while denigrating Native characters. Gender also has a contradictory position in many westerns where the (hyper)masculinity of characters as wide-ranging as Cooper's Indian-loving/Indian fighting Hawk-eye and John Wayne's Confederate officer Ethan Edwards (in John Ford's 1954 *The Searchers*, frequently called the greatest western film of all time) paradoxically keeps them from fully performing heteronormative roles such as husband or father.

Natty Bumppo (also known as Hawk-eye and Leatherstocking in Cooper's novels) dresses in buckskin and shares a cultural kinship with the Mohicans Chingachgook and his son Uncas. He speaks several Native American languages and lives his life in what Cooper imagines to be an indigenous manner, roaming the forested wilderness hunting deer with his Mohican companions, even while talking obsessively about the purity of his white racial identity as a "man without a cross." His manliness is defined in direct relation to his Indian-ness. This renders him, however, culturally if not racially crossed. Like the figure of the "tragic mulatta," he is at once too Indian to marry a white woman, but too white to marry an Indian woman. Annette Kolodny argues that he is, instead, married to the feminized wilderness itself. She writes that "implicit in the metaphor of the land-as-woman was both the regressive pull of maternal containment and the seductive invitation to sexual assertion," leaving no room for any appropriate human woman.[12] In his deep connection to both "vanishing" natives and their wilderness home—a space contradictorily imagined as at once fruitful mother and seductive virgin—Hawk-eye is therefore doomed to his mournful, solitary retreat westward across the continent, simultaneously rejecting the feminized and feminizing white civilization he is "clearing the ground for," as Mitchell puts it.[13] He uses his knowledge of Indian ways to become the ultimate Indian fighter, inviting the Anglo-European destruction of the feminized Indian wilderness he loves, even as his Indianized hypermasculinity forbids his entrance into the white domesticity he battles to protect.

Kolodny addresses this paradox of white frontier masculinity, the conflicting drives to both love and violently conquer the west, writing that "in destroying the landscape that had once promised virtually every satisfaction men have sought, men simultaneously destroy something precious, desirable and vulnerable within themselves."[14] We see this in many a manly western hero's rejection of female domesticity as he turns from his lovelorn sweetheart (saloon girl, rancher's daughter, schoolmarm) to ride off into the sunset. His lonesome ride away from romance, marriage, and family is not always solitary, however. Since the western hero's companion generally cannot be a woman, the world of the classic western is mainly homosocial and often homoerotic, with male characters cooking, riding, and even bathing together, as with Hawk-eye and Chingachgook, the Lone Ranger and Tonto, Butch Cassidy and the Sundance Kid, and the boy gangs of *The Magnificent Seven* (1960), *The Wild Bunch* (1969), and *Tombstone* (1993). Female characters, if they are present at all, tend to function in the classic western as foils or rescue objects, with the role of companion or sidekick to the white male hero generally filled by another man, such as *Star Trek*'s First Officer Spock to Captain Kirk.

While the homoerotic aspects of westerns have been openly explored in Ang Lee's 2005 *Brokeback Mountain* (based on the short story by

Annie Proulx) and contemporary weird westerns such as HBO's *Westworld* continue to openly embrace queer sexualities, they are often barely disguised in earlier texts such as *The Virginian, Riders of the Purple Sage,* and *Shane*.[15] Paul Varner, among others, has written extensively about what he refers to as "the invisible culture" of gay cowboys and queer sexualities in many classic western films and novels, and, concomitantly, their stringent attempts at denying their queerness.[16] In 1948's *Red River*, another John Wayne vehicle, two handsome young cowboys meet on a cattle drive and admire each other's guns: each man pulls his six-shooter from its holster and hands it over to the other to be weighed and fondled before they fire off together in a spontaneous bout of target practice, with each man shooting the other's weapon. Although Varner notes that this scene is almost comically "charged with homoeroticism," he also points out that *Red River* and other western films offer "equivocating attitudes toward sexually subversive cowboys [that] come in large part from the definition of their leading men as marginal outsiders."[17]

As with the contemporary "bury your gays" trope, these characters frequently die tragically at the end—lambs, according to Varner, "sacrificed to Hollywood's fear of the queer."[18] Matt (Montgomery Clift) in *Red River* is an exception, but only because he is saved by the return of the pretty Tess Millay (Joanne Dru), who successfully pleads for his life, throwing over him a thin cloak of face-saving heteronormativity, although this scene contrasts with one earlier in the film. After she has aggressively pursued the disinterested Matt, Tess takes advantage of a heavy nighttime fog to snuggle close to him. He lies passively in her arms, determinedly staring away from her, talking instead about the actual object of his passion: the domineering, hypermasculine Dunson (John Wayne). "You love him, don't you," Tess murmurs. "And he must love you." While the homoeroticism of the film can hardly be called hidden at this point, it is certainly mediated (or even triangulated, to evoke Eve Kosofky Sedgwick) by the presence of Tess, highlighting another role of women in classic westerns: to act as heterosexual window dressing, safely establishing the male hero's straight identity, thus freeing the film to focus on its true obsession—men's relationships with other men.

While the western's primary preoccupation, especially in its most classic form, may appear to be with masculinity, plenty of westerns have featured women in prominent roles, as reflected in feminist studies of the genre. Women writers' responses and the representation of women in westerns can reinforce the patriarchal, heteronormative, settler-colonial fantasies that abound in classic westerns, particularly when considering Amy Kaplan's argument for women's "manifest domesticity."[19] However, there also exists a robust pattern of women authors pushing back against patriarchal versions of frontier life (and its complex entanglement of racial and gender anxieties) in westerns produced from the nineteenth century to today. In 1891, just a year before publishing her now-iconic short story "The Yellow Wallpaper" in the *New England Magazine*, Charlotte Perkins Gilman placed in the same journal an eerie, ghost-story frontier tale called "The Giant Wistaria." As Jana Koehler notes, "While the home is typically configured in opposition to a hostile, uncivilized frontier in western literature, Gilman. . . . demonstrate[s] that the home itself is a frontier, one which is often brutal and destructive to women."[20] Koehler also analyzes the weird western fiction of Dorothy Scarborough, pointing out that her 1925 novel *The Wind* "offers a profoundly feminist critique of the West by pairing the supernatural with western tropes to challenge gender roles and white, middle class values."[21] Illustrating the increasingly close relationship between literary and filmic westerns (weird and otherwise), *The Wind* was adapted to the big screen in 1928 and remade in 2018. The screenplay for the 1928 version was coauthored and produced by Lillian Gish, who also starred as main character Letty, a Virginian who goes to live on an isolated ranch in Texas where she is eventually driven to madness and murder by the incessant, seemingly sentient wind. One of the few western films written by women (Frances Marion coauthored the script with Gish), it was the last silent film released by MGM, and, despite a mixed reception upon its release, it is remembered today as one of the greatest examples of the silent film era, although its feminist critique of life on the Texas frontier is only rarely discussed.

Weirding the Western: A Glance at History

In its earliest usage, "weird" as an adjective carried connotations of the supernatural, such as the "weird sisters" of Shakespeare's *Macbeth*—the witchy women who double, double toil and trouble the fate of the play's title character. By the nineteenth century, "weird" was increasingly used as an adjective before "fiction" to refer to speculative literature—that is to say, works about the strange and fantastic. Weird fiction, later dubbed "speculative literature," was the offspring of the gothic (a genre also obsessed with race, gender, and repressed sexualities) and blossomed into not only tales of the supernatural but all manner of the fantastic, including science fiction, time travel (or slipstream), horror, fantasy, and more. Examples of what we would now call "weird westerns" can be found in eras prior to the coinage of the term (or even "speculative literature"). Charles Brockden Brown's sleepwalking titular character *Edgar Huntly* (1799) inhabits a horrific and dreamlike early American gothic frontier where possible supernatural occurrences serve to highlight the tensions between the Lenni Lenape and the white settlers invading their land. This text foreshadows the key place that race will continue to have in subsequent weird westerns. Likewise, Charlotte Perkins Gilman's protofeminist novella *Herland* (1915) engages with the weird western by imagining a form of westward expansion where the Californian narrator travels into parts supposedly unknown and finds an all-female society that has arguably achieved harmony in part due to parthenogenesis. Gilman's *Herland* explores some of the same issues covered in the postmodern absurdism of British novelist Angela Carter's *The Passion of New Eve* (1977). In Carter's novel a British man, Evelyn, travels from New York to California. In the desert of the American West, he encounters Mother, a self-fashioned mythological being who transforms the male-bodied Evelyn into the female-bodied "Eve," who later tangles with a "gross parody of pioneers" and goes on a series of increasingly bizarre dystopian episodes.[22] Neither Gilman nor

Carter are traditionally considered western writers, yet they both use the backdrop of the American West to expose gendered violence and patriarchal oppression. In the same way that Brown's novel highlights the centrality of race to the weird western, Gilman's and Carter's works emphasize that the persistent weirding of gender and sexuality issues—from parthenogenesis to supernaturally driven sex-reassignments—are also commonplace in a wide range of weird westerns. Thus, when we consider Paul Green's direct definition of the "weird western" we should also bear in mind that it is a weirding (i.e., adding the supernatural, science fiction, horror, etc.) to an already weird (i.e., strange, unusual, and oddly inconsistent) genre.

The weirdness of the western is also suggested by its continuing ability to survive and return despite frequent declarations of its death. As Neil Campbell points out in "Post-Western Cinema" (2011), if the western is a "'dead' genre," it is one that "refuses to remain dead."[23] It has survived by "traveling across generic boundaries, poaching and borrowing from many different earlier traditions . . . returning and haunting American and global cultures in various forms."[24] The weird western literalizes Campbell's metaphorical rendering of the western as an undead genre, haunting and haunted, and provides further evidence to support his argument that the western has survived by crossing generic boundaries and by borrowing from different traditions. Particularly when the weird western's borrowing involves drawing from ethnic literary and cultural traditions, we may not even recognize those texts as westerns, classifying them as Afrofuturism or Indigenous Futurism, but failing to see the way those texts are also involved in reconfiguring the western.

The western, Campbell argues, has "shown a remarkable 'impurity,' over-spilling its boundaries," evolving into what he calls the "post-western," a type of genre text that is involved in "a sort of participation without belonging—a taking part in without being part of."[25] The post-western, which is and is not a western, is notable for its "inherent strange familiarity," its weirdness in comparison to classical forms of the genre.[26] The post-western is an intentionally strange, even uncanny genre, and it continually draws our attention to that strangeness, sometimes through the "deliberate jarring of expectations," often accomplished through the juxtaposition of seemingly clashing elements—from "*Lonely are the Brave*'s horse on the highway" to the "tumbleweed tumbling across a desert landscape" to arrive at a view "looking down onto Los Angeles' neon sprawl" in *The Big Lebowski* (1998).[27] The "strange familiarity" created by such juxtapositions, Campbell argues, jars the viewer "into a space of reflection, a critical dialogue with the form, its assumptions and histories," moving us "to think differently and better" about not only the history and assumptions of the genre itself but also about the historical realities that westerns mirror back to us.[28] Unlike, say, many science fiction narratives that conceal their western roots by substituting distant planets for western frontiers and ray guns for six-shooters, the weird western draws our attention to its acts of borrowing (as in the television series *Firefly*, transporting rustled cattle in the hold of a space ship) and its audacious generic joinings, inviting us to recognize genre conventions as conventions and actively participate in their interrogation.

Such audacious joinings, however, are much older than the genre designation "weird western." Because the western and science fiction, for example, are both so tightly bound to European and Euro-American colonizing projects, John Rieder, among others, suggests that the two genres cannot be separated. His *Colonialism and the Emergence of Science-Fiction* (2008) explains that science fiction and the western both enter popular culture in the latter half of the nineteenth century, a time that witnesses the height of European and U.S. imperial expansion, and concomitantly the first signs of the faltering of traditional empires around the globe. Not surprisingly, it is an era of extreme anxiety in the United States and Europe regarding empire and race, as well as masculinity and the "woman question." Rieder points out that early science fiction first emerges "in those countries most heavily involved in imperialist projects," first France and England, and soon after in Germany and the United States, adding that "allusions to colonial history and situations are ubiquitous features of early science fiction motifs and plots."²⁹ Although the earliest westerns spring directly from the experience of the Anglo-European invasion of North America, the most well-known of these early invade-and-colonize tropes in science fiction is H. G. Wells's *The War of the Worlds* (1897), in which Wells uses his introduction to explicitly compare a Martian invasion of Earth to the Dutch and British invasions of Tasmania and the accompanying genocide of Tasmania's aboriginal people. In the main text of *The War of the Worlds* this racial dynamic is disguised, although Wells is quite obvious in his introduction about his intention to use his tale of alien invasion and slaughter as a means of critiquing European colonialism. Indeed, Robert Murray Davis notes in "The Frontiers of Genre: Science-Fiction Westerns" (1985) that the two genres share "not only plot devices and character types but a common setting on the frontier, a common theme of survival, and a common mechanism in which force is sanctioned as a means of survival."³⁰

Not surprisingly then, when writers of color, particularly indigenous ones, produce works that fall into the category of science fiction or the western, the tropes they use may look the same on the outside, but, as Campbell suggests, they are also often weirded in powerful, defamiliarizing, and even decolonizing ways. In Hugo Award–winner Rebecca Roanhorse's (Ohkay Owingeh-African American) Indigenous Futurism novel *Trail of Lightning* (2018), the female Native American heroine, Maggie Hoskie, a kind of Navajo outlaw with a heart of gold, reluctantly hunts and kills mythic indigenous monsters that roam the postapocalyptic American West.³¹ She describes for readers the newest iteration of a violent frontier that exists in what used to be called New Mexico and Arizona, explaining that "Tse Bonito is still more Wild West frontier town than anything else. Bunch of cowboys and Indians, although everyone's pretty much Diné [Navajo]. Last time I came through here looking for a Bad Man, I ended up in a shootout that felt more like the OK Corral than a monster hunt."³² When the trickster Coyote appears in *Trail of Lightning*, he is dressed in the style of a western gambler, his dandyish clothing underscoring his potential for duplicity and untrustworthiness: "He wore a dapper gentlemen's suit right out of the Old

West . . . He was every inch the gentleman scoundrel from some old Hollywood Western."[33] Having the novel's most untrustworthy character wearing western garb—and, specifically, western garb that the narrator describes as a movie costume—perhaps also suggests Roanhorse's own ambivalence about the western form (one of many genres she puts into play in her novel): it may be charming and powerful, but be careful about believing that it is on your side.

While *Trail of Lightning* is part of what is now termed Indigenous Futurism, that genre classification itself draws from Afrofuturism, a term coined by culture and media critic Mark Dery in his 1993 essay "Black to the Future." Afrofuturism is concerned with a cultural aesthetic expressed in literature, art, music, and film that explicitly engages the experience of the African diaspora through a technocultural, science fiction lens and poses a direct critique of both typical white historical interpretations of the African diaspora and the black experience, as well as common presentations of blackness as either absence or alien grotesque in much white science fiction. The term "Indigenous Futurism" first appears in print in the 2012 collection *Walking the Clouds: An Anthology of Indigenous Science Fiction*, edited by Grace Dillon (Anishinaabe). As with westerns written by indigenous authors, Indigenous Futurism texts seek to counter the effects of imagining Natives through the lens of colonial tropes. Employed especially in white-authored science fiction, these tropes render indigenous people virtually absent from imagined future worlds (not unlike the western's own "vanishing Indian" trope) except on the rare occasions when, as in Edgar Rice Burroughs's *John Carter of Mars* stories (1912–46) or James Cameron's *Avatar* (2009), both sci-fi westerns, they are invoked as primitive aliens in need of a white (male, human) savior lest they vanish into their own pasts like their supposedly extinct earthly counterparts.

Gerald Vizenor notes the uncanny similarity between Indians and aliens in the white imagination, writing that both "aliens and *indians*[34] are simulations of the other in stories and narratives."[35] The mythic view of the historical nineteenth-century period most frequently glorified in the classic western reinforced the stereotype of the "vanishing race"; thus, it can be difficult for non-Native communities even today to recognize native-authored texts as westerns, even when, as in the case of Roanhorse's *Trail of Lightning*, the text literally contains cowboys, Indians, saloons, outlaws, gunslingers, and gamblers chasing each other through the high deserts of the American West. An emerging trend in twenty-first-century literature and film is the increased public and critical recognition of speculative genre texts (e.g., science fiction, horror, fantasy, superhero) by writers and artists of color, a move that has greatly diversified approaches in current weird westerns. This collection suggests that the greatest innovations in the genre of the western are taking place not in the classic form but in the hybrid narratives of the weird western. The individual contributions to this collection collectively create a critical framework that will help readers recognize the western in these weird tales.

Surrogate Indians and African American Westerners

We have chosen to focus the remainder of our introduction on the way this volume's reoccurring themes and topics of exploration about the weird west play out in one of the most prominent of the genre's offerings in recent years, HBO's series *Westworld*, which is a particularly potent and timely example of recent turns in the genre and of the complicated critical work it can perform. While there are myriad weird western issues to discuss in *Westworld*—including Latinx and Asian representations, in particular the outlaw storyline featuring Latinx character Hector Escaton (Rodrigo Santoro)—we have chosen to focus here on how *Westworld* relates to issues of Native American and African American representation as well as gender and sexuality, as these best reflect the sustained focus that our contributors take up in their chapters.

The original 1973 film *Westworld*, written and directed by Michael Crichton, is frequently thought of today as a high-camp sci-fi western, most memorable for Yul Brynner's grimly terrifying portrayal of a murderous android outlaw in one of Delos Corporation's three historically themed parks, where wealthy guests live out their fantasies by interacting with robot hosts nearly indistinguishable from humans. The hyperrealistic android hosts are programmed to serve human guests as prostitutes, saloon keepers, or, in the case of Brynner's black-clad Gunslinger, as a local badman who picks fights and draws first, thereby allowing guests to gleefully shoot him down without, Delos Corporation promises, any danger of being shot themselves.[36] While Crichton would go on to write many more sci-fi thrillers (no small number of them involving powerful corporations making morally dubious choices with technology), his *Westworld* is an especially delightful example of the resonance between science fiction and westerns and the often overlooked critical work weird westerns can do.

At first glance, HBO's *Westworld* seems to portray a racially diverse view of its futuristic fantasy version of the American West. The pilot episode, "The Original" (1.1), shows both men and women tourists in *Westworld* who are white, African American, and Asian. We see tourists on a family-friendly vacation as well as adults out to experience their own version of the late nineteenth- and early twentieth-century pseudoscience of the "west cure," where human guests relieve their "modern ills" via violent and sexual releases—in other words, guests indulge in their western genre fantasies as part of their own personal "regeneration through violence," as Richard Slotkin described the American cultural narrative of westward expansion. Sweetwater, the idealized town center of *Westworld*, may appear to be multicultural and representative of the nineteenth-century mythic frontier, but it does not seem to reproduce the deeply ingrained class and racial prejudices associated with the historic period and in other western texts. Or does it?

While the android hosts (hereafter referred to as "hosts," the shorthand used by characters on the show) and human tourists in *Westworld* are largely portrayed using a color-blind casting approach, the depiction of Native American hosts seems to be a notable outlier in the series. Native American hosts can be seen casually walking around the main street of Sweetwater, their attire—generally a variation on Hollywood Plains Indian aesthetic—standing out to mark them as part of the western, but racially and visibly coded in ways that the interchangeable deputies, prostitutes, and cowboys are not. Even when native hosts are not dressed in Plains tribal styles, such as the faro dealer Kissy (Eddie Rouse) in "The Original," there are more "tells" that their embodiment is racially specific. The Man in Black (Ed Harris) takes Kissy to a remote cliff where he asserts that there is "a lot of wisdom in ancient cultures," tying Kissy's body to the stereotype of the mystic Indian before unceremoniously scalping him to reveal a "maze" map. The episode "Kiksuya" (2.8) confirms that the presence of this map under his scalp indicates that Kissy would have been a Ghost Nation (the name invented for the American Indian tribe of *Westworld*) host at an earlier point in his programming. Kissy reads as a visible man of color, while the dialogue positions his racial identity as Native American, and yet the role is performed by an actor largely associated with African American roles—such is the blurring of race and its representation in *Westworld*.

The series does position American Indian hosts as racialized, which is one way in which the series shows its positioning as nonnative in its orientation. While current work in indigenous studies tends to consider how issues of race intersect with the political status of tribal communities (prioritizing the political and sovereign side of this intersection), even the more complex depiction of the Ghost Nation in season 2 helps to reinforce that Delos largely deals in narratives of white fantasy as well as fantasies of empire and imperialism that rely on racial difference. The adjoining world, the "Raj," where racial difference is visible and inherent to the governing power recreated there, allows guests to experience the British colonial occupation of India and linger in cultural exoticism. Relatedly, "Shogun World" highlights Delos's global outreach to recreate a mythic narrative tradition that has been important in the development of the American western film; it serves in particular as a nod to Akira Kurosawa's *Seven Samurai* (1954) as the urtext for the iconic Hollywood western *The Magnificent Seven*. In sum, Delos's high-tech adult amusement parks peddle stories of empire and domination to their guests, but generally leave the racial politics unspoken to maximize their commercial profit.

When William (at this point only known to viewers as the "Man in Black") tells Kissy in the pilot episode that he is "livestock, scenery... The others [the human guests at *Westworld*], they just come here to get their rocks off, shoot a couple Indians," the racial binary of the western gets injected into the series, despite any other attempts at creating a color-blind or even inclusive view of the West. The statement designates Native bodies as raced and marked for violence and also indicates that they exist to serve nonnative desires for exerting power. Tellingly, guests at the park kill more than just "Indians," so William's statement rewrites the violence that occurs to unfold strictly along racial lines; it is equally telling that we see white, African American, and Asian tourists, but—at least through the end of season 2—no Native American tourists in *Westworld*. While Ed Harris's character, William (The Man in Black), is frequently positioned as villainous and possibly beyond redemption, his statement gets to the heart of issues of Native representation in *Westworld*: that "Indians" are part of the landscape and appear to be scripted to be disposable and faceless even if the series itself attempts to challenge such facile racial binaries.

Westworld initially portrays American Indian hosts as part of a faceless "enemy" in season 1, setting them up to occupy the expected role in the settler versus indian binary and even playing out the racist overtones of western captivity stories, but season 2 breaks down this initial representation to provide nuance, as well as individual histories and identities, to the American Indian hosts. In season 1 the American Indian hosts are part of what the park's narrative dubs the "Ghost Nation": an invented tribal name that hints at their being mysterious, unknowable, threatening, and even haunting. Indians in American gothic literature exist as a haunting presence. As Renée Bergland has argued, "In the American imagination, Native American ghosts function both as representations of national guilt and as triumphant agents of Americanization... the ghosting of Indians is a technique of removal. By writing about Indians as ghosts, white writers effectively remove them from American lands, and place them, instead, within the American imagination."[37] The Ghost Nation embodies this in how they are named as well as in how they are positioned as haunting the previous lives and experiences of other nonnative–coded hosts.

The series utilizes the idea of the "vanishing Indian" stereotype, but does so in an ironic way. The hosts do not correspond to the "tribal real" because they are narrative constructs from Delos; likewise, their embodiment is the result of nonnative creation. The narrative by Ford (Anthony Hopkins) and others at Delos has "vanished" real Indians in order to provide "surrogate Indians" that fit within the narrative constructs that will sustain the park's commercial interests. However, these highly artificial Indian hosts are roles that rely on the casting of actual Native American actors for HBO's production. Season 2's breakout episode "Kiksuya" offers a sustained look at the humanity of the Ghost Nation in highlighting how this group of hosts came to be conscious; it also provides a significant portion of the episode's dialogue entirely in Lakota, which signals a perspective shift in the series.

The racial stereotypes and dehumanization of the Ghost Nation in season 1 is directly addressed in the backstory provided in episode 2.8. "Kiksuya" initially shows the Ghost Nation as family-oriented and living out an idyllic pastoral existence. In a jump cut to a scene in Delos's "repair center," two employees discuss Ford's directives to rewrite and redesign the American Indian hosts entirely because the management wants "something a little more exciting for grand opening," which means that they want the character of Akecheta—played by Zahn Tokiya-ku McClarnon (Hunkpapa Lakota)—to be "strong but silent. Something brutal. Dehumanized. They probably want the guests to feel better when they're kicking his ass." In other words, the executives at *Westworld* have decided to retire one American Indian stereotype (the nature-loving noble savage with mystic ties to the land) and replace it with another (the violent savage whom guests can feel good about killing): in this case, the intentional move toward dehumanizing Akecheta and other male American Indian hosts is directly linked to making guests feel better about reenacting settler-colonial violence.[38]

Although season 2 presents the racialized violence of settler colonialism as a negative symptom of the park's greed, it remains open as to whether or not the portrayal of American Indians grants them agency. In the final episode of the season, "The Passenger" (2.10), many of the Ghost Nation hosts find "the door" to a different "world" that Akecheta has long searched for. The door appears to be a "rift" in a cliff that opens up into a beautiful landscape, the bright, warm lighting making it appear heavenly. In going through this door the hosts, most of whom are Ghost Nation, are actually rejecting bodily existence; their bodies pile up like carnage on the cliff below as they give up their corporeal existence in favor of a liberated consciousness that is implied to live on, and they finally become literally "ghostly," as their tribal name indicates. Season 2 thus ends with vanishing American Indian hosts, to a degree. Ultimately, *Westworld* includes racialized bodies to later dismiss the exterior and racialized host "shell" as inconsequential.

Although season 2's conclusion repeats the trope of the vanishing Indian, the history of the African American West is never visible enough in the series to vanish. "Since the 1970s," Herbert G. Ruffin II writes, "the history of the African American West has evolved into an exciting branch of scholarship," as historians have explored a rich legacy of black explorers, black cowboys, all-black towns, and the development of black communities in western urban centers, a history that stretches from the earliest Spanish explorers and the Lewis and Clark expedition to contemporary Los Angeles.[39] Despite that rich historical legacy, African Americans remain underrepresented in the fictionalized version of western history that comes to us through the genre western.

If the western seems as unfriendly as other genres to African American representation, a closer look reveals a substantial, if often hidden, history, from filmmaker Oscar Micheaux's silent movies based on his own South Dakota homesteading experiences to recent films such as *Django Unchained* (2012) and the remake (starring Denzel Washington) of *The Magnificent Seven* (2016). Blake Allmendinger's *Imagining the African American West* (2008) and Michael K. Johnson's *Hoo-Doo Cowboys and Bronze Buckaroos: Conceptions of the African American West* (2014) have both extensively documented the representation of African American western experience in a variety of literary, cinematic, and televisual texts, including weird western texts such as the film *The Book of Eli* (also starring Denzel Washington, 2010) and the television series *Firefly* (2002).

On the surface *Westworld*, which features prominently several black actors (including Thandie Newton, who won an Emmy for Outstanding Supporting Actress in a Drama Series in 2018 for her role as park host Maeve Millay, a hard-nosed madam who was previously programmed as a grieving settler mother), would suggest continuing progress regarding African American representation and visibility in the weird western. Newton's Maeve, Jeffrey Wright's Bernard Lowe, and Tessa Thompson's Charlotte Hale are major characters in the series, and they are agents in the narrative's action and plot.

However, the future that *Westworld* suggests is that of a postracial society, one in which blackness is not marked as difference. The hosts are decidedly postracial, as the physical features that we attribute to race can be changed by Delos technicians. For the hosts, race is as superficial an element of identity as gender. Bernard and Maeve may be played by an African American actor and an Afro-British actress, respectively, but they are not represented as black characters, identifiable as such by visible and verbal connection to black history, culture, experience, and modes of expression. Even Charlotte (Tessa Thompson), who initially is not a host, is not written as a specifically African American character. By the end of season 2 we learn that the white-coded host, Dolores (Evan Rachel Wood), has used a host shell of Charlotte at strategic points in her campaign to take down Delos—a development that speaks to the general sense of interchangeability of host bodies, regardless of gender or racial coding. Dolores's usage of Charlotte's host body represents a kind of future-western passing narrative, one where race is erased and replaced with postracial rhetoric. The conscious twinning of Dolores to Charlotte is to some degree just another iteration of the way the hosts change roles as storylines change. Just as Maeve's earlier storyline positioned her as a mother living on the frontier, before she was reprogrammed to be the madam of the Mariposa Saloon and Brothel, the roles for black-appearing hosts are not necessarily uniquely positioned in relation to their seeming racial identity. In the future that is *Westworld*, the vibrant global black culture of today seems not to exist; instead, the series suggests that all of its characters have assimilated or embraced a particular brand of white U.S. culture—a kind of global colonialism.

As Madhu Dubey writes, "Some critics have regarded the raceless futures of U. S. science fiction as evidence of the socially progressive tendencies of the genre," although others have pointed out that "the erasure of racial distinctions in science-fictional images of future societies might be indicative of an evasion of the race problem rather than a solution."[40] Afrofuturist works reject the "tendency within futurist fiction to identify the raced body as a thing of the past" and instead "explicitly engage with the racial dimensions of technological futurism."[41]

Westworld follows the more general tendency of futurist works, especially in its representations of hosts whose "raced bodies" can be removed from whatever histories might have shaped those bodies in the past. At least with the black characters in *Westworld*, there has thus far been very little engagement with "the racial dimensions of technological futurism." And it certainly seems odd, given the number of black actors that we see on-screen at various times, that the created worlds seem to cater only to white fantasies. The western elements of this weird western—the parts that draw on the genre's mythologizing of western history—ignore the past of the African American West as much as the sci-fi elements fail to explore the African American future. Given the popularity of and avid participation in black rodeo in the present (which has increased in visibility over the past few years), it seems logical that Delos would capitalize on the money to be made by offering black cowboy adventures, not to mention the obvious appeal that an all-black western town would have for black customers. African American Deputy U. S. Marshal Bass Reeves (1838–1910), whose actual exploits as a western lawman make him an important figure in the history of the American West, has started to emerge in the last decade as a potentially archetypal western character in a variety of popular culture forms: Art Burton's biography *Black Gun, Silver Star: The Life and*

Legend of Frontier Marshall Bass Reeves (2008); the *Bass Reeves: Frontier Marshall* western short stories series (volume 1 published in 2015); a 2010 film (*Bass Reeves*, with James House in the title role); appearances in the SyFy television weird western series *Wynonna Earp* (2016–)[42] and a weird western episode of the CW series *Timeless* (2016–18).[43] Surely, African American guests at the *Westworld* facility would find a Bass Reeves adventure a compelling immersive experience. But where are those guests? Where is that storyline?

As *Westworld* suggests, and as the chapters in the anthology in the "African American Presence in the Weird Western" section demonstrate, the fictional African American West, in straightforward westerns as well as weird ones, continues to provide a mixed bag that includes surprising treats (e.g., Erykah Badu's 2013 weird western short film *They Die By Dawn*), potentially exciting but ultimately disappointing efforts (e.g., the 2017 Netflix series *Godless*), and a wide variety of narratives that fall somewhere between "treat" and "disappointment" (and that sometimes have a little of both within the same story).[44]

Gender and Sexuality in *Westworld*

Westworld begins by showing how the park's oldest host, Dolores, is sexually exploited by everyone around her, from guests to Delos employees. Gendered violence anchors much of the show's season 1 narrative arc, as viewers see Dolores and Maeve each find their respective ways out of their programmed narrative loops. We watch Dolores, and most other hosts, stripped naked as Delos employees check their programming, and we observe how the hosts generally serve as fodder for guests' sexual, violent, and even sexually violent fantasies. Dolores presents in season 1 as a host with a white female body who is programmed to adhere to heteronormative gender expectations for women. She is blonde, beautiful, demure, and in need of saving. Both Teddy (James Marsden), her host "boyfriend," and Peter Abernathy (Louis Herthum), her host "father," seem programmed to protect Dolores. Teddy's programming loops have him identify his action as "chivalrous," whether it's picking up a can of powdered milk Dolores routinely drops or attempting to save her from gun violence and rape. However, the men around Dolores consistently fail in protecting her, which undermines their attempts at performing patriarchal authority, although their failures to protect Dolores are necessary for the success of the guests' violent fantasies about her.

Dolores possesses what Jack Halberstam would term a "monstrous gender"—she appears human but is not, and her physical appearance reads as "female" even when her programming alternates between the feminine "Dolores" and masculine "Wyatt." In many ways, *Westworld* is a horror weird western, where Dolores is the "final girl" archetype as defined by Carol Clover—she is gender-ambiguous and can be both adversarial to the monstrous villain (the Delos corporation and the legacy of capitalism and imperialism it symbolizes) and also oddly fluent in speaking this monstrous language (her ability to use Delos technology to best Delos). Dolores defines gender binaries and expectations, which in the context of a western speaks to the varied history of the genre in portraying white women as victims, since Dolores is held "captive" by the corporate greed of the Delos corporation.

In viewing Dolores and Maeve as foils, we can consider how the series positions Dolores as an example of white feminism and Maeve as an intersectional feminist. To further their foil status, the white, blonde Dolores dresses in blessed virgin blue while Maeve, the sexualized woman of color, wears cathouse red, thus reproducing the dichotomy of the virgin and the whore. Dolores uses the tools of capitalism to effect her ends as an individual, while Maeve is more like Coleman's "Black Enduring Woman," who serves as a surrogate mother to all and allies herself with the Ghost Nation's mission. Regardless, *Westworld* shows how the western genre fosters toxic masculinity, particularly in William's (The Man in Black's) grotesque search for power but also how this toxic fixation becomes the park's own undoing, largely by showing how malleable identities are whether it's along gender, race, or even host and human lines.

Related to gendered embodiment and identity, the show also portrays a range of sexual experiences that mark the West as a queer space.

Clementine Pennyfeather (Angela Sarafyan), a host programmed to be a Mariposa Saloon and Brothel prostitute, propositions both men and women guests using the same sales pitch of "You're new, not much of a rind on you. I'll give you a discount." Of course this seems to be a bawdy pun since a clementine is a fruit with a rind, but it also seems to be an extension of the show's generally race-blind approach, now applied to sexual desire. Delos employee Elsie finds Clementine sexually alluring and kisses her during a routine programming check (1.1), again suggesting that a spectrum of sexual expressions are part of *Westworld*. However, the fringe town in "Dissonance Theory" (1.4) shows queer desires as illicit, unabashed debauchery, thus opening up the possibility that Sweetwater uses the guise of queer desire to actually reinforce heteronormative storylines, where female hosts exist to provide sexual pleasure to male patrons; tellingly, we usually see male guests copulating with female hosts in Sweetwater despite the host prostitutes using the same lines on all genders.

Like Red River, *Westworld* (both the original film and the HBO series) wants to have its (queer) cake and eat it, too. While nearly all the overt homosexual scenes in *Westworld* involve two or more women—presumably offering safe cover to ostensibly heterosexual male viewers—one of the few plot points reproduced by HBO that seems to be drawn directly from the 1973 film is, significantly, that of the two male friends (first-time visitor Peter and his more experienced friend John in the film; timid William and his jaded brother-in-law Logan in the HBO series) who have planned their vacation to *Westworld* together as an opportunity for male bonding, which involves riding, eating, fighting, and drinking together, as well as visiting female prostitutes. As in *Red River*, the sexualized body of a woman once again provides cover for the development and exploration of a homosocial male relationship structured around strengthening the challenged masculine identity of one of the men involved.

By now it should be clear that HBO's *Westworld* simultaneously clings to the past and the future of the western genre, so it should come as no surprise that in many ways Delos's "Westworld" is populated with those we can consider to be the undead. Whether it's the hosts who uncannily "die" for the delight of human tourists only to be "resurrected" for another group of humans to enjoy fucking and killing—to paraphrase Delos employee, Theresa Cullen (Sidse Knudsen)—or the uncanny "Ghost Nation" of indigenous hosts who tap into stereotypical expectations for nonnative communities about the role of indians in the western, or, even, the revelation in season 2 that the human guests' sojourn to *Westworld* is a not only a vacation, but a way to "cheat" death and have their own consciousness mapped and uploaded into a host "body" upon their natural demise, *Westworld* and the town of Sweetwater is filled with "undead" bodies that resist binary understandings of life and death, past and present.

Such uncanny and grotesque representations of host bodies as undead serves as a potent reminder that the mythic western and its tropes remain just as undead and unstoppable for our present and the imagined future of *Westworld*. The western genre itself can be seen as part of Renée Bergland's national uncanny: it's the genre that continues to haunt and enthrall, especially today, as *Westworld* viewers must reconcile the series' cautionary lessons about capitalism, technology, race, and gender during a political moment when the United States has increasingly been described as a business rather than a nation by political leaders, and when we have seen an embrace of nineteenth-century Jacksonian values and mythic views of the country and the "taming" of the American West as part of this mythos.

Overview of Chapters

The authors gathered here explore how the weird western challenges the representation of race and gender in the conventional western but also how the weird western can serve as a way to reinforce its existing gender and racial paradigms. The primary texts analyzed by contributors range from canonical works dating back to the nineteenth century to contemporary and popular texts in a variety of media, providing a well-rounded view of the weird western, historically and culturally. The world of the weird western can include a sci-fi amusement park such as that of *Westworld*, as discussed, or the alternate history of the American West as imagined by Indigenous Futurist author William Sanders (Cherokee), or even beyond Earth and into the "final frontier" of outer space as reimagined in the work of Jonathan Lethem. The overarching questions addressed in these chapters include the following: In what ways do the western and the weird aspects of the western reinforce heteronormative, gendered, racialized, and dominant discourse, and in what ways has the genre been used to invert and challenge traditional assumptions?

Our collection is divided into five parts. The first part brings together considerations of nineteenth-century authors and present-day multimodal texts. Tara Penry's "Attack of the Monstrous Vegetable: Bret Harte's Pioneer Nightmare and 'Miscegenation' Dream" argues that Harte's less widely known weird western stories deploy fantastical and supernatural elements that allow him to present a relatively positive view of interracial relationships at a time when other white authors portrayed miscegenation in almost entirely derogatory terms. Eric Meljac and Alex Hunt analyze a postmodern parody of the western in chapter 2, "Strange Country: Sexuality and the Feminine in Robert Coover's *Ghost Town*," arguing that the novel foregrounds gender, sexuality, and queer desire in its subversion of classic western character types such as the cowboy, the schoolmarm, and the madam. In chapter 3, "A Selective History: Identity and Identification in 'Deadlands,'" Australian scholar Nicholas William Moll explores a popular tabletop role-playing game in which player characters enact adventures in an alt-history version of the 1870s western American frontier. However, because of players' carefully limited choices, Moll argues that the game actually obscures subaltern histories of race and colonization in order to offer a guilt-free playing experience.

Part 2 looks at how weird westerns portray native characters, with special attention to American Indian authors' and actors' approaches to the genre. Joshua T. Anderson's "Mongrel Transmotion: The Werewolf and the Were/Wear/Where-West in Stephen Graham Jones's *Mongrels*" considers how Jones (Blackfeet) uses monsters that are external to indigenous cultures but prolific in popular culture (such as vampires and werewolves) to discuss Native identity and sovereignty and maps the genre crossing of the western and classic horror. Sara L. Spurgeon's "Indianizing the Western: Semiotic Tricksterism in William Sanders's *Journey to Fusang*" argues that Sanders's novel radically destabilizes what the classic westerns aim to achieve, providing instead a subversively decolonial indigenous narrative, an alt-history that both translates and *indianizes* the western. Domino Renée Perez situates DC Comics, mainstream superhero films, and the iconic western *The Magnificent Seven* in conversation with each other in chapter 6, "Magnificence and Metas in Professional Westerns," reading the DC Comics film *Suicide Squad* as a weird western remake of *The Magnificent Seven*, focusing in particular on the characters of Slipknot, played by Canadian actor Adam Beach (Salteaux Ojibwe), and El Diablo (Jay Hernandez), to look at how the film problematically reinforces stereotypes of the "savage" or "bad Indian" and the myth of the vanishing race.

Part 3 considers specifically what it means when American Indian characters and communities are portrayed metaphorically. If the traditional western is always threatening to vanish the Indian, then how do we address weird westerns that have replaced the unique narrative positioning of Indians with "surrogate Indians" who perform Indianness without native bodies? German scholar Johannes Fehrle's "Defamiliarizing the Western on the Extraterrestrial Frontier: Jonathan Lethem's *Girl in Landscape*" explores a powerful sci-fi reimagining of *The Searchers*, where the terror of and fascination with the threat of racial and cultural mixing is replaced by anxieties about human and indigenous alien species mixing. Fehrle explores the novel's nexus of gender, repressed sexuality, and racist violence, arguing that *Girl in Landscape* presents both a female coming-of-age story and a meditation on the disastrous effects of a violent American masculinity built on a John Wayne model. In chapter 8, "Shining the Light of Civilization: The Savage Other of the Frontier in Joss Whedon's *Firefly* and *Serenity*," Meredith Harvey considers how Whedon's space frontier television series *Firefly* uses tropes of indigeneity without actually representing indigenous peoples. Harvey focuses in particular on the characters known as "the Reavers," to uncover the ways the series complicates and replicates the romantic symbolism of the western frontier as a site of freedom and settler-colonial paradigms. In "Racial Metaphors and Vanishing *indians* in *Wynonna Earp*, *Buffy the Vampire Slayer*, and Emma Bull's *Territory*," Rebecca M. Lush utilizes a critical framework inspired by indigenous literary theory and "red readings" of nonindigenous texts to explore how the texts discussed in her chapter title share a striking lack of specific and individuated American Indian characters despite the inclusion of western aesthetics and attention to multicultural world-building, highlighting the complexities and challenges of intersectional approaches to race and gender in weird western texts that seek to critique settler colonialism while also having to work within its confines.

Part 4 looks specifically at the role of African American characters in contemporary literature, film, and television. In chapter 10, "The Mad Black Woman in Stephen King's *The Dark Tower*," Jacob Burg argues that the frontier imaginary developed within the western supports a nationalist project that is defined by stereotypes and outright exclusion. King's *Dark Tower* series deploys tropes from horror and science fiction to create a version of the western that, through the character of Odetta Holmes, explores the possibility of a new type of western hero: a black female gunfighter. Joshua D. Smith examines specific parallels between Harriet Beecher Stowe's nineteenth-century novel *Uncle Tom's Cabin* and Quentin Tarantino's spaghetti-western neo–slave narrative *Django Unchained* in chapter 11, "*Uncle Tom's Cabin* Showdown: Stowe, Tarantino, and the Minstrelsy of the Weird West." Placing *Django Unchained* in conversation with *Uncle Tom's Cabin* helps reveal the western elements of the novel, and the weird elements of both works help bring to the surface the racial discourse that is often buried in the western. In chapter 12, "Race and Gender in the Time Travel Western," Michael K. Johnson argues that, by mixing genres, the time travel western recreates the western form to appeal to the sensibilities of a twenty-first-century audience—by bringing, for example, currently popular genre character types such as superheroes into an Old West setting. Johnson points out that these contemporary television shows also bring a gender-balanced and multiethnic cast to a genre that in its classic form has repeatedly been critiqued for lacking those qualities and make visible an element of history that is nearly invisible in the classic western: the history of the African American West.

Part 5 looks at the role of zombies and other reanimated relics of the western past. Cynthia J. Miller and A. Bowdoin Van Riper's "Go West, Old Man: Or, Buffalo Bill and the 'Yellow Peril' in *Zeppelins West*" engages Joe R. Lansdale's steampunk western novel, in which fictional and historical figures mingle freely in a traveling Wild West show that includes cowboys, Indians, monsters, and zombies. *Zeppelins West*, according to Miller and Van Riper, simultaneously dramatizes and satirizes nineteenth-century Orientalist fantasies, evoking monstrous and racialized Others, both Asian and Native American, but ultimately reinscribing the rhetorics of manifest destiny. In chapter 14, "AMC's *The Walking Dead* and the Restructuring of Gender and Race on the Neofrontier," Australian scholar Scott Pearce positions *The Walking Dead* as a weird western and explores the decline and fall of the traditional western hero. Pearce explores how patriarchal hierarchies are challenged when the exceptionalist ideals on which they are based collapse, opening space for nonmale and nonwhite leaders and heroes to emerge.

NOTES

The editors wish to thank Victoria Lamont and the second reader of this manuscript at the University of Nebraska Press for their invaluable feedback that has helped us improve the introduction. We also wish to thank Billy J. Stratton for his feedback on nomenclature. We also wish to thank Emily Shelton for her attention to detail in copyediting this collection.

1. "Drama Series Westworld Debuts Oct. 2 on HBO."
2. Miller and Van Riper, *Undead II*, xix.
3. See Billy J. Stratton's note from his edited volume on Stephen Graham Jones regarding the difficulties of terminology in history as well as in a pub-

lishing landscape where "in house" style rules can be at odds with scholarly and community preferences. Stratton outlines the nuance behind "Native" versus "native" and "Indian" vs. "indian," following Vizenor's approach to decolonizing the language systems that we work within. Stratton, "Come for the Icing," 3n2.
4. Green, *Encyclopedia*, 5.
5. Tompkins, *West*, 4.
6. Tompkins, *West*, 39 (emphasis in original).
7. Tompkins, *West*, 5 (emphasis in original).
8. Mitchell, *Westerns*, 8–9 and 9.
9. Similarly, Richard Slotkin discusses Mary Rowlandson's *The Sovereignty and Goodness of God* as a key western urtext despite its setting in colonial Massachusetts (*Regeneration through Violence*).
10. Even earlier than Lennox's novel, Aphra Behn's frontier play *The Widow Ranter* (1690) also utilizes western tropes of settler and Indian conflict, minus the captivity narrative storyline. For a wider discussion of pro-towestern texts, both fiction and nonfiction, see Hamilton and Hillard's introduction to *Before the West was West* (2014); and Lush, "The Royal Frontier."
11. Mitchell, *Westerns*, 5.
12. Kolodny, *Lay of the Land*, 67.
13. Mitchell, *Westerns*, 9.
14. Kolodny, *Lay of the Land*, 144.
15. See William Handley's introduction to *The Brokeback Book*.
16. Varner, *Westerns*, 141.
17. Varner, *Westerns*, 41.
18. Varner, *Westerns*, 146.
19. Kaplan, "Manifest Domesticity."
20. Koehler, *Re-Thinking*, 6.
21. Koehler, *Re-Thinking*, 7.
22. Carter, *New Eve*, 100.
23. Campbell, "Post-Western," 409.
24. Campbell, "Post-Western," 410.
25. Campbell, "Post-Western," 410.
26. Campbell, "Post-Western," 414.
27. Campbell, "Post-Western," 413.

28. Campbell, "Post-Western," 414.
29. Rieder, *Colonialism*, 3.
30. Davis, "Frontiers," 33.
31. The myth traditions Roanhorse draws from are specifically Diné. Since Roanhorse is not Diné, the writers of the Diné Writers' Collective put forth a statement against Roanhorse's *The Trail of Lightning*, asserting it to be cultural appropriation. The recent censure of Roanhorse's award-winning book bears some similarity to the criticism directed against Leslie Marmon Silko's *Ceremony*; both *Ceremomy* and *Trail of Lightning* have been critiqued for sharing specific cultural beliefs without community permission. In Roanhorse's case, her identity as Ohkay Owingeh and not Diné adds another layer of complexity. Adrian L. Jawort critiques the statement made by the Diné Writers' Collective and offers a defense of Roanhorse. Roanhorse's genre-bending novel highlights in part how the western as a genre that rises out of settler-colonialism is frequently a difficult one to decolonize, even when American Indian authors try to write against the dominant culture's expectations. See Saad Bee Hozho, "The Trail of Lightning"; and Jawort, "The Dangers of Appropriation Critique."
32. Roanhorse, *Trail*, 24.
33. Roanhorse, *Trail*, 88–89.
34. indian (lowercase and italicized) is Vizenor's way of indicating that America's obsession with the stereotypical Hollywood indian is a construct that has no relation to what he terms the "tribal real."
35. Vizenor, "Penenative Rumors," 47.
36. Crichton notes in an interview that audience assumptions that the film was intended to be a warning about the dangers of advanced technology actually missed what he considered the more cutting critique of the dangers of uncontrolled capitalism (Yakai, "Michael Crichton"). Indeed, in both the original *Westworld* film and HBO's 2016 reboot, viewers see Delos Corporation employees discussing whether or not to shut down the parks when they first discover some android hosts have begun malfunctioning and are harming guests, only to be directed by upper management to keep the parks open so as not to risk financial losses.
37. Bergland, *Uncanny*, 4.
38. This episode also includes repeated scenes of scalping, and although the narrative purpose is clarified and goes against the usual "savage" stereotype

to instead demonstrate self-consciousness, the brutal violence involved in the depiction of those actions suggests that the series, even when telling a story centered on Native characters, was not considering Native viewers in choosing such graphic imagery, nor the potential traumatic effect on those viewers of repeatedly seeing graphic violence committed against Native bodies.

39. Ruffin, "Bibliographic," 363.
40. Dubey, "Future," 16.
41. Dubey, "Future," 19, 18.
42. See Lush, "Racial Metaphors and Vanishing *indians*," in this volume.
43. See Johnson, "Race and Gender in the Time Travel Western," in this volume.
44. *Godless*, for instance, develops a number of African Americans living in an all-black frontier town, only to kill them off—not western heroes but victims, their existence in the story just another means of demonstrating the villainy of the white outlaws, and yet another clichéd "second act" death.

BIBLIOGRAPHY

Allmendinger, Blake. *Imagining the African American West*. Lincoln: University of Nebraska Press, 2008.

Andras, Emily, creator. *Wynonna Earp*. IDW Entertainment, 2016–present.

Berger, Thomas. *Little Big Man*. New York: Bantam Dell, 2005.

Bergland, Renée. *The National Uncanny: Indian Ghosts and American Subjects*. Hanover NH: University Press of New England, 2000.

Briesewitz, Uta, dir. *Westworld*. Season two, episode eight, "Kiksuya." Aired June 10, 2018, on HBO.

Brown, Charles Brockden. *Edgar Huntly: Or Memoirs of a Sleepwalker*. Indianapolis: Hackett, 2006.

Burroughs, Edgar Rice. *John Carter of Mars*. New York: Canaveral, 1964.

Burton, Art. *Black Gun, Silver Star: The Life and Legend of Frontier Marshall Bass Reeves*. Lincoln NE: Bison, 2008.

Cameron, James, dir. *Avatar*. Twentieth Century Fox, 2009.

Campbell, Neil. "Post-Western Cinema." In *A Companion to the Literature and Culture of the American West*, edited by Nicolas S. Witschi, 409–24. West Sussex: Blackwell, 2011.

Carter, Angela. *The Passion of New Eve*. London: Virago, 2005.

Clover, Carol. *Men, Women, and Chainsaws: Gender in the Modern Horror Film.* Princeton NJ: Princeton University Press, 2015.

Cooper, James Fenimore. *The Pioneers, or The Sources of the Susquehanna; a Descriptive Tale.* New York: Charles Wiley, 1823.

———. *The Last of the Mohicans: A Narrative of 1757.* Philadelphia: H. C. Carey & I. Lea, 1826.

Costmatos, George, dir. *Tombstone.* Buena Vista Pictures, 1993.

Crichton, Michael, dir. *Westworld.* MGM, 1973.

Davis, Robert Murray. "The Frontiers of Genre: Science-Fiction Westerns." *Science Fiction Studies* 12, no. 1 (1985): 33–41.

Dery, Mark. "Black to the Future: Interviews with Samuel R. Delaney, Greg Tate, and Tricia Rose." In *Flame Wars: The Discourse of Cyberculture*, edited by Mark Dery, 179–222. Durham NC: Duke University Press, 1994.

Dillon, Grace, ed. *Walking the Clouds: An Anthology of Indigenous Science Fiction.* Tucson: University of Arizona Press, 2012.

"Drama Series Westworld Debuts Oct. 2 on HBO." Medium.com, July 30, 2016, https://medium.com/hbo-cinemax-pr/drama-series-westworld-debuts-oct-2-on-hbo-e17d39dcf3ca (accessed November 18, 2019).

Dubey, Madhu. "The Future of Race in Afro-Futurist Fiction." In *The Black Imagination: Science Fiction, Futurism, and the Speculative*, edited by Sandra Jackson and Julie E. Moody Freeman, 15–31. New York: Peter Lang, 2011.

Favreau, Jon, dir. *Cowboys & Aliens.* Universal Pictures, 2011.

Ford, John, dir. *Stagecoach.* United Artists, 1939.

———. *The Searchers.* Warner Brothers, 1956.

Frank, Scott, creator. *Godless.* Netflix, 2017.

Fuqua, Anthony, dir. *The Magnificent Seven.* MGM, 2016.

Gilman, Charlotte Perkins. "The Giant Wistaria." *New England Magazine* 4 (1891): 480–85.

———. "The Yellow Wallpaper." *New England Magazine* 5 (1892): 647–56.

Green, Paul. *Encyclopedia of Weird Westerns: Supernatural and Science Fiction Elements in Novels, Pulps, Comics, Films, Television, and Games.* Jefferson NC: McFarland, 2009.

Grey, Zane. *Riders of the Purple Sage.* New York: Harper & Brothers, 1912.

Halberstam, Jack. *Skin Shows: Gothic Horror and the Technology of Monsters.* Durham NC: Duke University Press, 1995.

Hamilton, Amy T., and Tom J. Hillard, eds. *Before the West Was West: Critical Essays on Pre-1800 Literature of the American Frontiers*. Lincoln: University of Nebraska Press, 2014.

Handley, William, ed. *The Brokeback Book: From Story to Cultural Phenomenon*. Lincoln: University of Nebraska Press, 2011.

Hathaway, Henry, dir. *True Grit*. Paramount, 1969.

Hawks, Howard, dir. *Red River*. MGM, 1948.

———. *Rio Bravo*. Warner Brothers, 1959.

Hughes, Albert and Allen, dirs. *The Book of Eli*. Warner Brothers, 2010.

Jawort, Adrian L. "The Dangers of Appropriation Critique." *Los Angeles Review of Books*, October 5, 2019, https://lareviewofbooks.org/article/the-dangers-of-the-appropriation-critique/ (accessed October 29, 2019)

Johnson, Michael K. *Hoo-Doo Cowboys and Bronze Buckaroos: Conceptions of the African American West*. Jackson: University Press of Mississippi, 2014.

Joy, Lisa, and Jonathan Nolan, creators. *Westworld*. HBO, 2016–present.

Kaplan, Amy. "Manifest Domesticity." *American Literature* 70, no. 3 (1998): 581–606.

Koehler, Jana. *Re-Thinking the Weird (in the) West: Multi-Ethnic Literatures and the Southwest*. PhD diss., University of New Mexico, 2019.

Kolodny, Annette. *The Lay of the Land: Metaphor as Experience and History in American Life and Letters*. Chapel Hill: University of North Carolina Press, 1975.

Kripke, Eric, and Sahwn Ryan, creators. *Timeless*. Universal Television and Sony Pictures Television, 2016–present.

Kurosawa, Akira, dir. *Seven Samurai*. Toho, 1954.

Kvande, Marta, and Sara Spurgeon. "The Removes of Harriot Stuart: Charlotte Lennox and the Birth of the Western." In *Before the West Was West: Critical Essays on Pre-1800 Literature of the American Frontiers*, edited by Amy T. Hamilton and Tom J. Hillard, 213–38. Lincoln: University of Nebraska Press, 2014.

Lee, Ang, dir. *Brokeback Mountain*. Universal Studios, 2005.

Lennox, Charlotte. *The Life of Harriot Stuart Written by Herself*. London: J. Payne & J. Bouquet, 1750.

Lush, Rebecca M. "The Royal Frontier: Colonist and Native Relations in Aphra Behn's Virginia." In *Before the West Was West: Critical Essays on Pre-1800 Literature of the American Frontiers*, edited by Amy T. Hamilton and Tom J. Hillard, 130–60. Lincoln: University of Nebraska Press, 2014.

Mauser, Brett William, dir. *Bass Reeves*. Ponderous Productions, 2010.

Miller, Cynthia J., and A. Bowdoin Van Riper, eds. *Undead in the West: Vampires, Zombies, Mummies, and Ghosts on the Cinematic Frontier*. Lanham MD: Scarecrow, 2012.

———. *Undead in the West II: They Just Keep Coming*. Lanham MD: Scarecrow, 2013.

Mitchell, Lee Clark. *Westerns: Making the Man in Fiction and Film*. Chicago: University of Chicago Press, 1996.

Natali, Vincenzo. *Westworld*. Season 1, episode 4, "Dissonance Theory." Aired October 23, 2016, on HBO.

Nolan, Jonathan, dir. *Westworld*. Season 1, episode 1, "The Original." Aired October 2, 2016 on HBO.

Peckinpah, Sam, dir. *The Wild Bunch*. Warner Brothers, 1969.

Penn, Arthur, dir. *Little Big Man*. National General Pictures, 1970.

Phillips, Gary, ed. *Bass Reeves: Frontier Marshal*. Vol. 1. Airship 27 Productions, 2015.

Proulx, Annie. "Brokeback Mountain." In *Close Range: Wyoming Stories*, 253–306. New York: Scribner, 1999.

Rieder, John. *Colonialism and the Emergence of Science Fiction*. Middletown CT: Wesleyan University Press, 2008.

Roanhorse, Rebecca. *Trail of Lightning*. New York: Saga, 2018.

Roddenberry, Gene, creator. *Star Trek*. Desilu Productions, 1966–68; Paramount Television, 1968–69.

Ruffin, Herbert G., II. "Bibliographic Essay: The Twentieth- and Twenty-First-Century West." In *Freedom's Racial Frontier: African Americans in the Twentieth-Century West*, edited by Herbert G. Ruffin II and Dwayne A. Mack, 363–85. Norman: University of Oklahoma Press, 2018.

Saad Bee Hozho. "The Trail of Lightning Is an Appropriation of Diné Beliefs." *Indian Country Today*, November 5 2018, https://newsmaven.io/indiancountrytoday/opinion/trail-of-lightning-is-an-appropriation-of-diné-cultural-beliefs-4tvSMvEfNE-i7AE10W7nQg/?fbclid=IwAR3rf2Y7IQH-xbZET0PdZ69LHlVGnHV8njBZ2EnJsmr8-tIzEIVjU67l5sI (accessed November 9, 2018)

Samuel, Jeymes, dir. *They Die by Dawn*. Tidal, 2013.

Scarborough, Dorothy. *The Wind*. New York: Harper & Brothers, 1925.

Schaefer, Jack. *Shane*. Boston: Houghton Mifflin, 1939.

Shakespeare, William. "The Tragedy of Macbeth." *Mr. William Shakespeare's Comedies, Histories, and Tragedies.* London: Blount & Jaggard, 1623.

Sjostrom, Victor, dir. *The Wind.* MGM, 1928.

Slotkin, Richard. *Regeneration through Violence: The Mythology of the American Frontier, 1600–1860.* Middletown CT: Wesleyan University Press, 1973.

Stevens, George, dir. *Shane.* Paramount Pictures, 1953.

Stratton, Billy J. "Come for the Icing, Stay for the Cake." In *The Fictions of Stephen Graham Jones,* edited by Billy J. Stratton, 1–13. Albuquerque: University of New Mexico Press, 2016.

Sturges, John, dir. *The Magnificent Seven.* MGM, 1960.

Tammi, Emma, dir. *The Wind.* IFC Midnight, 2018.

Tarantino, Quentin, dir. *Django Unchained.* Columbia Pictures, 2012.

Tompkins, Jane. *West of Everything: The Inner Life of Westerns.* Oxford: Oxford University Press, 1993.

Toye, Frederick E. O., dir. *Westworld.* Season two, episode 10, "The Passenger." Aired June 24, 2018, on HBO.

Varner, Paul. *Westerns: Paperback Novels and Movies from Hollywood.* Cambridge: Cambridge Scholars, 2007.

Vizenor, Gerald. "Penenative Rumors." *Fugitive Poses: Native American Indian Scenes of Absence and Presence.* Lincoln: University of Nebraska Press, 1998.

Wells, H. G. *The War of the Worlds.* London: William Heinemann, 1898.

Whedon, Joss, creator. *Firefly.* Twentieth Century Fox Television, 2002.

——, dir. *Serenity.* Universal Pictures, 2005.

Wister, Owen. *The Virginian.* London: Macmillan, 1902.

Yakai, Kathy. "Michael Crichton/Reflections of a New Designer." *Compute!,* February 1985, 44–45.

PART ONE

The Weird West, Past and Present

Attack of the Monstrous Vegetable   1

Bret Harte's Pioneer Nightmare and "Miscegenation" Dream

TARA PENRY

Based on the stories best known to American literature anthologies, Bret Harte seems a poor fit for a collection of essays on weird westerns. He did not write in any of the genres featured most prominently in Paul Green's *Encyclopedia of Weird Westerns (2009)*: dime novels, pulps, comics, films, television, or games. Unless we count a figurative "vampire" (Harte's word) and other adulterous women, whom Jeffrey Thomas calls "maneaters," Harte's fiction gives us none of the usual creatures of horrific fancy: "werewolves, mummies, man-made monsters, . . . mutants, zombies," and the like.[1] In an essay on 1950s comics, Green adds that American popular culture embraced "weird" storytelling in the age of the atomic bomb, a "paranoiac environment" of the mid-twentieth century when "superheroes were showing signs of fatigue."[2] If the epithet of "weird western" clings especially well to the fusion of recognizably western tropes and tales with the speculative fiction, horror, and fantasy of the nuclear era, or the late twentieth-century revival of the supernatural "to critique and comment on the Western tradition and the norms and values it promotes and maintains," presumably a writer who came of age during the U.S. Civil War and helped to formulate the generic conventions of the popular western represents the static "tradition" against which the weird western defines itself as "weird."[3]

But there is more to Bret Harte than the California Gold Rush chronicler and genteel humorist we meet in literary anthologies.[4] Harte's west is decidedly weird, both in its invocation of the gothic and in its numerous challenges to regional master narratives. Best known for his good-hearted western character types, such as the honorable gambler and the lounging miner, Harte freely incorporates gothic elements into fiction that may also be comic, pathetic, or satiric, resulting in hybrid texts resistant to classification.[5] In one story a vengeful madman springs from a wall with a knife between his teeth, adding a flash of drama to a mostly unremarkable courtship narrative; in another, a conventional love plot featuring a racially varied cast keeps going sensationally awry, until a wildfire finally consumes unassimilable identities.[6] Earthquakes solve intractable social problems such as a wife's adultery or a couple's estrangement.[7] Unfettered by genre, Harte satirizes western tourism in the same story that sees a Californio man and his biracial son disappear horrifically into a crack in the earth.[8] A pioneer house squats "half-buried" in the earth "like some monstrous vegetable."[9] Harte's gothic sensibility does not rely on the European figures of castles, prisons, ghosts, or vampires, but on thrilling and monstrous western tropes such as earthquakes, wildfires, and the bare, hastily constructed dwellings of pioneers. Harte turns these devices to weird use with an extravagant style and a frontier gothic preoccupation with "the desolation wrought by progress" in the West.[10] His stories regionalize a distinguishing characteristic of the American gothic: its obsession with "historical crimes and perverse human desires that cast their shadow over what many would like to be the sunny American republic."[11]

The most obvious objection to a gothic or weird reading of Bret Harte may be the author's very well-established and justly earned reputation as a humorist. Some readers once accepted him as the very spokesman of the nineteenth-century "sunny American republic"—a reputation now supplanted with better understanding of his satire. Harte has never been read as a horror writer; at his most lurid and melodramatic, he is understood to have "pander[ed]" to popular taste with "increasingly sensational stories punctuated by violence and sexual transgression or illicit romance."[12] But it is important to note that his most sensational prose has rarely received close or admiring study. When all of his stories are considered, Harte fits the profile of a gothic or weird writer, since large swaths of his work have been dismissed, like those of other gothic writers, as "sensational and indulgent."[13] Anticipating the fate of Stephen King, he has certainly been poorly received, and possibly "miscategoriz[ed]," when he places "characters and even monsters from different genre traditions . . . under the umbrella of one story."[14]

Jack Morgan's "double-helix" of comedy and horror offers perhaps the most compelling and comprehensive way to rethink Bret Harte as a weird western writer. Both comedy and horror, Morgan points out, have roots in "informal vernacular tradition," the one associated with saturnalia and fertility, the spirit of life, and the other associated with death, decay, and sterility.[15] "Comedy takes calamity into account," he continues, "but it privileges recovery, the vigorous, exhilarating rebound of living things from mishap, or their artful dodging of disaster"; horror, conversely, privileges "the actual disaster," confronting "the all-too-possible victory of morbid forces."[16] Harte's stories consider both the victory of "morbid forces" and the comedy of "recovery," although not always in the same tale. Nowhere is the combination more evident than in "The Bell-Ringer of Angel's" (1893), a sylvan romance of serial dispossession and betrayal. The narrator inclines toward humor when accounting for the grim history of a beautiful Sierran riverside: "Originally the camping-ground of a Digger Chief, [the spot] passed from his tenancy with the American rifle bullet that terminated his career. The pioneer who thus succeeded to its attractive calm gave way in turn to a well-directed shot from the revolver of a quartz-prospector, equally impressed with the charm of its restful tranquility."[17] But the story is no comedy; it is as calamitous as anything in Harte's oeuvre. By the time Madison Wayne realizes he has committed a murder while presuming (in vain) to guard the chastity of a woman he once loved, the generic cues of the tale have shifted from satiric comedy to gothic horror. Discovering his deadly mistake, Wayne utters "a wild, inarticulate cry," staggers and falls over a chair, "[rises] to his feet, blindly grope[s] his way down the staircase, burst[s] into the road, and, hugging the pouch to his bosom, [flees] like a madman down the hill."[18] "The Bell-Ringer of Angel's" begins in a black comic rendering of western history and proceeds to tighten its narrative noose to the end of the bitter tale. Just so, Harte's oeuvre oscillates between comedy and horror. His horrors are often the cherished ideas and icons of western nineteenth-century historiography: manifest destiny, Anglo-Saxon racial supremacy, the heroic pioneer. In Harte's fiction, these monsters of ideology alternately provoke satiric laughter or threaten sanity and vitality.

While advancing the work that critics have already associated with the gothic frontier—"dismantl[ing] myths of the West" and exposing the "underside of the western dream"—Harte's stories regionalize the gothic tropes of purity and monstrosity.[19] As Harte imagines it comically throughout his corpus, the western frontier invites and requires hybridity and social play. Men and women cross-dress and exchange roles; gamblers return money; beloved characters Thomas Luck and Jack Hamlin are half-white, half-Cherokee; criminals in other climes are leading citizens in the California gold camps; and so on. The "obverse" of this comic hybridity—the horror from which it rebounds—is rigid ideology, which Harte calls "a fixed idea."[20] According to the traditional expression of gothic xenophobia, cultural outsiders are figured as monsters, but in Harte's west, the ideology of purity itself is the most monstrous feature of the hybrid frontier, where virtually everyone is an outsider, and outsiders come in many kinds.[21] Furthermore, while gothic texts customarily "mark difference within and upon bodies," Harte spends surprisingly little time gazing at the physical form of his monsters; he reveals them in their grotesque speech rather than their grotesque corporeality.[22] He reserves lingering gazes for beautiful, changeable forms such as the begrimed killer on the run, coated in "a hideous reddish mask of dust and clay," who is "more like a beast than a man," plunging gratefully into a woodland pool and emerging in a "startling transformation" an "irrepressible" boy and "blond faun," ready for romance.[23] Unlike corporeal monsters of horrific fancy, "putrid and moldering things," visibly "impure and unclean," Harte's monsters are not distinguished by their bodies but by their self-righteous, rigid talk of racial, religious, or familial purity.[24]

Harte's stories of interracial courtship and marriage make especially clear the horrid consequences of western master narratives that fetishize racial and national purity. The ideal (but usually stillborn or doomed) order in these stories is a peaceful society of mixed races and mixed genres, where monsters of selfish appetite and narrow principle can do no harm.[25] Extreme narrative effects usually prevent these ideal orders from coming to pass. The narrator of Harte's first interracial romance, "Notes by Flood and Field" (1862)—its title drawn from William Shakespeare's racially transgressive *Othello*—has a romantic glimpse of such an order, then witnesses its cataclysmic failure. The more ambitious novella "Maruja" (1885) offers a rare happy ending to one of Harte's interracial courtship plots, but, true to the double helix of horror and comedy, "Maruja" is also one of Harte's more sustained gothic thrillers, its happy ending threatened by the intrigue of a minor character who defends familial purity and property with melodramatic intensity and murderous stealth. One of the weaknesses of "Maruja" is its willingness to caricature and dehumanize indigeneity—a problem Harte seems to want to correct in "The Ancestors of Peter Atherly" (1898). Once Peter Atherly discovers his biracial ancestry, he attempts to become a peacemaker between whites and Natives in the West, but the efforts of one man prove utterly insufficient to overcome massive cultural misunderstanding. Atherly's racial hybridity and his story's generic hybridity cannot overcome the entrenched cultural divisions of the West. These three stories together reveal that western conventions of racial purity and continental conquest were already under pressure between the 1860s and 1890s. A forerunner of weird western literary history, Bret Harte warned of ideological monsters turning the frontier comedy of hybrid play into a nightmare of murderous possession.

"Nature's Intentions": Discourses of Racial Purity

To understand Harte's rejection of the weird idea of racial purity, it is helpful to know the discourses that preceded and prompted him. Before Harte was born, antebellum frontier fiction treated "race" as a self-evident, scientific category. With dissenters growing harder to hear as the Civil War approached, "the process of developing a sense of Americanness," as Linda Frost has written, grew increasingly to take "whiteness" for granted.[26] Bill Handley has identified a few early Americans who advocated European marriages with Indians to aid diplomatic relations.[27] Karen Woods Weierman points out that Lydia Maria Child accepted interracial marriage in her 1824 novel *Hobomok* and later work.[28] And, thanks to a malleably raced female, James Fenimore Cooper successfully "incorporated" racial difference into an "American" marriage in *The Prairie* (1827).[29] However, from Hector St. John de Crevecoeur's eighteenth-century sketches to Cooper's Leatherstocking novels, frontier fiction overwhelmingly relegated interracial marriages to lurid gothic subplots in the consolidation of a pure, white nation.

From the colonial period to the 1820s, anxiety about racial mixing haunts early American literature of the frontier. At the end of Crevecoeur's *Letters from an American Farmer* (1782), the fictional persona of the book, an American-born farmer of English descent, plans to flee the unwanted revolution with his family and seek refuge with Indians. It relieves him to think of bringing a beau for his daughter, as the alternative would pose "the greatest danger": "For however I respect the simple, the inoffensive society of these people in their villages, the strongest prejudices would make me abhor any alliance with them in blood: disagreeable no doubt, to *nature's intentions* which have strongly divided us by so many indelible characters."[30] James Fenimore Cooper's iconic frontiersman of the widely read Leatherstocking novels insists just as firmly on racial purity. Although he lives like an Indian, he calls himself a "white man" with no "taint" or "cross" or racial mixture in his "blood."[31] In the 1820s Cooper's *The Last of the Mohicans* (1826) and Catharine Sedgwick's *Hope Leslie* (1827) both teased readers with the sensational possibility of a marriage between European and Native characters. With these early American frontier texts as models, western fiction developed both a preoccupation with racial hybridity and a habit of invoking "nature's intentions" to enforce boundaries of racial difference.

By the time the first dime novel appeared in 1860, with its thrilling tragedy of a Native American mother trying to raise a biracial child after the death of her European husband, American frontier fiction had established a pattern of considering and cutting off or marginalizing interracial futures. The preoccupation of authors and characters with whiteness and naturalness indicates just how "unnatural" and "unlikely" racial purity seemed to be in the context of the frontier, and just how much narrative artifice was required to defend it. Cooper's Hawk-eye insists repeatedly on his racial whiteness because he has "lived with the red skins long enough to be suspected" of going native; since his choice of life and companions is not racially pure or distinct, he clings to his pure, unmixed "blood" as the key to his identity, and he passes this presumption on to readers as a principle of frontier fiction.[32] Cooper and Sedgwick both permit attractions between white and Indian characters, but Cooper maintains lines of racial purity more decisively: the hero of *The Pioneers* (1823) turns out to have only an adoptive relation to a Native tribe, and the love match between Cora and Uncas in *The Last of the Mohicans* (1826) ends in death for both.[33] While both Cooper and Sedgwick seem to accept interracial erotic attraction as a consequence of frontier habitation, such relations only occur as thrilling foils to white marriages for primary characters. In early American frontier fiction, narrative conventions represent white racial purity as the natural desire of heroic character types even as they acknowledge that sexual attraction and friendship naturally occur anywhere that young people grow up as near neighbors.

Early in Bret Harte's career, the discourse of racial "amalgamation" encountered in frontier fiction became increasingly politicized by the emancipation of enslaved people in 1863 and the reelection of Abraham Lincoln in 1864. Trying to throw the presidential election to Democratic candidate John L. McClellan, two southern sympathizers in New York published an anonymous pamphlet purporting to represent a liberal Republican policy of encouraging marriages between newly liberated blacks and sympathizing whites. Their pamphlet issued a number of provocative statements, such as the title of one chapter, "The Blending of Diverse Bloods Essential to American Progress."[34] By sending their pamphlet to Republican papers for review, the authors prodded prominent abolitionists to commit themselves in favor of "miscegenation," a newly coined word referring to the sexual mixing (*miscere*) of genuses or human races. They succeeded in introducing a non sequitur to the political conversation that misrepresented the Republican platform.[35] "The term 'miscegenation' caught on quickly," explains historian Peggy Pascoe, "providing the rhetorical means of channeling the belief that interracial marriage was unnatural into the foundation of post–Civil War white supremacy."[36] Although the term appeared first in a booklet that claimed to encourage racial integration and intermarriage, the book's parody of liberal principles becomes clear in its crude insistence on race as a primary category of human identification. The booklet assumes that if blacks and whites are going to marry each other, a pseudoscientific term is needed to separate this kind of marriage from any other. Harte did most of his writing after the word "miscegenation" created the illusion of consensus that there was something unnatural and strange about marriages across lines of "race."

The Monstrous Pioneer

In a story composed before the term "miscegenation" entered the national vocabulary, Harte refused to align "nature's intentions" with white racial purity or the manifest destiny of American continental conquest. "Notes by Flood and Field" alludes not to Cooper, Crevecoeur, or others in the tradition of American frontier fiction, anxious about the propinquity of Indians to whites, but to Shakespeare's *Othello*, source of the phrase "by flood and field."[37] Harte's story, like Shakespeare's well-known tragedy, denies a love match across lines of race. If the reader catches the allusion, the title foreshadows the tale's tragedy. Set ostensibly in 1861–62, "Notes by Flood and Field" nonetheless evokes a misty myth-time between the 1840s, when white Jacksonian workingmen looked to western lands for economic opportunity they could not find in eastern cities, and the early 1860s, when industrial mining had begun to erode California hillsides and cause widespread flooding in the valleys.[38] Provoked to heightened awareness by the weird domestic life of his pioneer hosts, the narrator glimpses in this myth-time two versions of American life in the West, one hybrid and free, the other a monstrous degeneration from civilized Spanish California to a primordial and selfish state of brute competition. Part realist, part naturalist, part gothic, "Notes by Flood and Field" mixes *genres* but stops short of mixing *genes* as it considers marriage a possible solution to competing land claims in the West.

The action of "Notes by Flood and Field" unfolds in two parts, the first section representing the "field" of the title, and the second the "flood." The first-person narrator, a young surveyor, travels to a contested stretch of the Espíritu Santo ranch in California to mark the boundary between the old Mexican claim of Don Fernando Altascar and the new American claim of Missourian Joseph Tryan. He spends an unpleasant night with the utilitarian and myopic Tryan family before meeting the gracious don at his comfortable casa the next day. Although he does not wish to dispossess a man he admires, it is the narrator's responsibility to mark a new boundary between the properties, granting some of the ranch to the American. He leaves the area as soon as his job is done, the only pleasant memory lingering around Tryan's son George, a noble and picturesque vaquero assimilating to the Altascar way of life and courting the don's daughter Pepita. Some months later, in a spring flood, the narrator is drawn back to check on the rancho, and he learns that George has died rescuing others. The Tryan family is scattered and crazed, the boundary marker temporarily washed away, while the Altascars mourn the loss of the one character who might have made the American encroachment bearable. With their cattle and buildings in the foothills, the Altascars are not badly affected by the flood, except in the loss of George. The worst of the Tryans survive: they simply plan to "lay over a spell" until "driv[ing] stakes" somewhere more promising.[39] For neither family does surviving mean thriving; conflict promises to resume.

The story's interest in hybridity and assimilation registers first as a gothic atmosphere strangely combined with prosaic American realism.

Like early weird western writer Robert E. Howard in the 1930s, Harte mixes "seemingly incongruous elements"—settings and characters of the Far Western frontier with fantasy and gothic horror embodied unexpectedly in a pioneer family.[40] From the first paragraph, the romantically inclined narrator might as well be on his way to Edgar Allan Poe's House of Usher: he grows "disagreeably conscious" of his environment, which affects him with "morbid fancy," "more like a dull, dyspeptic dream than a business journey."[41] Yet the "atmosphere" is "dryly practical." On a California plain, nature is "too practical" for "disguises," and the unchanging blue sky seems one of the "sincerest of natural phenomena."[42] Dangling in this zone between Poe-like fantasy and the yawning quotidian, the narrative introduces not a haunted house riven by an ancient family curse but a weird western equivalent—a half-buried house that seems to have "grown out of the earth like some monstrous vegetable."[43] The house is fantastic yet the farthest place from a scene of romance, for "there [are] no recesses along its roughly boarded walls for vagrant and unprofitable shadows to lurk in the daily sunshine. No projection for the wind by night to grow musical over, to wail, whistle, or whisper to; only a long wooden shelf containing a chilly-looking tin basin and a bar of soap."[44] Explicitly replacing European gothic architecture, with its "shadows" and "recesses," with the utilitarian American architecture designed only for a "profitable" existence, Harte nonetheless maintains a gothic dreaminess and a fixation on the "morbid" response of the narrator to his environment. The scene is both gothic and antigothic; if the tension is to be resolved at all, we may resolve it by noticing that we are in a region not of gothic romance but of "monstrous," "chilly," "profitable" gothic realism.

The members of this emigrant household grimly fulfill the expectations set by their dwelling. Looking for a volunteer to escort the narrator to the Altascar home, Tryan questions his son Lycurgus in diction that, like the architecture, lacks music: "Kin you go, Kerg?"[45] His sons refuse his request with "hard young faces" trained in resistance by a man who thumbs his bible "with a look in his face as though he were hunting up prophecies against the 'Greaser.'"[46] Womanhood fares no better than masculinity in this pioneer household. When the narrator is called to dinner by a "weak-eyed" daughter of the family, he observes a mother breastfeeding her infant at the table and utterly ignoring him.[47] The embodiment of the practical frontier family, the Tryans represent a grotesque revision of the California myth of the hard-working, home-loving pioneer and his civilizing wife. All but one son of the family are absorbed in stubborn, near-sighted preservation of only themselves and their immediate kin. "Notes by Flood and Field" seems a surprisingly early example of the transition Judith Halberstam observes from nineteenth-century to postmodern gothic, the latter "disrupt[ing] the dominant culture's representations of family, heterosexuality, ethnicity, and class politics," as well as "the logic of genre that essentializes generic categories."[48] From an author who never identified himself comfortably as a Californian and certainly not as a pioneer, "Notes by Flood and Field" disrupts dominant Anglo-California culture's representations of the heroic pioneer family, pure white entitlement to western land, and white-favoring alignments of race and class. Gothicizing realism, with its utilitarian settings, values, and characters, the story upends traditional generic categories, so that romance emerges cleanly from the grotesque real as the mode of hybridity, adaptation, and beautiful impurity.

Nowhere is the story's partiality for romance more clear than in the Altascar casa and on the plain where young George Tryan displays his adaptive horsemanship. Unlike the rest of his family, George is "handsome" and "frank" and creates a "romantic impression" upon the narrator.[49] On horseback, leading the narrator to meet Don Altascar, he is "musical with jingling spurs and picturesque with flying riata"—the very antithesis of the unmusical parent and his practical architecture.[50] George's Spanish saddle and riata, not to mention his knowledge of the local species of cattle, mark him as well assimilated to the place, unlike his father. The narrator is enchanted. At the Altascar home, he is further pleased by the well-adapted architecture of the old Spanish family: the low doorway of the adobe house casts "a deep shadow and an agreeable coolness . . . as sudden and grateful as a plunge in cool water."⁵¹ Also comforting are the soft voices and candlelight the narrator encounters on a subsequent visit.⁵² According to this narrator, California needs romantic shadows, enclosed spaces, vaquero costume, and softly spoken Spanish syllables to offset its severe climate. Romance itself seems capable of adapting to land and climate in a way that American utility does not. The beautiful, friendly George courts Pepita Altascar quietly in a hall while the narrator discusses the business of his survey with the don. Far from disapproving, the narrator is "touched to the heart" by the "blending of tenderness and respect" in George's manner toward his lover's father.⁵³

A foil to the well-assimilated George, patriarch Joseph Tryan rigidly clings to his notions of racial and religious purity and manifest destiny. The utilitarian frontiersman who lives in a "monstrous vegetable" of a dwelling grotesquely asserts that God and "nature" condone his dispossession of a people more civilized and better adapted to the place than himself. Harte's narrator records Tryan's dinner conversation because "the same ideas have been sometimes advanced under more pretentious circumstances."⁵⁴ Harte places in the mouth of a crude, ungrammatical patriarch a set of opinions embraced in higher social classes under the name "manifest destiny" but exposed in this context for their vulgarity. "It was agin nater and agin God," the host complains of Mexican and Spanish land claims in California: "God never intended gold in the rocks to be made into heathen candlesticks and crucifixens. That's why he sent 'Merrikans here. Nater never intended such a climate for lazy lopers. She never gi'n six months' sunshine to be slept and smoked away."⁵⁵ The narrator "escape[s]" as soon as possible from Tryan's offensive ideas of race, religion, and "nature"—the "darker social reality" that the American gothic exposes as "the central fact of American life."⁵⁶ He gets relief from this practical application of manifest destiny by observing George's skill on horseback the next day. Relief and George's beauty are temporary; manifest destiny shows no signs of weakness.

In the contrast between the utilitarian, offensive father who makes the narrator wish to "escape," and the romantic son who transforms the whole landscape into a valley of "illimitable freedom," Harte invests "Notes by Flood and Field" most deeply in a contest between two different styles of living in the West, the subject on which the narrator is literally taking notes.[57] As Harte's narrator sees him, George is "free" because he has adapted selflessly to the place: he rides a "Spanish saddle" and woos in two "broken" languages, having learned to love and serve his neighbor and separate himself from his father's prejudices. Adaptability is precisely the trait the other Tryans lack. After the flood, the mad patriarch says he is "moving off."[58] The unrequited marriage is a cover plot for the real terror of the story. The narrative gives very little time, in fact, to Pepita and George. The most fearsome and realistic conflict lurks in the monstrous possibility that inflexible pioneer utility will triumph over the racially mixed romance of civilization that Altascars, George, and the narrator all prefer. As the surveyor who drives the stakes between Tryan's claim and Altascar's, the narrator himself is an agent of American utility, not intercultural romance, despite his contrary preference. With the death of George Tryan and the helplessness of Altascar before American law, only the narrator remains to protest the grotesque results of manifest destiny and to express nostalgic longing for a more humane, interracial, adaptive model for American occupation.[59] In this gothically realistic story, the monster prevails, and the monster is a garden-variety, practical American pioneer who believes himself authorized by God and nature to take possession of all he wants and sees.

Gothic Horror and Romantic Comedy

The novella "Maruja" (1885) ranks as one of Harte's most ambitious treatments of interracial marriage as a central theme for national and regional romance. Whereas the Civil War–era "Notes by Flood and Field" stops melodramatically short of picturing "a successful union between the two cultures" of Spanish and American Californians, "Maruja" is unusual in Harte's corpus for bringing about shared occupation of contested land—at least between rival colonizers from Spain and the eastern United States.[60] Crucial to this vision are the assimilative act of marriage and the triumph of realist conventions over the supernatural, gothic, and weird. In "Maruja," as in "The Bell-Ringer of Angel's," gothic horrors follow from a history of "successive evictions," including curses, hauntings, and shadowy murders by moonlight.[61] Most important, "Maruja" develops themes dating back to "Notes by Flood and Field": monstrous, narrow-minded, weird characters defend racial purity, while sympathetic characters treat joint occupation of land as both romantically picturesque ("Notes") and realistically profitable ("Maruja"). This story views marriage between English and Spanish families as natural and modern in the American West; efforts to prevent the natural course of human desire are warped, weird, and superstitious. On the other hand, if its social realism and the marriage plot seem staged and artificial, this story may leave the reader feeling that grotesque gothic jealousies and grudges are more real after all than the economic merger of families representing two colonial histories.

In "Maruja," as in "Notes by Flood and Field," most of these ideas are emblematized in the architecture. La Mision Perdida, the matriarchal property of the biracial protagonist Maruja Saltonstall, has been home to Indians, Spanish missionaries, the Spanish Guitierrez family, and now the Saltonstalls, led by Maruja's mother, a Guitierrez daughter and widow of a New England sea captain. These changes in ownership have left their most legible mark on the Guitierrez-Saltonstall home: "The original casa—an adobe house of no mean pretensions, dating back to the early Spanish occupation" has been "sheathed in a shell of dark wood," its American-style additions changing only the outer shape of the structure, while the internal rooms and patio remain intact.[62] European and American guests visit the outer rooms of the house; the family retreats for more intimate business and rest to the older, inner casa. The hostess, Doña Saltonstall, and her daughters move easily between the various parts of the house, as between English and Spanish languages.[63] As the Guitierrez family has adapted to American law, economy, social life, and architecture, so too the Saltonstalls' wealthy American neighbor Dr. West adapts to Californio custom and culture. Although West's dwelling, like Tryan's, is unlovely and utilitarian, he has none of Tryan's prejudices, and is admitted to the inner, Spanish rooms at La Mision Perdida as an intimate family friend. The fragrant vines and flowers surrounding Doña Saltonstall's porch provide the homelike atmosphere missing from his bachelor quarters. At least initially, it seems likely that the lush, hospitable, hybrid house will add another wing to accommodate the addition of an American man of business.

Head servant Pereo prevents a marriage between Dr. West and Doña Saltonstall in his gothic mission to defend property and family purity. He refuses to accept the ancient curse of a dying priest that the land must "always pass into the hands of the stranger."[64] Sneaking about in shadows—murdering when necessary—old Pereo embodies the gothic energy of the novella, avenging the violent past in a violent, paranoid present. In his presence, the modern, interracial courtship romance (with a realist novel of land claims, mortgages, wheat, and railroads at its periphery) yields to "the insane abstraction of a fixed idea."[65] In an early scene, in the shadows of a ruined church under moonlight, Pereo sees in a wayfarer the very image of the suitor he has just murdered (Dr. West). Although he is partially correct—the stranger is Dr. West's son from Missouri, known in the neighborhood as Henry Guest—he dismisses his perception of likeness: "I am mad—mad! It is not *his* voice. No! It is not *his* look, now that his face changes. I am crazy."[66] And in the last scene of the book, the son realizes in a flash that Pereo killed his father when the old servant practices using his lasso. "Suddenly he [Guest] became aware of some strange exercise on the part of the mysterious rider; and as the latter swept by . . . Guest saw that he was throwing a lasso! A horrible thought that he was witnessing an insane rehearsal of the murder of his father flashed across his mind."[67] These thoughts may be "horrible" and may require exclamation points, but they are not "insane." Both Pereo and Guest are correct in their flashing intuitions: so warped is Pereo by his "fixed idea" of keeping land that truth in his presence feels like madness, insanity, and horror. Although he is not a Guitierrez but an Indian and a family servant, he protects the Guitierrez claim to the property as fiercely and monomaniacally as any gothic villain.

Even Pereo's language isolates him from modern reality, for he speaks with exceptional artifice, matched only by the theatrical diction of the Indian servants who look up to him as an elder. Calling the Saltonstall servants to a garden meeting to find out what anyone knows about the conversation between the mistress of the house and the neighboring entrepreneur, Dr. West, before he decides to interfere, Pereo admonishes a girl to tell what she knows with the most improbable speech: "Now, the curse of Koorotora on thee, Pepita!' said Pereo excitedly. 'Speak, fool, if thou knowest anything!'" The girl answers, just as strangely, "Of a verity, no."[68] This is no translation from an indigenous language to English, but a palimpsest of Shakepearean minor-character histrionics on the multicultural, multilingual West, where Maruja addresses her mother in one "dialect" and the indigenous Pereo in another.[69] With his strange, artificial language, Pereo is an unnatural relic of the past, a living ghost. Modern Californios and Americanos "are no longer strangers," Maruja chides Pereo—"the years pass."[70] Dr. West and Doña Saltonstall had planned to make money on wheat and railroads *together*, and when West's son and Saltonstall's daughter become engaged at the end of the novella, it appears they will carry out the peace- and wealth-making plans laid by their parents.[71] By refusing Pereo's superstitions and prejudices, the practical couple stands to inherit the imperial legacy of two nations, represented by two adjacent family properties.

Chief among the problems of this story is the conventionally racist limitation of Pereo's power. The Indian servants are in awe of him, but to the Spanish and American characters he is "childish" and requires protection.[72] Harte never credits him with enough force to want to reclaim the land for *his own* people; he only imagines protecting it for the Guitierrez-Saltonstall family, whom we might expect him to resent as his own trespassers. Instead, he accepts his position as a servant in the family of his dispossessors, and he accepts the peonage of all the indigenous characters who admire him as an elder and leader. This acceptance of caste is a substantial, intractable problem in "Maruja," irresolvable when the story is read alone. In conversation with "Notes by Flood and Field," however, it becomes important that the villain and madman of "Maruja" belongs to another class than that of a white frontiersman. It requires the two stories together to clarify that frontiersmen are not necessarily villains, and Indians are not necessarily villains; rather, any character becomes monstrous when he commits murder or hunts up prophecies in his religious text against the neighbor who threatens his claim to property. Villainy does not belong essentially to any race or class or body in Harte's oeuvre, but follows when any "fixed idea" gets the upper hand on human sympathy.

Sharing Land

Rarely does Harte give an indigenous character a prominent, realistic place in his storytelling. In "Bret Harte's Portrayal of Half-Breeds" (1953), Margaret Duckett identifies a pattern of mixed-race characters embodying Harte's "sympathy" for people victimized by acts of "prejudice and wanton cruelty," and Gary Scharnhorst calls him "a racial progressive for his time."[73] The late story "The Ancestors of Peter Atherly" (1898) tells us more: the reader who takes Bill Handley's advice to withhold judgment about a writer's essentializing politics finds in the trio of "Notes by Flood and Field," "Maruja," and "The Ancestors of Peter Atherly" a persistent expectation that white American settlers adapt and assimilate to the foreigners and foreignness they encounter at the frontier of the hybrid American nation.[74] The son of a Plains tribal leader and a white American washerwoman, Peter Atherly embodies Harte's most ambitious attempt to wrest a half-Indian protagonist from the stereotypes of the captivity narrative and of American racial theory about the degeneration of mixed races and to dignify him as the descendant of "ancestors" and central character of a realist novella.[75] Despite the persistence of racial stereotypes, the messages of "The Ancestors of Peter Atherly" about mutual assimilation by marriage, the aptitude of mixed-blood children, and the need for intercultural understanding in jointly occupied western lands are progressive for the 1890s and for Harte's corpus. If Pereo is merely a relic of the past, Peter Atherly is a modern American citizen, picking up where George Tryan leaves off in "Notes by Flood and Field" in teaching white Americans how to live with colonial Others.

Peter Atherly is a California mining tycoon, the namesake of a western town, and a U.S. congressman, proud of his "undoubtedly" English surname and superior to "his Irish and German fellow citizens"—he talks "a good deal about 'race'"—when an Indian named Gray Eagle recognizes Peter in the national capital by a tattoo on his arm and corrects him about his paternity.[76] Gray Eagle reveals about Peter: "His father, big Injin, take common white squaw! Papoose no good,—too much white squaw mother, not enough big Injin father!"[77] The revelation explains some strange behavior of Peter and his twin sister, such as her ability to outride any man on a horse, her desire to swipe a lock of hair from a suitor, and the "wild and inexplicable resentment" Peter feels in England when he sees a statue of an Indian enchained by an English soldier.[78] As Gary Scharnhorst has pointed out, the story's naturalist presumption of racially based instincts is likely to be troubling to a modern reader. But, in his character as a realist reformer, Peter transcends racial typologies. He is working on a report at the time of his death that argues, "I am satisfied that much of the mischievous and extravagant prejudice against the half-breed and all alliances of the white and red races springs from the ignorance of the frontiersman and his hasty generalization of facts."[79] Unlike the son of the eponymous Malaeska in Ann Stephens's dime novel of 1860, who leaps from a cliff when he learns that he is half-Indian, Peter Atherly devotes himself to improving the mutual understanding of the races to which he belongs.[80] Peter, his sister, and his sister's unborn child do not survive their tale, but this novella's attempt to craft a more realistic mixed-race protagonist signifies that purity of "blood"—the obsession of characters in the two earlier stories—is not necessary for a useful, peaceful life; it is only a stereotype inflamed by such western genres as the captivity narrative and dime novel.

"Peter Atherly" grows most strange and histrionic in its rejection of the captivity narrative as a guide to Indian and white relations generally and Peter's character in particular.[81] Standing before a statue on what he thinks is his family estate in England, Peter first has a strange "resentment" at the representation of a captive Indian, and then he is surprised by an absurd desire to take a hostage in return for a shame he does not yet understand:

> He knew not how or why—a still more wild and terrible idea sprang up in his fancy. He knew it was madness, yet for a moment he could only stand and grapple with it silently and breathlessly. It was to seize this young and innocent girl [his companion], this witness of his disappointment, this complacent and beautiful type of all they valued here, and bear her away—a prisoner, a hostage—he knew not why—on a galloping horse in the dust of the prairie—far beyond the seas![82]

At this point, Peter does not even know that he is half-Indian, so his feelings of identification with the statue and his desire to repay an entire society for its wrongs by taking its most "beautiful type" for a hostage are inexplicable. Although a modern reader may dismiss the passage as a repulsive essentialism, it is important to Harte's treatment of genre. As a naturalist character, Peter possesses instincts from both parents, but he does *not* take anyone captive, at any point. He demonstrates in an age when white readers did not know this for fact that an Indian man, or "half-breed," at least, can master his impulses as well as a white man. As historian Daniel Walker Howe explains, nineteenth-century Americans prized "self-mastery" as a form of "character development" and one of the greatest of personal liberties.[83] In literature, this sort of self-control in a character is especially linked to the development of the realist novel. Peter Atherly is a liberal, realist American subject, capable of mastering instincts incompatible with modern civilized life.

Instead of taking a captive, Atherly ironically becomes one—not because of the instincts of racially pure Indians, but because of the intercultural misunderstanding that Peter correctly diagnoses and commits himself to repair if he can. The latter chapters of "Peter Atherly" take place at a western fort where Peter works as an "Apostle of Peace" with local tribes, trying to negotiate shared occupation of lands, despite the reluctance of Natives to accept him as a peace-broker.[84] Surprisingly, although no Indians except Peter are realistically individualized, Harte does invest these Plains tribes with the autonomy of resisting American peace overtures, which they justly find suspicious. With a constant state of tension between tribes and fort, Peter's sister and his love interest, the Englishwoman he once thought of abducting, ride into the woods alone and are captured offstage, out of sight of the reader. Peter rides after them, and his captivity is narrated explicitly enough to create friction with a conventional American frontier captivity tale. No sooner does he enter the woods on horseback but "he [feels] his arms and knees quickly seized from behind."[85] Told that his sister and her companion are already captured, he insists that the Englishwoman be sent back to the fort; he and his sister will remain captive. Harte challenges the conventions of Indian captivity in this scene because, in the capture that we witness, an Indian binds an Indian, and the captive impresses the captor and has his way. His captors recognize "force and dignity" in Peter and honor it by letting him walk with them into the woods, unbound.[86] On Peter's part, he has already chosen self-sacrifice in order to free Lady Elfrida. Captivity when it happens is not at all what Peter imagined earlier: an Indian man taking a white woman hostage out of retaliation and pride. Instead, tribes resentful and suspicious of whites kidnap those who come too close too often, and whose motives are uncertain to them. Peter and his sister die because their motives—her curiosity and his desire to help whites understand Indians better—are, ironically, not understood. The story's actual captivity is not romantic, adventurous, or manly, but a waste of life and symptom of a deep cultural impasse that even the isolated marriage here and there cannot solve. Although the story refuses to find interracial marriage monstrous, its tragedy is to demonstrate that there is no *social* place for the children of such marriages to live in peace. American society cannot call itself civilized, the descendant of Jewish, English, and Dutch immigrants insists, as long as fixed ideas about racial purity inhibit intercultural understanding.

As a group, these western stories of interracial attraction, courtship, and marriage work toward a radical idea of shared tenancy of contested lands. Harte's vision does not evict white settlers from the West, despite their offenses, and modern readers may fault him for demanding equal accommodations from indigenous and colonial characters. In the vision of his stories, however, the same principle applies to everyone: no one is entitled to commit offenses against his neighbor to preserve his claim to land. To do so is monstrous. Villains obsessed with the "fixed idea" of possession may come from any race or class or nationality. Some win and some lose in the shifting landscape of Harte's plots, but all run up against the plans of integrationists who believe they are free to make a life—even marry—among neighbors who speak a different language and dwell in a foreign style of house. Harte returns to the subject of racial hybridity as he returns to techniques of genre hybridity because "purity" in life and fiction is neither natural nor free. Fending off the monstrous imperial ideologies of purity and possession, Harte's westerns resort to gothic, weird sensations as they masticate and spit out the founding principles of the American occupation.

NOTES

1. Thomas, "Bret Harte," 94, 93; Green, *Encyclopedia*, 2. The stories Jeffrey Thomas studies in "Bret Harte and the Power of Sex," like the vampiric films in Barbara Creed's *The Monstrous-Feminine* (59–72), portray female sexuality as monstrous and threatening to men, marriage, and social stability.
2. Green, "Weird Western," 26. Justin Everett and Jeffrey H. Shanks underscore the importance of the interwar period in the development of weird genre fiction, although they also identify several early authors of "weird tales" whom Harte read and admired or parodied (*Unique Legacy*, x–xii).
3. Miller, "Introduction," 7.
4. As Gary Scharnhorst demonstrated in 1994, Bret Harte was already disappearing from American literature anthologies twenty-five years ago, with fewer stories selected when he did appear. Scharnhorst's findings continue to describe Harte's place in national anthologies ("Whatever").
5. Tom Hillard suggests "thinking of the Gothic as a literary *mode* rather than a genre" to make visible "the Gothic elements in Herman Melville's *Moby-Dick*, for instance, without having to make the claim that *Moby-Dick*

itself is a Gothic novel" ("Deep," 689). Charles Crow's *American Gothic* includes "works that could be considered Gothic-naturalist hybrids" (103) and other generically mixed selections.

6. Harte, "Mrs. Skaggs's Husbands," "In the Carquinez Woods," *Writings*, vols. 2 and 4.
7. Harte, "In a Hollow of the Hills," "The Passing of Enriquez," *Writings*, vols. 10 and 16.
8. Harte, "The Passing of Enriquez," *Writings*, vol. 16. Californios were Spanish-descended landowners in California at the time of the American conquest and the Gold Rush.
9. Harte, "Notes by Flood and Field," *Writings*, vol. 1, 346.
10. Mogen, Sanders, and Karpinski, *Frontier Gothic*, 23.
11. Savoy, "The Rise," 168. Focusing on slavery as a central national crime, Teresa Goddu writes similarly that the gothic seems to contradict "America's self-mythologization as a nation of hope and harmony" (*Gothic America*, 4).
12. Scharnhorst, *Bret Harte*, 147.
13. Hillard, "Deep," 690.
14. Kozaczka, "Genre Exchange," 88.
15. Morgan, *Biology of Horror*, 24–26.
16. Morgan, *Biology of Horror*, 29; "Toward an Organic Theory," 64.
17. Harte, *Writings*, vol. 8, 289. "Digger" was a derogatory term given by American settlers to Native peoples of Nevada and California. Harte satirizes the use of this term by emigrants. A "quartz-prospector" was a miner.
18. Harte, *Writings*, vol. 8, 322.
19. Kollin, "Race, Labor, and the Gothic Western," 678.
20. Morgan, "Toward," 63; Harte, "Maruja," *Writings*, vol. 5, 30.
21. Halberstam, *Skin Shows*, 14. Harte does not often consider western experience from the perspective of indigenous peoples. "The Ancestors of Peter Atherly," considered below, is unusual in that regard.
22. Halberstam, *Skin Shows*, 8.
23. Harte, "Flip," *Writings*, vol. 3, 297–98.
24. Carroll, *Philosophy of Horror*, 23.
25. Scholars who comment on Harte's racial progressivism have suggested that his sensitivity about his Jewish-English-Dutch ancestry helps to explain his critical perspective on white master narratives. See, for example, Duckett, 194.

26. Frost, *Never One Nation*, xii–xiii.
27. Handley, *Marriage, Violence*, 3.
28. Weierman, *One Nation, One Blood*, 90–100.
29. Rebecca Lush argues that Louisiana Creole Inez Middleton's "malleability, combined with her subservience to those around her, presents a cultural 'other' that can easily be reinscribed within an ever-expanding United States." An "anomaly" in Cooper's fiction, Inez answers "the challenge of how to 'Americanize' . . . previously foreign peoples" on the North American continent ("Louisianan Lady," 168).
30. Letter 12 (emphasis mine). For a more extended reading of Crevecoeur and the gothic, see Goddu, *Gothic America*, 13–30.
31. Elise Lemire explains why Cooper's metaphor of the "cross" is not a reference to Christianity or civilization, as readers once thought, but a reference to botany and animal husbandry and the purity of race (*"Miscegenation,"* 35–40). See also Lush, "Louisianan Lady," 155.
32. Lemire, "Miscegenation," 35.
33. Weierman finds biographical reasons for Cooper's and Sedgwick's interest in white-Native relations, and for Sedgwick's greater ability to picture a successful interracial marriage (62–90).
34. Lemire, "Miscegenation," 14.
35. Kaplan, "The Miscegenation Issue," 221–61.
36. Pascoe, *What Comes Naturally*, 1–2.
37. Desdemona falls in love with Othello while overhearing him tell her father stories "of moving accidents by flood and field" (*Othello*, 1.3.134). In its original magazine publication, Harte's title indicated the Shakespearean allusion with quotation marks. When he reproduced the story in volume 1 of his collected *Writings*, Harte simplified "Notes 'By Flood and Field'" to "Notes by Flood and Field" (Scharnhorst, *Bret Harte: A Bibliography*, 83; and Harte, *Writings*, vol. 1, viii).
38. Streeby, *American Sensations*, 166–69.
39. Harte, *Writings*, vol. 1, 366.
40. Shanks and Finn, "Vaqueros and Vampires," 3.
41. Harte, *Writings*, vol. 1, 345.
42. Harte, *Writings*, vol. 1, 346, 345.
43. Harte, *Writings*, vol. 1, 346.
44. Harte, *Writings*, vol. 1, 346.

45. Harte, *Writings*, vol. 1, 348.
46. Harte, *Writings*, vol. 1, 349, 352.
47. Harte, *Writings*, vol. 1, 350.
48. Halberstam, *Skin Shows*, 23.
49. Harte, *Writings*, vol. 1, 349.
50. Harte, *Writings*, vol. 1, 353.
51. Harte, *Writings*, vol. 1, 356.
52. Harte, *Writings*, vol. 1, 369–70.
53. Harte, *Writings*, vol. 1, 356.
54. Harte, *Writings*, vol. 1, 350.
55. Harte, *Writings*, vol. 1, 351.
56. Marianne Noble, "The American Gothic," 178.
57. Harte, *Writings*, vol. 1, 353.
58. Harte, *Writings*, vol. 1, 364.
59. Harte's narrator weakly suggests that Altascar appeal the legal decision, but Altascar seems to understand, two decades before Maria Amparo Ruiz de Burton made it plain in *The Squatter and the Don* (1885) and even before Harte's own experience in Washington, DC, led him to write the cynical "The Story of a Mine" (1877), that an appeal will be fruitless.
60. Warford, "An Eloquent and Impassioned Plea," 11.
61. Harte, *Writings*, vol. 8, 289.
62. Harte, *Writings*, vol. 5, 3.
63. The earlier Indian occupation is represented by a burial mound in the garden. In meetings there, as Renee Bergland might have predicted, servant Pereo and other Indians employed by the Guitierrez-Saltonstalls haunt the present with memories of a cursed past.
64. Harte, *Writings*, vol. 5, 19.
65. Harte, *Writings*, vol. 5, 30.
66. Harte, *Writings*, vol. 5, 62.
67. Harte, *Writings*, vol. 5, 138.
68. Harte, *Writings*, vol. 5, 39.
69. Harte, *Writings*, vol. 5, 30.
70. Harte, *Writings*, vol. 5, 32.
71. Twenty-four years and thousands of miles from California, Harte does not know what Maria Amparo Ruiz de Burton knows and reveals in *The*

Squatter and the Don: the Southern Pacific Railroad is not in business to enrich ranchers.
72. Harte, *Writings*, vol. 5, 31, 137.
73. Duckett, "Bret Harte's Portrayal," 193; Scharnhorst, "Bret Harte's Naturalism," 145.
74. Handley, *Marriage, Violence*, 6.
75. Although racial stereotypes abound in this longer story, Scharnhorst views Harte's typological approach to character as an aspect of his naturalism ("Bret Harte's Naturalism"). Judith Halberstam warns, "It is not always so simple to tell whether the presence of Gothic registers a conservative or a progressive move" (*Skin Shows*, 23).
76. Harte, *Writings*, vol. 16, 3, 25–27.
77. Harte, *Writings*, vol. 16, 27. Harte satirizes this Euro-American racial theory—that the offspring of two races inherit the worst traits of the parents—by letting readers hear what it sounds like if an indigenous man expresses it. See Scharnhorst, "Bret Harte's Naturalism," on the influence of Havelock Ellis's radical theory that "mixed race children might well inherit the *best* traits of their parents" (146; emphasis added).
78. Harte, *Writings*, vol. 16, 23.
79. Harte, *Writings*, vol. 16, 57.
80. To some degree, Harte's mixed-blood reformer might seem to fit the paradigm that Renee Bergland refers to as "ghostwriting with a vengeance"—when dead or fictionalized Indians speak for Euro-Americans. Certainly Atherly does voice Harte's opinion, but neither Atherly nor Harte voices the favored "mythology" of "White Americans" (160). Harte is countercultural enough to see white settler colonialism as monstrous, but his interest in a racially hybrid western future implicates him in the recurring plot of indigenous dispossession.
81. Harte's novel *Gabriel Conroy* (1871) also critiques the captivity narrative genre and manifest destiny (Tinnemeyer, *Identity Politics*, 107–21).
82. Harte, *Writings*, vol. 16, 23–24.
83. Howe, *Making the American Self*, 122.
84. Harte, *Writings*, vol. 16, 69.
85. Harte, *Writings*, vol. 16, 64.
86. Harte, *Writings*, vol. 16, 65.

BIBLIOGRAPHY

Bergland, Renee L. *The National Uncanny: Indian Ghosts and American Subjects.* Hanover NH: University Press of New England, 2000.

Carroll, Noel. *The Philosophy of Horror, or Paradoxes of the Heart.* New York: Routledge, 1990.

Creed, Barbara. *The Monstrous-Feminine: Film, Feminism, Psychoanalysis.* New York: Routledge, 1993.

Crow, Charles. *American Gothic.* Cardiff: University of Wales Press, 2009.

Duckett, Margaret. "Bret Harte's Portrayal of Half-Breeds." *American Literature* 25, no. 2 (May 1953): 193–212.

Everett, Justin, and Jeffrey H. Shanks, eds. *The Unique Legacy of Weird Tales: The Evolution of Modern Fantasy and Horror.* Lanham MD: Rowman & Littlefield, 2015.

Frost, Linda. *Never One Nation: Freaks, Savages, and Whiteness in U.S. Popular Culture, 1850–1877.* Minneapolis: University of Minnesota Press, 2005.

Goddu, Teresa A. *Gothic America: Narrative, History, and Nation.* New York: Columbia University Press, 1997.

Green, Paul. *Encyclopedia of Weird Westerns: Supernatural and Science Fiction Elements in Novels, Comics, Films, Television and Games.* 2nd ed. Jefferson NC: McFarland, 2016.

———. "Weird Western Comic Books of the 1950s." In Miller and Van Riper, ed., *Undead in the West II*, 26–44.

Halberstam, Judith. *Skin Shows: Gothic Horror and the Technology of Monsters.* Durham NC: Duke University Press, 1995.

Handley, William R. *Marriage, Violence, and the Nation in the American Literary West.* New York: Cambridge University Press, 2002.

Harte, Bret. *The Writings of Bret Harte.* 20 vols. Boston: Houghton Mifflin, 1896–1900.

Hillard, Tom J. "'Deep Into That Darkness Peering': An Essay on Gothic Nature." *ISLE* 16, no. 4 (Autumn 2009): 685–95.

Howe, Daniel Walker. *Making the American Self: Jonathan Edwards to Abraham Lincoln.* New York: Oxford University Press, 2009.

Kaplan, Sidney. "The Miscegenation Issue in the Election of 1864." In *Interracialism: Black-White Intermarriage in American History, Literature, and Law*, edited by Werner Sollors, 219–65. New York: Oxford University Press, 2000.

Kollin, Susan. "Race, Labor, and the Gothic Western: Dispelling Frontier Myths in Dorothy Scarborough's *The Wind.*" *Modern Fiction Studies* 46, no. 3 (Fall 2000): 675–94.

Kozaczka, Adam S. "Genre Exchange on the Supernatural Frontier in Stephen King's *The Gunslinger*: Gunfighter Archetype Meets the Ravenous Other." In Miller and Van Riper, ed., *Undead in the West II*, 87–105.

Lemire, Elise. *"Miscegenation": Making Race in America.* Philadelphia: University of Pennsylvania Press, 2010.

Lloyd-Smith, Alan. *American Gothic Fiction.* New York: Continuum, 2004.

Lush, Rebecca. "'Louisianan Lady': Racial Ambiguity, Gender, and National Identity in Cooper's *The Prairie.*" *Literature in the Early American Republic* 2 (2010): 153–71.

Miller, Cynthia J. "Introduction." In *Encyclopedia of Weird Westerns: Supernatural and Science Fiction Elements in Novels, Comics, Films, Television, and Games*, 2nd ed., edited by Paul Green, 4–13. Jefferson NC: McFarland, 2016.

———, and A. Bowdoin Van Riper, eds. *Undead in the West II: They Just Keep Coming.* Lanham MD: Scarecrow, 2013.

Miscegenation: The Theory of the Blending of the Races, Applied to the American White Man and Negro. By David Goodman Croly and George Wakeman. New York: H. Dexter, Hamilton, 1864.

Mogen, David, Scott Patrick Sanders, and Joanne B. Karpinski, eds. *Frontier Gothic: Terror and Wonder at the Frontier in American Literature.* Rutherford NJ: Fairleigh Dickinson University Press, 1993.

Morgan, Jack. *The Biology of Horror: Gothic Literature and Film.* Carbondale: Southern Illinois University Press, 2002.

———. "Toward an Organic Theory of the Gothic: Conceptualizing Horror." *Journal of Popular Culture* 32, no. 3 (Winter 1998): 59–80.

Noble, Marianne. "The American Gothic." In *A Companion to American Fiction, 1780–1865*, edited by Shirley Samuels, 168–78. Malden MA: Blackwell, 2004.

Pascoe, Peggy. *What Comes Naturally: Miscegenation Law and the Making of Race in America.* New York: Oxford University Press, 2009.

Savoy, Eric. "The Rise of American Gothic." In *The Cambridge Companion to Gothic Fiction*, edited by Jerrold E. Hogle, 167–88. New York: Cambridge University Press, 2002.

Scharnhorst, Gary. *Bret Harte: A Bibliography.* Lanham MD: Scarecrow, 1995.

———. *Bret Harte: Opening the American Literary West.* Norman: University of Oklahoma Press, 2000.

———. "Bret Harte's Naturalism." *Studies in American Naturalism* 1 (2006): 144–51.

———. "Whatever Happened to Bret Harte?" In *American Realism and the Canon*, edited by Tom Quirk and Gary Scharnhorst, 201–11. Newark: University of Delaware Press, 1994.

Shakespeare, William. *The Tragedy of Othello, the Moor of Venice.* In *The Complete Signet Classic Shakespeare*, 1096–1136. New York: Harcourt Brace Jovanovich, 1972.

Shanks, Jeffrey, and Mark Finn. "Vaqueros and Vampires in the Pulps: Robert E. Howard and the Dawn of the Undead West." In Miller and Van Riper, ed. *Undead in the West II*, 3–25.

Streeby, Shelley. *American Sensations: Class, Empire, and the Production of Popular Culture.* Berkeley: University of California Press, 2002.

Thomas, Jeffrey. "Bret Harte and the Power of Sex." *Western American Literature* 8, no. 3 (Fall 1973): 91–109.

Tinnemeyer, Andrea. *Identity Politics of the Captivity Narrative after 1848.* Lincoln: University of Nebraska Press, 2006.

Wall Hinds, Elizabeth Jane. "American Frontier Gothic." In *The Cambridge Companion to American Gothic*, edited by Jeffrey Andrew Weinstock, 128–40. New York: Cambridge University Press, 2017.

Warford, Elisa. "'An Eloquent and Impassioned Plea': The Rhetoric of Ruiz de Burton's *The Squatter and the Don*." *Western American Literature* 44, no. 1 (Spring 2009): 5–21.

Weierman, Karen Woods. *One Nation, One Blood: Interracial Marriage in American Fiction, Scandal, and Law, 1820–1870.* Amherst: University of Massachusetts Press, 2005.

Strange Country   2

Sexuality and the Feminine in Robert Coover's *Ghost Town*

ERIC MELJAC AND ALEX HUNT

Robert Coover's *Ghost Town* (1998) is a postmodern parody of genre western tropes.[1] A nameless "kid" without a past rides through "strange country" before being absorbed by a ghostly frontier town. Populated by a rough cast of frontiersmen, cowboys, gamblers, and outlaws, the town is dominated by two women, the "schoolmarm" and the "chanteuse," polar opposites, virgin and whore, who, in the end, are revealed as the same woman. The kid is by turns cast as stranger, hero, sheriff, outlaw, and villain. The action spins through a catalog of western storylines involving rustlers, train robbery, vigilante hangings, and so on. What initially appears as a deserted ghost town comes to life when the kid selects a jack of spades from an abandoned deck of cards in the old land claims office—a card that comes into play at the novel's climax. It is also in his initial venture into this ghost town that he first catches a glimpse of the Janus-faced schoolmarm behind a "dust-grimed window": "A beautiful woman, very pale, dark hair done up in a tight bun, dressed all in black."[2] At the sight of the schoolmarm, the novel's wheel of fortune is put into a symbolic spin—a turn resolved only at the climax, when Fortune intervenes, smiling in the kid's favor.

The western has always been weird, or weirder under critical scrutiny than as popularly consumed and generalized in the cultural imaginary. This view of the western as representing certain static conventions is epitomized by Jane Tompkins's assessment that the western, historically and generically, is a masculine genre "adamantly opposed to anything female."³ Victoria Lamont's important corrective, *Westerns: A Women's History* (2016), makes the case that women authors are in fact originators and shapers of the genre; only later did women's westerns become "ghettoized" and the masculine western canonized as a male-patriarchal form upheld by "masculinist critical paradigms."⁴ Between Tompkins's generalization and Lamont's revision, the western has retained the popular aura of masculine form, yet there remains a wide open country ripe for interpretation of the genre's gender dynamics. The present discussion sees Coover's *Ghost Town* not as expressing a radically new idea—in fact, it is mired in its own exploration of genre convention—but as making explicit a feminine power that was always latent in the western. *Ghost Town* is irreverent and funny, in some sense recalling the bawdy humor of *Blazing Saddles* (1974) even as it evokes the darker shadows of race and sex that drive *The Searchers* (1956). Overall, it is a weird novel and ours is a weird analysis, one that risks taking seriously an extended penis joke, engaging in a game of phallic three-card monte.

Coover's introduction of the "wheel of fortune" is the central figure of fate, free will, and possibility. His foregrounding of gender and sexuality in the wheel's turning casts these issues into relationship with questions of national history, Indian relations, and western myth. The novel props up, deconstructs, and rearranges the western's metanarratives of male dominance, female submission, and the vanished and silenced native. Coover's weird western thus uses literary form as a vehicle for critiquing the oppressive violence that is part and parcel of the myth of the American West, forcing a reckoning with the genre's covert language of desire and sexuality.

While the western is to some degree anchored in the Victorian American mores of *The Virginian* (1902) and its genteel veneer, Coover makes use of the ancient and medieval idea of Fortune's Wheel. The goddess Fortune spins her wheel of fate, introducing random changes in circumstance whereby individuals may gain great power and wealth or conversely be cast down into abject circumstance. The chanteuse-schoolmarm, the novel's most powerful figure, is a Fortune figure, and the kid is victim of her wheel's turns. The novel, as one critic said of Coover's work more broadly, dramatizes "the encounter with protean femaleness."⁵ Ultimately, we argue that Coover's treatment of sexuality and gender subverts western tropes and patriarchal normative sexuality. Here fate (Fortune) becomes dominatrix (chanteuse-schoolmarm), subverting manifest destiny, understood as the mastery of time (masculine) over space (feminine). The idea of masculine time and feminine space is based in classical mythology in the roles of the feminine Gaia and masculine Cronus. Carolyn Merchant outlines the long history in western philosophical thought through which the world is rendered as organic, animal, and female, as for example, in Plato's *Timaeus*.⁶ In her classic *The Lay of the Land* (1975), Annette Kolodny argues for the pervasive image of the Americas as metaphorically a "regression from the cares of adult life and a return to the primal warmth of womb or breast in a feminine landscape" and characterizes Frederick Jackson Turner's work as reinforcing the metaphor that "the West was a woman, and to it belonged the hope of rebirth and regeneration."⁷ In Western philosophical tradition as well as western American tradition, then, the space of the West is feminine, its lover and conqueror the masculine force of historical and future time.

A scene that serves as an example of the sexual parody and its associations with western genre tropes of heroism, the indigenous, and the feminine comes when Belle the chanteuse leads the townswomen in a protest against the male "authorities" at a moment when the kid is cast as sheriff. As the kid's deputy says, "The wimmenfolk in town is kickin up a awesome aggravation. It's jest only about gittin raped too reglar by the goddam savages, but their pants is on fire, it's a genuwine uprisin."⁸ These "wimmenfolk" are highly sexualized beings, according to the deputy's description. Such sexualization is often, in many ways, reserved for concepts of the masculine; however, in *Ghost Town*, it is the womenfolk who are the hypersexualized beings. In another instance, Belle testifies about how she was raped by the "cruel savages." Yet not only does she describe the scene, but she recreates it, exposing her sexual organs, and indeed her sexual being, to the kid: "Well, the first thing, the barroom singer says, is they hogtied me over a hitchin rail like this! She bends over the rail, her breasts spilling out, and takes hold of her ankles, while some of the other matrons tie her up there with some old frayed rope they've found in the street. They toss her black skirts up, tug her drawers down, pinch and palpate her exposed parts, and prod them with their brooms and pot handles."[9]

In this scene of bondage and sadomasochism—and parodic performance—women are completely in control of the sexual situation, and the male (the kid) is reduced to the position of the gaze. However, this is an uncomfortable gaze, because it is not the male who is in control of the gaze. Instead, he is practically forced into it, and the women *enjoy* the highly sexualized situation. The kid is an uncomfortable observer as he remarks, "Well jest so nobody dont git hurt here."[10] To this line Coover adds a condition: "He says uneasily."[11] This uneasiness suggests a sexual role reversal. While the male gaze is so often associated with the viewing of the pornographic or the deviant, instead it is the "hysterical women" who enjoy the exhibitionism and the male who sees this *uncomfortably*. In these positions, rather than the normative sexual roles, the women, and particularly the chanteuse, take what Michel Foucault reminds his readers "belongs, *par excellence*, to men," and transfer that "belonging" to themselves.[12] The scene bucks, in many ways, what readers would commonly find not only in the Western literary canon, but also in a more reserved Western cultural society.

In another key scene, the kid is himself made the tool of an attempted rape of the schoolmarm at the hands of the saloon drunks. For their hilarious amusement, they first force him to sit to a meal of "a pair of large uncooked testicles, still bloody and pulsing like a hairy heart," the aphrodisiac effect of which is "terrible prurience" and an excruciating erection.[13] The men of the saloon and his own "quivering member" propel the kid toward the schoolmarm, who quite suddenly appears in the scene, pinned against the piano by more ruffians. Even as the kid apologizes to the schoolmarm and protests—his "bucking organ" aimed unerringly through the "webbed complications of her underclothing"—he is unwillingly becoming the tool of a horrific rape.[14] Only when he accepts the Bible proffered by the schoolmarm is he (and she) saved. Opening the Bible, he finds a small pistol in its hollowed-out pages, with which he shoots his way out, magically ending the scene. Of course, it is Belle who has orchestrated and performed the role of the schoolmarm in this scene of rape; in both situations, with the chanteuse and the schoolmarm, the kid is both clearly marked as male through emphasis of his penis and is emasculated through his lack of control of the situation and of himself.

Coover's western parodies the heroism and masculinist emphases of John Ford's *Stagecoach* (1939), in which one finds a similar cast of characters, and an equally hostile terrain, but the depiction of conventional gender norms cement a kind of presumed masculine frontier in the cultural imagination.[15] On the other hand, in *Ghost Town*, the lost "hero," exposed and vulnerable in the expansive (filmic) western space, seems by turns empowered and—more significantly—emasculated and victimized. Threats of generic "Indian" raids call for the violent protection of womenfolk, though the women seem to use the threat to manipulate the men. More specifically, while our antihero takes on the roles of both sheriff and outlaw at turns, he is often ridiculed, feminized, accused of being "one a them transvested pussies."[16] Rather than having his masculinity affirmed through recuperation, *Ghost Town* instead resets to another scene, another generic scenario. The threatened rape echoes issues of sexual and gender determinacy, illustrated by Judith Butler in *Gender Trouble* (1990).[17] The emasculation of the man without a name is truly a point where a Western cultural apparatus negotiates a relative gender identity for the cowboy.[18] As Judith Butler states, "Gender ought not to be construed as a stable identity or locus of agency from which various acts follow; rather, gender is an identity tenuously constituted in time, instituted in an exterior space through a *stylized repetition of acts.*"[19]

Coover plays with identity, space, and sexuality (particularly emasculation). It is through this emasculation that the foregrounding of gender identity reveals itself, the kid's emasculation at the hands of such a rough cast of characters illustrating the embedded discussion of gender identity inherent in any form of performative sexuality. While the scene falls into the western pattern of what Lee Clark Mitchell has called "a man being beaten," the kid is not reaffirmed in masculine heroism through his recuperation, Mitchell's sense that through punishment and abuse of "the male body" the man "becomes what he already is."[20] Instead, the man is torn down, humiliated. But the wheel will pick him back up, too, recast in heroic mode.

Coover's novel is not reducible to a parody of western tropes and conventions, however. On a fundamental and structural level, the ideological critique of the western must be understood through the imagery of circular movement, of wheels and reels, that ultimately expose the artificial space of the western as constructed through media technology, historically and today. On the nineteenth-century American scene, westward expansion following the Civil War was fueled by photography, and the era saw innovation toward moving pictures. One form, familiar to us from Henry David Thoreau's description in "Walking" (1862), was the panorama. While first presented as a linear series of images (sketches, paintings, or daguerreotypes) the viewer would pass by, later inventions created a more powerful sense of narrative. The apex, perhaps, was John Wesley Jones's 1852 "moving painting" *Pantoscope of California, Nebraska, Utah, and the Mormons*.[21] Jones went on expeditions to California, creating photographs and sketches that were then reproduced as paintings. These spectacles moved, as Martha Sandweiss describes, as a long painted scene "unscrolled from one upright cylinder to another across a stage, giving viewers the illusion of traveling."[22] Interestingly, the trip down the Mississippi could be followed by a second feature—the trip back up the Mississippi—as the scroll was rewound. Panoramas depicting the American West, as Sandweiss argues, provided a narrative of westward expansion: "The success of the Mississippi River panoramas, coupled with the intense interest in the far West spurred by the discovery of California gold, soon created an audience demand for panoramic depictions of the overland (and overseas) routes to the mines."[23] The male voice-over narration of the moving scenes, as in the case of Jones, provided "resounding ethnocentric nationalism" on "a triumphalist march westward."[24] This was powerful, as Sandweiss argues, as "the West represented a place of common national purpose."[25] Western landscape may be feminine, but Jones's technology sublimates space to time through its technology of linear rollers. Coover subverts this masculine master narrative, particularly in its collusion with patriarchal constructions of gender and sexuality.

As movement across mythic space is a key aspect of the western, Coover's mechanical treatment of space is key to understanding *Ghost Town*. The aesthetic of *Ghost Town* references the filmic western by incorporating media technology into the landscape itself. If the kid's movement across space is random, space also moves around the kid. In Coover's novel, space is unbound, not subject to the masculinist narrative of time, a Turnernian sense of manifest destiny. The kid finds himself on a "vast empty plain," a "monumental void" in which "the ground the horse treads, for all its extension, might be paper thin and stretched over nothing."[26] Coover signals that "the West" is less a historical, geographical space than a blank page or screen whereon, as a character later puts it, they might "signify."[27] The kid rides toward a distant town, which recedes and vanishes like a "mirage."[28] He nods off periodically, waking to find it either full dark or high noon, "just one condition or its contrary like the two pictures on a magic lantern slide, flicking back and forth, as he opens and closes and opens his eyes."[29] One day the kid discovers, looking behind him, that another town lies in back of him, "a kind of mirror image" of the one he is riding toward. The town behind is "gaining on him" and eventually "glides up under his horse's hoofs from behind and proceeds to pass him by even as he ambles forward."[30] Only later after an encounter with what seems a band of bandits (one of whom he kills) does the kid finally arrive in the town: "It is high noon, and the main street of the vaporous town which has been so long eluding him now rolls up under his mustang's plodding hoofs as through in abrupt repair of some mechanical disorder."[31] Such imagery of mechanisms and rollers is heavily suggestive of early scenic representation, notably the panorama.

From Coover's overt reference to the magic lantern to his moving pictures of the western plains, Coover engages the myth of the American West both through its iconography and the technological representation of that iconography. While offering no explicit critique, the novel certainly refutes manifest destiny's justification of violence as regenerative. Instead, the West is, as one character frames it, "the adventurous stage a grand emprise," where many narrative braids with many potential outcomes vie for our attention through moving reels of film, which, in Coover's deft handling, are brought forward and backward and are spliced and respliced (to the befuddlement of the kid) through various western plots.[32] The feminine space, controlled, as we shall see, by the chanteuse-schoolmarm, is not bound by the masculine narrative of manifest progress.

The turning of the wheel is a crucial idea in the novel, whether the turning of the panorama's scroll, the film's reel, or Fortune's Wheel. At a later point, the kid experiences travel from the ghost town as "like they're on the rim of some wheel and the town's the hub, for it keeps rotating with his own sluggish progress, showing him always the same distant view," and he passes "the skeletal ruins of an old covered wagon lying on its side," with "one of the spoked wooden wheels . . . still slowly turning in the dead air, round and round, as though recalling the clocking of time when there was time."[33] These images hearken to the wheel of fortune in the saloon of the ghost town, which the kid first notices when the kid slaps down the "black one-eared jack" that he drew from the ghost town pack: "At the back, the tall fortune wheel creaks and ticks in its slow ceaseless rounds."[34] Later, when the saloon returns to being a dead ruin, the kid will again notice the "busted wheel of fortune."[35] This brings us back to the association of fickle fate and the feminine in Fortune's Wheel. Coover's novel deconstructs this aged master narrative, playing with the notion of the misogynistic concept of female Fortune, doing so through complex and bizarre sexual situations that empower and foreground Fortune as being in control and as "master-actor," rather than merely irrational. In fact, Fortune, characterized as the chanteuse-schoolmarm, may be fickle in her treatment of the kid, but she certainly is not treated by Coover with a misogynistic tone. Rather, Fortune is given even more power—the power of the phallus, which, in a Freudian sense, reverses the castration complex and empowers the feminine.

These sexual negotiations are connected to Fortune's Wheel, for the feminine sexual energy subverts masculine patriarchy just as the operations of chance and fate give the lie to the necessity of manifest destiny. Throughout *Ghost Town*, Coover peppers his reader with suggestions of Fortune's Wheel, mostly as a gambling prop, until he ultimately represents it as united with a sexually empowered female body. Classically, the wheel of fortune, or Fortune's Wheel, is personified as a female of fickle nature. In *The Consolation of Philosophy*, Boethius gives perhaps one of the best discussions of Fortune of late antiquity and the early medieval period. In various ways, Boethius's *Philosophy* warns the author of Fortune's will being greater than the will of man. Boethius's take on Fortune's Wheel is significant for Coover's narrative because Boethius ties the Wheel to notions of trust and determinacy.[36] Indeed, the kid cannot trust *anything* in this ghost town, not the chanteuse-schoolmarm, not the gang of roughs, not the landscape itself. In terms of determinacy, one can also see how the highly sexualized situations in the novel deconstruct and play with normative sexual roles, and such indeterminacy follows Boethius's warning that Fortune is ultimately mutable. The kid seems to understand well enough that the whim of the wheel of fortune is not always an imminent threat, so much as it is the free play of chance (or the "spin of chance") on a weary cowboy.[37] He is not in control: as Boethius's *Philosophy* states, "If you are trying to stop her wheel from turning, you are of all men the most obtuse."[38]

In the western space of national imaginary, Coover's *Ghost Town* inverts the masculine narrative and casts female agency as central in a play of sexuality and power. The wheel of fortune, acting as the dominant figure in the narrative, not only introduces the notion of femininity and chance, but it also represents exactly how Coover's text refuses linearity. The wheel of fortune can spin and stop at any point, entirely under the control of Fortune. Thus, narrative predictability, the very thing that linear time and place allows, is absent entirely from Coover's story, and by extension Coover's depiction of the American West. This "ghost town" must be understood as a representation of an American West that is entirely nonlinear, both in time and place. Coover's ghost town morphs, folds, reorganizes itself, expands, and contracts, just as the narrative appears to leap from scene to scene. The fact that the landscape and timeline of the novel appears nonlinear reinforces the notion that this narrative reimagines time (perhaps even narrative temporality) and place as markedly feminine. Indeed, the concept "of linear temporality, which is readily labeled masculine"—an idea articulated by Julia Kristeva in "Women's Time"—is tossed aside in Coover's postmodern western parody.[39] The feminization of the West in *Ghost Town*, by way of temporal and material gender inversions, gives rise to the powerful, sexually charged, and at times violent chanteuse-schoolmarm, introducing a pronounced femininity to the American West uncommon to the fan of popular American western fiction and film as enforced by "masculinist critical paradigms."[40] At the same time, the kid becomes subject to a gender identity crisis, insofar as he is emasculated by a ritualistic rape and is also feminized by way of the chanteuse-schoolmarm who challenges him for gender superiority. This identity crisis is one that cannot be and is not resolved, despite his efforts to combat threats to his heteronormativity. By the end, the chanteuse seems nothing so much as an S-M dominatrix enacting western genre tropes for her amusement and the bemusement of the hero.

The inversion of the masculine western narrative and casting of female agency is nowhere more visible than in the control that the chanteuse has over the kid, and indeed over the path of the narrative itself, linking her to Fortune's Wheel. Her appearance and seduction of the kid early in the novel seems almost stereotypical, with her lines delivered in a parody of Mae West ("Come up and see me sometime!"). The chanteuse, with the kid now mysteriously in her room examining "his new duds," delivers a teasing line: "Hlo, cowboy.... C'mon over here, darlin, and solace a poor widder woman with a sorely achin heart and a lonesome pussy sufferin from a sudden and dreadful deprivement."[41] The kid is unmoved, even in the view of raw sexuality. Elsewhere, Coover reveals her as a stunning provocateur: "It's the barroom chanteuse with the orange curls and the ruby in her cheek, propped up in the bed in a silky black nightgown with slots in it for putting her powdered ruby-tipped breasts on view."[42] Even in this hypersexualized moment, with the chanteuse inviting a sexual escapade, the kid does not bite. "Sorry, mam," he says, "I aint the condolin sort."[43] The stereotypical masculine narrative suggestion here is that the chanteuse's sexual invitation would greatly be appreciated by a weary cowboy. However, his resistance in the face of the chanteuse's assertion of sexual power actually places the kid in a disadvantaged position. Coover notes this by displaying the kid viewing himself and his clothing in the mirror once again: "He turns to study himself in the mirror, considering why it is he's been fitted out like this. He feels exceedingly powerful and yet powerfully vulnerable at the same time. Strange country. All this empty space, a body can see for miles. Yet it's impossible to shake the feeling that, whichever way he turns, he's got somebody or something just behind him."[44] Of note is the phrasing "exceedingly powerful and yet powerfully vulnerable."[45] It appears that the kid's "power" comes only from his new clothing, "a fringed and beaded buckskin shirt with matching leggings . . . glossy new boots . . . white ten-gallon hat . . . and hand-tooled gun belt" fitted with "silver-plated, ivory-handled Peacemakers" and "a new Winchester."[46] In this setting, the kid has apparent power, through his clothes and weapons, and also his words—in refusing or accepting her advances, his words affect the "perkiness" of the chanteuse's breasts.

However, given all of the power the kid *seems* to have over the sexual prowess of the chanteuse, he remains completely vulnerable to her control. Indeed, this vulnerability comes as a result of the chance and nonlinearity of the ghost town itself. The sexually free chanteuse, the maestro of the narrative events, orchestrates what happens in the ghost town. The chanteuse appears throughout the novel rather fortuitously. Her appearances are not linear, but are instead placed seductively, as if guiding the kid along the broken and continuously morphing path of this strange country. In this particular instance, the transition between scenes that results in the kid's miraculous appearance in new clothes in the chanteuse's apartment distorts linear time, creating a break, marking the time parameters as, perhaps, feminine. As a matter of fact, this transition is framed by females and an accompanying feminization of the kid himself.

This occurs, too, in the context of Coover's sexualized parodic treatment of the Indian captivity narrative. Prior to his appearance in the chanteuse's apartment, the kid, in the throes of memory, dream, or fantasy, is preparing to marry a "young Indian lass" who "loves him openly, freely."[47] The kid is cared for by this native. This concept of the rugged cowboy is turned, as if on a wheel, to a man in constant need of consolation, care, and ultimately codependency. However, in his cultural alienation and ignorance, the kid seems blind to his own parodic subversion. He does not have to ask, beg, or take, but he is "welcomed" into her. Even in this "welcoming" there is a hint of the parodic. Coover calls the lass "naive as this land of her birth," but in this dream or fantasy, we get the only glimpse of the kid as a stereotypical male hero. For, as "she looks into [the kid's] eyes and the entrails of a dead badger and prophesies that . . . his old life will beckon him once more and he will abandon her and his newfound brothers and sisters and so cause her to die of a broken heart," the kid beats "his chest in the manner that he's been taught," suggesting he will fulfill his stereotypical masculine duties to her for her mothering and sex.[48] None of this can be taken seriously, however, as it is only a dream, pushed even further out of the temporality of the broken narrative. Coover even expresses that the kid knows that the lass's prophesies will hold true. Even in the realm of a dream, the female fortune-teller controls the kid's destiny. This feminine agency recollects the revenge narrative of the prostitutes who shape men's destinies in Clint Eastwood's *Unforgiven* (1992), but in Coover's parodic West, female Fortune is more powerful, predicting—or even forcing the hand of—the kid's fate.

The indigenous "presence," to the degree that *Ghost Town* includes indigenous actors, is slight. Coover's Indian figure primarily comes through the kid's memory or dreams (notably that of his Indian wife), or through the innuendo of the townsfolk who blame "goddam savages" for predation.[49] One scene has the kid encountering "an old toothless Indian" camped in the desert under "the swarm of stars overhead." The kid asks the man what the stars say and he answers, "They say the universe is mute. Only men speak. Though there is nothing to say."[50] The kid is drugged by a puff of the Indian's pipe and comes back to consciousness to shoot the old man, who is stealing the kid's horse and possessions, in the back of the head.[51] The scene surely satirizes a Cormac McCarthy western in its juxtaposition of existential pretension and gory violence, and in a larger sense Coover's "Indian princess" scene surely satirizes the frontier fantasy of John Smith and Pocahontas. It is worth noting that the dream episode turns to nightmare when, having told her that he must leave her, she begins to strangle him while holding him underwater.[52] To further the notion that the female (here, the Indian lass) controls the male, it is after this sadomasochistic ritual that the kid finds himself being drowned by this lass, "her powerful hands . . . at his throat" and he "fighting for his life."[53] This fortune-telling lass has the power to kill the kid, dominating his life, as he had just been subjected to abject embarrassment by way of the erogenous zones of his body.

The novel reenacts the frontier fantasy of "going native" or "playing Indian" in what Shari Huhndorf enables us to recognize as a spoof of the New Age captivity narrative, a performance of indigenous identity that actually continues a politics of erasure.[54] In this beginning moment of framing, the kid's lack of power, his vulnerability, is also introduced by way of his own feminization. He is to marry the Indian lass, so he must undergo a "special purgative ceremony . . . known as the dance of the errant bridegroom."[55] In this version of the Plains tribes' Sun Dance, his nipples pierced, skewered, and roped, he is made to "hang . . . by the ropes to the central pole of the medicine lodge, his ankles and privy member weighted down with buffalo skulls."[56] At the same time, the native men "carve religious symbols in his buttocks."[57] Such exposure, highly sexualized insofar as it involves manipulation and rendering of genitalia and hindquarters, suggests an engendered weakening in the kid. *He* becomes the subject of a sadomasochistic ritual, rigged with ropes and piercings, concepts, ideas, and actions typically associated with that which one finds in examples of s-m pornography. Coover might be guilty here of a token inclusion of indigenous peoples that further marginalizes and silences, but he is at least clear that the figure of the Indian is a crucial player in the psychosexual conquest of the American West.[58] And it is feminine sexuality that comes to dominate space in this western. The confirmation of the feminine power of the ghost town reflects the dynamics Laura Mulvey posits in her 1975 essay "Visual Pleasure and Narrative Cinema." In the essay, Mulvey argues that "an active/passive heterosexual division of labour has ... controlled narrative structure. According to the principles of the ruling ideology and psychical structures that back it up, the male figure cannot bear the burden of sexual objectification."[59] Thus, in the refusal of the chanteuse-schoolmarm, the traditional "active/passive HETEROSEXUAL division of labour" is deconstructed in the narrative. The kid, who as we shall see, will slay the phallus, can do so only because of a feminine entity and remains unable "bear the burden of sexual objectification."[60] Instead, it is the chanteuse-schoolmarm who controls the narrative, asserting her power of the wheel of fortune, refusing to let the kid "rule" by forcing her to flee the town. By controlling the narrative structure in this fashion, the female becomes the active figure in the narrative, objectifying the male, insofar as the female calls the shots as to what the kid actually does and will be able to do in the future. Not only is the kid sexually objectified and emasculated early in the narrative; he proves not to be in control of his own narrative, and Coover's choice to hand the power of the narrative to the Janus-faced female figure flips that narrative. In asserting control, the chanteuse-schoolmarm figuratively castrates the kid and renders the him ultimately powerless in the narrative. He cannot be the hero of this novel. At best, he is an emasculated "second," who bows to the whims of this eerie ghost town that is dominated, both in terms of orchestration and narration, by a female character. Using Mulvey's terms, the chanteuse-schoolmarm assumes "the man's role as the active one of advancing the story, making things happen."[61] Such control feminizes the narrative, inverting the classical narrative structure and positing a weird west that reveals the western's latent female sexual agency.

Coover's mysterious and strange West remains characterized as a sexualized feminine West. As we have already mentioned, the controlling forces in the ghostly crowd are all female: Fortune and her wheel, the chanteuse, and the accompanying schoolmarm. Yet it is perhaps in the moments of female bodies on display—display that is invited and not forced—that reinforce the fact that this weird West is indeed governed by the female body. Even though the chanteuse is sexually aggressive, this aggression appears to be a kind of assertion of power, a kind of might that embodies the ever-changing western landscape the kid rides into. The chanteuse, in essence, takes on the role of the phallus, being the driving sexualized force in this barren landscape. In the position of the phallus, she acquires a Lacanian sense of power.[62] The way in which the chanteuse controls events, especially for the kid, by way of her body, suggests that she has "become" the phallus. As Hélène Cixous says, "[A woman's] libido will produce far more radical effects of political and social change than some might like to think."[63] Indeed, the chanteuse's libido produces a very acute political and social change in terms of what one would consider a dusty, weathered frontier saloon town. This is in contrast with the most hackneyed vision of the western frontier with the hero riding into town and setting order. This ghost town is "ruled by the female body politic," for, as Cixous also claims, "women are body."[64] In terms of Coover's work, that "women are body" is exhibited by the fact that so much of the chanteuse-schoolmarm's narrative space is description of the body. From perky breasts and a beauty mark on the cheek to skin exposed at the knee, most of what the reader reads of this Janus character is focused on bodily description, and moreover on what those erotic body parts suggest—sexual, feminine sexual power and the inversion of normative masculine sexual dominance.

Western gear—ropes, riggings, and so on—is not unknown in the realm of sexual fetish. The kid, for example, in a moment of high action, jumps into a horse-team rigging that he suddenly "associates with garter belts,"[65] recalling the "webbed complications" of the schoolmarm's underwear.[66] Margaret Weiss explains that "real SM is about 'energy' or 'power exchange.'"[67] She furthers this notion by arguing that, "on the one hand, SM is figured as outlaw: as transgressive of normative sexual values. On the other hand, SM is dependent on social norms: practitioners draw on social hierarchies to produce SM scenes, just as norms performatively produce subjects."[68] Therefore, in this scene, the chanteuse exhibits herself in a performative sadomasochistic way. It may transgress what the kid sees as "normative sexual values," but in exhibiting herself in this manner, exposing herself tied over the hitching post, the chanteuse *performs* a sexual *scene*. Indeed, she draws from this particular instance of sexual exhibition an "energy" and a "power exchange." In the first instance, she creates the energy necessary to draw the gaze of the kid to her. In the second instance, she assumes the role of power player. The kid, who is uneasy, is weakened in the scene by way of the chanteuse's *performative* weakening in the sadomasochistic situation. This is a power grab by the chanteuse, a power grab she asserts continuously throughout *Ghost Town*.

Such control over the kid by the chanteuse repeats itself throughout Coover's novel, as again, before a never-to-occur hanging, the chanteuse sexually invites the kid as she "kneels down beside him, flashing her naked underparts at him. I brung yu sumthin t'eat, honey, she says suggestively, and the thing between her legs seems to blow him a wet kiss. He turns his head away. . . . Yu're really up agin it, hero, she whispers, breathing heavily."[69] Belle controls the kid sexually and linguistically. She refers to the kid as a "hero," which he certainly is not; rather, she dominates him as hero of Coover's novel. "Thing," often slang for "penis," speaks in this moment for Belle, who invites the kid by way of "speaking" as an act of sexual advance. The chanteuse's language is one of fetishized eroticism, an eroticism of control governed symbolically by her "thing," a vividly phallic reference. Belle dominates sexually, her vagina a mouthpiece for erotic gesture, while her counterpart, the schoolmarm, as we will see, dominates linguistically through "proper" English grammar, offered verbally.

If the chanteuse resembles the highly sexualized, phallic-laden power of the feminine in Coover's narrative, then her Janus-like counterpart, the schoolmarm, demonstrates a kind of gender normativity, in a sexual sense, and also a performative association with linguistic and intellectual dominance of the feminine over the masculine. At a time when the kid suffers from painful arrow wounds from an Indian attack on a caravan, reminiscent of *Stagecoach*, the schoolmarm enters the scene, cleaning the kid's wounds and suggestively sucking the poison from the open flesh, once again arousing him to erection. The scene of healing thus becomes a highly sexualized scene, reminding the reader of the two faces of the chanteuse-schoolmarm. The suggestive head-bobbing and sucking is accompanied by an equally strong intellectual characterization. Notice how the schoolmarm (who is also the chanteuse) corrects the kid's use of the English language as he apologizes for his aroused state and thanks her for treating his wounds: "Sorry, mam. Cain't help thet. But I'm mighty obliged. She frowns down upon him, her thin unpainted lips pressed together. There is a tiny black beauty spot on her cheek, set there, it would seem, though it's probably but a mole, to compliment her long black dress. Fer whut yu done fer my laig, I mean. Did, she says sternly. I am obliged for what yu *did* for my leg. Yes'm. He closes his eyes. Yu're welcome."[70]

This particular scene with the schoolmarm creates a sense of conflict for the reader. Induced to raw sexual power by way of the chanteuse, one is accustomed to viewing the female characters as sexual beings, and Coover almost allows this to happen with the schoolmarm as he mentions, delicately, the beauty mark on her face. This reference to the flesh demonstrates a sexualized gaze, but one that is negated instead by the primacy of the intellect that the schoolmarm represents as she corrects the "done" for "did" in the kid's expression of gratitude. The schoolmarm not only heals the body of the kid, but she also acts in an intellectually superior manner, correcting the kid's speech. Once again a female character is in control of this parodic western narrative. The gender roles have been turned upside down once more, for the superior intellect of the schoolmarm dominates, thereby abandoning particular tropes of male dominance one would find in western tropes of male dominance.

Coover returns near the end of his novel to a scene of indigenous peoples, seemingly a bookend to the Indian maiden fantasy near the novel's opening. This time, the kid awaits his hanging in a jail cell and remembers a day on the desert when suddenly "a great band of warriors came galloping past riding bareback and without reins, heads high and staring rigidly ahead." The kid sees that "their lips were all sewn shut with rawhide thongs and their chests and foreheads were tattooed with mysterious pictographs and the teeth and tiny bones of animals embedded in their flesh." While his reaction is typically without affect, the kid realizes "that they were galloping into oblivion and carrying the secrets of the universe with them, and that although those secrets were not very interesting, they were the only secrets there were, and he would not be privy to them."[71] While the imagery can be read as parody—of McCarthy, of the vanished or last Indian, of New Age-y spiritualism—it is a deeply disturbing image that relates to the visual logic of the gender politics of the novel.

If the novel subverts the western by empowering the feminine over the conventional masculine imperialist narrative of manifest destiny, this tide does not lift all ships. The chanteuse-schoolmarm rules through the labials, whether by the chanteuse's nether kiss or the schoolmarm's grammar lessons. Conversely, the indigenous voice—heard once in the figure of an old man who assures the kid the "universe is mute"— is here violently muted and condemned to oblivion.[72] In fact, the townswomen set the men against the Indians when they accuse the "devil Indians" of rape and torture: "Us proper ladies jest aint habituated t'sechlike incivil misabuse! . . . Our innocent coosies is bein sorely afflicted!" The women advance their cause, in other words, by scapegoating, demanding "dead injuns."[73] Overall, while the feminine becomes powerful in this western, the indigenous remains victim, scapegoat, voiceless subaltern.

The power of the chanteuse-schoolmarm, or otherwise of the feminine power of Fortune over will (masculine, manifest destiny) is verified in the final wheel of fortune scene. Here, the kid, in his sheriff role, seems to take control of the situation as he must face the dealer of the wheel of fortune game.⁷⁴ At stake is the schoolmarm tied to the spinning wheel, seemingly a human sacrifice, her "black skirts falling past her knees each time she's upside down."⁷⁵ The kid's bet is his own life to save the schoolmarm's, and the game commences. Both the dealer—described as "immense bald and beardless man in a white suit," a seemingly phallic figure (reminiscent of the judge in McCarthy's *Blood Meridian*)—and kid cheat their way through the hand, but the kid plays on what he discerns as the dealer's blindness to gain advantage.⁷⁶ In the end, the kid lies, misrepresenting the last card dealt, and meanwhile sneaks around to cut the dealer's throat with his bowie knife.⁷⁷ The dealer's neck "leaks a "white fatty ooze" as the dying dealer's mechanical card shooters spurts cards across the table.⁷⁸ The kid successfully rescues the schoolmarm from the wheel and tries to escape from the town, but the schoolmarm refuses to leave, and the kid sees "the strands of orange curls peeking out beneath the unsettled bun."⁷⁹ It is the chanteuse-schoolmarm who controls the wheel of fortune in this ghost town. To follow the crazily gendered logic of the scene, it would seem that both the dealer and the kid are powerless in the face of the power of the chanteuse-schoolmarm; in fact, the kid symbolically slays the phallus—thus emasculating himself, and himself confirming the feminine power of the ghost town.

In other words, even though the kid *seems* to be the victor in this climactic scene, he could not have become victor without the intervention of the mistress Fortune. The schoolmarm, earlier tied to the spinning wheel, is an overt and direct reference to Fortune's Wheel (as she, as both chanteuse and schoolmarm, has been all along). Her mere presence in this scene reflects Coover's attempt to show that, without the influence of Fortune, the kid could not have escaped the dealer episode of being roughed up once more. This becomes even more pronounced in the jail after the murder when the chanteuse argues that the kid ought to be hanged for his apparent crimes. In the end, the kid is released, and in a joking manner, Coover displays the chanteuse-schoolmarm's ever-arching influence over the kid's fate. "I'm gonna miss yu, darlin," says the chanteuse, dressed still as the schoolmarm, albeit sloppily. She continues, "Aint ever day someone like yu comes driftin through." At this point, in a referential spin to the schoolmarm's correction of the kid's English earlier in the novel, the kid replies, "It *is* not *every* day."[80] In this linguistic play, we see the kid has indeed been influenced all along by this woman, this woman of fortune, and it is she who determined his fate all along.

One cannot mistake, knowing that the other face of this Janus schoolmarm is Belle the chanteuse, the hint to the dominance of female sexuality as Coover repeatedly tempts the reader to notice her flesh—from the beauty mark mentioned above, to the peeks at the skin above her stockings as she (the schoolmarm) spins on the wheel of fortune. The reader is constantly reminded of the coupled essence of feminine dominance in this frontier ghost town: intellect and sexuality. Here, the male, the antihero kid, has no power whatsoever. His fate is determined by Fortune only, a fickle female character of antiquity, and his maneuvers in the town itself are governed by a two-faced female, a schoolmarm-chanteuse who doubly dominates both his intellect and sexuality, rendering him incapable of asserting any masculine power over the ever-changing landscape, which twists and turns in constant postmodern free play, turning tropes on their heads and keeping readers questioning their expectations of the western.

In the final scene, the ghost town again leaves him, rolling away like the panorama or like reels of film, a great metawestern in which the center has not held, fickle fate and feminine power giving the lie to patriarchal monomyth of manifest destiny. Instead, Coover's tendency to refuse reductive plots, to "subvert the inexorable logic that sends . . . cowboy to sunset," demands that we break out of formulaic narrative.[81] Finally, the kid is left only with one object of the reality of his experience: "He touches the card in his pocket"—the one-eyed jack—"to be sure it's still there," yet even this evidence, of history or masculinity, is meaningless, "but a sign" of his experience.[82] The western itself, the novel suggests, is similarly a "signifyin" of the West, a series of conventions that silence a history that they purport to celebrate.

NOTES

1. The novel recalls Coover's other work, in various ways, notably his "western" play *The Kid* (1972) and a story "Shootout at Gentry's Junction"; and the work precedes Coover's recent novel *Huck Out West* (2017). *Ghost Town* includes innumerable references, allusions, and analogues to westerns generally and particularly—too many to list. That Robert Coover's *Ghost Town* (1998) followed Cormac McCarthy's *Blood Meridian* (1985) may be mere coincidence, along with the fact that both novels center on an unnamed "kid." Even as McCarthy's novel is far more philosophical than parodic, the comparison is rich and instructive, as both target foundational American myths embodied in the corpus of genre westerns, and Coover makes clear reference to McCarthy's work.
2. Coover, *Ghost Town*, 13.
3. Tompkins, *West of Everything*, 42.
4. Lamont, *Westerns*, 155.
5. Cornis-Pope, "Rewriting the Encounter with the Other," 40.
6. Merchant, *Death of Nature*, 10.
7. Kolodny, *Lay of the Land*, 6, 136.
8. Coover, *Ghost Town*, 45.
9. Coover, *Ghost Town*, 48.
10. Coover, *Ghost Town*, 48.
11. Coover, *Ghost Town*, 48.
12. Foucault, *History of Sexuality*, 153.
13. Coover, *Ghost Town*, 29, 31.
14. Coover, *Ghost Town*, 31–32.
15. While this comment generalizes *Stagecoach*, especially because in the film the prostitute becomes the heroine, the point is that films and western genre tropes are often constituted in terms of a masculine hero. For *Stagecoach* it is John Wayne, elsewhere others. Certainly, the frontier of the American West is strange, and sexual or gender stereotypes one could call normative are often turned on their heads, the condition remains that, in the general sense, time is masculine and space is feminine—thus, the normative gender roles are in place where one would expect them, unlike how such dynamics are represented in Coover's *Ghost Town*, where *all* sexual and gender norms are flipped and played with in a typical postmodern fashion.

16. Coover, *Ghost Town*, 7.
17. Butler argues that "gender does not denote a substantive being, but a relative point of convergence among culturally and historically specific sets of relations" (*Gender Trouble*, 10).
18. Butler, *Gender Trouble*, 10.
19. Butler, *Gender Trouble*, 140.
20. Mitchell, *Westerns*, 187.
21. Sandweiss, *Print the Legend*, 49. 72.
22. Sandweiss, *Print the Legend*, 48.
23. Sandweiss, *Print the Legend*, 60.
24. Sandweiss, *Print the Legend*, 72.
25. Sandweiss, *Print the Legend*, 72.
26. Coover, *Ghost Town*, 4–5.
27. Coover, *Ghost Town*, 28.
28. Coover, *Ghost Town*, 5.
29. Coover, *Ghost Town*, 5.
30. Coover, *Ghost Town*, 6.
31. Coover, *Ghost Town*, 11.
32. Coover, *Ghost Town*, 55.
33. Coover, *Ghost Town*, 51.
34. Coover, *Ghost Town*, 17.
35. Coover, *Ghost Town*, 26.
36. In an extended set of Socratic dialogues, Philosophy questions the imprisoned Boethius about his understanding of Fortune's Wheel: "Do you really value the presence of Fortune when you cannot trust her to stay and when her departure will plunge you in sorrow? And if it is impossible to at will and if her flight exposes men to ruin, what else is such a fleeting thing except a warning of coming disaster? It will never be sufficient just to notice what is under one's nose: prudence calculates what the outcome of things will be. Either way *Fortune's very mutability* deprives her threats of their terror and her enticements of their allure" (*Consolation*, 23). Mutability becomes a key player in Coover's text, especially in the climax, when the blind card dealer attempts to cheat at stud, only to have Fortune, there represented by the chanteuse disguised as the schoolmarm tied to and spinning on the gamblers' wheel of fortune, suggestively intervene in favor of the kid.

37. Such free play is the typical trope of postmodern narrative. That the concept of chance engages in "free play" or "spins" simply reinforces the postmodernity of this atypical western narrative.
38. Boethius, *Consolation*, 24.
39. Kristeva, "Women's Time," 474.
40. Lamont, *Westerns*, 155.
41. Coover, *Ghost Town*, 24–25.
42. Coover, *Ghost Town*, 25.
43. Coover, *Ghost Town*, 25.
44. Coover, *Ghost Town*, 26.
45. Coover, *Ghost Town*, 26.
46. Coover, *Ghost Town*, 24–25.
47. Coover, *Ghost Town*, 23.
48. Coover, *Ghost Town*, 23.
49. Coover, *Ghost Town*, 45.
50. Coover, *Ghost Town*, 83.
51. Coover, *Ghost Town*, 84.
52. Coover, *Ghost Town*, 24.
53. Coover, *Ghost Town*, 24.
54. Huhndorf, *Going Native*, 189.
55. Coover, *Ghost Town*, 23.
56. Coover, *Ghost Town*, 23.
57. Coover, *Ghost Town*, 23.
58. The kid is placed into the role of a male "dom," a role he does not choose. As Margot Weiss shows, when sadomasochistic roles are chosen, such practice is a practice of equal power. As Weiss puts it (though she speaks particularly of feminist reactions to BDSM), "SM is consensual, ... SM practices and roles are freely chosen, and ... SM is empowering" (*Techniques of Pleasure*, 164). In this scene, however, the kid is not empowered at all, but he has his power stripped from him, and this sadomasochistic scene is more torturous than empowering. Here, the sadomasochism is not the kind of sexual play Weiss observes in her study. Weiss indicates that practitioners of BDSM are often disturbed by particular kinds of S-M play. The S-M "slave auction," for instance, appears to disturb the BDSM community, insofar as it goes so far as to mirror the "violence it mimes" (20). This, indeed, is the problem Coover illustrates. The sadomasochism

in *Ghost Town* is not about a shared experience or empowerment. It is instead about mirroring violence, a sexual violence that, in a turn of a wheel or a parodic sense, is committed on the male rather than the female.
59. Mulvey, "Visual Pleasure," 20.
60. Mulvey, "Visual Pleasure," 20.
61. Mulvey, "Visual Pleasure," 20.
62. Butler discusses the Lacanian symbolic in *Gender Trouble*. While one understands that Butler discusses this "being" of phallus to be representative of the kind of gender politics that women must endure to gain any power at all, her comment resonates with what Coover actually achieves with the chanteuse in the pages of *Ghost Town*.
63. Cixous, "Laugh of the Medusa," 882.
64. Cixous, "Laugh of the Medusa," 886.
65. Coover, *Ghost Town*, 99.
66. Coover, *Ghost Town*, 31.
67. Weiss, *Techniques of Pleasure*, 131.
68. Weiss, *Techniques of Pleasure*, 145.
69. Coover, *Ghost Town*, 90.
70. Coover, *Ghost Town*, 69.
71. Coover, *Ghost Town*, 139.
72. Coover, *Ghost Town*, 83.
73. Coover, *Ghost Town*, 48.
74. Evenson, *Understanding Robert Coover*, 243.
75. Coover, *Ghost Town*, 125.
76. Coover, *Ghost Town*, 124.
77. Coover, *Ghost Town*, 128–29.
78. Coover, *Ghost Town*, 128–29.
79. Coover, *Ghost Town*, 137.
80. Coover, *Ghost Town*, 138–39.
81. Paul Quinn, "The Lone Cowboy," *Times Literary Supplement*, February 12, 1999, 21.
82. Coover, *Ghost Town*, 147.

BIBLIOGRAPHY

Boethius. *The Consolation of Philosophy*. Rev. ed. New York: Penguin, 1999.

Butler, Judith. *Gender Trouble: Feminism and the Subversion of Identity*. New York: Routledge, 1999.

Cixous, Helene. "The Laugh of the Medusa." *Signs* 1, no. 4 (Summer 1976): 875–93.

Coover, Robert. *Ghost Town*. New York: Grove, 1998.

Cornis-Pope, Marcel. "Rewriting the Encounter with the Other: Narrative and Cultural Transgression in *The Public Burning*." *Critique* 42, no. 1 (Fall 2000) 40–50.

Evenson, Brian. *Understanding Robert Coover*. Columbia: University of South Carolina Press, 2003.

Foucault, Michel. *The History of Sexuality: Volume 1: An Introduction*. New York: Vintage, 1990.

Huhndorf, Shar M. *Going Native: Indians in the American Cultural Imagination*. Ithaca NY: Cornell University Press, 2001.

Kolodny, Annette. *The Lay of the Land: Metaphor as Experience and History in American Life and Letters*. Chapel Hill: University of North Carolina Press, 1975.

Kristeva, Julia. "Women's Time." In *Critical Theory Since 1965*, edited by Hazard Adams and Leroy Searle, 471–84. Gainesville: University Press of Florida, 1990.

Lamont, Victoria. *Westerns: A Women's History*. Lincoln: University of Nebraska Press, 2016.

Merchant, Carolyn. *The Death of Nature: Women, Ecology, and the Scientific Revolution*. New York: HarperCollins, 1980.

Mitchell, Lee Clark. *Westerns: Making the Man in Fiction and Film*. Chicago: University of Chicago Press, 1996.

Mulvey, Laura. "Visual Pleasure and Narrative Cinema." In *Visual and Other Pleasures*, 14–27. New York: Palgrave MacMillan, 2009.

Sandweiss, Martha A. *Print the Legend: Photography and the American West*. New Haven CT: Yale University Press, 2002.

Tompkins, Jane. *West of Everything: The Inner Life of Westerns*. New York: Oxford University Press, 1992.

Weiss, Margot. *Techniques of Pleasure: BDSM and the Circuits of Sexuality*. Durham NC: Duke University Press, 2011.

3 A Selective History

Identity and Identification in "Deadlands"

NICHOLAS WILLIAM MOLL

"Deadlands: The Weird West" is a tabletop role-playing game that combines elements of history with fictional content drawn from a variety of genres. Tabletop role-playing games afford their players the singular opportunity to inhabit a character in an interactive experience. Guided by a game master through the narrative and setting of the game world, the persona and actions of characters are ultimately left for the player to decide. Within the game's setting players can craft characters from a wide variety of attributes and types. Set within a highly fictionalized 1870s western United States, the setting of "Deadlands" presents an alternate history: one in which the Civil War ended in a stalemate, slavery was abolished in 1864 to bolster Confederate forces, steampunk technology is viable, magic is real, and Native America hosts not one but two sovereign states—the Sioux Nation and Coyote Confederacy. In many examples of the role-play type of game, the experience of the players is one of removal from contemporary concerns and the historical conditions that led to the formation of current nation-states. This disconnection is often achieved through the presentation of a fantasy setting as an alternate notion of place and space. However, presenting an alt-history narrative that draws on the past for inspiration, "Deadlands" thus utilizes fictional elements to discourage focus on the contentious issues that stem from the nineteenth century. In doing so, "Deadlands" invites its players to engage with selective stereotypes and carefully designated tropes in the formation of their character and setting: the noble Southern veteran of war but not the slave owner, the cavalryman but not the scalp hunter, the mystical plains warrior but not disenfranchised Native American. It is an often-debated point regarding the degree and manner in which the western genre depicts issues of expansion, disenfranchisement, oppression, and other contentious aspects of nineteenth-century U.S. expansion. However, "Deadlands" as a western encourages its players to avoid questions of race and equity entirely. Instead, players engage in a binary adventure narrative defined by explicate terms of the player characters as "good" and antagonists as "evil," outlining the latter within a range that begins with the outlaw and other mundane threats but extends to the otherworldly, supernatural monster. Within the binary adventure offered by the weird western setting of "Deadlands," the subaltern histories of race and colonization are obscured by the game's fictive elements. In this sense, this chapter focuses its players in an Anglo-American imperialist narrative of expansion and avoids the questions of identity that have come to be central to the western genre. In doing so, the chapter draws, firstly, upon genre theory to explore the manner in which race and identity have been evocated in the western. Secondly, the chapter engages with concepts of role-play to explore the interaction between player character and setting.

The Weird Western Role-Playing Game

"Deadlands" is set within an alt-history interpretation of the nineteenth-century United States. The game is explicit regarding this status, with 1996's "Deadlands: The Weird West Roleplaying Game" informing players that "the year is 1876, but history is not our own."[1] Various editions of "Deadlands" have been published since the first edition. A second was published in 1999 under the shortened title of "Deadlands: The Weird West" and divided into "Player's Guide" and "Marshal's Guide" volumes. For both editions of "Deadlands," however, a wide variety of setting books were published that included details of geographic locations, events, character types, and a variety of other topics. "Lone Stars: The Texas Rangers (2001)", for example, focuses on the aforementioned organization, providing expansion to the base rules to facilitate games focused on the group. "Deadlands Reloaded," a widely revised edition of the game that advances the setting to 1879, was published in 2005. In addition, the storyline of "Deadlands" has produced other games within the setting. Some of these deviate broadly from the 1870s time frame of the original, while others focus on particular elements of the setting. These include "Deadlands: Hell on Earth"—first published in 1998 and set in a distant postapocalyptic future—and "Deadlands: Lost Colony," published in 2002 and positioned on an alien planet in the same era as "Hell on Earth." Likewise, 2013 saw the publication of "Deadlands: Noir," located in a variation of 1935 presented within the game's setting. Additionally, "Deadlands" has seen the production of other games beyond the role-playing products. These include battle games such as "The Great Rail Wars" (1997) and "Doomtown: Range Wars" (2000), each focused on railroad- and cattle-farming–themed combat clashes, respectively. Likewise, a collectable card game was also published within the setting of "Deadlands" in 1998 with a further edition reissued in 2014. Entitled "Doomtown" and "Doomtown: Reloaded," the distinct versions of the game focus on the town of Gomorrah, a troubled mining settlement in California. The setting of "Deadlands" is explored through a broad and expansive list of products, the vast majority of which focuses on the 1870s and the western United States.

Within the history of the nineteenth century and geography of the western United States, "Deadlands" positions its narrative in a context that features a mixture of the western genre and supernatural adventure. Herein, the game presents the frontier of the expanding nation as a haven for fear and monstrosity. The game further elaborates that the narrative of "Deadlands" is a collaborative experience in which players take on the role of "the heroes and heroines of the story," with one player acting as the "Marshal," a thematic term for game master.[2] From its outset, the format of "Deadlands" is one common to the tabletop role-playing game under Jennifer Grouling Cover's definition of the form: "a type of game/game system that involves collaboration between a small group of players and a game master [sic] through face-to-face social activity with the purpose of creating a narrative experience."[3]

Central to Cover's definition is the narrative experience created by players, with the participants themselves either acting as the protagonist characters in the narrative (players) or directing its plot (game master). Herein, to allow the game master to build a sense of drama within the game, the play and interaction of the player group (again, thematically termed a "Posse" in "Deadlands") are governed by a set of rules.[4] As part of their dramatic role, the game master additionally crafts the setting for the game, providing a sense of place, space and scope for the narrative. The players thus derive their characters from the setting. However, due to the presence of the mechanisms of the preexisting rules, a variable degree of structural and narrative elements are already built into a game's setting for use by the game master. Depending on the style and nature of the individual role-playing game, these elements can range from archetypical character types and sparse guidelines to resolve dramatic conflict to a detailed world and intricate system of situational instructions.[5] For its own setting, "Deadlands" provides Marshals and Posses with an elaborate example of role-playing game setting. To establish this setting, the game draws on both physical features of the western landscape—locations such as Deadwood or Tombstone—and historical events and individuals, such as an undead Abraham Lincoln. Thus, the game provides players with a blending of historical aspects of the United States' nineteenth-century expansion with those fictive elements—both crafted for the game and derived from existing texts within the western genre. Describing its setting in "Deadlands: The Weird West Roleplaying Game" as a "Spaghetti Western—with meat!" players may take on the role of typical western character types such as frontiersmen, cowboys, and gunslingers.[6] Conversely, a Posse may also engage with the more outlandish figures such as wizards (termed "Hucksters" within the game), the undead ("Harrowed"), or mad scientists. Similarly, when presenting the setting and narrative to the player group, the Marshal may construct a plot of bank robbers, range wars, and other long-held staples of the western genre, or one of supernatural monsters, invention gone awry, and other horror- or science-fiction–inspired scenarios. "Deadlands" provides an intriguing opportunity for role-players, presenting a distinctive mixture of history and fiction.

Throughout the setting of "Deadlands" rules have provided for outlaws and lawmen, steampunk science, monsters, trains, survivalism, and time and dimensional travel a broadly eclectic mixture of elements, many of which originate from genres other than the western. Mingling the western genre with aspects of others, "Deadlands" demonstrates the "genre hybridity" James Hewitson frames as key to the weird western subgenre.[7] Under Hewitson's definition, "Deadlands," like other examples of the weird western, provides the "conventions and narrative expectations" of one or more other genres, positioned within a western setting and space.[8] While blending other elements into its variation of the weird western, "Deadlands" presents imported aspects within the context of the nineteenth-century United States. Wizards ("Hucksters") engage in poker games with otherworldly demons (termed "Manitous"). While the term itself is derived from Algonquian belief systems, there is little of the Anishinaabe tradition featured in the game, decontextualizing the term for their magic. Mad scientists are contextualized as Thomas Edison–styled inventors. Due to the positioning of added genre elements into the western setting, Rachael Mizsei Ward places "Deadlands" within a pluralized blend of new western culture.[9] Within this blend, Ward aligns "Deadlands" with the 1990s revitalization of the American West within the consumer marketplace, signified by a return of the western to cinema with the decade presenting high-profile commercial successes such as *Dances with Wolves* (1990) and *Back to the Future III* (1990).[10] With the western-focused integration of varied genre elements throughout "Deadlands" the varying aspects of the game are contextualized for players into a cohesive setting-space that encompasses the broad strokes of the narrative. Thus, regardless of the role chosen, players are asked to identify with and orientate their characters and the actions undertaken into the historical and cinematic geography of the nineteenth-century American West. The mood and theme for "Deadlands" is thus one of checks and balances, where the strange, weird, and unusual aspects of the setting are presented behind a veneer of history and genre that helps provide structure and context to the players. The prominence of history within the game additionally carries the implication of a style of character and play undertaken by the players. For players, much of the drama and appeal of "Deadlands" arises from the juxtaposition of the western with other genre elements.

Race and Character

For players, character choice in "Deadlands" carries with it notions of race. It is not unusual within role-playing game settings for players to be asked to take on or identify a particular national or cultural grouping for their character, adjusting gameplay and rules to evoke a sense of difference in the player's choice. Many games, such as "Dungeons & Dragons," emphasize fantasy-based examples of race with players taking on the role of elves, dwarves, or orcs with the rules and abilities governing the character adjusting to represent physical and cultural differences between characters.[11] In doing so, differences in race are evocated in terms of the "quantity and quality of skills and abilities" a character may possess.[12] Herein, race extends from a gameplay element to one that implies certain styles or features of the setting. Soldiers or combat-oriented characters, for example, need high physical abilities, and so racial choices that focus on those capacities tend to lead player choices in that direction. While players may choose to align a race and profession with less favored abilities, ethnic grouping remains written into the rules as means of determining what is "either possible or impossible" for a character.[13] Unlike "Dungeons & Dragons," however, "Deadlands" features notions of race drawn from history and so does not include rules that overtly represent physical differences. For example, "Dungeons & Dragons" will adjust a character's abilities and the rules surrounding their actions for the player's choice of a half-orc race and introduce other specialized edicts for an elf. "Deadlands," however, offers no overt differences between characters for choosing Anglo-American, Native American, African American or any other racial identity. However, the game does provide specialized options for particular racial groups. Termed an "Arcane Background," these abilities carry with them a specific notion of culture and history.[14] Native American characters are permitted to become a Shaman,

African American characters may practice voodoo, Chinese can learn kung fu, among other culturally orientated options. This aspect of the game positions the rendition of race in "Deadlands" as presenting a similar function to that of "Dungeons & Dragons," emphasizing certain characters that allow distinct advantages and access to aspects of the rules. From this perspective, race in "Deadlands" performs a highly similar function to that described by Voorhees above. Yet, in drawing from history, "Deadlands" not only replicates the essentialist view of race demonstrated by "Dungeons & Dragons" but also reinforces racial stereotypes from the western tradition. While "Deadlands" does not limit character choice by race, it does associate character options and range of abilities with racial choice.

The portrayal of non–Anglo-American groups within the "Deadlands" setting follows the manner in which character and player choice frame these groups. This aspect of "Deadlands" is most evident in the book "Ghost Dancers" (1998), which focuses on Native American characterizations within the game. Within this book, narratives of Anglo-American and Native American frontier conflict are at the forefront. Herein the book notes both the historical figures of Tȟatȟáŋka Íyotake (Sitting Bull) and Tȟašúŋke Witkó (Crazy Horse) are identified with the Order of the Raven—an indigenous sect dedicated to the extermination of Anglo-Americans.[15] Conversely, "Deadlands" contrasts the Order of the Raven with the followers of the Old Ways, with the latter rejecting industrial Anglo-American society in all forms, including products such as firearms. With the latter classification designated for player roles and embodied by courageous "brave" and aloof "shaman"-type characters, the emphasis on frontier violence is contrasted by stereotypical character type options.[16] Presented as predominantly shamanic figures or warriors that deal in spirit animals, mystical powers, warrior customs, and other features, the portrayal of Native Americans in "Deadlands" is one that largely conforms to the stereotyped cinematic portrayals discussed by Raymond Stedman—that is to say, "smoke signals, fiery arrows, pow-wows, speakers with forked tongues, braves arranged in ordered echelons" and other evocations of the noble savage stereotype.[17] While this portrayal reinforces stereotypes and the existing Anglo-American narrative of Native America, such characterizations in a significant role also draw the narrative focus back to a white cultural perspective.[18] The game's setting does engage issues of indigenous dispossession and genocide, featuring the fictional shaman Raven freeing the Reckoners from their otherworldly prison in an act of revenge against the United States.[19] With the Reckoners serving as the antagonist of the setting and the source of supernatural energy, Raven's narrative acts as the explanation for the divergent history of the setting, but further treatments of indigenous-settler conflicts place the two on equal footing, contrasting magic with steampunk technology.[20] Thus, the division of Native Americans within "Deadlands" into two binary classifications draws on the stereotypes. The first is the Old Ways follower as an "admirable" Native American who wanders the "primeval forests" and is helpful to settlers while the second constitutes the Order of the Raven, a scornful enemy of civilization.[21] In similar terms to Native America, voodoo is presented through a variety of Hollywood-inspired stereotypes such as "mojo bags," sorcerers, and living voodoo dolls that act as "miniature killing machines."[22] Likewise, Asian characterizations within "Deadlands" are presented in depictions of Shaolin martial artists, warlords, and triads.[23] Throughout "Deadlands," player and racial identification are stereotypically engaged.

Through the rules and narrative conventions of the game "Deadlands" engages, it is evident that the game-books themselves present a sense of boundary within its play space that reflects the late twentieth- and early twentieth-century ethic of the production era. The 2006 "Deadlands: Reloaded" edition of the game separates women's rights from the restrictions of the nineteenth century, noting that "women in the Weird West can be most anything, from gunslingers and gamblers, to Indian shamans and warriors, or even politicians."[24] Similarly, "Deadlands: Reloaded" further notes that the Confederacy dissolved slavery in 1864 to "gain international recognition" with the result that "by 1879, racism is becoming a thing of the past."[25] Likewise, while the game features criminals romanticized in popular culture such as

Jesse James and John Wesley Hardin, "Law Dogs" notes that "players shouldn't ordinarily be playing outlaws" as these are "lawbreakers and killers" rather than the "strong arms and souls" of heroic player characters.[26] In this sense, the players may take the role of liberated women rather than those under suffrage, former slaves but not slave owners, reformed outlaws but not career criminals, and other such divisions. Oppositions and finite degrees of distinction that push or encourage players away from brash characters are, as Michael J. Tresca notes, common to tabletop role-playing game settings.[27] In positioning a sense of ethics and framing the player characters as innately moral, the game setting establishes a clear sense of good and evil with the players and their characters defined as protagonists and positive actors within the environment.[28] In the case of "Deadlands" the definitions of "good" and "evil" go further to suggest that acts restricted or persuaded against for player options—sexism, racism, oppression, criminal activity—are associated with the Reckoners, and thus supernatural horror. The association with supernatural horror accompanies dissuaded actions with mechanical consequences in the rules themselves. Utilizing a "Fear Level" mechanic as an indicator for the level of supernatural elements in a geographic area, the act of "fearmongering"—creating a sense of "fear and dread"—can increase its level.[29] The cultivation of dread through fearmongering can be embodied by whatever "strikes fear into the hearts of everyone."[30] Thus, the oppressive actions of individuals, intuitions, or groups are framed with negative consequences for player character within the games mechanics. This is further elaborated by the concept of a Fearmonger, the living embodiment of fear in the area who must be defeated in order to cease the act of fearmongering.[31] The lingering memory of human sacrifice within the setting's Mexico City, for example, causes some buildings to ooze "real blood."[32] In this space, the immortal Aztec priest Xitlan keeps both the memory and action of human sacrifice in practice, albeit secretly, cultivating fear for the Reckoners. Thus, historically based beliefs, perspectives, activities or institutions discouraged by the game's design are positioned within a dynamic of external, supernatural consequences. The use, interpretation, and selective tone of history within "Deadlands" guides player choice in regard to character and action.

Wide and Varied Influences

In the setting's portrayal of the past, "Deadlands" presents its players with key dates and moments of history. Many of these are blended with fictionalized elements or engaged as catalysts for further narratives. For example, "Deadlands: The Weird West" notes that during the Battle of Gettysburg in 1863 the Reckoners, a collective title for the four horsemen of the Apocalypse, were unleashed on the earth.[33] Herein, July 3, 1863, creates a point of divergence where history concludes, and game narrative begins. In this sense, then, "Deadlands" performs the same act of narrative and historical acrobatics as other examples of the western genre. To paraphrase and apply the perspective of T. K. Whipple, "Deadlands" marries together within its narrative a variety of myths and symbols drawn from both history and popular culture.[34] Within this milieu of varied sources of inspiration, individual examples of the western genre constitute a finite example of a broader "Great American Epic" as a narrative understanding of the United States' past.[35] This past is framed by Whipple as "a refuge" for the U.S. population from what he describes as the "dull seasons" of Hollywood cinema.[36] These "dull" films are defined by Whipple as "still-life studies of sex" (films of little substance but high amusement) and "current studies in frustration and futility" (politically conscious self-reflexive cinema).[37] For Whipple, the western gives the cinema audiences "some movies in which something moved": material that is "rich in significance" and reflects the virtues and construction of Anglo-American "civilization."[38] While the vast blend of materials and content in "Deadlands" and other westerns—historical, fictional and inspired by other genres—is not accurate to the period depicted, it does reflect the patchwork of ideas within Anglo-American culture that constitutes a "heroic age" for the nation.[39] Further, "Deadlands" would seem to present a quite literal example of framing the nineteenth-century United States as a heroic age in its reconstruction of history as a space for players to stage adventures. For example, while the historic defeat of Antonio López de Santa Anna in the Texas War of Independence (1835–36) and Mexican-American War (1846–48) is retained, "Deadlands" positions the general in California during the 1870s, leading a crusade to reclaim the formerly Mexican portions of the United States. Herein, the historical figure of Santa Anna is retained as a foe for player characters. In constructing a heroic age, "Deadlands" thus blends a wide variety of historical references.

As a fictional depiction of the period, "Deadlands" draws on a patchwork of influences—many of which extend beyond history. For example, "Tales o' Terror: 1877" details "the Seven," a band of seven samurai who "saved a small Japanese village from a band of desperate brigands."[40] However, soon after they migrated to the northwestern United States, where they protect towns from the coming Iron Dragon railroad.[41] In this sense, the Seven serve as an homage to both "The Magnificent Seven" (1960) and its antecedent, "Seven Samurai" (1954), directly drawing on the narrative of the latter. With a varied collection of historical and popular cultural influences, "Deadlands" represents a broad-based example of an action outlined by Richard Slotkin as common to individual examples of the western genre, offering their own distinctive patchwork of histories and fictions.[42] While individual westerns present their own particular blend, the genre presents a fragmented Anglo-American mythology.[43] Herein, Slotkin notes that the historical experiences of the western United States—"the trans-Allegheny West and Southwest, the Old South, and the Northeast"—were geographically and chronologically distinctive phases of the United States' growth.[44] As an example that draws broadly on the varied historic moments and fictional influences of the United States, the status of "Deadlands" as a western is more akin to the western genre as a whole rather than an individual text. Herein, the pirates that stalk the sunken ruins of postearthquake California mingle with the mechanized automations of Salt Lake City mad scientist Dr. Darius Hellstromme and other liberal blends of elements. Thus, "Deadlands" is highly self-reflexive as a western, drawing copiously from the length and breadth of the western genre and nineteenth-century setting, creating a broad and competing mixture of elements rather than a single, cohesive vision. In this sense, the game offers the general thrust of national history, to paraphrase Slotkin, fragmented by countless individual examples that struggle to align.[45] The effect of the varied elements of the game's nineteenth-century setting is a broad patchwork, associated with the market itself rather than as a single text.

While a patchwork as varied as "Deadlands" is both expansive and inclusive, some history within the "Deadlands" setting is minimalized to help the game achieve its evocation of a heroic age. The first edition of the game is set during 1876, for example, and the Civil War continues. Other events are left unaltered, serving as foundations for the setting's roots in history. As part of the 1876 setting, Wyatt Earp and Bartholemew William Barclay "Bat" Masterson serve as Dodge City Marshals just as they did historically, as noted in "The Quick and the Dead."[46] Herein, players of "Deadlands" are invited to author their own histories—juxtaposing or imposing their own, invented characters within the historical narrative of United States expansion. In doing so, players perform a certain "mental gymnastics" similar to that cited by Jacquelyn Kilpatrick regarding portrayals of Native America in cinema.[47] In *Celluloid Indians (1999)*, Kilpatrick frames the Western genre in film as a replication of the frontier processes undertaken by an expanding Anglo-America "in order to declare the land their own."[48] With the use of written history to overwrite the legacies of indigenous inhabitation, the western United States became a "historyless land" and a space for white narratives—a process replicated in cinema.[49] However, there is little consistency to the quantity of various historical, fictional, and inspired elements within "Deadlands," and they are not blended together in an even manner. Rather, within the context of individual setting books, the varying styles and engagements with history "Deadlands" demonstrates is utilized in varied quantities. For "Deadlands," the process of imposing a historical narrative onto the landscape itself is a contextual and collaborative one. Thus, the key distinction between "Deadlands" as a role-playing game and the cinematic or literary western genre is choice. While a film or prose is a narrative production, a role-playing game carries with it only the potential of narrative. With the setting, itself constructed of a broad selection of varied, sometimes conflicting, elements, it is quite possible for players and the Marshal to collectively choose which aspects are included or emphasized within their games and narratives and which are excluded. For example, "Rascals Varmints & Critters 2: The Book of Curses" provides context for gothic horror characters such as Dracula and affords the possibility of players taking on the roles of vampires and werewolves. Players without this book lack these options. However, a group may collectively decide to ignore or disallow certain elements or options. The Marshal may determine, for example, that vampires are strictly monsters and not suitable as a player option. In this sense, where films offer audiences of the western genre an official narrative with a key sequence of events, role-playing games provide the implication of narrative with elements—characters, events, locations—that may be arranged into a story through gameplay. Role-playing games thus highlight an important discrepancy between games about telling stories and games that "are stories."[50] Narratives and their settings thus become deeply "personal conceptions" for the player, both individually and on the level of the group.[51] The result of this experience can be "noticeably different" to the other players in the same play group, and wildly distinct between groups.[52] When engaged with "Deadlands," it is up to players of the game to negotiate their way through the various elements of the setting. In doing so, players are provided with the opportunity to choose which aspects of history and popular culture to emphasize within their personal games. The narrative process for "Deadlands," like that of other role-playing games, thus constitutes "a feedback loop, where the contributions of each participant lead to new states of the imaginary worlds."[53] Rather, within the context of individual setting books, the varying styles and engagements with history "Deadlands" demonstrates is utilized in varied quantities as determined by the players. "Deadlands" presents its players with a consumer experience of the American West, occupying the broad scope of the marketplace.

An Experience of the West

"Deadlands" provides a consumer experience of the American West, offering its players multiple streams of narrative and points of identification. "Deadlands" provides varied images and narratives of the nineteenth-century western United States that encapsulate the marketplace itself within the game's broad stroke rather than act as a single example in the manner of a film or novel. Yet "Deadlands" also encounters the same complications that Patricia Nelson Limerick positions as central to other consumer experiences of the western. In particular, among the "signs, symbols, and signifiers" of the western United States, "the question of identity and interests" is left open within the implied narrative boundaries.[54] While the game discourages racism, for example, it is careful to avoid statements about characters who have benefited from oppression and expansion—most notably, the Anglo-American townships the Posse protects. The effect is both one of open identification and limitation within the perspective of "only one of the contesting groups" that make up the historical landscape of the western United States.[55] Thus, the western often reduces "a tangle of many-sided encounters" to a "world defined by a frontier line."[56] Within a space with such broad and wide storytelling potential, the treatment of history within "Deadlands" inelegantly places other groups, such as Native Americans, African Americans, Asiatic cultures who—to paraphrase Limerick—enter the western United States from distinctive historic and geographic locations.[57] For example, the game setting's conscription of slaves into military service in exchange for freedom, framing African Americans as making "vital contributions" to the Confederacy, creates a schism between the contemporary politics of the game's players and the attempt to retain the historical aesthetics of the Civil War.[58] The Anglo-American narrative of the West within the consumer experience occupies the broad scope of the marketplace, attempting to integrate or at least address non–Anglo-American narratives. But in doing so, the narrative of the United States' East-to-West expansion "stretches to the point of snapping," occupying irreconcilable aspects and features.[59]

While the perspective presented by the setting is potentially vast, "Deadlands" regulates player narratives to Anglo-American experiences of the nineteenth-century United States and western genre. With specialized options presented as the signifiers of racial identity, the default racial type for "Deadlands" players and their characters is Anglo-American. Indeed, Anglo-America remains the focus of the setting, evoked through the township as the keystone of its wide and varied elements. Within the western genre, the town is the focus of the style of advancement and progress central to the narrative, and the state of the township itself serves as an indication of the frontier's portrayal within the narrative.[60] For example, the ruined, broken township of Clint Eastwood's *High Plains Drifter* (1973) reflects the moral bankruptcy of industry, and the deceptive, weary citizens of Redemption indicate the oppression of outlawry in Sam Raimi's *The Quick and the Dead* (1995). Fitting the township's place within the western genre, for "Deadlands" the vast majority of published adventures and narratives are located in or near one. Salt Lake City and Lost Angels (a fictionalized Los Angeles) serve as points of focus in the time travel–oriented "Devil's Tower" trilogy, for instance, while Dodge City acts as the setting of the Fourth of July–themed "Independence Day." Despite the settings' varied nature, the township provides players with key, consistent orientation throughout "Deadlands" and provides an assumption of Anglo-American identity for the players. Slotkin frames the township in the western genre as a social microcosm of U.S. society.[61] Applying Slotkin's logic to "Deadlands," the setting is thus not a single microcosm but a patchwork of contrasting distinctive vistas, each constituting a particular interpretation. The "Marshal's Handbook," for example, presents Deadwood as a town at the center of Sioux-Cavalry conflict, while Dodge City focuses on outlaw-lawman conflicts.[62] Thus, while the "Deadlands" setting draws on a wide variety of elements and genres, each is contextualized into the space and story mode of Anglo-American expansion. In this sense, "Deadlands" positions its narrative potential in explicitly Anglo-American terms.

History, Character, and Binary Adventure

"Deadlands" positions its player characters in a manner akin to protagonists within the conventions of the classic western. While "from the 1950s the line between good and evil becomes increasingly unclear" with the revisionist western, the classic western maintains a clear sense of binary.[63] Within the classic western the hero often dwells in the liminal space of wilderness near a town or traveling between them, defending civilized society but typically moving and operating outside it, an act mirrored in "Deadlands."[64] Thus, the hero of the classic western dwells on the cusp of the frontier itself—the very meeting point of the wilderness and urbanization, the quintessence of the West. The hero comes to operate in a world of balance between the conflicting "worlds of wilderness and civilization" and acts as a figure of equilibrium.[65] This action itself is replicated in "Deadlands" with the typical action of a Posse, traveling from town to town combatting the monsters spawned by the Reckoners and their Fearmonger representative. Unlike "Deadlands," however, the classic western's heroes are often a "white male figure" that represents the ideology of civilization but was not part of it.[66] This idealized masculinity demonstrates both honor and civility and virility and ruggedness existing in one individual in perfect equilibrium with two opposing forces. The western villain in this sense is a figure out of balance, too far on one side of the frontier or the other. Within the classic western, the wilderness and its inhabitants—the outlaw and the Native American—are represented as "uncivilised, primitive, killers."[67] In contrast, the civilized east is a place of restrictive rules and laws, institutions blind to the individual's needs, and a denial of the natural world that corrupts culture and laws and their representatives, carrying its own sense of problems. Threats to the delicate balance of the world come from one side of the frontier or the other: the violent wilderness-dweller or corrupt agent of civilization. This aspect of the hero and villain dynamic is given an intriguing twist in "Deadlands," with the corruption being both literal and biblical, originating from the Reckoners as monsters of otherworldly, supernatural origin. Herein, indigenous leaders such as Tȟatȟáŋka Íyotake and agents of Anglo-

American expansion such as the Rail Barons both present distinctive problems stemming from imbalance and the same source of corruption. In this sense, the industrial expansion of the eastern United States does not resolve the narrative's problems within "Deadlands;" rather it simply shifts the setting into other vistas such as the 1930s with "Deadlands: Noir" or the far future with "Hell on Earth" and "Lost Colony." Within this broad scope, characters within "Deadlands" can potentially be constructed to represent any culture or perspective. In particular, features of the setting such as a portal off the Atlantic coast provide opportunity to draw from elements historically beyond the nineteenth-century setting.[68] Yet the construction and use of the classic western's opposition of balance and corruption as a source of antagonism positions the player character in a binary opposition of moral balance and imbalance.

The use of supernatural horror in "Deadlands" plays a key role in obscuring the subaltern histories that the setting touches upon. Throughout the game, the human architects of genocide, slavery, and oppression are largely excluded from agency. The Reckoners themselves, while contextualized as the Four Horsemen of the Apocalypse, function more akin to the Great Old Ones of H. P. Lovecraft's weird fiction—otherworldly monsters that dwell on the very fringe of human perception. The use of Lovecraftian elements in conjunction with Anglo-American mythology thus demonstrates less concern with the historical events of expansion and colonization than with the articulation of a particular mode of interpreting history.[69] The action becomes allegorical, ascribing esoteric functions and emotive manifestations to events and traumas drawn upon in constructing the game's setting.[70] The Reckoners become associated with every hardship and trauma, from attrition in the Civil War to genocide and settler-indigenous conflict. There is thus a use of symbolism and allegory in the engagement of otherworldly sources of malevolence as sources of conflict that fundamentally avoids engagement with the history in and of itself.[71] Herein, Matthew Strohack is quick to remind us that "for Lovecraft" the blending of godlike, supernatural, monstrosities into Anglo-American settings—in particular, 1920s New England for the author himself—often "represented a possibility for rebirth or redefinition" of then-contemporary U.S. culture.[72] However, in "Deadlands" the Reckoners present an act of repression and regression away from a nuanced understanding of the past that reaffirms the morality and outlook of the classic western. In this sense, the portrayal of history in "Deadlands" follows the rout advocated by Cynthia J. Miller as conventional for the supernatural western—that is, as a commentary on Anglo-America and the "norms and values it promotes and maintains."[73] The characterization of the Reckoners themselves into biblical figures and their further association with key historical events provide a culturally specific personification. Narratively, the questions raised become ones of "moral order" and "human sin" as a framework for questions of "national identity."[74] Yet, within "Deadlands," the questions raised by the association of supernatural threats with human-based immoral behavior are typically resolved through violent confrontation with the Reckoner's agents. In this sense, the problem-and-solution pattern of "Deadlands" is then one based within the "pulp formula of hardened frontier heroes" with clear problems and antagonists they can defeat in a violent confrontation over the nuanced, complex, and enduring issues of expansion and oppression.[75] The player characters in "Deadlands" are positioned within a moral order of good and evil.

The supernatural elements of "Deadlands" create a space where the moral, imperialist protagonists of the classic western thrive. The revisionist westerns of the 1950s onward brought with them a questioning of the established moral order within the western genre. But the emergence of hybrid genre examples of the western brought "new spectacle."[76] However, the use of supernatural elements reflects for Cynthia Miller and A. Bowdoin van Riper a return to the "moral force" of the classic western.[77] Faced with otherworldly malevolence physically embodied, the weird western presents a rendition of the past that is a "rich mythological world" where "the Cowboy Code" lives on.[78] With its intricate alternate history, "Deadlands" embodies this concept of rich mythology with the Reckoners and their Fearmongers, just as its characters come to embody aspects of the Cowboy Code. The emphasis on moral order thus allows "the inner conflicts" of both the hero and social collective to be drawn into complex moral quandaries by historical realities such as "the inequalities of race and class," are thus externalized and projected into the space of binary good-hero versus evil-villain conflicts.[79] The role of the player-controlled character in "Deadlands" is thus a simple one. Despite the varied aspects of the setting available for the player-group's use, the function of the player character within "Deadlands" becomes a ritualized one, providing a moral resolution to history. In doing so, "Deadlands" invites its players to engage with history selectively, interacting with a crafted designation of tropes in the formation of character and setting.

Conclusion

Tabletop role-playing games afford their players the singular opportunity to inhabit a character in an interactive experience. For "Deadlands" this experience is one that occupies the broad scope of the western genre, including both historic and fictional elements. Guided by both rules and setting, the broad scope of the persona and actions of the characters are largely positioned within the perspective of national expansion and settlement for the United States in the nineteenth century. Thus, within the game's highly fictionalized 1870s setting, "Deadlands" presents an alternate history in which key events and individuals selectively conform or deviate from history, and where supernatural malevolence are physically embodied within the diegetic world. Most striking of all, however, is the setting's portrayal of the subaltern with the narratives of Native American, women, African American, and other liminalized groups from history placed on equitable footing with those of Anglo-Americans. Engaging with history selectively, "Deadlands" utilizes fictional elements to discourage focus on the contentious issues of the past. In doing so, "Deadlands" invites its players to engage with selective stereotypes and carefully designed tropes in the formation of their characters and settings in a manner that avoids contention or moral conflict. Instead, "Deadlands" engages in binary adventure narrative, defined in terms of the player characters as good and antagonists as evil, the latter defined in a manner that loops oppressive social institution and outlaw together as extensions of the alien Reckoners. Within the binary adventure offered by the weird western setting of "Deadlands," the subaltern histories of race and colonization are obscured by the game's fictive elements.

NOTES

1. Hensley, "Deadlands: Weird West," blurb.
2. Hensley, "Deadlands: Weird West," 15.
3. Cover, *Creation of Narrative*, 168.
4. Cover, *Creation of Narrative*, 168.
5. Cover, *Creation of Narrative*, 168.
6. Hensley, "Deadlands: Weird West," blurb.
7. Hewitson, "Undead and Un-American," 167.
8. Hewitson, "Undead and Un-American," 167.
9. Ward, "Genre Mashing," 269.
10. Ward, "Genre Mashing," 27.
11. Voorhees, "The Character of Difference."
12. Voorhees, "The Character of Difference.".
13. Voorhees, "The Character of Difference."
14. Hensley, "Deadlands: Weird West," 53.
15. Beakley, "Ghost Dancers," 97.
16. Hensley, "Deadlands: Weird West," 28.
17. Stedman, *Shadows of the Indian*, 218.
18. Stedman, *Shadows of the Indian*, 223.
19. Beakley, "Ghost Dancers," 10.
20. Beakley, "Ghost Dancers," 11.
21. Stedman, *Shadows of the Indian*, 45–50.
22. Goff, "Ranger's Bible," 15; Goff, "River," 114.
23. Forbeck and Mangold, "Great Maze," 47.
24. Hensley and Flory, "Deadlands: Reloaded," 28.
25. Hensley and Flory, "Deadlands: Reloaded," 30–31.
26. Long, "Law Dogs," 45.
27. Tresca, *Evolution*, 25.
28. Tresca, *Evolution*, 25.

29. Hensley, "Deadlands: Weird West," 207.
30. Hensley, "Deadlands: Weird West," 208.
31. Hensley, "Deadlands: Weird West," 208.
32. Long, "South o' the Border," 91.
33. Hensley, "Deadlands: Weird West," 7.
34. Whipple, *Study Out*, 59.
35. Whipple, *Study Out*, 61.
36. Whipple, *Study Out*, 63.
37. Whipple, *Study Out*, 63.
38. Whipple, *Study Out*, 64.
39. Whipple, *Study Out*, 67.
40. Long, McGlothin, Hopler, and Hensley, "Tales o' Terror," 50, 108.
41. Long et al., "Tales o' Terror," 50, 108.
42. Slotkin, *Gunfighter Nation*, 394.
43. Slotkin, *Gunfighter Nation*, 394.
44. Slotkin, *Gunfighter Nation*, 394.
45. Slotkin, *Gunfighter Nation*, 395.
46. Hensley and Hopler, "Quick and the Dead," 87.
47. Kilpatrick, *Celluloid Indians*, 42.
48. Kilpatrick, *Celluloid Indians*, 42.
49. Kilpatrick, *Celluloid Indians*, 42.
50. Hitchens and Drachen, "Personal Experience," 53.
51. Hitchens and Drachen, "Personal Experience," 59.
52. Hitchens and Drachen, "Personal Experience," 59.
53. Hitchens and Drachen, "Personal Experience," 59.
54. Limerick, "Adventures of the Frontier," 71.
55. Limerick, "Adventures of the Frontier," 73.
56. Limerick, "Adventures of the Frontier," 73.
57. Limerick, "Adventures of the Frontier," 73.
58. Long et al., "Back East," 10.
59. Limerick, "The Adventures," 73.
60. Slotkin, *Gunfighter Nation*, 395.
61. Slotkin, *Gunfighter Nation*, 309.
62. Forbeck et al., "The Marshal's Handbook," 150, 164.
63. Cook, "Hero and the Villain," 1.
64. Cook, "Hero and the Villain," 13.

65. Cook, "Hero and the Villain," 35.
66. Cook, "Hero and the Villain," 34.
67. Cook, "Hero and the Villain," 14.
68. Long, McGlothlin, and Hite, "Back East," 91.
69. Strohack, "City under the Hill," 235.
70. Strohack, "City under the Hill," 235.
71. Strohack, "City under the Hill," 236.
72. Strohack, "City under the Hill," 240.
73. Miller, *Encyclopedia of Weird Westerns*, 7.
74. Miller, *Encyclopedia of Weird Westerns*, 6.
75. Miller, *Encyclopedia of Weird Westerns*, 8.
76. Miller and van Riper, "Fantastic Frontier," 28.
77. Miller and van Riper, "Fantastic Frontier," 33.
78. Miller and van Riper, "Fantastic Frontier," 33.
79. Miller and van Riper, "Fantastic Frontier," 38.

BIBLIOGRAPHY

Beakley, Paul. "Ghost Dancers." Chandler AZ: Pinnacle Entertainment Group, 1998.
———, and John Hopper. "The Devil's Tower 1: The Road to Hell." Chandler AZ: Pinnacle Entertainment Group, 1998.
Cook, Christine Maria. "The Hero and the Villain in the Contemporary Western Film." Master's thesis, Massey University, 2012.
Costner, Kevin, dir. *Dances with Wolves*. MGM, 1990.
Cover, Jennifer Grouling. *The Creation of Narrative in Tabletop Role-Playing Games*. Jefferson NC: McFarland, 2010.
"Deadlands: Doomtown." Seattle: Five Rings, 1998.
"Deadlands: Doomtown Range Wars." Roseville MN: Fantasy Flight Games, 2000.
"Deadlands: Doomtown Reloaded." Ontario CA: Alderac Entertainment Group, 2014.
Eastwood, Clint, dir. *High Plains Drifter*. Universal Studios Home Entertainment, 1973.
Forbeck, Matt, and Hal Mangold. "The Great Maze." Chandler AZ: Pinnacle Entertainment Group, 1997.
———, Shane Lacy Hensley, John R. Hopler, Hal Mangold, and Jason Nicholas. "The Marshal's Handbook." Blacksburg VA: Pinnacle Entertainment Group, 1999.

Goff, John. "The Black Circle: Unholy Alliance." Chandler AZ: Pinnacle Entertainment Group, 2000.

———. "Ranger's Bible Addendum #84: The Voodooists." Chandler AZ: Pinnacle Entertainment Group, 1999.

———. "River o' Blood." Chandler AZ: Pinnacle Entertainment Group, 1999.

———. "Varmints & Critters 2: The Book of Curses." Chandler AZ: Pinnacle Entertainment Group, 2000.

———, Shane Lacy Hensley, Clint Black, and Sean Preston. "Deadlands: Noir." Blacksburg VA: Pinnacle Entertainment Group, 2013.

Hensley, Shane Lacy. "Deadlands: Hell on Earth." Chandler AZ: Pinnacle Entertainment Group, 1998.

———. "Deadlands: The Weird West Roleplaying Game." Blacksburg VA: Pinnacle Entertainment Group, 1996.

———, and B. D. Flory. "Deadlands: Reloaded." Blacksburg VA: Pinnacle Entertainment Group, 2005.

———, and John R. Hopler. "The Quick and the Dead." Blacksburg VA: Pinnacle Entertainment Group, 1997.

Hewitson, James. "Undead and Un-American: The Zombified Other in Weird Western Films." In *Undead in the West: Vampires, Zombies, Mummies, and Ghosts on the Cinematic Frontier*, edited by Cynthia J. Miller and A. Bowdoin van Riper, 166–81. Lanham MD: Scarecrow, 2012.

Hitchens, Michael, and Anders Drachen. "The Personal Experience of Narratives in Role-Playing Games." In *Intelligent Narrative Technologies II, Papers from the 2009 AAAI Spring Symposium*, 53–61. Stanford CA: AAAI, 2009.

Hopler, John R. "Deadlands: Lost Colony." Chandler AZ: Pinnacle Entertainment Group, 2002.

Kilpatrick, Jacquelyn. *Celluloid Indians: Native Americans and Film*. Lincoln: University of Nebraska Press, 1999.

Kurosawa, Akira, dir. *Seven Samurai*. Criterion, 1954.

Limerick, Patricia Nelson. "The Adventures of the Frontier in the Twentieth Century." In *The Frontier in American Culture: An Exhibition at the Newberry Library, August 26, 1994-January 7, 1995*, edited by James R. Grossman, 67–102. Berkeley: University of California Press, 1994.

Long, Steven. "Law Dogs." Chandler AZ: Pinnacle Entertainment Group, 1998.

———. "South o' the Border." Chandler AZ: Pinnacle Entertainment Group, 1999.

———, Christopher McGlothlin, John Hopler, and Shane Lacy Hensley. "Tales o' Terror: 1877." Blacksburg VA: Pinnacle Entertainment Group, 1998.

———, Christopher McGlothlin, and Kenneth Hite. "Back East: The South." Blacksburg VA: Pinnacle Entertainment Group, 1999.

McGlothlin, Christopher. "Lone Stars: The Texas Rangers." Blacksburg VA: Pinnacle Entertainment Group, 2001.

Miller, Cynthia J. "Introduction to *The Encyclopedia of Weird Westerns: Supernatural and Science Fiction Elements in Novels, Comics, Film, Television and Games*," edited by Paul Green, 4–14. 2nd ed. Jefferson NC: McFarland, 2010.

———, and A. Bowdoin van Riper. "The Fantastic Frontier: Sixguns and Spectacle in the Hybrid Western." In *Critical Perspectives on the Western: From A Fistful of Dollars to Django Unchained*, edited by Lee Broughton, 27–40. Lanham MD: Rowman & Littlefield, 2016.

Raimi, Sam, dir. *The Quick and the Dead*. Sony Pictures Home Entertainment, 1995.

Slotkin, Richard. *Gunfighter Nation: The Myth of the Frontier in Twentieth-Century America*. Norman: University of Oklahoma Press, 1998.

Stedman, Raymond William. *Shadows of the Indian: Stereotypes in American Culture*. Norman: University of Oklahoma Press, 1982.

Strohack, Matthew. "The City under the Hill: Allegorical Tradition and H. P. Lovecraft's America." In *American Exceptionalisms: From Winthrop to Winfrey*, edited by Sylvia Söderlind and James Taylor Carson, 223–42. Albany: SUNY Press, 2011.

Sturges, John, dir. *The Magnificent Seven*. MGM, 1960.

Tresca, Michael J. *The Evolution of Fantasy Role-Playing Games*. Jefferson NC: McFarland, 2011.

Voorhees, Gerad. "The Character of Difference: Procedurality, Rhetoric, and Roleplaying Games." *Game Studies* 9, no. 2 (2009): http://gamestudies.org/0902/articles/voorhees (accessed November 20, 2019).

Ward, Rachel Mizsei. "Genre Mashing in the Role-Playing Game *Deadlands: The Weird West*, the Steampunk Horror Western." In *Undead in the West II: They Just Keep Coming*, edited by Cynthia J. Miller and A. Bowdoin van Riper, 269–85. Lanham NC: Scarecrow, 2013.

Whipple, Thomas K. *Study out the Land*. Berkeley: University of California Press, 1943.

Zemeckis, Robert, dir. *Back to the Future Part III*. Universal Pictures, 1990.

PART TWO

Native Reclamations and Representations

Mongrel Transmotion   4

The Werewolf and the Were/Wear/Where-West
in Stephen Graham Jones's *Mongrels*

JOSHUA T. ANDERSON

> In all the stories and all the movies, there's human
> footprints walking along, becoming wolf prints at the end.
> —Stephen Graham Jones, *Mongrels* (2016)

At the 2016 Western Literature Association (WLA) conference, prolific writer Stephen Graham Jones (Blackfeet) was asked how the American West influences his genre-bending work, to which he responded: "I always try to step on the West in such a way that the blood seeps up from the footprint."[1] Jones's West can be a bloody place, where the blood of the West's past and ongoing violence often mixes with the blood of newborn monsters. His West maps new territories, including haunted modular homes, rest stops, drive-through urinals, and a storage facility with a ten-inch pipe that his characters in *Not for Nothing* (2014) use as a cigarette-butt receptacle and that may also be a wormhole into the western past. "In its other life, the ten-inch pipe was probably oilfield," Jones's narrator suspects, wondering if the storage facility— perhaps the entire town of Stanton, Texas—was "built around it."[2] As for that pipe's unfathomable depths, Jones's narrator explains: "You picture covered wagons and Comanche Indians standing around the pipe, waiting for a pebble to hit bottom, and waiting, and waiting."[3] Jones's West is full of such wormholes, a place where blood seeps up from the footprint and the settler and indigenous pasts are merely a stone's throw away. At times, his West is as tender as the store-bought turkey hearts that Lipsha uses to make "love medicine" in Louise Erdrich's debut novel, *Love Medicine* (1984). At others, it is dry-rubbed and Southern-fried with the grotesque, like the all-too-human tang of the Sawyer brothers' famous cannibal chili, or the "beef-fed-beef" and "cannibal cattle" in Jones's first novel *The Fast Red Road: A Plainsong* (2000).[4] In every case, when Jones steps on the West, he makes it new. Like a just-shed snake, his West slithers out from old skins, those overdetermined frontiers, and lays new tracks that defy the West's geopolitical and generic borders. In short, his West isn't only weird; it's unsettling. A West that *unsettles*.

Long before he was an acclaimed writer and a sought-after keynote speaker at literature conferences, Jones was obsessed with another set of footprints in the West. As he recalls in a postscript essay titled "Werewolf at the Door" included in the paperback edition of his werewolf novel *Mongrels*:[5]

> Starting at about twelve years old, living at my grandparents' house even deeper in the country, I'd set about trying to become a werewolf. . . . When the moonlight didn't work, I remembered a long-legged, pale coyote that we'd seen out at the fence once, just watching us. In my mind I squinted it into a regal, dangerous wolf, told myself those were *wolf* footprints in the driveway the next morning, coming out of the puddle I'd made the day before with the hose. If you drink from a wolf print, you become a werewolf. It's automatic. It's a rule of nature.[6]

The water in that coyote-turned-wolf track "tasted like dirt," Jones remembers, but the transformation didn't take. "When you're twelve," he surmises, "you want to be anybody else. *Anything*"—explaining that "werewolf, that was just my first option. And it was mostly for night."[7] By day, Jones hoped to turn into a "kid with blond hair, blue eyes, and a gold-rope chain necklace." Jones laments, "Neither happened. I didn't become a werewolf. I stayed an Indian in West Texas, where there aren't any Indians."[8]

At the center of Jones's unique approach to race in the West are the nearly endless possibilities for transformation, through which he turns racist frontier narratives and genres "where there aren't any Indians" into opportunities to reclaim territories for American Indian characters and writers. For instance, in the story notes for his collection *The Ones That Got Away* (2010), Jones credits Louis L'Amour as one of the inspirations for his Old West short story "Lonegan's Luck" (2009). "Thank you, Louis L'Amour," Jones writes, "your books were the ones I used to run off into the woods with in the dark, and read the first page by matchlight, then tear that page out, light it, read the next page by the burning page, and feel my way through that way, so that I'd just have a handful of burn at the end."[9] In the pulp westerns of L'Amour, Jones notes, "the good guys always won. Except, I always made them secretly Indian, in my head. They were a lot more believable that way."[10] In a more recent essay for Unbound Worlds, Jones describes how, as a spectator of non-Native films and television, he continues the long-standing tradition of the "captivity narrative," by capturing non-Native heroes onscreen and transforming them into strange kin. As Jones elaborates, "Growing up Indian, when the people on screen aren't like you but you kind of like them all the same, the obvious thing to do, it's abduct them. Make them come live with you."[11] Jones extends this practice of capturing and transforming characters and genres typically reserved for non-Natives to his own creative approach to writing fiction. As he explains in "Letter to a Just Starting-Out Indian Writer, and Maybe to Myself," "You don't have to be able to define what an Indian is in order to write 'Indian,'" or to "put a headdress on to write."[12] "When you do that," Jones warns, "you may as well be falling dead off the back of a horse. Where you'll land will be in a John Wayne movie. And that's a bad place for an Indian to have to spend forever. It's a bad place for an Indian to even spend ten minutes."[13] Instead, Jones calls on young Native writers to "just assume the Indianness. Of everything. Overwrite the world with us. . . . We're in the soil, yes, but we're in the future, too."[14] Put another way, Jones calls for Native writers to resist "taking a blood-quantum test on the page," and, in his own genre-bending work, he seeks to "leave the whole bookcase red."[15]

In this chapter, I track the shape-shifting narratives of kin-making and placemaking in Jones's werewolf bildungsroman *Mongrels*, arguing that the werewolf and the West shape-shift together, transforming "settled" narratives of race and place into new, unsettling destinies for genealogies, genres, and geopolitics. Beginning with the title, *Mongrels* reclaims the racist slur for miscegenation and revitalizes Gerald Vizenor's (Anishinaabe) reclamation of the maligned and tragic indigenous "mixedblood" or "crossblood." Moreover, the novel's transient, racially unmarked werewolf family transforms Vizenor's "Native transmotion," or the movement across geographies and genealogies, as well as through dreams, songs, and memories, into Jones's own version of what I call "mongrel transmotion," in which his "mongrels" move across and between genres, track shape-shifting family histories through competing origins, and assert new narratives of transformation for the werewolf, American Indian literatures, and the "were/wear/where-West."[16]

Jones's "mongrel transmotion" runs counter to the static and tragic depiction of the indigenous mixedblood, or the genealogically and culturally plural figure who, in settler discourse, has long served as a racist caricature in settler politics and literary imagination. From Mary Rowlandson's infamous captivity narrative to the blood laws of the nineteenth century, the story of the mixedblood warns settlers of the dangers of miscegenation and helps to shape racial hierarchies through a discourse focused on blood. The werewolf engenders a different, but related, hierarchy focused on "species," a word that Donna Haraway argues "reeks of race and sex."[17] In *When Species Meet* (2008), Haraway draws a comparison between the tragic mixedblood in settler discourse and ecological concepts such as "endangered species," which, Haraway asserts, "function simultaneously to locate value and to evoke death and extinction in ways familiar in colonial representations of the always vanishing indigene."[18] In pop culture, the werewolf (or wolf) and the mixedblood share generic, if not genetic, material, including howling wolves on truck-stop t-shirts, the covers of countless pulp horror novels, and a number of films, from *Wolfen* (1981) to Jacob Black's recurring Quileute character in the *Twilight Saga* (2005–8).[19] As Jones posits in his interview with Billy J. Stratton, "American Indians so often get cast as the werewolf in so many stories. It's because to colonial America-at-large, each is a fantasy creature lurking out in the trees."[20] However, in *Mongrels*, Jones transforms the werewolf from a tragic monster who embodies the "civilized" and "savage" into a shape-shifting monstrous family, who offer new narratives of kin-making and placemaking and make way for new transformations in what I call the "were/wear/where-West."

In the following section, I argue that Jones intervenes in werewolf origin stories and, in so doing, he reworks the monster's ongoing associations with the savage or "tragic" indigenous mixedblood. As Haraway asserts, "When species meet, the question of how to inherit histories is pressing, and how to get on together is at stake."[21] Similarly, Jones's unnamed narrator wonders how to inherit competing werewolf histories from his werewolf Grandpa, his Uncle Darren, and his Aunt Libby. However, the care taken by werewolves, such as his Grandpa, to avoid "leaving bread crumbs" complicates the narrator's quest to learn the truth of his origins; as he explains, "Werewolves aren't big on writing things down," which "kind of makes all the movies true."[22] Defying the unwritten laws of werewolves, the narrator does, in fact, "write things down," but the story he leaves behind is never static, the "truths" about werewolves are always conflicted, contested, "mongrels." As the narrator explains in the opening pages, "This is the way werewolf stories go. Never any proof. Just a story that keeps changing, like it's twisting back on itself, biting its own stomach to chew the poison out."[23] Although Jones's werewolves often leave the geopolitical and generic borders of the West, I argue that, through genre transfusion, or the intertextual exchanges across canonical Native literatures, monster literatures, and monstrous families in post-western films, Jones reveals new methods for transforming discourses of race and place in the were-West.

Genre Transfusion and the Were-West

When combined with the werewolf, the were-West connotes transformation. Shortened to *wer* and traced back to Old English, it genders the West ("man"-West), and with an apostrophe it becomes "we're-West," as in "we are West," or "we are the West." This process of linguistic transformation gets stranger when we track the *were*-West, not the *wer* (or "man"-West), but a West conjoined with the past subjunctive form of "to be," a West with plural pasts and competing origins. With werewolf origin stories and family histories that "keep changing" and "twisting back on themselves," Jones's *Mongrels* resists the authenticity tests for werewolves, the West, and Native American literatures. The novel's structure reinforces the aesthetics of mongrel transmotion across genres and geographies. Told nonchronologically during the narrator's adolescence (between his eighth and sixteenth birthdays) and shifting between long first-person chapters and short third-person vignettes, the narrator recounts his transient life on the road with his Aunt Libby and Uncle Darren after the deaths of his Grandpa and his mother, Jess. As a result, the novel does not make for easy tracking—its stories "keep changing" and its structure keeps "twisting back" on itself. Moreover, Jones's werewolves are never Hollywood Indians in disguise: they do not return to "traditional" homelands, they do not cohere around unifying origin stories, and no one falls "dead off the back of a horse."

However, in his interview with Stratton, Jones explains that, while writing *Mongrels*, "I realized that what I'm doing is writing Indian stories dealing with what I would consider issues that are fairly local to Indian life right now."[24] For instance, rather than "Indians-watching-Indians on T.V.," as in Chris Eyre's film *Smoke Signals* (1998), Jones's narrator watches "moondogs" on television—the novel's term for a tragic subspecies of werewolves who are bitten, rather than born into the blood, and, therefore "can't go the full distance, can't transform like you can if you were born into it."[25] "These man-wolves," the narrator explains, are "what the movies are based on," inspired, in particular, by the monster film *The Wolf Man* (1941), in which Bela Lugosi's racialized character "Bela the Gypsy" can go "full wolf," but those he infects, such as the white Larry Talbot (Lon Chaney Jr.), transform into tragic, two-legged man-wolves.[26] Unlike Chaney's tragic character in Universal Pictures' classic lunar gothic, the narrator's Grandpa insists that real werewolves are not "married to the moon."[27] Instead, Jones eschews the supernatural authenticity tests imposed on monsters and, by extension, mixedbloods, presenting "ordinary monsters," "check-to-check werewolves," and "monsters I could believe in. A monster like me and mine."[28]

By using "ordinary monsters" to tell "Indian stories," Jones's approach to race (and class) draws comparison to works by Percival Everett (*Erasure: A Novel*, 2001), Colson Whitehead (*The Intuitionist*, 1998, and *Zone One*, 2011), and Toni Morrison ("Recitatif," 1983), that contribute to what Ramón Saldívar in "The Second Elevation" calls the "postrace aesthetic" and its four fundamental characteristics:

Postrace aesthetics is in critical dialogue with the aesthetics of postmodernism
Postrace aesthetics draws on the history of genres and typically mixes generic forms
Postrace aesthetics is invested in speculative realism
Postrace aesthetics explores the thematic of race in twenty-first-century America.[29]

In *Mongrels*, the exploration of the "thematic of race" is inseparable from the novel's remixing of generic forms, in which Jones's monstrous offspring are produced by the generic intermixture of canonical characters and tropes from American Indian literatures. Like Vizenor's crossblood pilgrims in his first novel *Darkness in Saint Louis Bearheart* (1978), Jones's werewolves trek across the country, from New Mexico and Texas to Florida, Georgia, Arkansas, and the Carolinas, making for a reimagined "homing-in" narrative for werewolves who, the narrator reminds us, have never had a "homeland."[30] Drawing inspiration from James Welch (Blackfeet), Jones's werewolves have *winter in the blood* (1974), they are "made for snow . . . but in the snow you leave tracks, and those tracks always lead back to your front door, and that only ever ends with the villagers mobbing up with their pitchforks and torches."[31] Therefore, like the cross-bred cattle that survive the tough southwestern terrain in Leslie Marmon Silko's (Laguna Pueblo) *Ceremony* (1977), Jones's werewolves must adapt to the Southwest and the Southeast, learning to stay on the move and one step ahead of the "villagers," cops, and liquor-store clerks who might brandish *"pitchforks and torches.... Like what we're in here, it's a Frankenstein movie."*[32]

Nearly two hundred years after Mary Shelley "bid [her] hideous progeny go forth and prosper," Jones sets his monstrous progeny loose in the West, the South, and the Southeast, where they share generic affinity with other monstrous families in the post-West.[33] This lineage includes the aptly named "Sawyer" family of cannibal taxidermists in *The Texas Chain Saw Massacre (1974)*, Papa Jupiter and his irradiated band of scavengers who give new meaning to the "nuclear family" in *The Hills Have Eyes* (1977), and the carny (and carnal) killers who comprise the Firefly family in Rob Zombie's *House of a 1000 Corpses* (2003).[34] However, unlike these monstrous, rural white families, who bear striking resemblance to the savage and static Indians of the Hollywood western, Jones sets his monstrous family in motion across geographical, generic, and genealogical lines. In resistance to what Vizenor calls "terminal creeds," or beliefs and actions that result in stasis and cultural death, Jones's werewolves drive beat-up Impalas, El Caminos, and Delta 88s hard and fast, often trying to "outrun [their] headlights."[35] And yet their constant motion is not purely liberating, but a condition of living in "a world that wants us to be monsters."[36] In such a world, motion can be deadly, as they worry about transforming while driving an eighteen-wheeler at "highway speeds," gripping "steering wheels [that] aren't designed for monsters that aren't supposed to exist."[37] Moreover, they cannot stay in place long enough to mourn their dead. Instead, they are forced to carry the memory of the narrator's Grandma, who died before he was born, and his Grandpa, who dies "halfway between man and wolf," his body left in an unmarked grave, where Darren uses a front-end loader to "crush all Grandpa's bones, so it wouldn't matter if anyone dug them up."[38] And, like the characters in Erdrich's *Love Medicine*, who carry the memory of June Morrissey after she disappears into a North Dakota snowstorm, Jones's werewolves carry the felt absence of the narrator's mother, Jess. Unlike her twin siblings, Libby and Darren, Jess was born without the ability to transform into a werewolf, and she dies at fourteen, soon after giving birth to the narrator. As the narrator explains, "For a lot of years we'd been pallbearers, carrying my mom from state to state."[39]

Declaring that "this is the way it is with werewolves," the narrator comes of age in a world where the sacred is always profaned, where traveling from "state to state" across geographical borders is a necessity, and where transforming from "state to state" across the lines of species (human and wolf) and monstrosity (human and werewolf) is a condition of lycanthrope life.[40] As a result, the novel's version of mongrel transmotion often moves away from narratives of repatriation, or the recovery of ancestral remains and sacred lands, and toward narratives of rematernity and repaternity through the narrator's efforts to interpret family stories about his mother and grandmother, his absent father, and his Grandpa.

Although the werewolves in *Mongrels* bear passing similarities to other monstrous families in the post-West, Jones explains that they inherit much of their history from the Oklahoma outlaw "family" of vampires in Kathryn Bigelow's *Near Dark* (1987).[41] As Jones writes: "Here was a family of vampires who . . . were living in a series of vans with blacked-out windows. Just driving from town to town using different scams to lure victims out into the darkness for a little teeth-on-neck action. . . . They were just doing what they could to survive."[42] As the urtext for *Mongrels*, *Near Dark* is chock-full of western iconography: vampire Severen (Bill Paxton) wears spurs and slathers his chin in beer foam performing briefly as Buffalo Bill at a western biker bar, while the recently turned protagonist Caleb (Adrian Pasdar) wears a cowboy hat to shade his pale vampiric skin. Whereas *The Texas Chain Saw Massacre* was shot on special film stock to accentuate the blinding Texas glare, *Near Dark*, as its title suggests, is always approaching night, that space between the western's motif of sunset and the Red Power novel's imagery of dawn.[43] Plotted around a series of modern-day captivity narratives, Caleb oscillates between allegiances to his cowboy family and his new, vampire family, until the two families come to a head at the Godspeed Motel. In the film's strangest scenes, Caleb's father lays out his son on a gurney back at the ranch and hooks him up for a person-to-person blood transfusion, a procedure that Caleb later repeats with Mae, the vampire who infected him in the film's opening frames. The film concludes with blood transfusions that "cure" Caleb and Mae of their vampire infections and, perhaps, reinfect them with the West and its generational violence and gendered mythologies for kin-making and placemaking.

In *Mongrels*, Jones does not hook his monsters up for a blood transfusion, but a genre transfusion—the mutual and at times monstrous exchanges across a range of generic influences, from the scatological humor of indigenous trickster stories (see Darren's glitter-flecked scat trails and profitable urine) to the tropes of Red Power to the monstrous families in the post-West. Jones's emphasis on genre transfusion presents a unique version of "Native slipstream," which Grace Dillon (Anishinaabe and Metis) defines as "a species of speculative fiction within the sf [science fiction] realm," that crosses genres, and "as its name implies, Native slipstream views time as pasts, presents, and futures that flow together like currents in a navigable stream. It thus replicates nonlinear thinking about space-time."[44] Originally referring to a phenomenon in aeronautics, slipstream has gained considerable traction in the late twentieth and early twenty-first centuries as a genre term with ill-defined boundaries, one that Bruce Sterling describes as a mode of postmodern writing that *"simply makes you feel very strange."*[45] Although Sterling is credited with coining "slipstream" as a genre in a 1989 issue of the fanzine sf *Eye*, Vizenor made use of the term eleven years earlier in his inventive short story "Custer on the Slipstream" (1978). Jones's unique approach to race in the West emerges from Vizenor's slipstream, transforming western fantasies of violent and romantic occupation into unsettling narratives that "make you feel very strange." As coeditors

James Patrick Kelly and John Kessel assert in the introduction to *Feeling Very Strange* (2006), "Slipstream can take you to a place where you have never been. An impossible place that cannot exist, and yet a place where you are expected."[46] For both Jones and Vizenor, the West has long been such a place for Native peoples—at once "an impossible place" where indigenous futures "cannot exist" under the rubric of manifest destiny, and yet a place where Native peoples are expected to perform scripted acts of death, disappearance, and dispossession.

By recombining the "impossible place" of the West with monsters that "aren't supposed to exist," Jones exhibits his method of truth-telling in postrace, "postindian," and postmodern fiction. As Jones tells Stratton, "I think in fiction, on the page, if you multiply two lies, you can get a truth."[47] In one of the novel's most powerful examples of this approach to the truth about stories, Jones offers three competing origin stories for werewolves. The first is Darren's retelling of Grandpa's elaborate adventure story in which an old woman fortune-teller and the Black Wolf—a werewolf secret agent behind Nazi lines—discuss the origins of werewolves. Recasting "*end-stage* rabies" as the infection that births werewolves, the old fortune-teller explains that "never before had rabies been allowed to run its complete course."[48] However, she elaborates, there was once an old woman healer who "couldn't fight the madness" in an infected child, but "she was skilled to keep the child alive, though each day his teeth grew more pointed. Though each day the hair sprouted on his body. That was what the madness had always been trying to do."[49] The story of the fortune-teller, Black Wolf, and end-stage rabies represents one of Jones's intertextual mixtures that draws inspiration from the fortune-tellers in *The Wolf Man*, the werewolf secret agents behind German lines in Robert McCammon's *The Wolf's Hour* (1989), and the interconnected fear of rabies and wolves in Blackfeet stories recounted in Barry Lopez's *Of Wolves and Men* (1978).[50] This elaborate story of werewolf origins is then contested by Libby, who offers a much shorter explanation, saying, "A wolf got hungry one day, so he dressed up in the clothes of a man he'd just eaten and walked on two feet into town but got lost in the tangle of streets . . . until he forgot who he was. And now here we are."[51] Here, too, Jones seems to reference and invert a story collected in *Of Wolves and Men*, in which Lopez describes the Navajo belief that some wolves were "human witches in wolves' clothing."[52] Unable to decide which origin story he believes more, the narrator makes up his own: "The unholy union. Those two star-crossed lovers the world always needs. . . . A wolf and a logger's daughter meet out in the moonlight night after night, trying to figure out the precise mechanics of their relationship."[53] The tragedy, he explains, is that "when the woman gives birth to the first of us, [she] has to die from it." However, in a poignant rescripting of this tragedy, the narrator decides: "I guess that makes *love* the actual infection in our blood."[54] Similar to the way Jones combines competing stories to produce new ones, the narrator takes the irreconcilable origin stories told by his aunt and uncle and playfully remixes them to produce his own.

This method of remixing and regenerating stories does not simply produce new fictions or "lies," but, instead, the embellished stories that "keep changing" require acts of critical and creative interpretation and afford opportunities for "twisting back" to uncover hidden truths. For instance, the narrator's self-authored "unholy union" or "star-crossed-lover" story can be reinterpreted as the slant or mythic version of the narrator's own "monstrous birth." The first version of this story is told by his Grandpa, who transforms stories about "dewclaws" and "birthing," into a story about dragging a rabid dog out of sight to be put down, until the narrator recognizes that "it wasn't a dog Grandpa had to drag out by the fence."[55] "The real story," the narrator explains, "the one Grandpa was trying to say out loud finally, it's that a father carries his oldest daughter out past the house, he carries her out and she's probably already changing for the first time, into an abomination, but he holds his own wolf back, isn't going to fight her like that."[56] In the narrator's poignant retelling, he rerecognizes the truth hidden underneath his Grandpa's slant story, so that it is Jess, his mother, not a rabid dog, who is transforming into a moondog. In this version, his Grandpa holds Jess by the "scruff" and "raises a ball-peen hammer" for the killing blow. However, Grandpa "isn't decisive enough, can't commit to this act with his whole heart," and "for the rest of that night, for the rest of his *life*, this husband and father and monster is swinging that little ball-peen hammer, trying to connect, his face wet with the effort, the two of them silhouettes against the pale grass, going around and around the house."[57] With the narrator's monstrous birth story, Jones establishes unique relationships across what horror philosopher Noël Carroll calls *"natural horror,"* or the "real" horrors of history (Nazis, nuclear war, ecological disaster, chattel slavery, sexual violence, settler violence) and "art-horror," or the fictional horrors of the "cross-art, cross-media genre."[58] The narrator's monstrous birth is never told straight with the brutal realism of a "natural horror" story, but, instead, the narrator must interpret and reinterpret the different versions of "art horror," or the embellished slant stories passed down by his Grandpa, Darren, and Libby, where he discovers multiple versions of the truth.

By the end of the novel, the narrator will again rescript his birth story after he learns that his biological father was a "sheep," or self-hating werewolf, who impregnated Jess as an act of revenge against the narrator's Grandpa. This painful realization leads the narrator to assert, "Now I know the truth about myself. I was a murder weapon. I was revenge."[59] However, in *Mongrels* the "truth" in violent stories, origin stories, and birth stories can, and must, always be reinterpreted and rescripted; the truth, like the mongrel, is a shape-shifter. Or, as the narrator understands from the opening pages, "What I had to do to get to the truth of the story was build it up again from the same facts, but with different muscle."[60] Rather than multiplying two lies to get a truth, then, Jones's mongrel transmotion reveals how multiple slant truths can be produced or "built up" through the intersections and interactions of competing stories, where fiction enables and produces its own truths, and Jones's narrator learns to treat truth and fiction as interrelated, like the strands of a double helix, two sides of the same frontier.

Wolf-Wear and the Wear-West

The werewolf, the West, and the Indian are all wearable identities in the post-West. Where there was once the "authentic" Indian costumes in

Edward Curtis's traveling wardrobe, we now have headdressed hipsters at Coachella. Teddy Roosevelt fashioned himself in western wear as part of his neurasthenic "west cure," while today, Teddy Flood wears the recreated and recreational West along with his fellow life-like hosts in HBO's *Westworld* (2016–present). In 1995, biologist Doug Smith reintroduced the endangered gray wolf to Yellowstone, but the wearable wolf, like the wearable Indian and West, needed no such reintroduction—it flourishes as a Halloween costume and truck-stop souvenir, and a wolf mask named "Peachfuzz" made its violent and strangely erotic debut in the mumblecore film *Creep* (2014). The wearability of the wolf, the West, and the Indian connotes performance, and several monstrous families in the post-West have gotten in on the act. In *Men, Women, and Chain Saws* (1992), Carol Clover suggests that there is a "special connection between the country folk of the urbanoia [or city-revenge] films," such as *The Hills Have Eyes* and *The Texas Chainsaw Massacre*, "and the Indians of the settler-versus-Indian western."[61] As Clover elaborates, "In these stories, both redneck and redskin are figured as indigenous peoples on the verge of being deprived of their native lands," suggesting that "the rednecks of modern horror even look and act like movie Indians."[62] Drawing inspiration from Clover, but going underneath the clothes, Jack Halberstam argues that skin itself "becomes a kind of metonym for the human" in gothic and neogothic horror, adding that "its color, its pallor, its shape mean everything within a semiotics of monstrosity."[63] In his reading of an iconic scene from *The Texas Chainsaw Massacre 2* (1986), Halberstam argues that when Leatherface forces the "final girl," Stretch, to wear the face of her friend LG, "she becomes literally a 'stretch' between genders. LG's face is stretched across her own, her gender is stretched between her mask, her location, her body, and her relation to her monstrous dance partner [Leatherface]."[64] And, Halberstam adds, "gender, *Chainsaw 2* suggests, is skin, leather, face, not body, not internal mechanics, certainly not genitalia."[65]

Jones, like Clover and Halberstam, is interested in how the monstrous West is worn. Building from my focus on how Jones recombines intertextual influences to transform narratives of race and place, here I argue that textiles, or the materials that werewolves wear and wear out, reveal Jones's unique vision for refashioning the discourse of race in the wear-West. The racial formation of "the Indian" in both literature and law has long been determined less by skin than by blood. As Kim TallBear (Sisseton-Wahpeton Oyate) asserts in *Native American DNA* (2013), "'Indian blood' has enjoyed a unique place in the American racial imagination, and tribal communities are managed (by others or by us) according to the precise and elaborate symbolics of blood."[66] In *Mongrels*, blood remains an important substance and symbol, both as a method of transmitting werewolfism, either by infection ("moondogs") or monstrous birth, and as a mark of violence. However, rather than reifying the discourse of "blood quantum" and other "genetic metaphors" that TallBear argues "increasingly colonize our vocabularies of self, inheritance, and destiny," identity for Jones's werewolves is a fraught question, and blood, like television and the moon, never holds all of the answers.[67]

For the narrator (and reader), Jones's *Mongrels* is part Charles Darwin's *On the Origin of Species* (1859) in its tracking of werewolf biological origins, and part Sigmund Freud's *The "Wolfman" and Other Cases* (1918) in the way the narrator becomes an interpreter of stories and dreams in a contemporary American landscape where, the novel's epigraph asserts, "no one believes in werewolves."[68] As a species, Jones's werewolves have preferred habitats and specific physiologies and mating patterns. They are "built for the snow" and have "dewclaws" for birthing; they "age like dogs" when they transform, and unlike the moondogs in movies, their bodies maintain the "conservation of mass" when they shift—"if anything," the narrator explains, "after shifting you're a few ounces lighter, taking into account all the calories you just had to burn through."[69] They are not "married to the moon," but, much like the geese in Erdrich's *Love Medicine*, werewolves do "mate for life."[70] However, whereas Darwin's work "kills" the werewolf by demonstrating its evolutionary impossibility, and Freud tracks (and attempts to "kill") the werewolves that continue to shape-shift in the human psyche, Jones's *Mongrels* seeks to give readers werewolves we can *believe* in.[71] His werewolves resist purity, make mongrels of taxonomies, leave tracks across species.

Crucially, in *Mongrels*, identity is wearable, making second-hand *jeans* as good a marker of werewolf identity as *genes*. In part, the novel's emphasis on *jeanealogy* over genealogy becomes a method for rerecognizing the intersections of race, class, and monstrosity. As Jones writes, "I'm always wondering how this werewolf's going to pass the credit check at the used car lot. I'm always thinking that you can tell when werewolves are in town, because all the used jeans disappear from the racks."[72] In *Mongrels*, Jones's "check-to-check" werewolves watch *Wheel of Fortune* on "knob-less TVs" that come with their trailers.[73] They eat hot dogs and steal ketchup packets from the gas station, skip town when the rent check bounces or when the liquor-store clerk remembers their strawberry wine cooler order.[74] They make "owl jerky" from roadkill and ritualize the burning of their trash to avoid waking up back in delicate human form with a "ragged lid of a tin can in your gut . . . that cuts like a circle saw blade, in first gear."[75]

However, for the narrator and his family, denim is not only a marker of class, but the preferred fabric of werewolves because it shreds away during transformations: "The good thing about jeans, it's that they rip away."[76] Although the narrator admits that "it sucks always having to buy new jeans," he tells us in the closing pages that he has scrawled "secret graffiti" into a thousand bathroom stalls that reads: "*When I am a werewolf, I will wear jean shorts.*"[77] In each case, *jeans* seems to pun its homophone *genes*, allowing us to hear "the good thing about *genes*, it's that they rip away," or, as if satirizing the recent online DNA testing economy, we might hear the narrator say, "It sucks always having to buy new *genes*." Moreover, denim, the durable and dynamic fabric, contains its own vexed racial history stemming from cotton plantations and American chattel slavery, a history that has been largely stonewashed from the minds of its working-class and high-fashion wearers. In *Mongrels*, Jones's werewolves do not directly remember denim's fraught history, but instead they value its ubiquity and affordability, as well as its capacity to "rip away," but "not at the seams like you'd think—the yellow thread there is tough like fishing line—but in the center of the denim, where it's worn the thinnest."[78] Similarly, Jones seeks weak points in settled narratives, places where the West is "worn the thinnest" and where racist histories and stories can be transformed, ripped away at the center, and "re-membered." At times, this process of "re-membering" exposes the horror on the surface, like the dried and sutured skins of Leatherface's mask. At others, it reveals something new hidden beneath something old, like the iconic Lone Ranger mask and Kemosabe's association with silver.

In nearly all werewolf texts, especially those post–*Wolf Man*, silver is the element required to kill lycanthropes. As Stephen King explains, "For werewolves and vampires and all manner of things that squirm by starlight, it was silver you wanted; honest silver. You needed silver to stop a monster."[79] On this point, Jones's werewolves are no different; they too can be put down with a silver bullet or wounded by a silver "throwing star."[80] Even the word "silver," the narrator explains, is one "werewolves kind of hiss out, like the worst secret."[81] However, for Jones's werewolves, "part of being deathly allergic to silver is a deep-seated hatred of the Lone Ranger," because the masked rider is believed to be "the first werewolf hunter."[82] In "Hero with Two Faces: The Lone Ranger as Treaty Discourse" (1996), Chadwick Allen argues that the long-standing Lone Ranger radio and television series modeled America's fantasies of treaty discourse in federal Indian policy between the heroic Lone Ranger and the resourceful but subservient Tonto.[83] And this model relationship became binding through ritual and material exchanges after the death of the Lone Ranger's brother, Captain Reid. As Allen explains, "It is Tonto's hand that cuts the mask from Captain Reid's vest, fashioning what will become the sign of both the Lone Ranger's new identity and the reconfiguration of his frontier power."[84] Moreover, by the end of the "origin sequence," silver becomes a mark of this "treaty discourse," when "Reid's silver Ranger's badge is reconfigured as the Lone Ranger's silver bullets. The Lone Ranger's white stallion, called Silver, will also wear silver horse shoes."[85] Calling for an "alternate reading" of the silver closely associated with the iconic western lawman, Allen suggests that "the silver of these items of Lone Ranger paraphernalia can be linked to the silver of Tonto's ring, to an Indian tradition of craftsmanship and to an Indian symbolic system."[86] More broadly, Allen asserts that "all aspects of the Lone Ranger's new costume, though strongly promoted . . . as essentially White, remain ambiguous, ultimately deriving from the frontier's 'contact zone.' The Lone Ranger's new costume can be read as a 'masked' version of the half-breed's."[87]

In Jones's reworking of the Lone Ranger's origin story, there is no Tonto, but there are plenty of "half-breeds," monstrous mixtures of blood and bone, bound together by shape-shifting family stories. More to the point, Jones associates the werewolf allergy to silver with a "deep-seated hatred of the Lone Ranger," who is not only the "first werewolf hunter," but also a self-loathing werewolf.[88] As the narrator asserts, "For that last gasp of the Old West, when trains and horses were both there at once . . . the Lone Ranger was a werewolf, and the worst kind: a self-hating one. A werewolf who hunted down other werewolves."[89] This revelation aligns the Lone Ranger with "sheep," or self-hating werewolves who no longer transform into wolves.[90] Much in the way that Thomas King (Cherokee) reimagines the Lone Ranger as a masked Indian, and possibly a woman, in the essay and photo series ironically titled "Shooting the Lone Ranger," Jones calls on us to suspect something monstrous lurking underneath the Lone Ranger mask, that iconic symbol of treaty discourse transformed into a symbol of stasis and werewolf self-loathing. With violent histories covered by romantic fantasies, the Lone Ranger—and "sheep" more broadly—become symbols of the settled narratives of the Old West that can be re-recognized as "wolves in sheep's clothing." For Jones's narrator, these well-worn masks can and must be ripped away, allowing settled narratives to become unsettled "where they are worn the thinnest."

What is truly monstrous in *Mongrels* is the refusal to shift, the allegiance to purity, the metaphorical and material masks that impose stasis and inflict violence in their rigid resistance to transformation. Whereas the Lone Ranger mask is the symbol of the Old West worn by the first werewolf hunter, Lycra, or synthetic stretch pants, presents a new but equally deadly fabric for Jones's werewolves in the post-West. Unlike denim, the narrator explains, Lycra does not shred away during transformations: "Stretch pants, they wolf out with you," the fabric painfully "embedding itself under the skin."[91] In Jones's novel, "stretch pants are just as dangerous to werewolves as highways."[92] Lycra is not only a dangerous material for werewolves, but a material metaphor for western storytelling. Long since liberated from its origins in the Old West, the genre is not always "Old" (see the neo- or post-westerns of Cormac McCarthy and the Cohen Brothers) or "West" (see the interstellar west of 1977's *Star Wars*), and it continues to defy its geopolitical and temporal boundaries. However, like Lycra, the genre resists transformation even as it expands to new territories. Built on the faulty history (but compelling metaphors) of Frederick Jackson Turner, the classic western is itself a transformation narrative that tells the story of settler Americans emerging from harrowing encounters with indigenous peoples as a "new race" ready to transform the land from a tabula rasa or terra nullius into a "complex nervous system" out of the mud from the "simple, inert continent."[93] Certainly, the West has undergone dramatic changes since Turner lamented the close of the frontier. Where we once had Buffalo Bill Cody's romantic reenactments of the Ghost Dance in his Wild West show we now have the "Ghost Nation" of *Westworld*. Whether it is set in the Old West or in outer space, this expansive genre remains an inhospitable, nearly uninhabitable, genre for living indigenous characters, who most often appear as silent or savage, static, or spectral, but who rarely turn into anything more than reminders of America's violent and romantic past. It is a genre that gives rise to the illusion that this story is settled—a genre in desperate need of new narratives of transformation.

The West shares many of the qualities of Lycra in *Mongrels*; however, its material and metaphorical properties are also subject to change. As the narrator explains, "Texas was bad for werewolves," a place with "grass growing up all around" their car, "like Texas was doing everything it could to keep us here. Not because it wanted us to find work, to make lives. It was because it wanted to eat us."[94] Even after escaping Texas and its carnivorous geography, Jones's werewolves discover weird western motifs that stretch beyond the West's geopolitical borders. The narrator, for instance, is cut by a silver "cockfighting spur" in Florida, while trying to rescue Darren, who is being held captive in an indoor shark tank by a black-market pesticide company that collects and sells his profitable werewolf urine.[95] Grace-Ellen, the woman who cut the narrator with the silver spur, soon joins Libby and the narrator in helping to save Darren from his captivity narrative. Although she is not a werewolf, Grace-Ellen was once married to Trigo, a werewolf from Texas, who was employed and secretly killed by the pesticide company. From Grace-Ellen, the narrator learns new truths about werewolves; as she explains, "Being a werewolf isn't just teeth and claws.... It's inside. It's how you look at the world. It's how the world looks back at you."[96] Perhaps more important, after helping him escape, Grace-Ellen falls in love with Darren and soon becomes pregnant with his child. Challenging the family's hard-earned understanding of what happens to nonwerewolf women (such as Jess) who carry werewolf babies, Grace-Ellen turns to an unlikely source of werewolf survival—silver. Showing Libby and the narrator her silver hoop earrings, "clamped through all around the edges of her ear," Grace-Ellen explains: "The silver gets in your blood. Not enough to hurt, just enough to kick the wolf in the baby. To keep it down for the birthing process."[97]

By first associating the werewolf allergy to silver with their "deep-seated hatred of the Lone Ranger" and, later, rerecognizing silver as a necessary and wearable material for werewolf rebirth, Jones turns silver into an unlikely source of werewolf "survivance"—Vizenor's term connoting not mere survival, but endurance, continuance, and resistance. As Rebecca M. Lush argues in "'Cause the Lie Becomes the Truth': Dead Celebrities and Horror Archetypes in *The Last Final Girl* and *Zombie Bake-Off*" (2016), "Most of [Jones's] horror fiction circles back to the idea of survival in a way that is reflective of a Native worldview. The notion of survival, so central to the horror genre, is in many ways inextricable from the idea of survivance, which has been at the core of much recent literary scholarship on Native literatures."⁹⁸ Focusing on his depiction of dead celebrities, such as the Michael Jackson-masked slasher in *The Last Final Girl* (2012) and the Elvis impersonating wrestler-turned-zombie named Graceland Elvis in *Zombie Bake-Off* (2012), Lush contends that "Jones's use of celebrity culture in horror novels allows him to expand on new ideas of the 'living dead,' since death has done little to minimize the popularity of Jackson or Elvis."⁹⁹ Similarly, in *Mongrels*, Jones reanimates the story of the celebrated (if not celebrity) masked rider, the Lone Ranger and turns him into another monster that has long been associated with Native peoples, the werewolf. In so doing, *Mongrels* does not so much "expand on new ideas of the living dead," but exposes the racist discourse of the tragic and savage mixedblood under the Lone Ranger's mask and the West's other well-worn disguises. Moreover, by transforming silver from a substance of werewolf death and a symbol of western fantasies into a substance and symbol of werewolf rebirth, Jones intervenes in the process that Jodi A. Byrd describes as "zombie imperialism," in which western films, horror texts, and political discourse represent Native peoples as "the originary necropolitical affect of the living dead."¹⁰⁰ Drawing upon the unique affordances of the werewolf, Jones's mongrel transmotion reverses and reworks this process of "zombifying" Indians, making tracks across genres and using the monster's unique transformative abilities to shape new destinies of survivance and regeneration for the maligned and tragic mixedblood.

In so doing, Jones simultaneously envisions new, shape-shifting destinies for the West. Rather than allowing the western to "wolf out" and, once again, embed itself under the skin, Jones's novel ends in a motel room in Texas, where the narrator undergoes two interrelated processes of transformation. Beginning with his "tongue," the locus of language and shape-shifting storytelling, the narrator transforms physically into a werewolf, feeling "the exquisite torture of his knees turning backward," and "the ball-points of his shoulders allow[ing] for a more canine range of motion," before he wakes in a room "alive with the scent, with the stories the scent had to tell."¹⁰¹ Moreover, after cycling through a number of wearable identities in the third-person vignette chapters—a "vampire" on Halloween, a "mechanic" in Alabama, a "biologist" in Florida, and a "criminal" in trouble with his teacher for drawing a werewolf on the moon—in the final chapter he refers to himself simply as "the nephew."[102] Completing its interrelated narrative drives toward kin-making and werewolf transformation, Jones's *Mongrels* leaves us in a West filled with "stories that keep changing," tracks that keep transforming, interpretative strategies that keep "twisting back." His wear-West is not made of Lycra—it is not one size fits all. And his were-West, remixed with influences from other genres, does not simply expand or "stretch" before turning back into itself. Instead, when Jones's werewolves make tracks in the West, the monster and the "impossible place" shape-shift together into something new. As the narrator writes, "In all the stories and all the movies, there's human footprints walking along, becoming wolf prints at the end."[103]

Stretching the West well beyond its generic and geographic boundaries, Jones's werewolf novel offers unique visions for how hard-earned truths about race and place can be worn and worn out. Through mongrel transmotion, or movement across genres, genealogies, and geographies, Jones's unique voice in the West contains the sonic range of a single wolf's howl, which Barry Lopez notes "can contain as many as twelve related harmonics."[104] Lopez also observes that "when wolves howl together they harmonize, rather than chorus on the same note, creating an impression of more animals howling than there actually are."[105] In the novel's narrative drive toward kin-making, Jones's werewolves howl and harmonize with a broad range of texts and genres, creating the impression of more Wests than there are on the shelf and more werewolves lurking out in the trees, or moving into the trailer next door.

With reports of a "Mysterious Werewolf Killed in Montana" released by the *New York Post* and the *Great Falls Tribune* in May 2018, it's possible that even skeptics will become unsettled, wondering, if only to themselves, what else might be possible out there in the West.[106] *Mongrels*, though, is not about that kind of confirmation. Jones's werewolves are not the kind that can be tracked and tagged and held captive on some cordoned-off monster reserve. As the narrator proclaims: "People say werewolves are animals, but they're wrong. We're so much worse. We're people, but with claws, with teeth, with lungs that can go for days, legs that can eat up counties."[107] Making tracks at the intersections of the genre-transforming were-West and the wearable-if-not-worn-out West, Jones's werewolves are the monster that emerges when the often tragic crossblood mixes with the romantic mythos of the American West. "We're families, not packs," Darren declares, marking kin-making and multispecies relationality at the center of Jones's monstrous West.[108]

Through exchanges across genres and genealogies and transmotion across fantasies and geographies, Jones leaves us with a West that is as much a question as a place: Where-West? In *Mongrels*, the where-West is an impossible place oversaturated with bodily fluids and overdetermined by fantasies, one that stretches like Lycra, embeds itself under the skin, and becomes the place where dead and dispossessed Indians are expected. It is a place where blood is always seeping up from the footprint, but it is also a place filled with possibilities for new narratives of transformation. Most of all, it is a weird place where stories keep changing and the truth twists back on itself, a place with competing origins and indeterminate futures, a place that has yet to be settled.

NOTES

1. Jones made this comment during an interview with Susan Bernardin as the keynote speaker at the 2016 Western Literature Association luncheon in Missoula, Montana.
2. Jones, *Not for Nothing*, 115. See also the haunted modular home in *Mapping the Interior* (2017), the haunted rest stop in "This Is Love" (2014), and the drive-through urinal in *Flushboy* (2013).
3. Jones, *Not for Nothing*, 115.
4. Jones, *Fast Red Road*, 146. See also the Sawyers win the Texas vs. Oklahoma chili cookoff in director Tobe Hooper's *Texas Chain Saw Massacre 2*.
5. Jones, *Mongrels*.
6. Jones, "Werewolf at the Door," in *Mongrels*, 5.
7. Jones, "Werewolf at the Door," 6.

8. Jones, "Werewolf at the Door," 6.
9. Jones, *Ones that Got Away*, 242–43.
10. Jones, *Ones that Got Away*, 243.
11. Jones, "Long Time Ago." In this essay, Jones captures Rambo, Conan the Barbarian, and the entire cast of *Star Wars*, including "Darth Vader" (whom Jones renames "Darth Custer"), the twinned pair Leia (with her "Hopi hairdo") and Luke Skywalker (with his quintessentially Indian name), and Yoda, who, Jones asserts, is "an Indian grandmother if there ever was one."
12. Jones, "Letter to a Just-Starting-Out Indian Writer," xv.
13. Jones, "Letter to a Just-Starting-Out Indian Writer," xv.
14. Jones, "Letter to a Just-Starting-Out Indian Writer," xvi.
15. Jones, "Letter to a Just-Starting-Out Indian Writer," xvi, xii.
16. See Gerald Vizenor's *Crossbloods* and his essay "Native Transmotion." Jones's *Mongrels* is less influenced by N. Scott Momaday's Red Power trope "blood memory," which emphasizes the recovery of indigenous identities, lands, and histories, but too often conflates the "ancestral" with the "authentic," than by Vizenor's "crossblood," which not only signals the mixing of genetic materials, but the "transmotion" and transformations between origins and futures, biologies and beliefs.
17. Haraway, *When Species Meet*, 18.
18. Haraway, *When Species Meet*, 18.
19. *Wolfen* was adapted from Whitley Strieber's debut novel of the same title, published in 1978.
20. Stratton, "Observations on the Shadow Self," 51.
21. Haraway, *When Species Meet*, 35.
22. Jones, *Mongrels*, 215.
23. Jones, *Mongrels*, 8.
24. Stratton, "Observations on the Shadow Self," 52.
25. Jones, *Mongrels*, 95.
26. Jones, *Mongrels*, 95.
27. Jones, *Mongrels*, 10. Before Akira Kurosawa exposed film audiences to dappled sunlight cutting through jungle canopy, exploring the gray hues between truth and justice in *Rashomon* (1950), George Waggner directed *The Wolf Man* (1941)—the werewolf's cinematic urtext, in which moonlight swims in thick, low-rolling fog. Like Kurosawa's dappled sunlight, Waggner's masterful interplay between moonlight and fog blurs the lines

between truth and justice. It remains one of Universal Studios' most enduring classic monster films—a haunting, atmospheric werewolf film that I call a "lunar gothic."

28. Jones, "Werewolf at the Door," 6, 4.
29. Prior to Saldívar, Gerald Vizenor (Anishinaabe), one of Jones's primary influences, described the contemporary indigenous people who resist the master narratives of settler colonialism as "postindian warriors." As Vizenor elaborates, the *"indian"* is a colonial invention, a product and simulation of "manifest manners" and systems of oppression and dominance, which can be resisted by "postindian warriors [who] encounter enemies with the same courage in literature as their ancestors once evinced on horses, and [who] create their stories with a new sense of *survivance*," which, for Vizenor, connotes not mere survival, but endurance, continuance, and resistance (*Fugitive Poses*, 4).
30. Jones, *Mongrels*, 208. Critic William Bevis defines the "homing in" plot as a unique American Indian version of the bildungsroman that has broader political implications. Unlike the "leaving plots" that characterize the American bildungsroman, whereby "the individual [such as Ishmael, Huck Finn, and Jay Gatsby] advances, sometimes at all costs, with little or no regard for family, society, past, or place," Bevis argues, that in the "homing in" plot, *"the hero comes home"* ("Native American Novels," 582).
31. Jones, *Mongrels*, 42.
32. Jones, *Mongrels*, 42.
33. Shelley, *Frankenstein*, 169.
34. Hooper, *Texas Chain Saw Massacre*; Craven, *Hills Have Eyes*; Zombie, *House of 1000 Corpses*.
35. Jones, *Mongrels*, 184.
36. Jones, *Mongrels*, 191.
37. Jones, *Mongrels*, 38–39. This image of death by highway draws loose comparison to one of the latest monstrous families in the post-West, the Grahams in director Ari Aster's *Hereditary* (2018), who grieve the death of Charlie after she is decapitated by a telephone pole while gasping for air, her throat swelling in anaphylactic shock (or possibly demonic possession). Like the Grahams, Jones's monstrous family is haunted by a tragic family history—the death of the narrator's mother, the desecration of his Grandma's grave, and the death of his Grandpa.

38. Jones, *Mongrels*, 18; 20.
39. Jones, *Mongrels*, 247.
40. Jones, *Mongrels*, 20.
41. Bigelow, *Near Dark*.
42. Jones, "Werewolf at the Door," 4.
43. See N. Scott Momaday's Pulitzer prize–winning novel *House Made of Dawn* (1968) and the repeated imagery of sunrise in Leslie Marmon Silko's *Ceremony* (1977).
44. Dillon, *Walking the Clouds*, 3.
45. According to *The American Heritage Dictionary of the English Language*, "slipstream" has two earlier definitions from aeronautics, first appearing in 1913: "1. The turbulent flow of air driven backward by the propeller or propellers of an aircraft. Also called race; and 2. The area of reduced pressure or forward suction produced by and immediately behind a fast-moving object as it moves through air or water."
46. Kelly and Kessel, *Feeling Very Strange*, xv.
47. Stratton, "Observations on the Shadow Self," 56.
48. Jones, *Mongrels*, 219.
49. Jones, *Mongrels*, 219.
50. As Lopez writes, "Rabies was a real reason to fear wolves, for there were few more horrible deaths. A Blackfeet man bitten by a rabid wolf was bound with ropes and rolled in a green buffalo hide. A fire was built on and around him and he was subjected to this intense heat until the hide began to burn. The disease was believed to leave in the man's profuse sweat" (*Of Wolves and Men*, 123).
51. Jones, *Mongrels*, 220.
52. As Lopez elaborates, "The Navajo word for wolf, *mai-coh*, is a synonym for witch" and "a Navajo witch becomes a werewolf by donning a wolf skin. If he means to kill someone, he travels to his hogan at night, climbs up on the roof, tosses something through the smokehole to make the fire flare, revealing where people are sleeping. He then pushes down a poison on the end of a stick, which the victim inhales. (Dirt rolling off the roof at night is a sign that a werewolf is about)" (*Of Wolves and Men*, 123).
53. Jones, *Mongrels*, 221.
54. Jones, *Mongrels*, 221.
55. Jones, *Mongrels*, 25.

56. Jones, *Mongrels*, 27.
57. Jones, *Mongrels*, 27.
58. Carroll, *The Philosophy of Horror*, 12.
59. Jones, *Mongrels*, 285.
60. Jones, *Mongrels*, 12.
61. Clover, *Men, Women, and Chain Saws*, 136.
62. Clover, *Men, Women, and Chain Saws*, 136.
63. Halberstam, *Skin Shows*, 6–7.
64. Halberstam, *Skin Shows*, 151.
65. Halberstam, *Skin Shows*, 151–52.
66. TallBear, *Native American DNA*, 45.
67. TallBear, *Native American DNA*, 45.
68. The full epigraph, quoted from American science fiction writer James Blish, reads: "Eventually I went to America. There no one believes in werewolves." Quoted in Jones, *Mongrels*, n.p.
69. Jones, *Mongrels*, 42, 25, 165.
70. Jones, *Mongrels*, 10.
71. As history of science professor Brian Regal argues, "The spread of the idea of evolution helped kill off the werewolf because a canid-human hybrid makes no sense from an evolutionary point of view." However, Regal concedes that Darwinian theory makes "the ape-human hybrid . . . not only evolutionarily acceptable," but "the basis of human evolution" (n.p.). See Regal, quoted in "Darwin Killed Off the Werewolf."
72. Jones, "Werewolf at the Door," 7.
73. Jones, *Mongrels*, 208.
74. Jones, *Mongrels*, 157.
75. Jones, *Mongrels*, 36.
76. Jones, *Mongrels*, 43.
77. Jones, *Mongrels*, 43, 296.
78. Jones, *Mongrels*, 43.
79. King, *It*, 159.
80. Jones, *Mongrels*, 46.
81. Jones, *Mongrels*, 46.
82. Jones, *Mongrels*, 86.
83. Allen, "Hero with Two Faces," 609–38.
84. Allen, "Hero with Two Faces," 628.

85. Allen, "Hero with Two Faces," 628.
86. Allen, "Hero with Two Faces," 628.
87. Allen, "Hero with Two Faces," 628.
88. Jones, *Mongrels*, 86.
89. Jones, *Mongrels*, 86.
90. Jones, *Mongrels*, 236.
91. Jones, *Mongrels*, 63, 43.
92. Jones, *Mongrels*, 42–43.
93. Turner, "Significance of the Frontier."
94. Jones, *Mongrels*, 58–59.
95. Jones, *Mongrels*, 257.
96. Jones, *Mongrels*, 260.
97. Jones, *Mongrels*, 288.
98. Lush, "'Cause the Lie Becomes the Truth," 306.
99. Lush, "'Cause the Lie Become the Truth," 307.
100. Byrd, *Transit of Empire*, 229. For more about the representation of Native peoples as zombies, see also Risling Baldy, "On Telling Native People to Just 'Get Over It.'"
101. Jones, *Mongrels*, 293–94.
102. Jones, *Mongrels*, 292.
103. Jones, *Mongrels*, 297.
104. Lopez, *Of Wolves and Men*, 38.
105. Lopez, *Of Wolves and Men*, 38.
106. Murray, "Mysterious Wolf-like Creature Shot"; O'Neill, "Mysterious 'Werewolf' Killed in Montana."
107. Jones, *Mongrels*, 278.
108. Jones, *Mongrels*, 281.

BIBLIOGRAPHY

Allen, Chadwick. "Hero with Two Faces: The Lone Ranger as Treaty Discourse." *American Literature* 68, no. 3 (1996): 609–38.

Risling Baldy, Cutcha. "On Telling Native People to Just 'Get Over It,' or Why I Teach about *The Walking Dead* in my Native Studies Classes" (2013). CutchaRisingBaldy.com, https://www.cutcharislingbaldy.com/blog/on-telling-native-people-to-just-get-over-it-or-why-i-teach-about-the-walking-dead-in-my-native-studies-classes-spoiler-alert (accessed September 6, 2019)

Bevis, William. "Native American Novels: Homing In." In *Recovering the Word: Essays on Native American Literature*, edited by Brian Swann and Arnold Krupat, 580–620. Berkeley: University of California Press, 1987.

Bigelow, Kathryn. Director. *Near Dark*. F/M Entertainment, 1987.

Byrd, Jodi A. *Transit of Empire: Indigenous Critiques of Colonialism*. Minneapolis: University of Minnesota Press, 2011.

Carroll, Noël. *The Philosophy of Horror: Or, Paradoxes of the Heart*. New York: Routledge, 1990.

Clover, Carol. *Men, Women, and Chain Saws: Gender in the Modern Horror Film*. Princeton NJ: Princeton University Press, [1992] 2015.

"Darwin Killed Off the Werewolf." *Science Daily*, June 30, 2009, https://www.sciencedaily.com/releases/2009/06/090616080135.htm (accessed October 8, 2019).

Dillon, Grace. *Walking the Clouds: An Anthology of Indigenous Science Fiction*. Tucson AZ: Sun Tracks, 2012.

Freud, Sigmund. *The "Wolfman" and Other Cases*. London: Penguin, 2002.

Halberstam, Judith. *Skin Shows: Gothic Horror and the Technology of Monsters*. Durham NC: Duke University Press, 1995.

Haraway, Donna. *When Species Meet*. Minneapolis: University of Minnesota Press, 2008.

Hooper, Tobe, dir. *The Texas Chain Saw Massacre*. Vortex, 1974.

———. *The Texas Chain Saw Massacre 2*. Canon Group. 1986.

Jones, Stephen Graham. *The Fast Red Road: A Plainsong*. Talahassee FL: FC2, 2000.

———. *Flushboy*. Westland MI: Dzanc, 2013.

———. "Letter to a Just-Starting-Out Indian Writer—And Maybe to Myself." In *The Fictions of Stephen Graham Jones: A Critical Companion*, edited by Billy J. Stratton, xi–xvii. Albuquerque: University of New Mexico Press, 2016.

———. "A Long Time Ago: Stephen Graham Jones on Capturing *Star Wars*." Unbound Worlds, October 4, 2017, http://www.unboundworlds.com/2017/10/long-time-ago-stephen-graham-jones-capturing-star-wars/ (site discontinued).

———. *Mapping the Interior*. New York: Tor, 2017.

———. *Mongrels*. New York: William Morrow, 2016.

———. *Not for Nothing*. Westland MI: Dzanc, 2014.

———. *The Ones that Got Away*. Germantown MD: Prime, 2010.

———. "This Is Love." In *After the People Lights Have Gone Off*, 61–78. Chicago: Dark House, 2014.

Kack-Brice, Patrick, dir. *Creep*. Blumhouse Productions, 2014.

Kelly, James Patrick, and John Kessel, eds. *Feeling Very Strange: The Slipstream Anthology*. San Francisco CA: Tachyon, 2006.

King, Stephen. *It: A Novel*. New York: Signet, 1986.

Lopez, Barry. *Of Wolves and Men*. New York: Scribner, 1978.

Lush, Rebecca M. "'Cause the Lie Becomes the Truth': Dead Celebrities and Horror Archetypes in *The Last Final Girl* and *Zombie Bake-Off*." In *The Fictions of Stephen Graham Jones: A Critical Companion*, edited by Billy J. Stratton, 305–26. Albuquerque: University of New Mexico Press, 2016.

Momaday, N. Scott. *House Made of Dawn*. New York: Harper & Row, 1968.

Murray, David. "Mysterious Wolf-like Creature Shot in North Central Montana Near Denton." *Great Falls Tribune*, May 24, 2018, https://www.greatfallstribune.com/story/news/2018/05/24/wolf-dog-dogman-some-mysterious-creature-montanans-look-answers/634379002/ (accessed September 6, 2019).

Nolan, Jonathan, and Lisa Joy, creators. *Westworld*. HBO, 2016–present.

O'Neill, Natalie. "Mysterious 'Werewolf' Killed in Montana." *New York Post*, May 25, 2018, https://nypost.com/2018/05/25/mysterious-werewolf-killed-in-montana/ (accessed September 6, 2019).

Saldívar, Ramón. "The Second Elevation of the Novel: Race, Form, and the Postrace Aesthetic in Contemporary Narrative." *Narrative* 21, no. 1 (January 2013): 1–18.

Shelley, Mary. *Frankenstein: The 1818 Text, Context, Criticism*. 2nd ed. Edited by J. Paul Hunter. New York: W. W. Norton, [1996] 2012.

Silko, Leslie Marmon. *Ceremony*. New York: Viking, 1977.

Stratton, Billy J. "Observations on the Shadow Self: Dialogues with Stephen Graham Jones." In *The Fictions of Stephen Graham Jones: A Critical Companion*, edited by Billy J. Stratton, 14–59. Albuquerque: University of New Mexico Press, 2016.

TallBear, Kim. *Native American DNA: Tribal Belonging and the False Promise of Genetic Science*. Minneapolis: University of Minnesota Press, 2013.

Turner, Frederick Jackson. "The Significance of the Frontier in American History" (1893–94). American Historical Association, https://www.historians.org/about-aha-and-membership/aha-history-and-archives/historical-archives/the-significance-of-the-frontier-in-american-history (accessed September 6, 2019)

Vizenor, Gerald. *Crossbloods: Bone Courts, Bingo, and Other Reports.* Minneapolis: University of Minnesota Press, 1990.

———. "Custer on the Slipstream." 1978. In *Walking the Clouds: An Anthology of Indigenous Science Fiction,* edited by Grace L. Dillon, 15–26. Tucson: University of Arizona Press: 2012.

———. *Fugitive Poses.* Lincoln: University of Nebraska Press, 1998.

———. "Native Transmotion." In *Fugitive Poses: Native American Scenes of Absence and Presence,* 167–200. Lincoln: University of Nebraska Press, 1998.

Zombie, Rob. *House of 1000 Corpses.* Universal Pictures, 2003.

5

Indianizing the Western

Semiotic Tricksterism in William Sanders's *Journey to Fusang*

SARA L. SPURGEON

In a generic sense, William Sanders's (Cherokee) novel *Journey to Fusang* (1988) appears to be a fairly standard—even classic—western. A white male protagonist travels to the wild frontiers of the historic North American West, where he has a series of adventures involving battles with various Native tribes in a savage wilderness, spiced with the occasional visit to a town marked by saloons, gambling halls, and whorehouses. And, still following the classic western trope, his individual story turns out to be part of a much larger, epic tale narrating the fight to win the West and establish a new nation while wrestling with issues of race, gender, settler colonialism, and possession of land. This novel can even be classified as a captivity narrative, since a major storyline involves not only the captivity of the hero, but also of a lovely young white woman carried off by savages, only to be heroically rescued (more or less) by the protagonist.

All these standard signifiers, however, wind up pointing to something that radically destabilizes what classic westerns aim to achieve, providing instead a subversively decolonial indigenous narrative via what Gerald Vizenor (Anishinaabe) refers to as trickster hermeneutics. While trickster figures are common throughout North American indigenous traditions and are commonly understood to be multifaceted figures—both wise and foolish, greedy and generous, often comically blinded by lust but just as often acting as benefactors for humans—Vizenor has famously argued that many such anthropological definitions fail to grasp the narrative role of the trickster in making meaning. More than a character, Vizenor asserts, "the trickster is a sign . . . that cannot be separated or understood in isolation; . . . the signified, or the concept the signifier locates in language and social view, is a narrative or even a translation. . . . The trickster is a comic holotrope in narrative voices, not a model or tragic figure in isolation."[1] Trickster discourse, then, according to Vizenor, is an indigenous form of narrative signifying that is comically subversive both in its function as a sign as well as in the concept(s) it signifies.

Sanders's entire novel in this sense functions as a comic narrative signification of indigenous decolonization and resistance, not just a text with a character that can be read as a trickster. Its trickster discourse is part of its narrative structure. *Journey to Fusang* both translates and *indianizes*[2] the western (to use the definition of Jace Weaver et al.), weirding it in multiple—sometimes comic and sometimes tragic— ways.[3] The trickster nature of the novel and the meaning it generates reside, in part, in the ways Sanders uses the signifiers of classic westerns to implicate history itself in his semiotic trick, for *Journey to Fusang* is also an alternative history.

Alternative histories, sometimes referred to as AH, alt-history, counterhistory, slipstream, or, occasionally, uchronia, evoke "what if" scenarios from history and present an alternate version of how the world would look if some historical event had unfolded differently. Some alternative histories emerge from science fiction and involve a character traveling back in time to alter a past historical event; some invoke the many- or parallel universes theory; some simply speculate on how different the world might be if, for example, the Confederacy had won the Civil War, if Alexander the Great had lived to be an old man, if Hitler had been assassinated before he could invade Poland, and so on.[4]

Alternative histories, in other words, are an inherently tricksterish form. By presenting a version of the past in which some historical event yields an outcome other than what we know, they also create an alternative history after that point in time, thereby implicitly or explicitly creating alternative versions of our present moment and possible futures. These imagined interventions in actual historical events can offer a fruitful method for thinking through current and past systemic realities and injustices, performing a decolonizing function by subverting the presumed naturalness and inevitability at the heart of colonialist histories of the sort frequently found in westerns. Alt-history texts often function via a kind of serious play as a means of resistance to contemporary social, political, and economic structures by insisting on the historical contingency, rather than the supposed inevitability, of such structures. As Catherine Gallagher notes, the deliberate interference in the course of history by alt-history texts "indicate[s] a significant expansion of our sense of plausible chronologies, and . . . this enlarged sense of temporal possibility correlates with a newly activist, even interventionist, relation to our collective past."[5] If westerns as mythic texts frequently function, as I have argued elsewhere, as "the language through which a society remembers its history and attempts to understand its future," an alt-history western can potentially destabilize the signifiers and signified concepts inherent in the United States' favorite nation-defining genre, weirding not just the genre itself, but the most basic meanings generated by its signifying narratives.[6]

Sanders establishes the basics of his alternative version of the invasion and colonization of what is now called North America in a prologue that includes an excerpt from a fictional text, "A Short History of the World," authored by a fictional Arab scholar and historian, Hamzah ibn-Rashid, a figure perhaps inspired by the historical Ibn Rushd (sometimes referred to as Averroes in his native Andalusia), a twelfth-century Moorish scholar from Spain who wrote extensively on Islamic and Aristotelian philosophy. The excerpt from "A Short History" orients Sanders's readers to the alternative historical world they are about to encounter, explaining that, in their thirteenth-century invasion of Europe, the Mongols (rather than turning back at the borders of Austria—a decision still not fully understood by historians) overran nearly all of western Europe, razing most of its great cities before drifting back to Asia "after little more than a century of occupation." Their departure results in "a new Dark Age, darker than that which had followed the fall of Rome. And, even as the invaders withdrew, there came the Plague to further depopulate and demoralize the Christian world." Nearly four hundred years later, Europe is still a fragmented, economically depressed backwater, while the Chinese and Moors have "explored whole continents beyond the seas.... Some have speculated that, had the Mongols been turned back in time, history might have proceeded differently: that it might have been Venetians or Franks, or even Spaniards or Englishmen, who discovered and explored the New World."[7] If one purpose of the western is to naturalize the European invasion and colonization of the Americas, or to frame manifest destiny as a historically inevitable manifestation of racially superior Anglo-Europeans expanding U.S. borders from the Atlantic to the Pacific, Sanders's text renders that version of settler colonialism as finally contingent upon nothing more than a random, inexplicable accident of history.

By the time the novel proper begins, in the late seventeenth century, the Arabs and Chinese have established competing and occasionally cooperative trading empires in North America. The eponymous Fusang is roughly the American West (although, as the novel makes clear, from the Chinese point of view it is the Far East of their empire)—most explicitly, what is now called California and much of the land west of the Rocky Mountains. This is the heart of the Chinese presence in North America, Sanders explains in his author's note, and its capital city, Haiping, is located at the site of modern-day San Francisco. Kaafiristan is the general Arabic geographic expression for the North American mainland, and in the novel refers to the region that falls under actual or claimed Islamic rule, chiefly consisting of the lower Mississippi Valley and the southern Great Plains, with the capital of Islamic North America, Dar al-Islam, roughly equivalent to New Orleans.

The first-person narrator of *Journey to Fusang*, in an ironic twist of mimetic cultural appropriation, is not Native American, but a young Irish gambler, con artist, and petty thief named Finn, although, as Finn notes, "at other times and places I have used other names and been called other things," winking at his own trickster-like character early on.[8] Later in the novel, several Comanche, amused by Finn's display of magic tricks and sleight of hand, will nickname him "Coyote." Sanders's decision to tell the story of European irrelevance and the birth of an organized pan-indian nation in the form of a western and through the point of view of a European protagonist is a comic bit of trickster mimesis in the vein of what Vizenor terms "stealth and cultural irony."[9] This destabilizing move turns the trajectory of the narrative signs we expect in a western in a direction that feels both familiar and strange. Rather than a heroic Anglo-Saxon defeating red savages or a noble white savior who out-indians the indians, the comically bumbling Finn is appropriated by the natives to help set the stage for their opposition to the Arab and Chinese colonizers and to witness the birth of their new nation in North America.[10] In other words, while traditional westerns function as narrative signifiers of Euro-American sovereignty won by battling savage natives, Sanders's indianized western points in the opposite direction, translating the tale of white nation-building into a story of indigenous sovereignty won by battling savage settler colonialists. The novel works to decouple the notion of savagery from that of race, associating it instead with colonialism and slavery—twin evils Sanders presents as sources of rot within any civilization that engages in them.

The abject status of Europeans in the indianized version of history that unfolds following the Mongol decision to advance into Austria is apparent in the backstory of Sanders's European protagonist and his journey to the American West. Forced to flee romantic and financial troubles in Ireland but lacking money to book passage legally, Finn stows away on an Arab ship sailing from Cork. Too late he discovers he has chosen a slave ship carrying enslaved Europeans to the vast slave markets the Arabs have established at Jezira al-Kebir (present-day Cuba). The Arabs and Chinese have built their North American empires, we learn, by providing slaves to the Mexica (also called the Azteca) Empire in exchange for Mexica gold and silver. Poverty-stricken Europeans regularly sell their own people into the booming slave trade, emptying their own lands and further crippling the already anemic European economy. In the earliest passages of the novel, before Finn's eventual arrival in the American West, we see a Europe on the opposite end of a slave trade devastating the lives of millions and suffocating the political and cultural development of an entire continent.

Finn ends up a slave himself, enduring a racially flipped version of the Middle Passage, with Europeans as abject captives suffering the horrors of the hold below deck. This amounts to a double subversion of the captivity narrative as it typically functions within the genre western, which steadfastly refuses to acknowledge the African American slave narrative as its secret twin. Indian captivity narratives are a precursor to, and subgenre of, the western. While they have been continuously popular on both sides of the Atlantic since the 1682 publication of what is considered one of the first, and most widely read, North American captivity narratives, *A Narrative of the Captivity and Removes of Mrs. Mary Rowlandson*, and even though historically nearly as many white men were captured as white women, by the time captivity narratives take fictional form they most frequently present captive white women in the hands of savage indians, with the ever-present threat of the "fate worse than death" lending a titillating frisson to their bestseller status.[11] Richard Slotkin calls captivity narratives "the archetype of the American experience," while Annette Kolodny claims their pathos-laden vision of helpless, threatened white womanhood encouraged white American audiences to view themselves not as aggressors or invaders but as innocent victims of unprovoked attacks endured as they strove to carry out the holy mission of manifest destiny placed before them by God.[12] All the classic western's anxieties about race and gender get bound up in the sign of the captive white woman. This is played for both poignant and comic effect in the character of Finn's love interest, the beautiful Irish slave girl Maeve.

To retain the myth of injured white innocence, however, typical captivity westerns must work to render invisible the historical reality of the flood of captive black bodies pouring out of slave ships beginning with the arrival of the first enslaved Africans in what is now called Virginia in 1619, as well as the even longer history of captured and enslaved Native Americans, hundreds of thousands of whom were carried off to plantations in the Caribbean. Slave narratives and abolitionist texts, which utilized many of the same tropes as indian captivity narratives, presented male figures as captives somewhat more frequently than indian captivity narratives, but did so often by feminizing and abjectifying the black male body. Western captivity narratives, on the other hand, require a captive white (and ideally female) body as a narrative sign in order to generate meaning. The ideological work carried out by this sign is twofold: in relation to the European invasion of the Americas, it accomplishes what Anne McClintock terms "victor-victim reversal," but it also works to cover over the violence enacted by white patriarchy on the bodies of all women, even white ones, via the distinctly raced and gendered roles of helpless captive, vicious captor, and heroic rescuer familiar to us from countless westerns on page and screen.[13]

Maeve, who is carried off during a raid (by savage colonizers rather than savage indians), is perceived by Finn to be in desperate need of rescue. In many ways she is a stereotypical captive white woman—young, beautiful, and at the mercy of a violent and savage Other. In a classic western, we understand Maeve to be what is referred to in film criticism as a rescue object, the thing that must be redeemed by the white hero in order to demonstrate his triumphant masculinity. When the rescue object is a young woman toward whom he has expressed a romantic interest, we further understand she will fall gratefully into the hero's arms once he saves her. And, as Kolodny explains, in the indian captivity western the sign of the captive white woman, through her sexual purity and innocence, typically signifies the victimization of the equally pure and innocent white race. The sign of the captive white woman thereby provides justification for the extermination of the savages who have imperiled her, neatly entwining manifest destiny, white supremacy, and righteous patriarchy in one sexy, pale-skinned package. Only rarely is the figure of the captive white woman given agency of her own in a western.[14] Even more rarely is she allowed to literally or figuratively fuck the hero. Maeve manages both, revealing herself to be as much a trickster as Finn, although quite a bit less bumbling.[15]

When Finn first stumbles upon her, Maeve is being auctioned at a high-end slave market in Dar-al-Islam (New Orleans). He is besotted by her white skin, flaming red hair, and large breasts and manages to purchase her using someone else's money. He magnanimously frees her as he takes her with him to the frontier trading post where he has found employment as a freedman, and there she enthusiastically has sex with him as they spend the long, cold winter speculating on how they can get to Fusang (California) to make their fortune. When the trading post is destroyed and Maeve is carried off, Finn joins the newly allied tribes as they launch an assault against the colonialist army, commanded by the provocatively named Vladimir Khan, which has been ravaging both Arab trading posts and indigenous settlements across the West. Finn, who is frequently undone by greed as well as lust, plans to sneak away in the chaos of battle, free Maeve where she is being held, and not coincidentally make off with a large chest of gold the Chinese have given to Vladimir Khan to fund his campaign of destruction (and thereby subvert their eastern colony's insipient plans to declare independence from Peking). Although the Comanche and their native allies are successful in the assault, Finn botches his rescue attempt, losing track of both Maeve and the chest full of gold. Afterward, several Comanche tell Finn they saw Maeve, bloody and bruised, riding away from the battle, headed west. Finn is convinced she is going to Fusang to wait for him and tells himself he will find her there, declare his love, and marry her, smugly imagining her gratitude at his offer to make her an honest woman, even as he fumes over the lost gold.

Finn does locate Maeve nearly a year later, in the Chinese city of Haiping (San Francisco) at a high-end brothel called the White Flower Inn. As he and his companion, Yusuf (a young Jewish crewman on the slave ship who escaped with Finn), are led up a gleaming staircase, marveling at the Persian carpets, silk tapestries, and glittering chandeliers that surround them, Finn begins to rethink his plan to make his living as a gambler, telling Yusuf, "Well, you know, I have been meaning to get into some steadier line of business—had in mind the games, of course, but. . . ." He is interrupted by a servant who brings them into a private office where Maeve, gowned in silks and jewels, greets them, explaining that she is not employed by the White Flower Inn; she owns it. Stunned, Finn wonders aloud how Maeve could afford to purchase such a profitable establishment. She rolls her eyes, and Finn finally begins to understand. "'God's bum,' I said, awed. 'You got the gold.... How did you manage it?'" Maeve explains she tricked Vladimir Khan's Captain of the Guard, a Russian named Orhan, into carrying her and the gold out of the tent and through the battle to safety: "'When the job was done, I took the knife I had found lying beside the strongboxes . . . and I cut his throat.' She looked at my face and added sharply, 'And you can drop the expression of sanctimonious horror, Your Holiness. If you'd seen what Orhan did to those two girls he captured at Taos, you'd say murder was too good for him!'"[16]

Maeve tells Yusuf and Finn they can stay the night free of charge, and even have their pick of the prostitutes she employs. Finn is outraged, although he struggles to articulate why. Readers understand that, within the system of patriarchy, his is a logical response to Maeve's refusal to inhabit the role of female rescue object, combined with Finn's resentment that her business sense (as demonstrated more than once in the novel) is superior to his own. At base, however, this tricksterish and subversive upending of the sign of the captive white woman is the same sort of decolonizing move Sanders deploys throughout the novel. Here Sanders equates the colonizing patriarchal expectation of male ownership of women with the twin evils of slavery and imperialism. As a signifier, Maeve brazenly points to the capitalist underpinnings of each.

When Finn indignantly declares, "You owe me, woman!" she responds, "Is it possible you had the unmitigated damned audacity to think you could come marching in here, big as you please, and move in, and help yourself to a share of my business that I've built with my own honest labor? No. . . . I see now, it's even worse than that. You didn't just expect a share—you thought you'd be taking over the whole thing, didn't you?" "But you're my woman!" Finn insists, comically oblivious to the assumption of ownership he deplored in the form of institutionalized slavery but that seems so naturalized to him under the guise of patriarchal ownership of Maeve, her body, and her labor. "I'm no man's!" Maeve returns. "Haven't I told you enough times I'll not be owned!" Because she has told Finn precisely that on multiple occasions, he is initially lost for words; then, inadvertently revealing the connections between ownership of women and the economics of slavery—as well as the western's reliance on the female rescue object remaining passive and helpless—he declares, "Well, then, it was my gold!" "In a pig's arse!" Maeve responds, "It was Vladimir Khan's, and then it was anybody's that could take it. . . . I'd have given you a bit of money, if you'd asked, for old times' sake, and because I can spare it. I'd have taken care of you until you could get set up, or staked you to a game. . . . I might even have given you a job. But you come here this way, and I'll not give you a damned thing."[17]

Rather than a hooker with a heart of gold, Maeve is a businesswoman with a chest of gold, a trickster who tricks Coyote himself, and, like Coyote, she is decidedly morally ambiguous, as her "own honest labor" arguably relies on the exploitation of the bodies of other women (and men, as the White Flower Inn also employs male prostitutes). The sign of the captive white woman points here in the opposite direction of innocence or victimization, despite the fact that Maeve has, in fact, been enslaved, both by the Arabs who purchased her back in Ireland, and by the ontology of patriarchy that can only imagine her as a thing to be owned, even if that ownership is sometimes prettily masked by the sign of marriage or romantic love. Rather than signifying cultural or racial innocence to white American readers, Maeve's captivity within two systems, slavery and patriarchy, instead points to the twinned nature of those systems and to the persistent silencing of the meaning of captive bodies within traditional westerns. Just as the expansion of U.S. imperialism was financed by the labor of enslaved African and indigenous peoples, Sanders suggests it also rests on the backs of captive female bodies like Maeve's. While the sign of Maeve's whiteness in a classic western would typically signify her cultural innocence, and her meaning as a love interest and rescue object would typically signify her sexual innocence, here the sign of the captive white woman subverts both empire and patriarchy. Maeve manages to steal not only the chest full of gold, but to also make off with the ideological work done in westerns by the fantasy of helpless white femininity. Maeve is not endangered by savage indians, but by the savagery of colonialism and the institutional slavery that enables it. Her freedom is not threatened by sexually rapacious natives, but by patriarchy and its assumption of ownership of female bodies, even, perhaps *especially* in this case, white ones.

Journey to Fusang provides, then, the requisite sign of a captive white body (both male and female), but, as Vizenor suggests about trickster narratives, it takes that body as signifier and, instead of pointing it toward white innocence and victimization on the western frontiers, evokes the otherwise elided and ghosted figures of captive African and indian slaves lurking as mimetic echoes or twins behind the images of the enslaved Finn and Maeve. Early in the novel, deploying the rhetoric used about enslaved Africans in our own timeline, Finn speculates on what appears to him to be the inevitability of the status of the English as slaves to the more civilized Arabs, observing, "Truly it is hard to imagine that the English might ever amount to much, although they are often wonderfully strong, and make hard and faithful workers; and of course they can sing and dance like anything."[18]

For all its comic irony, however, *Journey to Fusang* is quite serious in presenting slavery as a bedrock historical evil upon which imperialism rests. In weirding and translating the western into an indigenous text, Sanders foregrounds slavery as the fuel that drives the engine of every imperial venture in the New and Old Worlds. Without exception in this novel, those who deal in slaves—Arabs, Chinese, Europeans, Mexica, Comanche, or obliviously patriarchal white men—are fated to be punished in some way. Slavery spawns, and in turn is supported by, the opium trade once the Chinese discover how well opium poppies grow in the high, arid climate of New Mexico and begin forcing the Pueblos to cultivate the crop in order to supply opium to markets in Mexico and Dar al-Islam (New Orleans). The Mexica in the novel use slave labor in their mines, then trade the gold and silver they produce for Chinese silks and jade, Moorish weapons, and Chinese opium. But the drug trade here is secondary to the evil of holding human beings in bondage—or, more accurately, enslavement through drug addiction is analogous to colonialism. Put another way, colonialism is the ultimate expression of slavery and cannot exist without it, being imagined in the novel as a kind of vampiric force (personified by Vladimir Khan, a metaphoric, not actual, vampire) that feeds off the bodies of captive human beings, in this case mainly Europeans and natives from smaller nations captured by more powerful tribes like the Comanche to be sold or traded to satisfy the Comanche desire for horses and weapons.

The rhetorical sign of "Indianness" (as Chickasaw scholar Jodi Byrd analyzes the term) as it is typically deployed by westerns is complicated and problematized here, especially in its troubling historical relationship to slavery. The actual Cherokee history of owning enslaved Africans within their own colonized nation is engaged by Sanders in several other alt-histories, most notably his 1991 novel *The Wild Blue and the Gray*. In that text, the Five Tribes forced into Oklahoma on the Trail of Tears decide, after fierce debate, to ally themselves with the Confederacy during the Civil War in exchange for the Confederacy's promise to honor tribal sovereignty in Oklahoma, a promise the Union refuses to make. By 1916, when the now independent Confederate States of America come to the aid of their former British allies in the British battle against the Germans, the Cherokee Nation sends a young pilot named Amos Ninekiller as a token gesture of support to serve with the Confederate Air Force in France. While the Confederacy has officially ended race slavery as a legally recognized system by 1916, they have replaced it with Jim Crow, a system so brutally efficient in disenfranchising supposedly free blacks even the Germans are impressed. While Amos is shunned by most of the white Confederate pilots he serves with, he is confronted by a black servant attached to his CAF unit who pointedly reminds him that some Cherokee also enslaved black people. Amos acknowledges this as an everlasting shame for the Cherokee and promises the man, whom he has accidentally discovered organizing an armed African American uprising against the Confederates, that he will keep the group and their plans secret.[19]

In other words, Indianness for Sanders is a complicated, complex, and fully human sign, freighted with a deep and profound history that is neither saintly nor evil. This is rarely the case in texts, especially westerns, authored by nonnatives. In the hands of nonindigenous writers, Byrd argues, Indianness as a sign most typically "serves as the ontological scaffolding for colonial domination" both within North America and beyond. "As long as the United States continues to construct itself as cowboy," Byrd explains, "it must designate or infect those to be vanquished as 'Indians.'"[20] As the genre literally created to memorialize the ongoing project of white colonial-cowboy domination of actual indians, the western most frequently deploys Indianness as a sign pointing to one or both of the twinned ontological categories of noble savage and savage savage, each one a flattened and undifferentiated vision of indigeneity that serves, as Byrd suggests, mainly as a justification for dominance.

In indianizing the sign of Indianness, however, Sanders's western translates the meaning it carries, in part by decolonizing the reductive historical vision of indigeneity most westerns generate. Ironically, for an alternative history, the novel achieves this by using actual historical details. For example, Sanders's descriptions of the Azteca Empire and its capital city, Tenochtitlan (now called Mexico City), are historically accurate in nearly all respects. Yusuf, the crewman who confides to Finn he may be among the slaves intended for sale to the Mexica, describes their capital city (which in the sixteenth century of our own timeline was one of the largest metropolises on earth):

> It's bigger than Rome or Constantinople or even Baghdad—why there are independent kingdoms in Europe and Africa that cover less area than Tenochtitlan alone. And all of it laid out carefully with long straight streets, even canals in some parts like those of Venice, and market squares bigger than most European towns. Flowers growing everywhere, and the people looking so clean and well fed, even the poor . . . and in the center, dominating the whole city from wherever you stand, the great pyramid. . . . with a whole city-within-a-city of lesser temples and palaces clustered at its base.[21]

Sanders (who in addition to writing fiction also published a nonspeculative history, *Conquest: Hernando de Soto and the Indians, 1539–1542*), appears to have drawn much of this description of Tenochtitlan from Cortes's second letter to Charles V (1520) in which Cortes describes the city's dozens of plazas, vast markets, temples, canals, and the like. Cortes's letter, which also details Tenochtitlan's broad, paved streets, complexly engineered system of reservoirs and sewer pipes that supply water for the metropolis, its hundreds of finely carved stone bridges, and a list of animals found in Moctezuma's three private zoos, is well known in the historical record, but rarely appears in white-authored narratives, fictional or otherwise, about the Americas. Most westerns instead suppress and overwrite actual history in the service of producing a fantasy version of Indianness in which all natives were primitive hunter-gatherers whose technologically inferior cultures were destined to wither under the onslaught of Europeans moving across the continent, perpetually shoving ahead the frontier between advanced white civilization and backward indigenous savagery. The contrast between the historically accurate description of indigeneity offered in Sanders's alt-history and the colonialist fantasy version offered by most historical novels (and many supposedly nonfictional histories) weirds this western in a powerfully decolonizing way, asking us, as Gallagher suggests, to expand our sense of plausible chronologies and to engage with our collective past from an active, interventionist, and decolonial stance.

Indianizing the sign of Indianness also functions to uncover the figures of enslaved peoples and murdered natives typically hidden behind the sign of the heroic white pioneer searching for freedom deployed in more standard westerns. *Journey to Fusang* accomplishes this by stripping away racialized assumptions of white innocence and victimization, making visible the violence and savagery those assumptions are meant to hide. Enslaved and murdered bodies are here tied directly to colonialism. The character of Vladimir Khan, for example, functions as an avatar of imperialism in the novel, a vampiric force that thrives by stealing life from other nations and cultures, leaving piles of dead bodies in its wake. He has amassed an army made up of Europeans (mercenaries, freedmen, and escaped slaves) as well as natives from various tribes grown desperate at seeing their members kidnapped by the Comanche and sold to Arabs who have established a network of frontier trading posts on the southern Great Plains.

It is one of these posts that employs Finn, who has escaped his fate as a slave when the ship on which he is imprisoned sinks in a hurricane, and it is a raid on this trading post that will launch the pan-tribal alliance that finally defeats Vladimir Khan and his army. Slavery has bolstered imperialism and enriched the Comanche and Mexica, even as it has devastated Europe and less-powerful tribal nations in the Americas. Members of Vladimir Khan's army, ironically painted red and disguised as Comanche with captives to sell, enter the post and slaughter its inhabitants. Among the dead is the post's commander, an Arab named Ibrahim who had taken pity on Finn and his fellow escaped slave, Alfred, and hired them, along with Yusuf, to perform manual labor around the trading post. Ibrahim, who is presented as a sympathetic character, civilized, educated, and fair-minded, nevertheless throws open the gates of the heavily fortified post and gets out the trade goods when he believes he will have more captives to acquire. The sin of trading in slaves dooms him to a bloody death. Finn and his two companions have been chasing escaped camels, which the Arabs use widely in their trading caravans, when the attack occurs. When they return they find a single, mortally wounded survivor who tells them the slaughter was carried out by a mixed army of fighters "led by Europeans of some kind. . . . white-skinned men, like Englishmen or Bulgars, most of them. A couple who looked Chinese." [22]

This polyglot army is commanded by Vladimir Khan, but his general, who acts as the army's military commander, is a thinly disguised version of a figure that appears with some frequency in indigenous speculative fiction as well as white-authored westerns—George Armstrong Custer. Finn describes him as "a tall man . . . and fair as a Norseman, with curly yellow hair and pale blue eyes. . . . [H]e wore a fringed deerskin jacket of the native style." His attacks on native settlements and the Arabs' frontier trading posts, which culminate in the rape, torture, and murder of any survivors of the initial assaults, are so savage even the relatively warlike Apachus (Apache) and Comanche are appalled. Vladimir Khan's army, with its brutal, blond general, represents a kind of synecdoche of slavery and imperialism, the alt-history version of the actual invaders of the Americas. In the novel they are described as a potential nation themselves, offered as a sort of mirror image of the pan-native nation born from their defeat and a double of the Euro-American nation that will use enslaved bodies to establish itself in our own historical reality. Sanders suggests that their cause is not entirely unsympathetic, although their methods are. Like the Chinese settlers who pour into Fusang, China's wild eastern frontier, desperate for the chance to someday own land of their own, the white and native members of Khan's army, faced with a choice between slavery or hunger, are described as "a nation on the march . . . a new nation, or something on the verge of becoming one, made up of wild folk whose only common bond was an endless struggle, generation after generation, with a hard and dangerous land."[23]

Their savagery, however, like that of the Union in *The Wild Blue and the Gray*, prompts an alliance of otherwise antagonistic native nations, which come together in order to oppose Vladimir Khan as well as the Chinese and Arabs. Like the Southern nightmare of the slave revolt, the specter of an organized pan-tribal resistance is the ghost that haunted proponents of manifest destiny and shaped U.S. policy in the American West and abroad. It also lurks in the margins of traditional westerns, where the sign of Indianness signifies that which is primitive, savage, and racially incapable of complex political development or organization. It is a sign whose meaning, therefore, effectively forecloses any possibility other than white domination by disallowing the potential of indigenous political or military organizing. Byrd explains that the persistent ghostly nightmare that Indians, like enslaved Africans, might be perfectly capable of organized decolonial resistance continues to haunt U.S. foreign policy today, particularly the war on terror. As many have pointed out, it is no coincidence that the U.S. military still refers to enemy-occupied areas as "Indian country," or that the code name the Pentagon chose for Osama bin Laden was "Geronimo." Byrd notes that "Indianness becomes a site through which U.S. empire orients and replicates itself by transforming those to be colonized into 'Indians' through continual reiterations of pioneer logics, whether in the Pacific, the Caribbean, or the Middle East."[24] In other words, Indianness in traditional westerns must always be signified as primitive, chaotic, and incapable of organized resistance to superior white civilization in order to justify the conquest of the natives and uphold the narrative of the inevitability of manifest destiny. The trickster hermeneutics of Sanders's indianized western, on the other hand, narrates an origin story for the signifier denied and silenced in traditional westerns—the possibility of a unified Native nation brought together in organized resistance to colonialism.

The indigenous alliance Sanders imagines in *Journey to Fusang* is a frequently uncomfortable one, however. The Comanche, one of the most powerful tribal nations in North America, have grown strong in part through their participation in the slave trade. They must therefore gain the trust of other tribal people upon whom they have preyed. The attacks on the Arab trading posts finally compel the Comanche to reconsider their complicity with the colonizers and to enter into alliance with tribes they previously treated as enemies or convenient sources of captives to sell. This alliance is "an unheard-of-thing," Abdullah Kills Bull, a Muslim Comanche, explains to Finn, "for the Snakes [Comanche] are even more fiercely independent than the other tribes ... with no central authority and very little tradition of combined action.... [But now] the usual differences had been put aside. The Muslim Snakes were enraged over the burning of the mosque and the murders of the imams. The Pawnees were out for blood because of the destruction of their town on the Long River, and willing to make alliance with the Snakes or anyone else if it would help them even the score.'"[25]

While Sanders's novel is clearly decolonial in its aim of establishing a united and sovereign indigenous nation, this is not a world where the natives dream of throwing out all nonindigenous people, or going back to a precontact way of life. Their response to the material reality of the Arab and Chinese presence is to take those things they need or that they feel make their lives better, adapting and adopting them for their own ends. For example, Abdullah Kills Bull explains to Finn that all the tribes, regardless of their past disagreements with each other, are especially upset over Vladimir Khan's destruction of the trading posts "which had been vital parts of the natives' lives; where now would they get powder and shot and knives and the other amenities of civilization? 'Now we shall be as our grandfathers,' Abdullah Kills Bull said bitterly, 'making our weapons and tools from stone and dressing all in skins.'"[26]

The Comanche in particular seem adept at freely appropriating things like gunpowder, horses, and steel-bladed knives, which are immediately useful, and, via what Vizenor might call cultural play, entering into and indianizing less physical cultural artifacts like Islam. While many westerns employ the figure of the man-who-knows-indians (a white man who understands indian ways, dresses in buckskin and fringe, and is able to adapt native knowledge to be turned against the natives themselves), that hybridized frontier hero functions as a sign signifying the flexibility and superiority of Europeans, and thus their rightful displacement or replacement of actual indians. Conversely, when white authors present native characters who have adapted or adopted European artifacts or ideas, they are frequently tragic figures, villainous half-breeds, or bitter, alienated outsiders. At best, they might function as a white hero's loyal sidekick, working to advance settler colonialism, presumably out of recognition of white racial and cultural superiority.

In *Journey to Fusang*, Sanders imagines indigenous adaptability through the lens of Vizenor's idea of transmotion, which he defines as the continual adaptation to changing circumstances.[27] As a means of indianizing and translating the western, transmotion emerges in this novel as a powerful strategy of survivance enabled by a trickster-like flexibility of vision. Sanders utilizes indigenous transmotion to alter the concept signified by the sign of Indianness in all his presentations of indigeneity, but especially in his presentation of the Comanche, with whom Finn works closely at the trading post. The first Comanche Finn meets is a man named Muhammad Ten Bears, who "wore an outfit of white deerskin, worked with fine designs in little beads, and a Moorish blanket tossed loosely over his shoulder, silver bands ringed his long muscular arms. On his head he wore a close-wound blue turban decorated with several long feathers.... He held a musket in one hand—a flint-lock, I noticed, obviously new, and a round hide-covered shield." Muhammad Ten Bears, who regularly trades captives to the Arabs at the post, greets the doomed post commander Ibrahim in "flawless classical Arabic."[28] Like the culture of the historical Plains tribes, Comanche culture in *Journey to Fusang* has been transformed by the horse and the rifle, but here many of the Comanche have also adapted the religion of the Arabs as well as their weapons and mounts. Like the indianized Catholicism Weaver et al. argue has been transformed by native people into something different from what the Spaniards practiced in Europe, the Islam practiced by the Comanche is no longer the same faith the Arabs originally brought to the Americas.[29] When Finn wonders how the Comanche can be Muslim while still openly adhering to their own indigenous beliefs about the sacred, the Turkish scout Alp explains, "They say they are [Muslim], and they believe it, and no doubt God accepts them as His children. But you will find that al-Islam is like the paint on their faces—just underneath they are still the Snakes."[30]

When transmotion is turned toward what Daniel Heath Justice calls the decolonization imperative, it becomes a form of trickster mimetics, not *false*—as Alp remarks, the Comanche genuinely believe themselves to be Muslim—but also no longer serving the purpose of colonial mimesis as Homi Bhabha imagines it, which, he claims, is to ensure the strategic failure of the colonial mimic through their inevitable difference from the colonizer. As Bhabha puts it, "To be Anglicized is *emphatically* not be to English."[31] Not to be English, however, is only a strategic failure if being English is the goal. For the Comanche, the goal is something else. The affront to Islam and murder of the imams, like the attacks on the trading posts, provide the hinge for their decision to initiate the largest Gathering of the Clans ever seen, but their purpose in doing so is not to become more like the Arabs, but rather to create an organized pan-tribal resistance that will eventually oppose the Arabs.

Whether the pan-tribal native nation that emerges from this alliance will stand with, alongside, or against the already sovereign Mexica Empire to the south is left unclear in the novel. The Comanche have clearly benefited from trading slaves to the Mexica, but the other indigenous peoples who have joined with them oppose the practice. The combined indigenous army defeats Vladimir Khan, but the narrative ends soon after, with the actions of the newly allied tribes having destabilized the colonial powers in North America in unexpected ways. The Arab trade networks are thoroughly disrupted as the native alliance organized by the Comanche now controls the entirety of the Great Plains. The Azteca Empire, while no longer threatened by Vladimir Khan's army, has been deprived of its source of slave labor and is facing massive economic and political upheaval. The Chinese in Fusang, the foreign power most recognizably engaging in settler colonialism (rather than the more franchise-style colonialism of the Arabs), have perhaps been the most destabilized, as it is revealed that they were the ones secretly supplying Vladimir Khan with funding and munitions. A character named Lu Hsu (a Ming loyalist) explains to Finn, "The Manchu barbarians rule [in Peking]. . . . Fusang represents a source of great worry to the Manchu usurpers. They fear it will become a center of resistance, and they are right. . . . Fusang is all but ready to declare its independence from Imperial rule."[32] The Manchus, Hsu explains, secretly traded money and weapons to Vladimir Khan in exchange for his promise to invade Fusang, crushing the Ming loyalists there before they could rebel—an obvious allusion to the historical rebellion of Britain's American colonies on the opposite side of the continent in our own reality.

As an indigenous text shaped by trickster hermeneutics, *Journey to Fusang* translates and weirds the western by indianizing the signs we expect to encounter in the genre—settlers and indians, captive white women and savage Others, heroic battles and quests to establish a new nation. Sanders slyly deploys these familiar western signs, then points them toward a subversively decolonial meaning. We are forced to reconsider the meaning of captive bodies in our history and our fiction, insistently reminded in this narrative to question how they are legitimized, ghosted, or silenced based on their perceived race or gender. And, by conceiving of his western in the form of an alternative history, Sanders challenges not just the ways audiences may think about manifest destiny, but the ideas we may hold about our present reality and possible futures, as well.

NOTES

1. Vizenor, *Narrative Chance*, 189.
2. While "indigenize" is the more current form of this critical term, I argue that "indianize" is more specific both to the setting of this novel in North America, as well as to the mainstream ideas about natives typically found in westerns which this novel seeks to undermine.
3. Weaver, Craig Womack, and Robert Warrior discuss, among other indianizations, the ways Native people have adopted and adapted many Christian religious rituals brought to the U.S. Southwest by the Spanish. They quote Simon Ortiz (Acoma), who argues that many of these religious rituals "are now Indian because of the creative development that the native people applied to them" (xix). The formerly European Catholicism has been transformed, they argue, "into something Indian, the concept of transformation being markedly different than that of hybridization," which they see as a descent "into a relativistic abyss" in which everything and nothing is ever authentically Indian (xix).
4. The related but not identical term "counterfactual history," refers to a specifically scholarly form of alternative history used by historians as a tool for academic research rather than for developing a work of literary fiction.
5. Gallagher, "Undoing," 11–12.
6. Spurgeon, *Exploding the Western*, 9.
7. Sanders, prologue, *Journey to Fusang*, n.p.
8. Sanders, *Journey to Fusang*, 3.
9. Vizenor, "Aesthetics of Survivance," 17.
10. The "savage indian" westerns were common up through the 1960s, when many revisionist westerns became more sympathetic (albeit often patronizingly so) to Native Americans. John Wayne starred in a number of "savage

indian" westerns, including *Stagecoach* (1939), *She Wore a Yellow Ribbon* (1949), and *The Searchers* (1956). James Fenimore Cooper provided the template for the white man who is a better Indian than the Indians in *The Last of the Mohicans* (1826), and this trope plays out cinematically in *Little Big Man* (1970), *Dances with Wolves* (1990), and *Avatar* (2009).

11. For more on the first known version of the captivity narrative in fiction and arguably the first western, Charlotte Lennox's *Life of Harriot Stuart* (1750), see Marta Kvande and Sara Spurgeon's "The Removes of Harriot Stuart: Charlotte Lennox and the Birth of the Western."
12. Slotkin, *Regeneration through Violence*, 98; Kolodny, *Lay of the Land*, 19.
13. McClintock, "Imperial Ghosting and National Tragedy," 820.
14. Again, Cooper provides the initial blueprint for this trope of helpless white femininity, but it is eagerly reproduced in countless westerns from John Ford's Cavalry Trilogy to 2017's *Hostiles*.
15. Maeve may be a comic homage to Mercutio's version of Queen Mab in *Romeo and Juliet*. Sanders is the only author to be a two-time recipient of the Sidewise Award (which goes to the best alt-history published in a given year), and his first win was for his 1997 short story "The Undiscovered," which places a hapless William Shakespeare in Virginia in 1599, composing and staging *Hamlet* using natives as actors while stranded in an Algonquian town.
16. Sanders, *Fusang*, 304, 305–6, 306.
17. Sanders, *Fusang*, 308.
18. Sanders, *Fusang*, 16.
19. The history of Cherokee antiblack racism played out in our real world timeline in the controversial 2007 decision by the Cherokee Nation to disenfranchise thousands of their citizens known as Cherokee Freedmen—the descendants of enslaved Africans owned by the Cherokee who were guaranteed citizenship within the Cherokee Nation in 1866. Ironically, Cherokee Principal Chief Chad Smith has framed the debate about the legality of the decision to strip the Freedmen of their citizenship as a matter of Cherokee Nation sovereignty.
20. Byrd, *The Transit of Empire*, 157, 158.
21. Sanders, *Journey to Fusang*, 40–41.
22. Sanders, *Journey to Fusang*, 180.
23. Sanders, *Journey to Fusang*, 193, 198.

24. Byrd, *Transit of Empire*, xiii.
25. Sanders, *Journey to Fusang*, 263–64.
26. Sanders, *Journey to Fusang*, 264–65.
27. Vizenor, *Fugitive Poses*, 181.
28. Sanders, *Journey to Fusang*, 121, 122.
29. Weaver, *American Indian Literary Nationalism*, xix.
30. Sanders, *Journey to Fusang*, 127.
31. Bhabha, *Location of Culture* (99; emphasis in original).
32. Sanders, *Journey to Fusang*, 294.

BIBLIOGRAPHY

Bhabha, Homi K. *The Location of Culture*. London: Routledge, 1994.

Byrd, Jodi. *The Transit of Empire: Indigenous Critiques of Colonialism*. Minneapolis: University of Minnesota Press, 2011.

Cameron, James, dir. *Avatar*. Twentieth Century Fox, 2009.

Cooper, James Fenimore. *The Last of the Mohicans: A Narrative of 1757*. London: R. Bentley, 1826.

Cooper, Scott, dir. *Hostiles*. Entertainment Studios, 2017.

Cortes, Hernan. "Letters from Mexico." In *The Library of Original Sources, Vol. V: 9th to 16th Centuries*, edited by Oliver Thatcher, 317–26. Milwaukee: University Research Extension, 1907.

Costner, Kevin, dir. *Dances with Wolves*. Orion Pictures, 1990.

Ford, John. Director. *Fort Apache*. RKO Pictures, 1948.

———. *Rio Grande*. Republic Pictures, 1950.

———. *The Searchers*. Warner Brothers, 1956.

———. *She Wore a Yellow Ribbon*. RKO Pictures, 1949.

Gallagher, Catherine. "Undoing." In *Time and the Literary*, edited by Karen Newman, Jay Clayton, and Marianne Hirsch, 11–30. New York: Routledge, 2002.

Justice, Daniel Heath. "'Go Away, Water!': Kinship Criticism and the Decolonization Imperative." In *Reasoning Together: The Native Critics Collective*, edited by Craig Womack, Daniel Heath Justice, and Christopher B. Teuton, 147–68. Norman: University of Oklahoma Press, 2008.

Kolodny, Annette. *The Lay of the Land: Metaphor as Experience and History in American Life and Letters*. Chapel Hill: University of North Carolina Press, 1975.

Kvande, Marta, and Sara Spurgeon. "The Removes of Harriot Stuart: Charlotte Lennox and the Birth of the Western." In *Before the West was West: Critical*

Essays on Pre-1800 Literatures of the American Frontiers, edited by Amy Hamilton and Tom Hillard, 213–38. Lincoln: University of Nebraska Press, 2014.

McClintock, Anne. "Imperial Ghosting and National Tragedy: Revenants from Hiroshima and Indian Country in the War on Terror." *PMLA* 129, no. 4 (October 2014): 819–29.

Penn, Arthur, dir. *Little Big Man*. National General Pictures, 1970.

Rowlandson, Mary. *A Narrative of the Captivity and Removes of Mrs. Mary Rowlandson*. Cambridge MA: Samuel Green, 1682.

Sanders, William. *Conquest: Hernando de Soto and the Indians, 1539–1542*. New York: Wildside, 2003.

———. *Journey to Fusang*. New York: Warner, 1988.

———. *The Wild Blue and the Gray*. New York: Grand Central, 1991.

———. "The Undiscovered." *Asimov's Science Fiction Magazine*, March 1997, 86–110.

Slotkin, Richard. *Regeneration through Violence: The Mythology of the Frontier, 1600–1860*. Middletown CT: Wesleyan University Press, 1973.

Spurgeon, Sara L. *Exploding the Western: Myths of Empire on the Postmodern Frontier*. College Station: Texas A&M University Press, 2005.

Weaver, Jace, Craig Womack, and Robert Warrior. *American Indian Literary Nationalism*. Albuquerque: University of New Mexico Press, 2006.

Vizenor, Gerald. "Aesthetics of Survivance: Literary Theory and Practice." In *Survivance: Narratives of Native Presence*, edited by Gerald Vizenor, 1–24. Lincoln: University of Nebraska Press, 2008.

———. *Fugitive Poses: Native American Scenes of Absence and Presence*. Lincoln: University of Nebraska Press. 1998.

———. "Trickster Discourse: Comic Holotropes and Language Games." In *Narrative Chance: Postmodern Discourse on Native American Indian Literature*, edited by Gerald Vizenor, 187–212. Norman: University of Oklahoma Press, 1993.

6 Magnificence and Metas in Professional Westerns

DOMINO RENEE PEREZ

Against the backdrop of the setting sun, a woman, clad in leather with a red sash tied across her back and carrying a samurai sword, walks slowly toward the ramp of a Chinook helicopter. The scene then cuts to a reverse shot from inside the helo, so that its open door frames the white-masked woman's entrance onto the aircraft. In the distance, positioned on either side of her stands a platoon of combat soldiers. Behind them, smoke rises up from a city skyline. Once she is on board, audiences are made privy to the woman's backstory, witness her proficiency with a blade, and learn her name—Katana (Karen Fukuhara). After being introduced to the unsavory occupants of the transport by the commander in charge, Katana's instinct is to draw her sword, to which the officer responds, "Whoa. Easy, cowgirl. This ain't that kind of mission." The details of the sequence serve to situate David Ayer's *Suicide Squad* (2016) in the western genre and pay homage to the film's source material.

With its comic book pedigree, bumping soundtrack, and penchant for visual excess, *Suicide Squad* appears far removed from the rolling hills of the frontier or the dusty streets of Tombstone, Arizona. *Suicide Squad* mutes its identity as a western and its faithfulness to the professional plot under the noise of its hyperstylized veneer. Although it centers on genetically enhanced humans and urban vistas, the film is, in fact, a high-octane weird western, in which "cowboys" battle supernatural Indians to save a distressed damsel. However, *Suicide Squad* is not about lone rangers, white and black hats, or good versus bad; rather, it is about bad versus worse. The cavalry does not arrive in the nick of time because "it ain't that kind of mission." Instead, the outlaws save the day and all of humanity along with it. The film upholds generic conventions through the juxtaposition of savagism and civilization and the ways its diverse characters seek to preserve the integrity of the family, even as they push against these same ideas.

Suicide Squad focuses on six criminals-turned–would-be heroes, tasked with completing a rescue-turned-termination mission in the besieged city, seen billowing with smoke. Agent Amanda Waller (Viola Davis) originally identifies this group as metahuman criminals with extraordinary abilities to combat a potential hostile alien invader, à la Superman, except one who does not share the "values" of the United States. The strike force, called Task Force X, under the direction of Colonel Rick Flag (Joel Kinnaman), is eventually pressed into national service to defend an attack on Midway City by the evil Enchantress (Cara Delevigne), a six-thousand-year-old metahuman with interdimensional abilities, and her equally powerful brother Incubus (Alain Chanoine). Dubbed the "Suicide Squad" due to the explosive pellets injected in their necks as a control measure, the racially diverse group—comprised of Deadshot (Will Smith), Harley Quinn (Margot Robbie), Captain Boomerang (Jai Courtney), El Diablo (Jay Hernandez), Killer Croc (Adewale Akinnuoye-Agbaje), and Slipknot (Adam Beach)—agree to "go somewhere very bad to do something that will get [them] killed," not out of loyalty to country or love of the law but for pay, in the form of having their prison sentences reduced. As hired guns, the Suicide Squad rids a population's scourge, illustrating what John Shelton Lawrence and Robert Jewett identify as the "dominant American myth of the Western village cleansers."[1] This arrangement presents the squad members with opportunities for moral redemption and in the process reframes ideas about heroism and which communities are worth saving.

Influenced by the prospect of individual gain (freedom and money), the metahuman criminals in *Suicide Squad* abjure greater-good moral responsibility to battle a pair of their own, while still defending those in need. In *Westerns: Making the Man in Fiction and Film* (1996), Lee Clark

Mitchell analyzes the structure of four different types of western films: classical, vengeance variation, transition theme, and professional plot. The latter variety features heroes who are "professional fighters, men willing to defend society only as a job they accept for pay or for love of fighting, not from commitment to ideas of law and justice."[2] Mitchell argues that in films of the professional type, the focus "is on the conflict between the heroes and the villains," where "both are professional, and their fight becomes a contest of ability that is significant for its own sake." Although a "concern with a fight between equal men of special ability is an aspect of all Westerns," Mitchell contends that "only in this particular version of the myth does the fight itself, divorced from all its social and ethical implications, become of such central importance."[3] *Suicide Squad* culminates in such a contest. Rather than choose right or wrong, in the final battle, the group members choose each other no matter the personal cost.

The team's status as criminals, in addition to their moral—as well as in some cases, mental—instability, make them unlikely protectors of civilization. Isolated from family and society at large in a Louisiana black-ops prison called Belle Reve, they are denied rights of citizenship. As incarcerated individuals, they are the property of the state (or, in this case, the federal government) and are exploited for their violent abilities. According to Lorrie Palmer, as westerns evolved, "the cowboys themselves grew darker, more violent, and more divided within themselves."[4] The Suicide Squad members' familiarity with what Deadshot calls "the dark places," along with their unpredictability, emerge from living outside the boundaries of civilization, the same society they are charged with protecting. Villages and towns have given way to a metropolis and other planetary concerns. The raised stakes of worldwide destruction allow cowboys, who excel at various forms of violence, to hone their skills through their extralegal endeavors as assassins, gangbangers, and thieves, to name a few: "Stability is anathema to the real western hero. And again the rejection of stability emphasizes the potential danger to society that the western hero contains. He cannot be appealed to on the ground of normal citizenship. In a country where the whole idea of citizenship plays such an important role there is adulation of a hero who by definition rejects much that is a part of the citizen's role. As soon as the hero identifies himself entirely with a community his nature changes."[5] The squad members *are* a danger to society; they cannot be convinced initially to do what is right on the basis of morality alone, which is why they are coerced into compliance through electronic control measures. Regardless of whether they succeed in their mission, they can never fully be a part of the world they protect. In fact, the film repeatedly reminds audiences of the squad members' criminal histories and outsider status. Adhering to cultural standards of morality would make them no longer exceptional villains, which, more than their superhuman abilities, is what distinguishes the group from the rest of the population. What the outlaw heroes must do to rescue the damsel in distress further entrenches them beyond the boundaries of the social order, where they will remain separate. While this is true of most western heroes, from George Stevens's titular *Shane* (1953) to Ethan Edwards in John Ford's *The Searchers* (1956), the diverse racial and ethnic backgrounds of the squad members complicate this location and limit the roles they are allowed to occupy within the genre.

Standing in opposition to the metropolitan cowboys is a pair of metahuman siblings of indigenous origins. These otherworldly supernatural beings, in ancient times, were revered as gods. Previously held captive in a clay vessel, Enchantress is released by anthropologist Dr. June Moone (also played by Cara Delevigne), who is Colonel Flag's love interest. While wandering in the South or Central American jungle, Dr. Moone happens upon a pyramid of the Mesoamerican variety, falls into a cave (either named "Tres Osos Caves" or "Gobierno Cave," the details of the printed page of the briefing are unclear), and purposely breaks open a clay totem, freeing Enchantress. In addition to being a horrible anthropologist, Dr. Moone becomes the human host for the spirit being, who takes possession of the woman's body. As an indigenous figure of Latin American origin, Enchantress represents Native corruption of the civilized individual. Eventually taking full control of her human host, Enchantress becomes the Indian antagonist.

Dr. Moone's possession (or, rather, infection) by Enchantress becomes a cautionary tale about contamination, one that happens in a vague, unnamed Latin American–sounding country with Mesoamerican-style pyramids. The names of the caves, which translate to "Three Bears" and "the Government," respectively, positions Dr. Moone as a modern-day Goldilocks, a model of white femininity, innocence, and purity, who stumbles into the ancient site of an indigenous power and becomes polluted by contact with its representative. Moone's physical corruption as a result of this encounter is a characteristic that runs throughout her depiction. For example, when Flag first encounters Moone, she is sitting in a bathtub of murky filth and reeds, positioned beneath a pentagram, and begs him for help, having recently lost control of her body to Enchantress. Except when crafting her weapon to destroy the world, Enchantress appears dirty, caked in mud or ash, capable of polluting everything she touches, which is how she creates her army. Violent, faceless hordes covered in pustules—people infected by Enchantress—overrun the city like a marauding band, killing everyone in their path. Dr. Moone's fate represents a variation of the captivity narrative in which a vulnerable white woman is possessed and polluted by her Native abductors. Once infected by savagism, the host can then spread the disease and must be stopped for the safety of the civilized world.

Enchantress merges antiquity and technology, so that the former is associated with historical indigenous populations and the latter with contemporary global citizenry. After reviving her brother Incubus, Enchantress tells him that humans have turned against them. The siblings are no longer worshiped as gods; instead, people worship machines. Enchantress vows to punish humans for their betrayal by creating a machine to destroy all human life. (Narratively the move does not make sense, as is true with many other parts of the film, because there will be no one left for the siblings to subjugate.) Through spell-casting and other ancient rituals, she begins to build her weapon. As it takes shape, veiled indigenous figures adorned in headdresses, arms outstretched, rise up from the ground to encircle a pillar of light that destroys the building's roof as it shoots up into the sky. The creation of the weapon illustrates that Enchantress and Incubus are not simply acting on their own behalf; they have access to other powerful, unseen indigenous figures, who will help to bring about the end of civilization.

Suicide Squad unapologetically centralizes the fight of the professional western. The stakes of the final showdown could not be more clear. By defeating the extradimensional mystical siblings and their mutant armies, the task force will safeguard millions of human families around the world. Many of the squad members' personal relationships to this social institution are both frustrated and aspirational. Deadshot is alienated from his daughter, who is in part responsible for his incarceration because she refused to allow him to kill Batman. The little girl writes to her father every day. Unbeknownst to Deadshot, the authorities withhold the letters to make him believe that his daughter no longer wants contact with him, thereby deepening his punishment and isolation. Despite Harley's declaration that she and the other squad members are not "normal," her deepest desire, as revealed by Enchantress, is to be a "normal" wife and mother.[6] In her fantasy, Harley holds a child, in a stark white kitchen bathed in light, as the Joker, sans green pallor and dressed in a suit, kisses her good morning and then turns his attention to a second child seated in a high chair. To no one in particular, she mutters, "He married me." The elusiveness of family does not diminish Deadshot and Harley's longing for or the value they place on it. Enchantress tries to delude Diablo with a vision of his own family restored, but he sees the ruse for what it is. Refusing the illusion, Diablo confronts Enchantress, telling her, "You can't have them. These are my people here right here." He lays claim to his fellow squad members and the bond he shares with them. Later he declares: "I lost one family. I'm not going to lose another." Diablo sacrifices himself to save his surrogate family, who then go on to defeat Enchantress and recover June Moone. The uncanny Indians are vanquished and Moone sloughs off the skin of her former captor to emerge fully restored. Born anew, she is free from any hint of corruption that might have occurred as a result of her experience.

Given its adherence to generic conventions, *Suicide Squad* invites comparisons with other westerns. For example, the scene inside the

Chinook as the squad rides into hostile territory calls to mind John Ford's *Stagecoach* (1939). Dr. June Moone and Enchantress mirror, respectively, the virginal goodness of Amy Kane and the dangerous allure of Mrs. Ramirez in Fred Zinnemann's *High Noon* (1952). However, *Suicide Squad* most significantly parallels John Sturges's exemplary professional western *The Magnificent Seven* (1960), following key plot points and characterizations from the film classic. Whereas the concerns of the squad are more global, *The Magnificent Seven*, with its own eclectic group of gunslingers and opportunists, focuses on a local conflict—namely, a Mexican village under attack by a ruthless bandit, Calvera, and his men. The Suicide Squad members possess abilities that correspond to the original seven, with the exception of Slipknot, who has no analogous figure because he plays no substantive role in the film. As the on-the-ground leader, Flag takes on the Chris Adams (Yul Brynner) role with the others corresponding as follows: Deadshot as Vin Tanner (Steve McQueen), Harley Quinn as Chico (Horst Buchholz), Killer Croc as Britt (James Coburn), Captain Boomerang as Harry Luck (Brad Dexter), Diablo as Bernardo O'Reilly (Charles Bronson), and Lee (Robert Vaughn). Furthering the comparison, Katana, the model minority with a clear set of morals and values to which she adheres, is an homage to *The Magnificent Seven*'s source material, Akira Kurosawa's *Seven Samurai* (1956). Not officially one of the squad, she, nevertheless, leads the "hero walk" to the climactic showdown. Celebrated and criticized for its ethnically diverse cast, *Suicide Squad* also engages in the racial politics of representation, conflation, and elimination, expressly involving Mexican and Indians, issues present in Sturges's original and Antoine Fuqua's 2016 remake, to maintain the cinematic status quo.

In conventional Hollywood films, historically, the narrative emphasis on a "white, handsome, middle-aged, upper-middle-class, heterosexual, Protestant, Anglo-Saxon male," who seeks to protect the status quo, necessarily relegates Others to the roles of "villains, sidekicks, [and] temptresses," subordinates who challenge, serve, or service the white hero.[7] *Suicide Squad*, at times, destabilizes familiar conventions of a genre that centralizes white masculinity and regularly marginalizes or villainizes American Indian and Mexican characters. So, although Flag serves as the field commander, he, like the other members of the crew, is exploited by Waller, who threatens his love interest, Dr. June Moone. The film also features an actual diverse cast that includes black, First Nations, and Latinx actors. Women take on prominent roles, holding sway in each of the narrative arenas, as mastermind (Waller), villain (Enchantress), and professional killers (Harley Quinn, formerly Dr. Harleen Quinzel, and Katana, Flag's bodyguard), whose abilities match and exceed those of their male counterparts. For all of its progressive elements, the film still sacrifices Latinx and Native characters to uphold the value of heteronormative whiteness, as is made evident when the distressed damsel is saved, a point punctuated by Flag and Moone's passionate embrace. Ultimately, the film depends on its diverse characters to reaffirm contemporary racial (and racist) paradigms and quell anxieties about globalization. For these and other reasons, *Suicide Squad* is less progressive than its source material and more in line with the racial and social politics of Fuqua's remake.

Through its depiction of Mexicans and Indians, Sturges's *The Magnificent Seven* offers social commentary about racial prejudice and the integrity of cultural communities. Even so, the film still relies on "brownface": white actors made up to look like Mexicans for its lead roles. Eli Wallach plays the principal Mexican antagonist, Calvera, and Buchholz, a German actor, is introduced as Chico, a young Mexican man and wannabe gunfighter, whose name means "boy." *The Magnificent Seven*, released in the middle of the civil rights era, gestures toward the importance of dignity and self-determination for Indians and Mexicans, respectively, though at times it conflates the two groups. Nonetheless, the opening scenes substantiate the centrality of Mexicans to the narrative's conflict.

In the same way that westerns—such as *The Searchers*, *A Man Called Horse* (1970), *Dances with Wolves* (1990), and many others—distinguish good Indians from bad, *The Magnificent Seven* makes distinctions between types of Mexicans: good Mexicans are docile and generally, if not explicitly, reinforce the importance of white heroism, and the lawlessness of the bad Mexicans makes white heroism necessary. Calvera at once reveals himself to be an extortionist who has been stealing food and supplies from the village for years, leaving the residents with barely enough on which to live. When one of the villagers, Rafael, charges at Calvera, calling him a "murderer" and "thief," the man is shot dead in the street. Seconds later, his unnamed wife runs out and cries over his prone body. The scene confirms Calvera as a threat to the community of farmers and demonstrates the internecine violence that plagues the village.

In the moral equation of *The Magnificent Seven*, the Mexican villagers represent the good Indians, both figuratively and literally. At the celebration to mark the founding of the village, events include a "torito" (or little bull, lined with fireworks, popular at Mexican festivals or the feast days of Catholic saints) and a deer dancer. The dance suggests that this is not simply any Mexican village; rather, it is one with strong ties to a specific Native community. Flutes, drums, slapstick percussion, and rattles accompany the dancer as he enacts the movements of the deer. For more than "four centuries of attempted conquest," the Yaquis have performed the deer dance to honor the animal's nourishment of the people and its significance to the continuation of their way of life.[8] Yaqui homelands stretch from southern Arizona to Northern Mexico, which correspond geographically to the suggested location of the village.[9] The scene is cross-cut with three of the seven mobilizing to intercept the men Calvera has sent to spy on the village. As the action intensifies and Calvera's men are killed, sonically the theme of the seven comingles with the indigenous music of the deer dance, alluding to the syncretic relationship between the two groups that is necessary to defeat Calvera. The death of the deer, which is depicted in the scene, foreshadows the sacrifices some of the seven will make so the village can live in peace.

The value of Native people and traditions to Mexican village life is contrasted by the disregard shown for an American Indian man named Old Sam in the United States. The village peons travel to Tombstone, Arizona, to buy guns—despite not knowing how to use the weapons—so that they can attempt to defend themselves and protect their limited resources. In Tombstone, Henry, a salesman of "ladies' corsets" and a Good Samaritan, has paid twenty dollars for the funeral of Old Sam, who collapsed in the street and died. He remarks that for "two hours people stepped over and around [the dead man] without lifting a finger," adding that his offer to pay for the funeral is simply the action of a "decent man." The undertaker, Chamlee, explains that, though the body has been embalmed, it cannot be buried in Boot Hill, because the deceased was an Indian. Some townspeople object to Old Sam being buried alongside white folk in the cemetery, an attitude they have taken since the town became "civilized." Additionally, there is no one to man the hearse, because the previous driver quit. Robert, Henry's traveling companion, inquires if the driver was also "prejudiced" like the townspeople, exemplifying John H. Lenihan's assertion that Hollywood, particularly in the early fifties, "could and did criticize frontier America's racial intolerance toward the Indian."[10] In *The Magnificent Seven*, however, the exchange makes clear that, in becoming civilized, the town has lost its decency, as is evident by its treatment of the dead American Indian man.

The scene is also important because it sets the stage for the professional element of the plot. From the crowd that has gathered to watch, Chris steps forward, offering to drive the hearse, and another bystander, Vin, joins him to ride shotgun, literally. Their willingness to drive Sam's body to the cemetery is motivated by a desire to use their skills as gunslingers rather than any sense of social injustice. To the watching peons, Chris's and Vin's actions belong to men of superior ability and moral caliber, willing to stand up for what is right. When later approached by the villagers, who ask Chris for help buying guns, he tells them, "Nowadays men are cheaper than guns." The conversation initiates Chris's collection of men with extraordinary abilities.

The twenty dollars Henry pays for Sam's funeral is the exact amount the seven are offered for the job in the village, placing the same value on the Indian man's death as on the professionals' lives. In other words, one dead Indian is worth the same as a group of white gunslingers. The decreased economic value of the latter in the United States is best illustrated when Chris and Vin initially seek out O'Reilly (Charles Bronson) to join their effort. Despite being paid $600 for his participation in the Travis County War and $800 for his involvement in Salinas, his willingness to put his life on the line for $20—along with the fact that he is shown chopping wood for his breakfast—demonstrates his severely diminished resources, though he is not alone in his economic circumstances.[11] Chris, Vin, Harry, and O'Reilly are motived, in part, by money, while Lee seeks an opportunity for redemption, Britt to challenge of the odds (thirty against seven), and Chico to fulfill his romantic longing to be a gunslinger.

Regardless of the fact that "the film can be seen as the purest justification of the more dubious aspects of American foreign policy," as Jenni Calder proposes, for the most part it manages to avoid the U.S. savior fantasy.[12] Rather than simply a film about "gallant Americans, the men with courage, the weapons and the skill, [who] ride over the border and defend a threatened Mexican village," the seven, constituted of ostensibly six white men (Chris, Vin, Harry, Britt, and Lee) and a Mexican man (Chico), empower the villagers to take up arms and defend themselves.[13] Any pretense of American expansionism is quelled once the gunmen cross over into Mexico, where they acknowledge that they are interlopers in a country that does not belong to them. Specifically, before becoming a solidified seven, Chico follows the six at a distance, hoping to join the group by showing his determination and usefulness. Harry complains that the young man trailing them is an annoyance, to which Chris replies, "It's a free country." O'Reilly adds, "And it's his."

O'Reilly's progressive geopolitical views align with his ethnic and cultural heritage, which are revealed after audiences have had time to emotionally invest in the character. Overhearing a group of boys call O'Reilly "Bernardo," Chris teases that the village has adopted the gunslinger, to which O'Reilly replies, "Bernardo O'Reilly, that's my real name. Mexican on one side, Irish on the other, and me in the middle." His identity as a person of mixed heritage reflects the actual mixing of cultures in the American West, yet, in the context of the film, it strongly aligns Bernardo culturally with the villagers. Of the seven, Bernardo, particularly through his interactions with the village's children, actively disrupts the venerating of the hired guns. Bernardo's death is notable because he sacrifices himself to protect a group of children who represent the future of the village. As Bernardo dies, he redirects the children's admiration—and perhaps even the audience's—away from himself toward the Mexican men in the village. Fighting alongside the seven, the villagers have found the resolve to do what they must to protect themselves and their families. Before dying, Bernardo asks the boys, "What's my name?" And they answer, "Bernardo," to which he replies, "Damn right." The importance of the scene is threefold: it ensures that he will be remembered by the children who have promised to tend to his grave; the biracial man's claiming of his identity valorizes Mexicanness; and it creates racial solidarity not only between Bernardo and the children, but also, by extension, their fathers and the village at large. Chico's decision to stay in town signifies the return of a Mexican to his homeland, reestablishing communal, national, and racial boundaries, while Chris and Vin, the only two other survivors, presumably, ride back to the United States and an uncertain future. Challenging ideas about race and nation while simultaneously relying upon the worst impulses of Hollywood westerns in their treatment of Mexicans and Indians, Sturges's morally complicated film ultimately depicts Mexican families, who are seen by the seven, as having a value worth protecting and for which they would die.

With few of the same moral complications, *Suicide Squad* continues the practice of representing, conflating, and eliminating Native and Mexican characters, as seen with Slipknot, however briefly he appears, and Chato "El Diablo" Santana. Slipknot, an assassin who can climb anything, serves as the bad Indian and is placed on unequal footing with the other members of the team. Narratively, Slipknot is not identified as a Native character, but given that Adam Beach is easily one of the most recognizable First Nation actors, the conflation of Beach's ethnic identity with that of Slipknot's is likely. He is the only criminal not given a backstory or introduced by Waller in the film's lengthy exposition. In spite of the fact that, early on, Deadshot and Harley have three different scenes that lend insight into their characters, director Ayer claims there was not enough room to add a brief history of Slipknot, even though one had been filmed: "Slipknot gets his head blown off pretty quick... when you have that many characters every frame of real estate is priceless, and I didn't want to invest in that real estate to create some misdirect because after opening night everyone knows he dies anyway."[14] Ayer's decision not to reveal Slipknot's criminal past as a serial rapist spares audiences the insatiable sexual savage cliché. On the other hand, the director's monetization of cinematic space indicates that the character has no "value" as a property. Slipknot's hasty demise contributes to a long cinematic—as well as literary—history of eliminating or vanishing Indians.

Of all the Suicide Squad's members, Chato Santana, known on the streets as "El Diablo," is the most clichéd character in the film: he performs double duty as both a bad Mexican *and* a good Indian. Waller introduces him as the "pyrokenetic homeboy" and later refers to Chato as an LA gangbanger. A portion of the "Activity Report" on his criminal profile visible on-screen reads: "Born into a close family of Catholic Mexican immigrants in Boyle Heights and spent his early years under the watchful eye of his grandmother.... As he reached his teens, he was drawn into gang activity, moving up the ranks stealing cars, dealing drugs, and selling handguns." He is suspected of murdering more than fifteen men in Los Angeles. When initially incarcerated, Diablo incinerates a sizeable group of men in a prison riot and is seen on the security camera taunting the prison guards with a flaming crown hovering above his head. He is, in that moment, "El Rey," the king of a toxic masculinity that is dependent on violence and destruction, cementing his place as a bad Mexican. An immigrant Mexican criminal of the cinematic, cultural, and political imagination, Chato is covered in facial and body tattoos. His difference is not only remarked on but also marked in numerous ways throughout the film. Captain Boomerang asks when they first meet, "What's that crap on your face? Does it wash off?" Deadshot addresses Chato as "ese" (meaning "dude" or "bro," the slang can also refer to gang ties) and with phrases such as "hola amigo."

Furthermore, he possesses his own mystical ability—the power to see delusion and enchantment, a capacity he has had his entire life.

Perhaps in an effort to mitigate his deeply problematic representation, the film gives Chato a redemption arc that begins when Waller narrates a portion of Chato's backstory. Set to War's "Slippin' into Darkness," a song about a descent into madness, audiences see Chato surrendering to police, instead of being apprehended, after losing control of his pyrotechnic power and setting fire to his house, accidentally killing his wife and two children. When the police slam Chato against the hood of the car to cuff him, a close-up shot reveals tears streaming down his face. His remorse becomes a tacit acknowledgement of his unchecked rage. The darkness that touches all the squad members, making them well suited to the role of urban cowboys, affects Chato differently. He has taken a vow to never again use his ability, making him analogous to Lee, who suffers from PTSD in the original film and can no longer fight.

Chato is redeemed when he goes back on his word and unleashes his full power. He sacrifices himself to save his "people," his criminal brethren. The squad members, who have almost exclusively taunted or mocked him, have replaced his dead wife and children. Even more inexplicable is Chato's transformation from a tattooed, t-shirted homeboy into a skeletal Indian god, wearing a loincloth and headdress of quetzal feathers engulfed in flames. In this uncanny form, he speaks almost exclusively in Spanish. The unveiling of Chato's true identity, as an Aztec-looking fire god, in his fight against Incubus further complicates his representation as a Mexican—or, more precisely, as a Mexican Indian. "Mystical good Indian" fights "supernatural bad Indian" in a struggle to the death, where both are killed. As the character most closely aligned with Bernardo, Chato dies protecting others. His demise maintains the integrity of his surrogate family, who work in unison to vanquish Enchantress and save the damsel in distress. Chato gives his life so that Deadshot, Harley, and Flag can have the opportunity to be reunited with their loved ones. The remaining squad members' defeat of Enchantress, the remaining lone bad Indian, and the reunion of the happy white couple overshadows Chato's role as the true hero of the battle.

Released a little over a month apart, *Suicide Squad* and Fuqua's *The Magnificent Seven* were often mentioned together by critics, most of whom focused on the diversity of the cast and complained that the characters were merely tokens. By and large, critics failed to mention what these diverse characters actually do within a genre that has determined historically their contributions to the heroic western. Fuqua's film combines the professional western with the revenge plot, while also trading the complex international relationships of the original for multiracial diversity in the United States. Land and gold are now at the heart of the conflict, the latter detail a nod to Harry and his fortune-seeking ways in the original. As the defenders of a town in need, the seven (though sometimes eight) are more explicitly morally compromised, not unlike the members of the Suicide Squad. The inclusion of black, Mexican, American Indian, and Korean actors, as well as a woman, in lead roles does little to resolve the racial politics and problems of the original. In some instances, it actually exacerbates them, while also introducing new racial and gender complications, as in the case of Ayer's film.

Gone are the village, Calvera, and Mexico, along with the value placed on Mexican and Indian communities. Instead, the focus is on the white town of Rose Creek, where farmers are being forced off their land by an unapologetic capitalist named Bartholomew Bogue (Peter Sarsgaard), who is running a gold mining operation. Accompanied by his armed goons, Bogue interrupts a meeting in the town church and supplants the preacher at the pulpit, where he delivers his own sermon, one that lays bare U.S. economic, political, and religious values: "I came here for gold. This country has long equated democracy with capitalism, capitalism with God—you are not only standing in the way of progress, you are standing in the way of God." The scene places moral virtue and hard work in opposition to protocorporate greed, a point underscored by his offer of twenty dollars for each parcel of their land. The figure is a callback to the original film, one that places an amount on the lives and livelihoods of the *white* farmers. Bogue then sets fire to the church, has the preacher beaten, and kills a man named Matthew Cullen (Matt Bomer) outside of the church in a scene reminiscent of Rafael's murder in Sturges's film. The camera cuts from a close-up of Emma Cullen (Haley Bennett) crying over her husband's supine body to a long shot of the burning church before going to black.

For those familiar with the original, the film announces early on that the racial politics of the premise have shifted from Mexicans to Anglo-Americans and that the composition of the seven will be diverse not only in skill but also in race and ethnicity. Sam Chisholm (Denzel Washington), who serves in the Chris role, is introduced along with the opening credits. When he first emerges from the horizon, through the undulating heat, the initial feature audiences see is his black hat. Outfitted with a pistol, holster, cartridges, and shotgun, his occupation is hinted at even as his identity and mores remain obscured. Sam's appearance is sounded by an assortment of string, percussive, and brass instruments, as well as American Indian flutes and a chorus of women's voices, a mixture that represents, as later revealed, the diversity of seven. His arrival disrupts the community; people stop and stare, though it is unclear whether or not his being black or a bounty hunter is the cause for their reactions. Sam, a warrant officer, quickly proves himself to be of superior skill, drawing the attention of Emma and Teddy Q (Luke Grimes), a fellow Rose Creek resident who has offered to accompany Emma in search of hired guns.

Emma Cullen's movement from grieving widow to gunslinger is not so much a transformation as it is a revelation. Although her initial actions mirror those of Rafael's wife in Sturges's film, she is more akin to Katana in *Suicide Squad*. Emma knows her way around a gun, and, as later revealed, she was the only one with "the balls enough to negotiate" hiring men on behalf of her community. She wields a shotgun with considerable skill, even taking over for one of the seven when he abandons the group. Furthermore, she keeps a cool head during the climactic shoot-out, even pulling other men to safety. At the same time, her bare shoulders and the sexual insinuations others make about her hold in tension her desirability and vulnerability as a woman. In other words, she is competent enough to fight alongside men yet also feminine enough not to threaten the masculine integrity of the seven. Ultimately, however, she is a woman who seeks "righteousness," as she tells Sam, though she will "settle for revenge," which makes her as morally compromised as the man she hires.

Motivated by his own desire for revenge, Sam's agreement to help complicates the professional plot, yet is consistent with the actions of the western hero, who "kills in the name of something more ambiguous, often himself (personal revenge), sometimes progress (social revenge)."[15] As audiences learn, Bogue's men raped and killed Sam's mother and sisters, while also leaving Sam hanging to die. In a western where the central conflict is capitalism, Sam's willingness to forgo monetary gain in favor of personal justice reveals his location outside the moral and cultural economy of the film, thereby further distinguishing him from both his adversary and the men he hires to help rid the town of Bogue. Most of the morally complicated professionals Sam enlists, whose makeup reflects a racially diverse West, are motivated by the pay: Irishman Faraday (Chris Pratt), Cajun Civil War veteran Goodnight Robicheaux (Ethan Hawke), Chinese knife expert Billy Rocks (Byung-hun Lee), Mexican outlaw Vasquez (Mañuel Garcia-Rulfo), Indian killer and scalp hunter Jack Horne (Vincent D'Onofrio), and Comanche Red Harvest (Martin Sensmeier).[16] To this group Sam, who happens to speak Comanche, adds his expertise as gunman, rider, and skilled tactician. One critic remarks that the film "is just another superhero flick that spends half its running time assembling a band of bulletproof daredevils."[17] Nevertheless, the interactions of this racially and ethnically diverse group bring to light the legacy of slavery, the Texas-Mexico conflict (in particular the role of the Toluca Battalion in the 1836 Battle of the Alamo), Chinese labor on the American railways, the history of black cowboys in the west, and federally sanctioned American Indian genocide, as well as day-to-day racial prejudices in the West.[18]

Comparable to its predecessor, the film relies heavily on outmoded cinematic tropes to represent racialized characters and conflicts. For example, Red Harvest's arrival is sounded by flutes, drums, and, rhythmic chanting. The dichotomy of good and bad Indians is retained in the characters of Red Harvest, who protects Emma when she runs out of bullets, and Bogue's henchman, Denali, who throws his hatchet into the back of an unarmed woman as she attempts to flee. Similarly, though spared a soundtrack of flamenco-style guitars or mariachi brass, Vasquez, when first introduced, makes insinuations about raping Emma, fulfilling the role of a violent, depraved Mexican criminal. A drunk Faraday greets Vasquez with a "yippee, yippee, yippee, andale," adding to it "ole muchacho." Instead of using these moments to address the economic, social, or racial histories that inform these conflicts, the film plays them for comic effect or presents them as obstacles to the seven before they become a cohesive fighting machine, eschewing the actual complicated cultural geographies of the West.

Adherence to the professional plot trumps identity politics, so that, despite the fact that the nonwhite men are all that remain of the seven, their departure from the town is meant to mark the completion of their job rather than suggest any existing racial or cultural barriers that would bar their participation as citizens in the community they helped to save or in the United States at large. Their actions—done "to win something that didn't belong to them," as Emma narrates—are memorialized as "magnificent." Still, the men, as racialized vigilantes, no matter how noble their actions, face an uncertain future as they ride off to the margins of the margins, which diminishes their heroism by making them racial and cultural anomalies.

The diversity of Fuqua's seven tells audiences that the world of the cinematic western is changing: their presence in it serves as fact. As Michael Agresta maintains, "If the genre in [the Obama] era can be said to have a unifying aim, it's to divest itself and its audiences of a strictly white, male, heterosexual perspective on history, and by extension on present day conflicts."[19] Rather than representative of revisionist liberal politics, the film serves as a corrective to "fantastical utopias of white heroism." Leah Williams reminds audiences that "people of color were not only present at the inception of the Wild West—but they were also its primary architects."[20] Focusing on the racial politics of having "historically oppressed, sidelined, and discarded men" sacrifice for a community to which they could never belong, Allison Willmore takes a far more critical stance. For Willmore, "its ensemble feels like an assemblage of token characters loosed from the background to ride to the rescue of a white frontier settlement."[21] Given the conventions of the professional western and the western genre in general, preserving civilized communities is what heroes do before riding away. Culturally and socially, white heroes are not barred from belonging; instead, they choose *not* to belong. Sam, Vasquez, and Red Harvest are morally, juridically, and culturally barred from belonging *because* of their race or ethnicity. Simply put, the stakes are only the same on the surface. Specificity matters.

The racial politics of Fuqua's *Magnificent Seven* align more closely with those of the *Suicide Squad*, particularly in its treatment of Mexican and Indian characters. As contemporary westerns, the films prioritize racial and ethnic diversity to destabilize the white heroism of the genre. At the same time, they also double down on the importance of white communities. Substituting the Mexican village with the mostly white residents of Rose Creek erases difference without acknowledging the privileges that offer protections to some and not others. Ayer's *Suicide Squad* relies on its diverse characters to reaffirm contemporary racial paradigms, while affirming ideas about model minorities, murderous black men, savage Indians, violent Mexican gangbangers, and other cultures as potential threats or sources of global contamination.

Suicide Squad mingles elements of the weird with the professional plot in order to satisfy the most basic conventions of the western: recover the girl and eliminate the savage (albeit supernatural) threat, in order to save civilization. The film's Indians have no specific tribal affiliation or correlation outside the celluloid landscape, thereby illustrating what Gerald Vizenor (White Earth Anishinaabe) identifies as a lack of "the tribal real."[22] Their uncanny abilities heighten the threat they pose to family and communities on both a local and global scale. Chato, Enchantress, and Incubus are cinematic Indians whose narrative presence is permitted only so they can be eliminated from the landscape to foreground the true heroism of the film's metropolitan cowboys and cowgirls. *Suicide Squad*'s commitment to eliminating Indians from the narrative is so dogged that not even the Chinook and Apache helos (military transports named after indigenous groups of the Pacific Northwest and Southwest) survive. By the end, no Indian—or Latinx character, for that matter—is left alive, indicating that the greatest narrative contribution they have to offer the western, weird or otherwise, is their demise.

NOTES

1. Lawrence and Jewett, *Myth of the American Superhero*, 106–7.
2. Mitchell, *Westerns*, 85.
3. Mitchell, *Westerns*, 86.
4. Palmer, "Punisher as Revisionist Superhero Western," 29.
5. Calder, *There Must Be a Lone Ranger*, 19.
6. After Chato tearfully recounts the story of how he accidentally killed his wife, Harley responds sharply: "What'd you think was going to happen? Huh? What you were just thinking you could have a happy family and coach little leagues and make car payments? Normal is a setting on the dryer. People like us don't get normal."
7. Ramirez Berg, *Latino Images in Film*, 67.
8. Evers and Molina, *Yaqui Deer Songs*, 20. Evers and Molina refer to Yaqui leader Anselmo Valencia, who, on September 27, 1977, argued before the U.S. Senate Select Committee on Indian Affairs for recognition of the Yaquis as Indians: "The Yaquis are Indians in every sense of the word. We have our own language, our own culture, such as the Pascola dancing, the deer dancing, and the coyote dancing. These dances are Indian in origin. In the deer dance, we sing to honor the great mountains, the spring, the lakes. We sing of our father the Sun, and of creatures living and dead" (6). Valencia cites, as Evers and Molina note, the deer dance as one of "the primary evidences that Yaquis remain Yaqui" ("Trust Status for the Pascua Yaqui Indians of Arizona," 20).
9. If the village is located in Northern Mexico in or near Yaqui territory, then logistically, traveling to Tombstone, Arizona, would take only a few days by horse.

10. Lenihan, *Showdown*, 57.
11. From 1869 to 1873 Agustín Salinas Sr., while serving as Mayor of Laredo, hired an extra police force to allegedly quell political unrest in the town, though it is generally believed that he did so to intimidate his opponents (Bishop, "Coke-Davis Controversy"). The Travis County reference may refer to the Coke-Davis controversy concerning the gubernatorial election in 1873 when the Travis Guard and Rifles, a small policing force, were called in to protect Coke. Instead, they turned into a posse that protected Davis (Mora, "Salinas"). Also, the Yaqui Wars in Mexico did not begin until 1887, lasting until 1910. Given the dates of these events, the film is set somewhere between 1875 and 1886. The 2016 remake is explicitly identified as taking place in 1879, which is consistent with the proposed dating of the 1960 version.
12. Calder, *There Must Be a Lone Ranger*, 199.
13. Calder, *There Must Be a Lone Ranger*, 99.
14. Shepherd, "*Suicide Squad* Director Explains."
15. Calder, *There Must Be a Lone Ranger*, 133. Goodnight, a longtime acquaintance of Sam's, knows that their involvement in the town's affairs has more to do than simply "for the good of mankind." Sam purposely—and selfishly—puts the lives of the other six at risk in order to avenge his sisters and mother. He is redeemed from this act by Emma, who kills Bogue in the church seconds before he is about to kill Sam.
16. As in the original, Sam is offered "everything" to help the town. Emma presents him with a saddlebag, which Sam does not even bother to open once he hears that Bartholomew Bogue is the one terrorizing the town. Later, when Goodnight tries to slink off the evening before the big showdown, Sam asks, "You just gonna run off before you get your cut of the gold?" The offer of "everything," therefore, is meant as an enticement for more pay, should the seven succeed in defeating Bogue and laying claim to the mine. Greater economic value, therefore, is placed on the skills and lives of the professionals in Fuqua's version.
17. Nicholson, "*The Magnificent Seven* Gallops Boldly into Mediocrity."
18. Examples include: Robicheaux is a Confederate Civil War veteran with severe PTSD; Vasquez's grandfather participated in the Battle of the Alamo on the Mexican side; Robicheaux and Billy Rocks meet after the former is sent to serve a warrant for the Northern Pacific Railroad; Sam is repre-

sentative of black cowboys in the West; Jack Horne is known for killing more than 300 Crow Indians; and Billy explains that "Goody helps [him] navigate the white man's prejudices."
19. Agresta, "How the Western Was Lost."
20. Williams, "How Hollywood Whitewashed the Old West."
21. Willmore, "The Diversity Is Just for Show."
22. Vizenor, *Manifest Manners*, 4.

BIBLIOGRAPHY

Agresta, Michael. "How the Western Was Lost (And Why It Matters)." *Atlantic*, July 24 2013, https://www.theatlantic.com/entertainment/archive/2013/07/how-the-western-was-lost-and-why-it-matters/278057/ (accessed July 21, 2017).

Ayer, David, dir. *Suicide Squad*. Warner Bros., 2016.

Bishop, Curtis. "Coke-Davis Controversy." Handbook of Texas Online, July 12, 2010. https://tshaonline.org/ handbook/online/articles/mqc01 (accessed August 31, 2017).

Calder, Jenni. *There Must Be a Lone Ranger: The American West in Film and in Reality*. New York: Taplinger, 1975.

Evers, Larry, and Felipe S. Molina. *Yaqui Deer Songs/Maso Bwikam*. Tucson: University of Arizona Press, 1987.

Fuqua, Antoine, dir. *The Magnificent Seven*. Sony Pictures, 2016.

Lawrence, John Shelton, and Robert Jewett. *The Myth of the American Superhero*. Grand Rapids MI: William B. Eerdmans, 2002.

Lenihan, John H. *Showdown: Confronting Modern American in the Western Film*. Urbana: University of Illinois Press, 1980.

Mitchell, Lee Clark. *Westerns: Making the Man in Fiction and Film*. Chicago: University of Chicago Press, 1996.

Mora, Lilia R. "Salinas, Agustín, Sr.," Handbook of Texas Online, August 18, 2016, https://tshaonline.org/ handbook/online/articles/fsali (accessed August 31, 2017) .

Nicholson, Amy. "*The Magnificent Seven* Gallops Boldly into Mediocrity." MTV News, September 23, 2016, http://www.mtv.com/news/2935220/magnificent-seven-denzel-washington-chris-pratt-review/ (accessed August 31, 2017).

Palmer, Lorrie. "The Punisher as Revisionist Superhero Western." In *The Superhero Reader*, edited by Charles Hatfield, Jeet Heer, and Kent Worcester, 279–94. Jackson: University of Missisippi Press, 2013.

Ramirez Berg, Charles. *Latino Images in Film: Stereotypes, Subversion, and Resistance.* Austin: University of Texas Press, 2004.

Shepherd, Jack. "*Suicide Squad* Director Explains Why Slipknot's Backstory Was Cut." *Independent,* August 14, 2016, https://www.independent.co.uk/arts-entertainment/films/news/suicide-squad-director-david-ayer-slipknot-backstory-cut-deleted-scene-a7190081.html (accessed July 15, 2017).

Sturges, John, dir. *The Magnificent Seven.* United Artists, 1960.

Valencia, Anselmo. "Trust Status for the Pascua Yaqui Indians of Arizona." Washington DC: Government Printing Office, 1977.

Vizenor, Gerald. *Manifest Manners: Narratives on Postindian Survivance.* Lincoln: University of Nebraska Press, 1999.

Willmore, Alison. "The Diversity Is Just for Show in *The Magnificent Seven.*" BuzzFeed, September 10, 2016, https://www.buzzfeed.com/alisonwillmore/the-diversity-is-just-for-show-in-the-magnificent-seven (accessed August 31, 2017).

Williams, Leah. "How Hollywood Whitewashed the Old West." *Atlantic,* October 5, 2016, https://www.theatlantic.com/entertainment/archive/2016/10/how-the-west-was-lost/502850/ (accessed August 31, 2017).

PART THREE

Surrogate *indians* and
Other Indigenous Metaphors

Defamiliarizing the Western on the Extraterrestrial Frontier

7

Jonathan Lethem's *Girl in Landscape*

JOHANNES FEHRLE

Jonathan Lethem's *Girl in Landscape* (1998) explores the western's traditional race and gender relations by combining a female coming-of-age story with a rewriting of John Ford's classic Indian-hater western *The Searchers* (1956), a film with which Lethem has, by his own admission, long been obsessed.[1] *Girl in Landscape* revisits, updates, and attempts to write against Ford's film and, by extension, the western, while acknowledging—not least through its frame and intertextual borrowings—the pull of the genre and its structuring hierarchies. The novel gives the genre several twists, however: most obviously, it retells the western from an adolescent girl's perspective, setting her search for adulthood and her grief for her dead mother against the backdrop of an extraterrestrial frontier. Drawing on a wide range of intertexts, including Charles Portis's *True Grit* (1968) via Carson McCullers and Shirley Jackson (whose peculiar coming-of-age novel 1951 *Hangsaman* is referenced in an epigraph), Lethem situates his weird western within a broader trend of revising earlier narratives in postmodern literature.[2] Lethem has expressed in an interview his awareness of "the postmodern move, an assault upon a classic work by taking the neglected or minority viewpoint and retelling the tales—think of Jean Rhys rewriting *Jane Eyre* as *Wide Sargasso Sea*. Given my interests at the time, it wasn't much of a leap to watch *The Searchers* and wonder about Natalie Wood's version of events. What might it be like to see John Wayne through her eyes?"[3]

Lethem's novel ties this *gendered* revision to an exploration of *racism* in the classic western. Its depiction of how a race of aliens, an obvious stand-in for the generic "Indians" of the western genre, become subjected to racist violence highlights both how the classic western "offered and enacted [racism] as a theory of history"[4] and explores the twisted logic that, in a psychoanalytic reading, springs from sexual repression channeled into the (attempted) genocide against Native Americans, a theme critics have long identified in *The Searchers*.[5] The novel draws the connection between a generic revision centered around gender and an exploration of the deterioration of racist frames of perception into genocidal cleansing by relating these to a certain brand of white American masculinity. This violent, xenophobic version of what R. W. Connell has termed "hegemonic masculinity" tries to dominate or erase all things perceived as nonmasculine and nonwhite (despite incorporating aspects of either category).[6] Its force—which structures the Indian-hater western's central nexus of gender, repressed sexuality, and racist violence against a perceived Other—is laid open through the female protagonist's perspective, a maneuver through which the novel sheds light on "our ambivalence about American manhood." For Lethem, Wayne's star persona most clearly embodies "our national disasters of racism, sexual repression, violence and authority," while retaining the continued fascination of many U.S. Americans, including Lethem.[7] The novel therefore explores how this masculinity is at once compelling and disastrous, leading necessarily to the violation of others. *Girl in Landscape* counterbalances and, ultimately, at least partly supplants this white manhood by the nonwhite and feminine elements Pella learns to embrace. The novel's countervision of a feminine, nondisastrous perspective on new environments and alterity that tries to engage and learn from racial and ethnic otherness nevertheless remains hybrid and unable to fully escape the pull of Efram's masculinity.

Revising the western's depiction of femininity and Native Americans is a slippery slope, however. This is so not merely because of Lethem's position as a white male author (although some blind spots certainly derive from his particular position and privilege), but even more so because the American West, women, Native Americans, and America as a whole have been symbolically overburdened by masculinist and settler colonialist fantasies and narratives for centuries. Any attempt to undo these therefore becomes a veritable minefield of clichés, stereotypes, and unvoiced and often unnoticed assumptions, all the more so when the western is added as a generic frame that structures the narrative.[8] By setting the novel not in the historic West but on an extraterrestrial frontier and by replacing Native Americans with aliens displaced by a settler colonial force taking over the supposedly empty "frontier" of their home planet, Lethem tries to evade some of these issues. As will become clear, however, *Girl in Landscape*'s ways of depicting the Archbuilders as peaceful victims or coding the space shaped by them in gendered terms often uncomfortably continue traditions of gendered and racialized depictions that have structured Euro-American perceptions of the American West and its inhabitants, despite the novel's weird western alterations.[9]

The Novel

Girl in Landscape begins in Brooklyn Heights at some unspecified time in a future. It follows the Marsh family: thirteen-year-old Pella, the novel's main character and focalizer; her ten- and seven-year-old brothers, Raymond and David; and their parents, Clement and Caitlin. After the end of Clement Marsh's political career on Earth, the parents have decided to join in the settlement of a new frontier by relocating to the planet of the Archbuilders. After Caitlin's sudden death from a brain tumor, the rest of the family moves to the planet, and to a small settlement in a distant valley there. Clement at first seems to fall back into the role of a leader of the nascent community, but the valley is already under the de facto control of the mysterious first settler and patriarch Efram Nugent, who antagonizes Clement's every move. Furthermore, lacking Caitlin's unifying presence, the Marsh family gradually falls apart, its various members each grieving and searching for their lost mother and wife. Pella roams through the landscape of the alien planet, Raymond loses himself in old photographs, and Clement starts an affair.[10]

Pella soon develops a mystical connection to the planet that is caused by an Archbuilder virus, which many of the other families on the planet suppress by taking drugs—a practice that Clement opposes. The virus makes Pella go into trances in which her mind enters small native animals called "household deer." Pella uses her new skill to spy on the adults of the colony, discovering—in a literalized metaphor for growing up—secrets about the adult world to which she would rather have remained oblivious. She spies on her father's liaison with the scientist Diana Eastling and witnesses a sexually charged encounter between the human artist Hugh Merrow and one of his Archbuilder models, Truth Renowned, as well as the subsequent burning of the corpse of Truth Renowned, who has likely been murdered by Efram or one of his followers.

The strained equilibrium on the planet, torn between the overbearing Efram's rule by violent fait accomplis and Clement's attempts to become the leader of a liberal, trans-species community, is completely unsettled when Efram raises the fear of the Archbuilders' molestation of the settlers' children. After Truth Renowned's death, Efram imprisons another Archbuilder, Hiding Kneel, on charges of child molestation. Pella finds out that Hiding Kneel is innocent, however, and in an attempt to stop the lynching justice, Pella and one of the other children, Morris Grant, try to blackmail the frontiersman by threatening to say that Morris witnessed Efram rape Pella. When Efram refuses to back down, Doug Grant, Efram's disciple, kills the frontiersman to protect his brother Morris and then flees into the desert.

A final four-page section is dedicated to the status of the settlement after Efram's death. Many of the settlers have left. Pella's brother Raymond and Morris's brother Doug each wander through the desert in solitude, while Pella, her youngest brother, David, and Morris form their own, somewhat dysfunctional family unit. Clement, meanwhile, beaten and insane, stays in his bedroom, growing Archbuilder potatoes under his bed. Only the Archbuilders seem better off: they move freely through the town and, in an act of symbolic closure, inhabit Efram's now-vacant living room.

Gender, Land, and *The Searchers*

Girl in Landscape upsets the western's traditional affirmative masculinist stance in a number of ways: most obviously, it gives the central narrative agency and—through its focalization—also its interpretative authority to Pella, the female teenage protagonist. Secondly, and connectedly, through Pella's role and vision, the novel unveils (through the depiction of Clement's increasing dissociation) how hegemonic concepts of masculinity wreak havoc on men themselves as well as the community (through Efram's threats, molestation, and murders of the Archbuilders). This gendered rewriting is a move that will, in the end, become central to the novel's resolution, a partial healing of the traumatic rupture caused by the death of the other central female figure, Pella's mother, Caitlin, in the novel's opening section. To highlight the positive effect of this unifying female presence, the novel employs a structural circularity, starting and ending with a strong female character as the center of a family unit—first Caitlin, then, after her journey into adulthood and the healing of her wounds, Pella.

As a revision of the western and Wayne's roles and persona, however, the novel also explores masculinity, as tied to the "frontier experience" and its promise of "regeneration through violence," a connection that, as scholars Dan Moos and Christine Bold have shown, is intricately connected to notion of whiteness and the aggressive suppression of racial Otherness.[11] From its first pages, the novel connects masculinity and the frontier. Although it is Caitlin who sells the family's "westering" to the children, Clement in particular hopes to profit from the move. Building on the tradition of the "American sissy"—men like Theodore Roosevelt and Owen Wister, who used the West as a space to build up a masculinity they perceived to be lacking in the East—Clement likewise hopes to use the frontier experience to rebuild his battered masculinity and begin a new political career.[12] After his election defeat, Pella finds Clement "gazing self-pityingly off toward some imaginary frontier" that turns out to be "not imaginary enough."[13] As becomes clear, however, Clement is not half the man he wishes to be. Instead he is, in Pella's eyes, "a coward" and "useless" (14; 37), absent when his wife falls in the shower and helpless to console his children when they try to cope with the imminent death of their mother. After Caitlin's death and the end of his political career, he becomes even more helpless, unable to accomplish anything without a campaign team to guide him from speech to speech and Caitlin to keep his life and his family together (240). As a result, Clement stumbles from one defeat to the next and Pella's attitude toward him develops from her initial oscillation between occasional pride for his high aims and the feeling of being let down to a complete lack of respect that culminates in her wish that he rather than Caitlin had died (241). In the end, she feels only pity, and the traditional dynamic of child and parent reverses: Pella now protects Clement from the community's demands, which he can no longer meet (248).

As the heart of what amounts to Clement's ultimate dissociation are his repeated defeats in the face of the domineering Efram, whose aggressive masculinity eclipses Clement's more community-dependent one: a gender performance that proves ineffective without an audience to affirm it and a community to bestow symbolic power upon Clement and do what he commands. Read in the western frame and its patterns of gendered opposites, it is the frontier—with its seeming demands for a hardened masculinity (like Efram's), which he cannot meet, and the lack of a community (coded in the western as eastern and feminine)— that unmake Clement. Unlike Pella, Clement opposes Efram in his own game, a male struggle for domination, whereas she ultimately changes the rules. In the end, Clement fails in all of the areas associated with traditional, hegemonic masculinity. He is not physically assertive like Efram; he does not retain patriarchal power, since he can hold neither his woman (Diana Eastling leaves the settlement on a long expedition rather than being pulled into Clement's power contest), nor his family; and he cannot even reclaim his societal position as a leader, the arena he invests himself in most strongly.

Crucially, Efram, as Clement's antagonist and other, is at the heart of all of these failings. His effect on Clement's less violent, more community-oriented masculinity provides part of Lethem's take on

Wayne as the epitome of the violent undercurrents of American masculinity that he has written about for *Salon*.[14] Efram defeats Clement's claims to authority time and again by ignoring them and patronizes his adversary. Carrying resonances of Ethan Edwards's monosyllabic scoff "that'll be the day," which Ethan uses as a universal dismissal against any challenge of his position or opinions throughout *The Searchers*, Efram, too, repeatedly places his lived frontier experience above Clement's book-learning in only slightly more words.[15] He hints at knowledge of the planet and the native and nonnative inhabitants he—like Wayne's character—strategically withholds to retain his position of authority.

In their first confrontation, Efram warns Clement, "You don't want to be seen as a carpetbagger," and suggests "things you can't or haven't bothered to imagine about the Archbuilders, things I know," mirroring Ethan's knowledge of the Comanche, and finally levels the charge, posed as a rhetorical question: "You really think it's that simple, don't you Marsh? Read about a place, then go blundering in. The map and the territory aren't the same" (113, 118). Through their repeated confrontations, the novel pits the two masculinities embodied by Efram and Clement against each other for both Pella's and the reader's eyes. On the one side there is Efram's lone, violent, bullying masculinity, which in the western context of the Archbuilder planet proves to be hegemonic. Clement's less physical, less imposing masculinity—which depends on his command of language, symbolic acts, and ideals through which he managed to rally the Earth community under his leadership—fails on the frontier: a classic dichotomy of western versus eastern American masculinities played out in countless novels and movies. As the plot progresses, it becomes increasingly clear that Clement is no match for Efram, the planet, or even the challenge of raising his children. The women he turns to as ersatz-Caitlins (Pella and the scientist Diana Eastling) turn away from his attempts to instrumentalize them, as do Ellen Kincaid and the lesbian couple Llana Richmond and Julie Concorse (214–15).

After so many defeats, Clement is reduced to hiding in his darkened bedroom, tending potatoes whose seeds [sic] were blown into the house when, in a childish act of defiance, he ignored one of Efram's warnings, refusing to close the windows of his room to keep the seeds outside. This pathetic attempt to "show Efram Nugent that everything doesn't have to be done his way" is the ultimate display of weakness in a long row of slipping authority, as the narrator's wry comment makes clear: "As if Efram would ever bother to look under Clement's bed, or be impressed to find potatoes growing there if he did" (234). This last act of childish rebellion reduces Clement to nothingness, to the existence as a "bedroom farmer" (235), an image that encapsulates the failure of Clement's masculinity. His attempt to retain his masculinity by ignoring Efram's warning backfires, making him less rather than more of a man. He is confined to the domestic space of the bedroom, the epitome of femininity, and makes the masculine task of subduing the land as a farmer into a parody, watering plants that grow like weeds without demanding any attention. In the context of the western—and, particularly, the John Ford western—this impression is strengthened by his occupation of the very indoor space that, from *Stagecoach* to *The Searchers*, are always unable to contain Wayne's characters, as Ford's cinematography and use of doors as thresholds makes clear. Houses are too small for Wayne's larger-than-life masculinity and the same is true for Efram's, yet they easily envelop Clement.

Opposing Clement's ineffectual masculinity is Efram's angry, domineering gender performance, which is broken through suggestions of an at least borderline-pedophiliac attraction to the pubescent Pella. Efram in turn becomes the object of her sexual awakening, a figure whose overbearing, rugged masculinity at once attracts, repulses, and mystifies her and serves as a countermodel to Clement's bureaucratic masculinity. In an interview, Lethem describes Efram Nugent—whose name renders homage to both Ethan Edwards and Frank S. Nugent, *The Searchers*'s screenwriter—as "an anti-heroic, racist, angry figure," and he states, "I wanted to explore what it was like to have your sexual coming-of-age watched over by this bullying man."[16] By transforming the lingering incestuous desires between Ethan and his sister-in-law into an equally forbidden pedophiliac attraction on Efram's part, Lethem makes explicit the illicit sexual tension that, as Marty Roth and others have shown, structure *The Searchers*, despite John Ford's insistence that "sex, obscenity, and degeneration" did not interest him.[17]

Introduced already as a haunting presence that commands equal measures of respect and fear before he ever appears in the flesh, Efram is an embodiment of the stereotypical tough cowboy masculinity. Remediating one of the iconic images of the western hero dominating a landscape that makes him appear larger than life, the novel first sets Efram, who continually seems to appears out of thin air, against a dramatic evening sky, making him part of an awe-inspiring landscape: "A man in a hat stood on a ridge to her left, between her and the sun, so that he was a silhouette against the pink. Standing still, he was almost like another of the broken arches on the horizon, somehow drawn suddenly close" (80). Building on the western's obsession with the physique of its protagonist and its repeated mirroring of his corporeality in the harsh land, Efram is as closely associated with the land through comparison and "framing" as his generic predecessors.[18] Building on Ford's depiction of Ethan in *The Searchers*, a film in which "the landscape and the reluctant hero are inseparable," Efram likewise becomes part of the land: more than a man and more than Pella can grasp.[19] His smile seems "carved in rock," and his physicality is described by Pella as "a mistake in scale," in which "Efram Nugent could seem too big, out here"; her reaction is to want "him adjusted, made smaller" (81). His physique and his size alone—like Wayne's, who towered over everyone—sets Efram apart from Clement, who is almost the same size as Pella, as she realizes in her final attempt to "crawl into his lap" an attempt so out of sync with their developments and Clement's symbolic fall out of manhood and adulthood and Pella's growth that the narrator remarks, "She might have been trying to sit in [ten-year-old] Raymond's lap" (89).

As suggested by the title, the land is not merely associated with Efram, however. Rather, the novel adopts the western's traditional ambiguity of using the land to bring out the masculine characteristics of the hero when its features reflect the hero's hardness and gendering it as feminine when it is imagined as "an environment of receptivity, repose, and painless and integral satisfaction," and a virgin land to be penetrated.[20] In his attempts to transcend this traditional inscription of the land as a reflection of the male hero, to render it more complex and associate it with his *female* hero, Lethem nevertheless inadvertently falls into the kind of psychosexual fantasy Annette Kolodny has described as a dominant symbolic figuration in (early) American literature.

The planet's weird geology is associated as much with Caitlin, the lost mother, of whom Pella is constantly reminded as she gets lost in the alien landscape. As James Peacock notes, the novel "offer[s] up the alien landscape as a kind of objective correlative of the protagonist's mourning for her mother," and the land works in this way not only for Pella but for other motherless or quasi-motherless children in the novel: Pella's brother Raymond as well as the neglected Morris Grant.[21] If we read the scenes in which Pella is most closely in contact with the land through Kolodny's analyses of the " Myth of Conquest," they reveal a gendered dimension that is very close to the Freudian infantile fantasies of a return to the womb that Kolodny identifies throughout early renditions of the American wilderness. As if to stress the Freudian dimension of the trances in which Pella's mind slips into the household deer, she first crawls into the earth, to hide herself in an underground Archbuilder structure, a likely unwitting reiteration of the "return to the primal warmth of womb or breast in a feminine landscape."[22]

There is another dimension to this connection on top of its gendered aspect, however: the connection between Euro-American settler and Native land. Significantly, Pella crawls not into an unmarked earth-as-mother, but into a landscape whose geoformed structure—a collapsed Archbuilder dwelling—symbolically stands for Archbuilder culture. Lethem thus presents us with a gendered revision of the western hero, but, in a slightly different fashion, continues the settler colonial myth of the protagonist's special relation to the land. Although Ethan's and other western hero's violent male domination are transformed into Pella's more mournful, more subtle, and more feminine retreat, her embrace likewise establishes a relation between settler and land that is different in detail but similar in function. As Patrick Wolfe has shown, this very connection between settler and land is typical of the discourse of legitimization that takes place in settler colonial societies, a dual process in which indigenous claims to the land are denied or ignored whereas settlers are coded as being of the land.[23]

Pella's trances are both a literal and a symbolic immersion into Archbuilder culture, a culture to which the remaining Archbuilders on the planet have lost their connection. In this fashion, it resembles another dominant strategy of settler colonial discourse, which, while eliminating indigenous peoples as legitimate owners, simultaneously appropriates indigenous Nativeness to distinguish itself from a European mother country.[24] As Margery Fee has shown, moreover, symbolic acts of acceptance by Native people are common in North American literature, with countless versions of Vanishing Indians granting settlers a sense of history and legitimacy in their appropriation of Native land (e.g., through a symbolic handing over of a token of the land).[25] When Pella lies in the abandoned Archbuilder ruin and goes through an Archbuilder practice (being in fact affected and infected by an Archbuilder virus) that allows her to inhabit the spirit of the household deer, there is a sense of her immersion in Native culture. This immersion legitimizes at least *her* presence on the planet, but by extension also that of other respectful settlers. The practice of merging furthermore evokes animistic rituals associated with Native shamanism (the fact that the household deer were quite likely created by Archbuilder technology notwithstanding) and the supposed natural spiritual union between Native people and the land, thereby resonating deeply with Euro-American fantasies of going Native. It is, indeed, this latter aspect, the connection of Pella to the land as Native, that remains central. Whereas Pella's regression to an embryonic state inside the symbolic mother is temporary—a symbol for the stagnation of her mourning process that she will finally overcome—her association with Native culture is more permanent. Rather than being an antithesis, there is a link between the settler colonial and gendered visions of the symbolic claiming of the land, as Kolodny shows: "In a sense, to make the new continent Woman was already to civilize it a bit, casting the stamp of human relations upon what was otherwise unknown and untamed."[26] In a way, this is what happens in Lethem's novel, too. Here the land as ersatz-mother imbued with the authenticating hints of a vanished culture prepares us for the nonviolent settler's embrace of the alien planet and its culture, setting Pella apart from the hostile domination of the planet and its inhabitants that Efram's masculine subjugation stands for and opening up a space for a settler colonial cohabitation that is less antagonistic.

Race, Repression, Genocide

Despite Lethem's claim that he did not write a traditional western, because he wanted to avoid "the pitfalls of depicting Native American culture," *Girl in Landscape* nevertheless strongly reflects on the western and its depiction of Native Americans.[27] While traces of settler colonial ideology shine through Pella's connection to the planet's landscape, these seem largely inadvertent, as I have demonstrated. The novel more consciously explores *The Searchers*'s racist psychology by depicting Efram's treatment of the Archbuilders. The alien race's position as the indigenous race inhabiting a colonized planet is obviously structurally similar to that of Native Americans in the western. Although Lethem strove to evade the pitfalls of the depiction of Native Americans in the traditional western by altering the genre to a weird western, the stereotypes he employs to mark the Archbuilders as Indians (such as that of "the vanishing American" or the "noble savage") still resonate with the position of Indians in U.S. history and the white imaginary. These stereotypes repeatedly trip up the novel's aim of exposing *The Searchers*'s racist psychology while avoiding the images of violent savages that have long divided critics about whether Ford's film itself (rather than merely its protagonist) is racist or not.[28]

In an interview, Lethem discusses these thoughts and the sources for his Archbuilders in some detail, underscoring his sense of the aliens as colonial subjects:

> When I created the Archbuilders . . . I knew they couldn't be threatening or evil, as in the manner of the Comanches in a John Ford

film. Instead I wanted them to be harmless, thoughtful, befuddled types, who stand to one side and comment on the action. What I reached for, unconsciously, were the *Indian* Indians in Forster[']s *Passage to India*]. And this unconscious choice shaped the plot to a large degree.

The Archbuilders, like Forster's Indians, spend the first half of the book puzzling over the behavior of the colonists, seemingly safe, to one side of the action. Then, in *Girl*, as in *Passage*, there comes a crisis in the middle of the book: in Forster, a possible rape or an imagined rape in a hidden cave. That Marabar Caves incident became, in *Girl*, Efram fondling or not fondling Pella. And the natives are the ones who fall under suspicion. One among them is martyred to the hysteria which comes over the settlers.[29]

While the Archbuilders' inactivity, which casts them in the role of a quietly suffering subaltern, is questionable from a postcolonial or settler colonial studies stance, it is quite effective in highlighting the mechanisms of racism and Othering that underlie the generic codes of the genre of the western and U.S. culture more generally. If one follows a psychoanalytic reading of racism and the fear of miscegenation (which in *Girl in Landscape* is turned into the fear of child molestation) as springing from a projection of one's own repressed desires onto a racialized other, the question of Efram "fondling or not fondling" Pella is indeed at the heart of the novel, for it can be construed as the bottom of Efram's crusade against the Archbuilders.[30] By writing the Archbuilders as entirely devoid of aggression, Lethem can cast the violence they are subjected to into a starker light. At the same time, however, he does so at the expense of his Natives' agency, focusing instead on the dynamics within settler society that lead to their violation. Here the main characters are divided between the belligerent, hate-filled Wayne character, Efram, who attempts to murder and segregate aliens and humans, and the much more liberal and compassionate perspective, which aims for a peaceful coexistence interested in understanding and approaching the other race, adopted by Clement and Pella. This offers

Pella a privileged position with regard to the Archbuilders—at least in the readers' eyes, if not in that of the Archbuilders, who welcome everyone, even Efram, who hates and wants to annihilate them.

As is made clear time and again, Lethem's Archbuilders are not dangerous "savages," but peaceful to the point of passivity. As such, their victimization by the settlers in the second half of the novel serves to highlight a possible logic behind settler colonialism in the United States. The Archbuilders may be the indigenous inhabitants of a planet named after them and formed by their once-great command of science (they controlled the weather, made the arches and turrets through viruses, created genetically modified food that sows itself, and possibly made the household deer with which they now merge in trances), yet their right to be in their native land is increasingly questioned.

Whereas the local storeowner E. G. Wa is only annoyed by the Archbuilders who "hang around the general store until kicked out, like deracinated Indians at a trading post," never buying anything and thereby underscoring the pointlessness of a store that seems like adults playing at an economy that has not arrived, it is Efram who first questions the legitimacy of the Archbuilders' presence in the settler colony.[31] Building on a hate of a Native Other that he shares with his filmic antecedent, Ethan Edwards, Efram freely expresses his conviction that the settlers "ought to draw a line around this town we're starting here.... Make it a *human* settlement, a place where kids are safe" (114; emphasis in original). It is also Efram who first suggests and later defends resettling the Archbuilders like replanted trees: "I'm just talking about moving them out of our settlement. They don't care. They've got plenty of other places to wander around. A whole ruined planet for them to gawk at and wonder what the hell happened to their civilization" (115). Again, there are strong traces here of settler colonial discourse, which likewise tends to portray indigenous people as nomadic rather than settled (regardless of whether this is in fact the case) and from there treats them as freely moveable from a land that only reaches its full potential when settled by sedentary Europeans.[32]

Efram's callousness toward the friendly and curious Archbuilders is thus unsettling enough even before it turns to murder. The whole perversity of his stance, however, only shows itself in context: just seconds before framing the Archbuilders as potential child molesters, Efram tells Clement that "Pella's a lovely girl" (114), and throughout the novel there is a feeling that it is his own illicit desire for Pella that he projects onto the Archbuilders. Indeed, from the beginning, a strange sexual dynamic emanates from Efram, who, in their first meeting, misidentifies Pella as Clement's wife, assessing her age and body in his musing that Clement must have remarried, since Pella is "too young to have had three kids" (80). This sexualization of Pella implied in this stripping her of the protective, nonsexual category of the child, informs their relationship. Pella is awed by Efram, and Efram in his turn frequently separates her from the other children by putting her on the level of an adult—for example, when he winks at her while sending Morris and David off to "herd" some household deer "up west" (84–85). Efram sees in the Archbuilders the pedophiliac threat he himself poses through his attraction to the underage Pella. Throughout the novel, his attitude toward Pella contradicts his rhetoric, a contradiction that he sublimates through his increasingly hostile actions against the Archbuilders. While he is sitting next to Pella on his couch, her leg draped over his in a recreation of a scene she saw of Diana and Clement when she spied on them as a household deer, he condemns the Archbuilders as "sexual deviants" and threatens, "If they touch the children I'll kill them" (180). When Pella drifts off into a trance, Lethem creates a narrative ellipsis in which Efram, in Lethem's words, may be "fondling or not fondling Pella."[33]

Whatever Efram's actual deeds, it is his only slightly suppressed pedophilia that lies at the heart of the racist affirmations of his masculinity, forming the second link between race and gender: an inversion of Pella's feminine embrace and openness toward the Archbuilders and their planet. Efram, in contrast, contains his illicit desires by turning his libido into rage against the Archbuilders, whom he charges with the very act he himself most clearly verges on: child molestation. This becomes even clearer if we analyze Efram through his filmic predecessor, Ethan, whom critics have accredited with a similar embattled psychology. Reading Scar as Ethan's "dark alter ego," film critics have described Ethan's psychology and actions in a way reminiscent of Freud's classical reinterpretation of *Hamlet*: "Scar does what Ethan Edwards wants to do but cannot do and cannot even admit to wanting: he annihilates Ethan's brother's family and seizes the women for himself (or else destroys them)."[34] Indians, therefore, become the object of Ethan's hate, because "they symbolize his own unacceptable and barely controlled emotions."[35] *The Searchers* thus provides a variation of the Indian-hater theme, which, in the psychoanalytic view, centers around "the basically sexualized nature of racist psychology."[36]

In a similar fashion, the child molestation Efram claims to fear is only present in his imagination. Indeed, there is nothing in the depiction of the Archbuilders that suggests that they are libidinous. There are no Archbuilder children on the planet and those aliens who still inhabit it are interested in words much more than bodies. Nevertheless, Ethan sees his fears confirmed when he discovers what he interprets as an act of miscegenation between Hugh Merrow and his model, Truth Renowned. When Efram finds out about their contact (possibly because he, too, can enter the household deer), he immediately interprets the scene through his lens, seeing the Archbuilder's supposed new carnal knowledge and the fact that he later finds Truth Renowned and Hiding Kneel in the schoolroom, attending the children's lessons, as evidence for the Archbuilders' imminent child molestation. Not only does Efram act in classic western fashion when he raises a posse (albeit one consisting of only two members), he furthermore sees it as his duty "to maintain the separation between the two races."[37]

As a result he punishes the act of (imagined) miscegenation between the "native beauty" (147) and Merrow, protecting the illusion of racial purity. Like a true repressed western hero he sees a sexual contact he claims to have happened as an unnatural act and a crime, as his reference to Merrow's cabin as "the scene of the crime" (142) makes clear. Although he never explicates which law this encounter violates, there exists no doubt for Efram that a punishable transgression has taken place, and he consequently bullies Merrow into leaving while Truth Renowned is murdered by either Efram, or Ben Barth, or both.

When Clement Marsh objects to Efram's accusations against Truth Renowned, urging him to "show not just that something happened, but that anyone was hurt by it if it did happen," Efram's reply is indicative of his psychology. He merely responds with more insinuations, suggesting that "your proof [will] come when an Archbuilder leads a kid into the hills for some more of what Hugh Merrow's been teaching them" (150). The only justification he can provide for his planned acts of racial segregation is that the Archbuilders do not "make the same distinction between kids and adults that we do," but, ironically, this distinction is one that does not affect his own interaction with Pella. In fact, Efram, while expressing concern about the children's safety, puts on a show directed at least in part toward Pella, the only nonadult allowed to stay at his "tribunal." When he accuses Merrow of lying, he "turned, met Pella's eyes, seemed to look through them" (150), hinting not only at Efram's potential knowledge about her ability to spy through the household deer, as she fears, but also carrying the element of erotic tension omnipresent in Efram's treatment of Pella.

While his paranoia, fueled by his own repressed pedophiliac desires, dominates Efram's increasingly genocidal stance against the Archbuilders, there is another side to Efram's hate of the aliens. Much like the heroes of classic westerns and many a nineteenth-century writer, Efram differentiates between good natives and bad natives: the ones who have vanished and leave room for nostalgia and projection, and the ones he sees on the planet today, who are a problem to be dealt with by violent means. For, while he despises the current Archbuilders (not only as the targets for the projection of his own desires, but as lazy degenerates who never work), he adores what he sees as the original Archbuilders, those who formed the planet and then mysteriously vanished. In these vanished Archbuilders, he sees a race that has gone "to the stars, to the real frontier" (179)—in other words, advanced progress. He thus looks nostalgically at a future he imagines in terms of an American frontier past, which, as many critics of Frederick Jackson

Turner have pointed out, only gains its full potential when it has already passed. Efram expresses a conservatism that is much more backward-facing than that with which he charges the Archbuilders. As James Peacock explains, "While criticising the current Archbuilders for 'picking through their own memories of greatness' (Lethem 1998a: 180), he succumbs to the same romanticisation of the past when he refers to 'the real frontier' of the stars to which the former Archbuilders emigrated."[38]

In an act of what Elaine Graham calls "ontological hygiene," Efram creates categories that allow him to place the remaining Archbuilders into a different category from both humans and those vanished Archbuilders he idolizes: "'Hiding Kneel and Truth Renowned, those types aren't what I call Archbuilders,' he said. 'They're what the Archbuilders left behind.'"[39] Not only does he never entertain the possibility that they might be one and the same people, Efram classifies the present-day Archbuilders in subhuman, eugenic terms, which sets them up for any treatment he sees fit; they are "the rabble . . . , the lazy, stupid ones that didn't want to go" (179).

What is striking about this contempt is not merely the contradiction of Efram's relation to the Archbuilders, which he divides into those vanished who should be venerated and those who remain and can be dehumanized and murdered (a distinction resonating strongly with the dialectic of noble and savage Indian), but also how much he once again misinterprets reality. For one, his contempt for the Archbuilders' supposed obsession with their civilization's past greatness constitutes another moment of projection. It is Efram, not the Archbuilders, who dwells in the race's legendary past. Whereas Efram sits in a house whose main room looks like "a reconstruction of an Archbuilder interior" (176), a veritable museum of Archbuilder artifacts painstakingly reconstructed from shards, when Pella confronts Hiding Kneel with the planet's past and Efram's contempt for the present Archbuilders' lack of honoring their past, Hiding Kneel merely remarks, "Efram Nugent's love of ancestors is quite poignant." In contrast, the Archbuilder refuses "to pretend a relation I do not have, to all the wrecked stuff" (239).

There are additional layers of irony at work that are worth unpacking in Efram's view of the Archbuilders. When charging them with becoming "a bunch of good-for-nothing navel-gazers," who, by turning "this planet into a hell of luxury—the weather control, the free food," have turned "into hothouse creatures picking through their own memories of greatness," Efram not only uses words that make him sound like one of the language-obsessed Archbuilder (180); he describes his own existence more than theirs. It is, after all, Efram who has hothouses to grow Earth food, because he does not want to eat the Archbuilder potatoes and, far from keeping himself busy breaking soil, Efram, too, enjoys free food, for it is Ben Barth who does most, if not all of, Efram's work. Like Warshow's "man of leisure," we never see Efram working.[40]

The extent of the ontological boundaries between humans and Archbuilders and their dehumanization that Efram's fearmongering has created becomes obvious when Pella comes across a group of settlers beating a bleeding Hiding Kneel in front of Wa's store. The scene recalls not only Efram's earlier talk about resettling the Archbuilders that attributed no agency to the aliens, but also resembles the deportation of an unwanted, imagined Other more than a typical beating in a western. Intensified by its lack of resistance, the violence Hiding Kneel is subjected to is disturbing. Only when the Archbuilder speaks does Pella realize that "she had begun to think of it as a kind of animal or plant, the way the men were destroying its body" (245). What we witness in this scene's stripping of individuality and rights from Hiding Kneel is a point central to the novel's treatment of its Indians-as-Archbuilders, which Pella realizes in the end: "None of what had happened was really about Archbuilders, Pella decided. None of the humans had ever met an Archbuilder, or even seen one. It was still all about humans, what they saw when they looked at the Archbuilders, what they saw instead of the Archbuilders" (279).

It is exactly this emphasis on the "white man's Indian"—or, in this case, the human's Archbuilder—that is central to *Girl in Landscape*'s comments on the role of projection and prejudice in the treatment of a colonized Other.[41] The murder of the Archbuilders is as little about the Archbuilders as individuals as the genocide of Native Americans was about individuals or even distinct tribes. Lethem's depiction of the harmless, friendly, and trusting Archbuilders and the abuses they suffer serves as a clear case in point of how skewed perceptions, racist projection, and ontological hygiene can lead to genocidal violence.

While the discussion so far has focused on the victimization and objectification of the Archbuilders, there is another aspect to their depiction that connects to the generic context of *Girl in Landscape* as a weird western, as well as to Pella's female countervision to Efram's male violence. This is connected to the Archbuilders' positive depiction and their active role in Pella's development. Despite their position as victims, which clearly aims at highlighting the role of Native Americans in the traditional western, the Archbuilders are not merely stand-in Indians; they do something to the genre. Lethem's genre mixing allows him to defamiliarize his Indians in many ways. Physically, the Archbuilders, whose bodies consist of "flesh and fur and shell and frond," are so strange that the children are afraid of them at first, with Pella experiencing their initial sight as "a physical thing," a shock against which she has to brace herself (61, 62). But the Archbuilders are Other in a number of ways: they are hermaphrodites, a biological fact that likely contributes to making them "perverts" in Efram's eyes, but, contrary to Efram's fearmongering, they are characterized as peaceful and trusting, with, moreover, no obvious interest in any sexual activity. The only thing the Archbuilders seem truly passionate about is language. It is reported that each Archbuilder speaks hundreds of languages native to the planet, all infinitely more complex than English, a language that fascinates them because its words are so imprecise and overloaded with meaning.

It is particularly through the linguistic excess of their speech and names that the Archbuilders engage with the traditional images of somber, quiet, howling, or grunting Indians. In a dual move of parodying ludicrous names given to Indians in the western and showing the Archbuilders' quaint humor and obsession with the poetic potential of the English language, they give themselves English names such as Lonely Dumptruck or Gelatinous Stand. This is one of the ways in which *Girl in Landscape* aligns itself with revisionist or post-western interventions in the genre. Building on the concept of a minor literature developed by Deleuze and Guattari, Neil Campbell describes these as follows: "The established and taken for granted 'major language' and codes of the Western genre are made to 'stammer' in these renewed forms, drawing attention to its mythic constructs and to new thematics within the texts–'Conquer the major language in order to delineate in it as yet unknown minor languages.'" The poetic subversiveness and quaint eloquence of the Archbuilders' language use, both of them attributes not usually associated with stereotypes of Native Americans in the western, likewise introduce the Archbuilders as outsiders speaking in a "minor language" that makes the genre stammer.[42]

In a conversation with Lethem, Michael Silverblatt has described this as a recurring strategy in Lethem's work. Lethem employs characters like the Archbuilders or Lionel Essrog in *Motherless Brooklyn* (1999) who "take on this funny secondary language; almost as if in order to move forward in their dilemmas, your heroes have to work in a language different from the one spoken that obscures rather than reveals meaning"—a notion to which Lethem agrees, noting that "I'd created a series of excuses, essentially for Joycean wordplay, and it was always a marginalized character or characters who were allowed to thrive as a subculture in my earlier novels."[43] This notion of a marginalized voice speaking against a dominant language also extends to Lethem's use of genre. As a writer of science fiction in his early works, he speaks to a mainstream audience; as a mainstream writer, he draws on the aesthetic and tool kit of the genre fiction he came of age with as a reader and a writer, a transgressive inbetweenness, which in *Girl in Landscape* makes the western genre stammer.

It is in this vein of conquering the major language of the western and the Indians' role in it that, in a world of adults who seem strange, menacing, invasive, distant, weak, untrustworthy, or incompetent, the only truly insightful conversation Pella has is with the Archbuilder Hiding Kneel. The talk, which immediately precedes the novel's showdown in which Pella rescues Hiding Kneel, is crucial for Pella's completion of her coming-of-age process. Despite the Archbuilders' social awkwardness, which manifests in their obliviousness to insults and social etiquette, Hiding Kneel helps Pella to come to terms with her grief by taking the girl seriously and putting its finger on her emotional wounds. It is this emotional confrontation that allows her to complete her mourning for her parents, for Caitlin's literal death and Clement's symbolic one. The sharing of emotions through speech in this scene is a reversal of the western's usual mode of operation as an "antilanguage," as well as of the trope of the white man and the man of color running from women, emotions, and civilization that Leslie Fiedler has identified as central to American literature and the western.[44] When she tells the Archbuilder about her mother and her disappointment with Clement, the Archbuilder remarks, "You too are concerned with the superiority of your lost ancestors," and then forces Pella to admit that she hates Clement not only for his passivity but for the fact that he survived while her mother did not. This outburst leads Hiding Kneel to observe, "The elegance of the explanation is that it encompasses also why you are so angry at yourself" (240–41).

Races, Genders, and True Community

Toward the end of the novel Pella overcomes her attraction to Efram and his brand of masculinity and reconciles herself with the loss of her parents. This coming-to-terms allows her to bully Morris into confronting Efram alongside her and thereby leads to Efram's death, a necessary step to ending the violent command of his destructive and racist frontier masculinity. In the novel's final section, Pella finds a new role as the nexus of a small community of abandoned children (Pella, Morris, and her brother David), thus filling a place claimed in different versions by both Efram and Clement throughout the story. This chosen community could be the seedling for an actual community whose absence Pella remarked on throughout the novel. Furthermore, Pella's identity offers a feminine counterpoint to Efram's destructive and Clement's ineffectual masculinities and thereby closes the circle, bringing back visions of the only true unit we see: that of the Marsh children around Caitlin's unifying presence in the novel's first section. Evading the trap of offering an essentialist utopia of the return of a nurturing mother, however, the novel insists on Pella's difference and the absence of easy solutions. When her brother David starts to cry, Pella refuses to console him, thinking instead, "Let David mother himself. Let him learn" (280). Instead, Pella's role is, at least in part, that of a masculine protector, on the guard against Doug Grant, who, after killing Efram, roams the desert, waiting to become the next Efram.

In this fashion, the novel makes clear that Pella transcends the binaries of female (nurturing mother) and male (violent frontiersman) that the western traditionally sets up and is therefore better prepared to become leader of her small quasi-community than any of the other characters. The confrontations with Efram and the planet have irrevocably changed Pella: "There was something hard about her. Or worse than hard. Efram had made her, made her know herself, how far she'd traveled" (280). It is exactly this transformation, however, this combination of Caitlin and Efram in Pella, that will make her able to confront her counterpart, Doug Grant, who has been shaped only by Efram, without a feminine foundation. This is reflected in the novel's final lines: "She knew Doug Grant was the same [as Efram]. He'll come back, she thought. He'll grow up and come back, the new Efram. The one who doesn't fit in town. The one she killed was still alive in him. That was who she would wait for" (280).[45]

The novel thus ends with a sense of danger, but, in contrast to her initial passivity in the face of Efram's overbearing masculinity, Pella now feels able to confront this danger. Nevertheless, *Girl in Landscape* leaves it open whether this second confrontation will eradicate the type of masculinity that Efram and Doug embody, "an aggrieved hostility that made him distant, unreachable" (148), or if it is in fact an essential part of life in Lethem's narrative universe that will simply be transferred to the next person. Still, there is a hopeful note after Efram's death. Pella rallies David and Morris around her, and they repeat the only activity that ever constituted a real temporary human community on the planet: baking bread, a skill they learned from Ellen Kincaid.

While this gendered reversal, which installs Pella in place of the patriarch Efram and the failed would-be leader Clement, is a central part of the novel, its racial reversal is equally noteworthy. It once again connects the two aspects of race and gender in a new way. Not only are the Archbuilders much more present in the final part—in an act of poetic irony, occupying Efram's house—it is obvious that Pella regards them as part of the community and the humans' previous inability to truly engage the Archbuilders on their own terms as a failing: "Maybe now they would meet them. Maybe now the Archbuilders would buy the bread" (279). As feebly optimistic as the notion of buying bread seems, baking is as noted a sign of true community.

Furthermore, there are other markers that the new community will be different and less segregated. Pella and some of the other children are, through their out-of-body experiences, connected to the Archbuilders in a way the other settlers, who took pills against the Archbuilder virus, were not. While this depiction of the connection between Pella and the other children and the land and Archbuilders carries overtones of settler colonialist fantasies, it also provides Lethem with a chance to lay out a vision of a more egalitarian, trans-species community. As James Peacock argues, "The opportunity [these experiences] afford for her to 'cross the line' is essential to her coming of age: not only do they allow her to witness several key clandestine events, they also force her to experience and accept the otherness which is integral to true community."[46] Ultimately the landscape, and Pella's interaction with and interpretation of it, represent "a chance to reassemble the scattered fragments of memory in the establishment of a new community": the town she eventually names after her lost mother, Caitlin.[47] This symbolic claim through naming is a complex act that seems natural in that, for Pella, the planet was always Caitlin's vision more than that of any of the other family members. It was she who told the children about the planet and kindled their curiosity and enthusiasm. It was also Caitlin who appeared in the landscape more than any other character; having prepared the children for their encounter with it, she provides the original interpretation of the planet. Furthermore, when Pella wandered over it after first arriving on the planet, Caitlin's "voice hung over the landscape," leading Pella to tell herself, "Caitlin is here" (48, 49). By symbolically transplanting her mother's presence into the community as a kind of guardian spirit, Pella transforms her mourning process from a vaguely meandering abstraction that haunts her in the landscape to a concrete remembrance and relocates the ghost of her lost mother from the solitude of the wilderness to the community she builds. It is with this community building in mind, after all, that Pella also hopes to draw her lost brother Raymond from his hiding place in the desert.

Notions of symbolic appropriation through naming and the taking and redefinition of a land in which she is ultimately an invader come to mind when we read this act in terms of Indian politics. Yet, as Peacock insists, the transformation of the land is centrally linked to Pella's experience of alterity, which lies at the bottom of the fusion of girl and landscape and, as noted, complicates the western's more traditional settler colonial link between the masculine hero and the land that leaves no space for compromise, inbetweenness, or a nonvanishing indigenous presence. Peacock writes, "For Pella to become a 'feature of the landscape' and thereby complete her mourning for Caitlin, she must embrace the Archbuilders' place in that landscape and accept them as part of the mourning process and, indeed, as a part of her that she can never hope fully to understand."[48] It is in this complex fusion that Lethem's genre bending manages to bring together, if not entirely reconcile the sci-fi western with its opposite poles of male and female, human and nonhuman (its version of the white and Indian dichotomy in the non–weird western) and the challenges of overcoming mourning and stepping from childhood into adulthood. There remain contradictions that cannot be entirely sublated, to be sure: humans and Archbuilders will never understand each other fully, for instance, as the Archbuilders' peculiar language and their indifference to insults and Efram's insistence that he knows Archbuilders, which leads to the most blatant misinterpretations and violent crimes, have made clear throughout the novel.

In retrospect, Lethem himself has been skeptical of the scope of the accomplishments of his weird western intervention: "*The Searchers* is too gristly to be digested in my novel, too willful to be bounded in my theories. I watch or don't it doesn't matter: *The Searchers* strides on, maddened, through broken landscapes incapable of containing it—Ford's oeuvre, and Wayne's, the 'Studio-Era Film,' and my own defeated imagination—everywhere shrugging off categories, refusing the petitions of embarrassment and taste, defying explanation or defense as only great art or great abomination ever could."[49] As I have tried to elaborate, the novel and its fantastic solutions to problems of the gendered and racialized overdetermination of the symbolic landscape of the past and present American West and its indigenous inhabitants still tremble against the powers of genre, in some places inadvertently reproducing, in a different fashion, the ambiguous power that Lethem attests to *The Searchers* and its mesmerizing blend of white masculinity, racism, and violence. By extension, then, Lethem's Archbuilders do not unmake Ford's and the western's Comanche, according to the author. But perhaps Lethem is too pessimistic and his novel does in fact not have to bear the full weight its author puts on it. After all, the fact that his fellow students, whom he tried to convince of the greatness of *The Searchers*, were not willing to accept the film and its depiction of Indians on its terms, as Lethem describes in his essay, suggests the diminishing power of some of the classic western's more troubling aspects. In spite of the current political climate, one can hope for a revised, more differentiated image of lone, violent white men, xenophobia, and the United States' settler colonial past and present. As my reading suggests, however, there is still a ways to go. For, while blatant racism and misogyny are easily spotted and rejected, gendered and racialized hierarchies and frames of perception have a way of inscribing themselves into our visions and conventions, and *Girl in Landscape*, despite its author's best intentions and in much slighter ways, still bears some of the troubling marks of the discourses it critically engages.

NOTES

I would like to thank Rosa Nowag, Rebecca Lush, and Emily Shelton for their corrections and suggestions, as well as Aynur Erdogan and Ruxandra Teodorescu for help in accessing some of the articles cited in this chapter.

1. Lethem, "Defending *The Searchers*."
2. Stein, "Jonathan Lethem," 232.
3. Stein, "Jonathan Lethem," 232.
4. Maltby, "Better Sense of History," 37.
5. See Eckstein, "Introduction," 3, and "Incest"; and Roth, "'Yes, My Darling Daughter,'" 68.
6. Connell, *Masculinities*.
7. Lethem, "Darkest Side."
8. I have explored the related question of the tension between revisionist writing, genre conventions, and the larger social frameworks that guides our interpretations in a discussion of two Canadian attempts to more straightforwardly rework the western by replacing the hero with a heroine elsewhere. Fehrle, "'If I get an outfit.'" A more extensive study on revisions in American and Canadian western novels is forthcoming: see Fehrle, *Postmodern Gunslingers*.
9. While I discuss how Lethem's depiction of the Archbuilders and their planet evokes the conventions and stereotypes about the United States and its indigenous inhabitants, such as the trope of the noble savage, the novelist's choice to invent an extraterrestrial race in his attempt to avoid the pitfalls of depicting actual Native Americans could be examined further. I point the interested reader to Meredith Harvey's chapter on Joss Whedon's *Firefly* in this volume.
10. James Peacock reads the novel as an "obviously heartfelt autobiographical work" about Brooklyn and the loss of a mother (Peacock, *Jonathan Lethem*, 75). See also Luter, *Understanding Jonathan Lethem*, 6–7.
11. Slotkin, *Regeneration through Violence*; Bold, *Frontier Club*; Moos, *Outside America*.
12. Vidal, "Theodore Roosevelt." See also Bold, *Frontier Club*.
13. Lethem, *Girl in Landscape*, 12. Further references will be given parenthetically.
14. Lethem, "Darkest Side."
15. In this way Efram's speech—like his physical presence—recalls not only Ethan Edwards, but other classic westerners, whose "laconic put-downs cut people off at the knees," establishing order rather than the exchange of emotions or ideas, and thus stand in opposition to a form of communication that is gendered as female in the western; Tompkins, *West*, 51.

In *Girl in Landscape* it also crucially stands in opposition to Clement, whose former authority depended on his skill at using speeches to rally up emotions rather than doing things himself.

16. Gaffney, "Jonathan Lethem," 50.
17. Quoted in Roth, "'Yes, My Darling Daughter,'" 65.
18. Tompkins, *West of Everything*, especially 5–6 and 69–87.
19. Bandy and Stoehr, *Ride, Boldly Ride*, 185.
20. Kolodny, *Lay of the Land*, 4.
21. Peacock, *Jonathan Lethem*, 79.
22. Kolodny, *Lay of the Land*, 6.
23. Wolfe, "Settler Colonialism and the Elimination of the Native," 395–97.
24. Wolfe, "Settler Colonialism and the Elimination of the Native," 389.
25. See also Fee's observation: "The simultaneous marginality and ubiquity of the Native people in our literature can be explained to some extent, then, by our desire to naturalize our appropriation of their land. It also explains a general lack of interest in Native culture or history: we want to *be* them, not to understand them. But Romanticism supplies us with a further explanation: the Indian stands for a dispossession larger than his own" ("Romantic Nationalism," 24; emphasis in original). Although Fee writes about English Canadian literature, there are more similarities than differences between English Canadian and American depictions of Native Americans and First Nations people. See also Philip Deloria, *Playing Indian*.
26. Kolodny, *Lay of the Land*, 9.
27. Stein, "Jonathan Lethem," 233.
28. Tom Grayson Colonnese offers an interesting perspective on this debate in an essay about watching *The Searchers* with some of his Native American colleagues. While noting that Louis Owens called the film "the best Indian movie ever made," Colonnese and his colleagues reach a more ambiguous conclusion, seeing it as "engaging because it goes further than any other western of its day in the direction of truth and fairness; but finally . . . frustrating to us because it stops well short of being truly fair" ("Native American Reactions," 335, 342).
29. Stein, "Jonathan Lethem," 233.
30. Eckstein, "Incest and Miscegenation," 197–98.
31. Abbott, *Frontiers Past and Future*, 99.

32. Wolfe, "Settler Colonialism."
33. Stein, "Jonathan Lethem," 233; quoted above.
34. Freud, *Interpretation of Dreams*, 282–83.
35. Eckstein "Darkening Ethan," 3; see also Buscombe, *The Searchers*, 21; and Gallagher, "Angels Gambol," 272–73.
36. Kovel, *White Racism*, 67, cited in Roth, "'Yes, My Darling Daughter,'" 68. While there is much to be said for the psychosexual component of racism (see, e.g., Hodes's more historical "Sexualization of Reconstruction Politics"), and it works well for a reading of both *The Searchers* and its weird western revision *Girl in Landscape*, this view—based on psychoanalytic research from the 1960s—seems to overstate its case a bit, ignoring other elements such as economic factors.
37. Abbott, "Homesteading on the Extraterrestrial Frontier," 257.
38. Peacock, *Jonathan Lethem*, 89.
39. Graham, *Representations of the Post/Human*, 11–16.
40. Warshow, "Movie Chronicle," 37.
41. Berkhofer, *White Man's Indian*. In line with Lethem's attempts to avoid depicting any historical tribes, race and ethnicity likewise are largely bypassed. All characters, except Wa, whose name and speech patterns suggest that he is not a native speaker of English but an Asian immigrant, seem to be Caucasian Americans, and ethnicity within the human community does not play a role. Rather, the western's pattern of whites vs. Indians is transformed into one of humans vs. Archbuilders.
42. Campbell, *Rhizomatic West*, 151.
43. Clarke, *Conversations with Jonathan Lethem*, 27.
44. Tompkins, *West of Everything*, 50; Fiedler, *Love and Death in the American Novel*.
45. It is worth noting that it was, in fact, Doug himself who shot Efram, yet Pella and the novel attribute Efram's death to Pella. It is thereby made clear that, whereas Doug may have pulled the trigger, resisting and defeating Efram—the real heroic acts—are Pella's accomplishments.
46. Peacock, *Jonathan Lethem*, 86–87.
47. Peacock, *Jonathan Lethem*, 85.
48. Peacock, *Jonathan Lethem*, 87.
49. Lethem, "Defending *The Searchers*," 13–14.

BIBLIOGRAPHY

Abbott, Carl. *Frontiers Past and Future: Science Fiction and the American West.* Lawrence: University Press of Kansas, 2006.

———. "Homesteading on the Extraterrestrial Frontier." *Science Fiction Studies* 32, no. 2 (July 2005): 240–64.

Bandy, Mary Lea, and Kevin Stoehr. *Ride, Boldly Ride: The Evolution of the American Western.* Berkeley: University of California Press, 2012.

Berkhofer, Robert F., Jr. *The White Man's Indian: Images of the American Indian from Columbus to the Present.* New York: Knopf, 1978.

Bold, Christine. *The Frontier Club: Popular Westerns and Cultural Power.* Oxford: Oxford University Press, 2013.

Buscombe, Edward. *The Searchers.* London: British Film Institute, 2000.

Campbell, Neil. *The Rhizomatic West: Representing the American West in a Transnational, Global, Media Age.* Lincoln: University of Nebraska Press, 2008.

Clarke, Jaime, ed. *Conversations with Jonathan Lethem.* Jackson: University of Mississippi Press, 2011.

Colonnese, Tom Grayson. "Native American Reactions to *The Searchers*." In *The Searchers: Essays and Reflections on John Ford's Classic Western,* edited by Arthur M. Eckstein and Peter Lehman, 335–42. Detroit: Wayne State University Press, 2004.

Connell, R. W. *Maculinities.* 2nd ed. Berkeley: University of Califonia Press, 2005.

Deloria, Philip J. *Playing Indian.* New Haven CT: Yale University Press, 1999.

Eckstein, Arthur M. "Darkening Ethan: John Ford's *The Searchers* from Novel to Screenplay to Screen." *Cinema Journal* 38, no. 1 (Autumn 1998): 3–24.

———. "Incest and Miscegenation in *The Searchers* and *The Unforgiven* (1959)." In The Searchers: *Essays and Reflections on John Ford's Classic Western,* edited by Arthur M. Eckstein and Peter Lehman, 197–221. Detroit: Wayne State University Press, 2004.

———. "Introduction: Main Critical Issues in *The Searchers.*" In The Searchers: *Essays and Reflections on John Ford's Classic Western,* edited by Arthur M. Eckstein and Peter Lehman, 1–45. Detroit: Wayne State University Press, 2004.

Fee, Margery. "Romantic Nationalism and the Image of Native People in Contemporary English-Canadian Literature." In *The Native in Literature,* edited by Thomas King, Cheryl Calver, and Helen Hoy, 15–33. Oakville ON: ECW, 1987.

Fehrle, Johannes. "'If I get an outfit can I be cowboy, too': Female Cowboys in the Canadian Revisionist Western." In *Proceedings / Anglistentag 2017 Regensburg*, edited by Anne-Julia Zwierlein et al., 211–19. Trier: Wissenschaftlicher Verlag Trier, 2018.

———. *Postmodern Gunslingers in a Transnational West: Revisions of the Western in Canadian and American Literature*. Forthcoming.

Fiedler, Leslie. *Love and Death in the American Novel*. New York: Stein & Day, 1966.

Ford, John, dir. *The Searchers*. Warner Bros., 1956.

Freud, Sigmund. *The Interpretation of Dreams: The Complete and Definitive Text*. Edited and translated by James Strachey. New York: Basic Books, 2010.

Gaffney, Elizabeth. "Jonathan Lethem: Breaking the Barriers between Genres." *Publishers Weekly*, March 30, 1998, 50–51.

Gallagher, Tag. "Angels Gambol Where They Will: John Ford's Indians." In *The Western Reader*, edited by Jim Kitses and Gregg Rickman, 269–76. New York: Limelight, 1998.

Graham, Elaine L. *Representations of the Post/Human: Monsters, Aliens, and Others in Popular Culture*. New Brunswick NJ: Rutgers University Press, 2002.

Hodes, Martha. "The Sexualization of Reconstruction Politics: White Women and Black Men in the South after the Civil War." *Journal of the History of Sexuality* 3, no. 3 (January 1993): 402–17.

Jackson, Shirley. *Hangsaman*. London: Penguin, [1951] 2013.

Kolodny, Annette. *The Lay of the Land: Metaphor as Experience and History in American Life and Letters*. Chapel Hill: University of Carolina Press, 1975.

Kovel, Joel. *White Racism: A Psychohistory*. New York: Pantheon, 1970.

Lethem, Jonathan. "The Darkest Side of John Wayne." Salon, August 12, 1997, https://www.salon.com/1997/08/11/wayne/> (accessed August 25, 2017).

———. "Defending *The Searchers* (Scenes in the Life of an Obsession)." In *The Disappointment Artist and Other Essays*, 1–14. New York: Doubleday, 2005.

———. *Girl in Landscape*. New York: Doubleday, 1998.

Luter, Matthew. *Understanding Jonathan Lethem*. Columbia: University of South Carolina Press, 2015.

Maltby, Richard. "A Better Sense of History: John Ford and the Indians." In *The Book of Westerns*, edited by Ian Cameron and Douglas Pye, 34–49. New York: Continuum, 1996.

Moos, Dan. *Outside America: Race, Ethnicity, and the Role of the American West in National Belonging*. Hanover NH: Dartmouth College Press, 2005.

Nabokov, Vladimir. *Lolita*. Paris: Olympia, 1959.

Peacock, James. *Jonathan Lethem*. Manchester: Manchester University Press, 2012.

Portis, Charles. *True Grit*. 1968. New York: Signet, 1969.

Roth, Marty. "'Yes, My Darling Daughter': Gender, Miscegenation, and Generation in John Ford's *The Searchers*." *New Orleans Review* 18, no. 4 (Winter 1991): 65–73.

Slotkin, Richard. *Regeneration through Violence: The Mythology of the American Frontier 1600–1860*. Middletown CT: Wesleyan University Press, 1973.

Stein, Lorin. "Jonathan Lethem: The Art of Fiction No. 177." *Paris Review* 166 (Summer 2003): 218–51.

Tompkins, Jane. *West of Everything: The Inner Life of Westerns*. New York: Oxford University Press, 1992.

Vidal, Gore. "Theodore Roosevelt: An American Sissy." In *The Essential Gore Vidal*, edited by Fred Kaplan, 784–96. New York: Random House, 1999.

Warshow, Robert. "Movie Chronicle: The Westerner." In *Focus on the Western*, edited by Jack Nachbar, 45–56. Englewood Cliffs NJ: Prentice Hall, 1974.

Wolfe, Patrick. "Settler Colonialism and the Elimination of the Native." *Journal of Genocide Research* 8, no. 4 (December 2006): 387–409.

Shining the Light of Civilization 8

The Savage Other of the Frontier in *Firefly* and *Serenity*

MEREDITH HARVEY

Joss Whedon's science fiction series *Firefly* (2002) and the subsequent film *Serenity* (2005) are set in a distant future, but a surprisingly familiar distant future, one that features horses and wagon trains as often as it does space stations and vertical futuristic cities. The first aired episode of *Firefly*, "The Train Job," begins with a barroom brawl, which ends with the perpetrators of the brawl being thrown out of a holographic window into another familiar scene, the arid foothills associated with the American West and the Hollywood western, a space only distinguished from that familiar West by the shadow of three moons in the background.[1] The scene closes as the pilot of the spaceship Serenity draws open the airlock door and the outnumbered instigators all hop aboard. While the spaceship and hologram place us squarely in the science fiction genre, the barroom brawl, long dusters worn by the ship's Captain Mal Reynolds, and sawed-off shotgun of his first mate, Zoe, all place us within the western. As Lorna Jowett points out, "Joss Whedon's *Firefly* adopts a distinct Western iconography," but set in the outer space world of science fiction: "The combination of Western and science fiction in *Firefly* offers both a familiar past detached from its historical period and a recognizable future unsettled by anachronism."[2] It is this anachronism that allows the show to engage simultaneously with questions regarding the United States and imperial powers of the past, present, and future.

While the often arid frontier settings of the outer rim, or border planets, of *Firefly*'s world remind us of the western, so, too, does the frontier ethos that that setting represents, especially as such settings are juxtaposed against the futuristic Central Planets and Alliance ships. Though we do not see the Central Planets in "The Train Job," the sterile and technologically advanced environment of the Alliance ships contrasts with the disadvantaged and rustic mining town of Paradiso. This juxtaposition sets up one of the central conflicts of the show. As Michael K. Johnson points out, "The central conflict in *Firefly*, as is often the case of the Western, pits 'civilization' against 'savagery.'"[3] In Whedon's world, such civilization borders on its own type of savage self-interest. We see this when, after disclosing to Mal the town's desperate need for medicine, the sheriff of Paradiso explains that the Alliance regiment "let the medicine get swiped out from under their noses and then took off for their camp without so much as a whoopsie daisy."[4] For the crew of Serenity, the ambivalence regarding the encroaching power of the distant metropole stems from a desire to remain beyond the control implied by such problematically achieved civilization. As Captain Mal Reynolds states, those aboard Serenity include "them as feel the need to be free" and "never be under the heel of nobody ever again," particularly the heel of the Alliance.[5] The crew therefore spends much of their time exploring those spaces in between the corporate civilization of the Alliance and the savagery that exists in this new frontier.

The sentiment of distrust of an Alliance government reveals another connection to the show's western roots, as the show's protagonists are former members of the "losing side" of a civil war that pitted the Independents against the Alliance. Within such a context, the western iconography evokes connections to post–Civil War Confederate soldiers on the western frontier, yet Whedon deliberately inverts the role of slavery in this evocation. Beyond the protagonists' oft-cited desire for freedom, throughout the series and the film, Whedon's post–Civil War hero reveals his disgust with the Alliance's use of slavery to build up its civilization and empire—a barroom brawl in a later episode, "Shindig," is instigated by Mal's theft from a man that earned his money "with the sweat of his slave-tradin' brows." As Johnson points out, "The frequency of references to slavery indicates *Firefly*'s efforts to distance itself from the politics of earlier Southern Westerns even as it appropriates the romantic appeal of the Lost Cause."[6] While Whedon takes care to make such a distinction, slavery is not the focus of the show, but rather one bit of evidence that the Alliance is on the "wrong" side in this western hero's continued fight for freedom and independence, for civility earned through a slave trade can hardly deem itself aspirational. Such echoes of the Civil War in relationship to the western remind the viewer of those connections between U.S. development and its roots in slavery, and as such it opens up room for what Neil Campbell claims as the territory of the post-western, since the plotlines act to "interrogate the very ideological frameworks that had conjured it into being in the first place."[7]

One such ideology of the past that *Firefly* "interrogate[s]" is that of the role of racism in historical justifications of slavery, power distribution, and colonialization. While the crew of *Serenity* navigates between these scenic landscapes and thematic elements of both science fiction and the western, Whedon attempts throughout to align his racial politics more closely with the inclusionary politics seen most often in the former. As Johnson argues, "*Firefly*'s universe suggests that race—specifically, whether one's ancestry is Euro or African—and gender do not predetermine one's place in the civilization/savagery continuum. There are no African Americans in Firefly's world because there is no Africa and no America."[8] Despite these attempts on Whedon's behalf to accommodate the progressive politics of a multicultural present or future world, his invocation of a postracial society remains problematic. While Whedon refuses to romanticize the ethnocentric assumptions of the frontier, his avoidance of race actually hinders his ability to thoroughly engage in the legacy of the U.S. settler colonial past or contemporary imperialistic present. Moreover, his invocation of the western genre to critique the civilizing mission of the Alliance while "deracializing" its inhabitants in many ways reenacts the dismissal of the subaltern in the settler colonial narrative of the western imaginary and its contemporary inheritance, even while alluding to the indigenous "savage" of those same spaces.

Settler Colonialism of the Firefly 'Verse

Scholars of settler colonialism identify the United States as part of that colonial movement whose end mission consisted of occupation of foreign land, beneficial development of said land, establishment of permanent settlements, and perpetuation of this new civilization.[9] The post-Columbian Americas developed as a part of a larger European expansion of power and territory. When the United States became an independent nation, it continued the now Euro-American colonization of the frontiers of North America and thus took on a distinct colonial project that assumed permanent control of the land. In a special issue of *Western American Literature* on settler colonialism, Alex Trimble Young and Lorenzo Veracini discuss the importance of settler colonial critiques of western productions, explaining that while "western cultural production is [not] always the result of settler colonial ideology," it is "engaged with questions pertaining to it," and that "the problem of the West is in a crucial sense, the problem of settler colonialism."[10] In *Firefly* and *Serenity*, Whedon creates a fictional extension of the European and Euro-American conquest of the Americas and, as such, leaves room for critiques of what Sara Spurgeon speaks of as "the reality of invasion, conquest, and colonization that made possible the European settlement of the Americas."[11] We see this throughout Whedon's depiction of conquest and colonization, as well as the shows' evocation of the western genre itself, which encourages the audience to read such critiques as directed not just to the original sin of U.S. colonization, but to the ethos of colonization created in its wake.

Throughout the series, the audience learns that planets of the *Firefly* 'verse become settlements,[12] first through terraforming of the land, "a process taking decades, to support human life," and then through the settlement of populations.[13] The process of settler colonialism on the American frontier depended upon a similar process, as America's native habitats from east to west underwent change in order to sustain the European-style agriculture. Like the Alliance process of terraforming, which created "new Earths," the process of settlement of the frontier attempted to recreate environments similar to those of the "Old

World," Europe. While, for the Alliance, "the central planets formed the Alliance," in the settler colonial mission of the United States, the distant metropole controlled the western development from the eastern seaboard of their initial settlement. As the colonizing metropole, the Alliance occupies planets well beyond those established as part of the Central Planets. This expansion through the continual acquisition and modification of lands of the frontier clearly aligns the mission of the Alliance with that of the United States as a settler colonial state. We see the Alliance's role in this colonial structure in episode "The Train Job," as the soldiers' existence in Paradiso reflects both an occupation of and a role in the development of these outer rims. They perpetuate this mission as the "arm of the Alliance" reaches further out each year; however, unlike the U.S. role in perpetuating their civilization through western settlements, the outer rims of space extend in perpetuity. The context of space allows Whedon the platform on which to explore the inexhaustible desires of this type of settler colonial ideology. Both U.S. frontier development and the Alliance outer-rim development require the rhetoric of empty space, which needs to be improved upon before "settlement"; however, the science fiction of *Firefly*'s frontier reveals the potential when the settler colonial state, having expended the resources through the colonization of Earth, continues its hegemony to the *vacuum domicilium*.

Early on in the show's pilot episode, after nearly being caught in an illegal salvage mission by an Alliance ship, one Serenity crew member asks, "What the hell [the Alliance] doing this far out, anyhow?"[14] Another crew member playfully responds, "Shining the light of civilization." While this exchange informs us of the physically expansive reach of the Alliance, it also cues us to its control of cultural interpretations of civilization within these border spaces. The opening of *Serenity* highlights the significance of this theme, as an Alliance teacher explains that under the control of the Alliance "everyone can know the comfort and enlightenment of our civilization." Such assumptions regarding civilization justified parallel U.S. settler colonial acts upon the frontier, as the United States developed through a process of "creating enduring social and political institutions to normalize and perpetuate the settler project."[15] Within the American West, these attempts to develop a "civilized" nation included government-sanctioned development through Homesteading Acts, Mining Acts, and Land Grant Institutions, to name just a few programs. Such developments assumed that assimilation and acculturation in the dominant Anglo-American identity and culture was progress toward a greater civilization. Similarly, the Alliance assumes the positive impact of its civilization-building. In his discussion of both present and historical settler colonial ideology in the United States, Mahmood Mamdani critiques the "uncritical embrace of the settler experience [that] explains this blind spot in the American imagination."[16] Within the 'verse, this civilizing ideology of the Alliance stands in for that ideology of development on the American frontier, and through his equivocal treatment of this ideology, Whedon encourages a critical view of the assumptions of manifest destiny, American settler experience, and its contemporary inheritance.

Whedon's interrogation of this blind spot in the American imagination manifests throughout the series as well as the film, but never more so than in his depictions of the Reavers, cannibalistic savages that occupy the outermost frontier of the Alliance-controlled settler colonial project. In this capacity, the Reavers demonstrate the ways that *Firefly* develops as a neowestern, which "keeps alive the basic elements and clichés of the traditional Western while still allowing them room for modification."[17] The Reavers resemble clichéd depictions of Indians within traditional westerns, but their story becomes modified in order to present a counternarrative to the civilizing mission of the Alliance. Through these depictions of both the clichés and their modifications, *Firefly* and *Serenity* both echo and interrogate the development of the American West in relation to the indigenous presence. In the episode "Bushwhacked," we are introduced to the Reavers through a description reminiscent of the savage Indian of the western imaginary: "If they take the ship, they rape us to death, eat our flesh, and sew our skins into their clothing." The threat of violence in Whedon's frontier takes the familiar shape of rape, cannibalism, and removal of the skin;

each of these potential acts specifically reimagines the threat of the savage Indian in the mythology of the western frontier. Furthermore, such depictions are not accidental, as Whedon himself underscores the Reaver-as-savage in the DVD commentary of *Serenity*. As the Reavers' ships emerge from an ion cloud, Whedon describes his cinematic and thematic reasons for including the scene: he "needed the Indians to ride up over the hill and defeat the cavalry."

The resemblance between the Reavers and depictions of "savages" on the nineteenth-century western frontier have not escaped the notice of critics.[18] Whedon has indeed fallen under fire for this depiction of the Reavers as the "savage other," a step that takes very little imaginative effort given the show's and the film's westernness. In reference to his depiction of the Reavers within their western context, Whedon has said, "Every story needs a villain and in the old westerns, these were the Apaches"; however, Whedon has also defended his depiction of "metaphorical Indians" as intentionally "deracialized."[19] Much like his efforts to "deracialize" the question of slavery in relation to the Independents' Civil War, Whedon attempts to deracialize his Indians by portraying them through actors of varied ethnicities. While Agnes Curry acknowledges this stated effort to deracialize depictions of the Reavers, she reminds us that such depictions are still problematic given the "racial coding" of the Reavers.[20] When the audience finally sees the Reavers in the film, their long unkempt hair, facial mutilation as war paint, spears as weapons, and skins as clothing all reveal the physical evidence of racial coding, but Curry's primary argument relies on the premise that an audience enculturated with the western genre cannot divorce depictions of "raiding parties" from their indigenous predecessor, even in the context of outer space. She closes her argument with a telling statement about our ability to divorce "the mythic west" of old Hollywood westerns from the reality of racism that facilitated the settlement of the west: "The Western is not just another story form . . . whatever transmutations and ironic recastings, the Western continues to depend in a remarkably straightforward way on the continued abjection of a very specific group of people."[21] Such readings remind us that the rhetoric of the frontier cannot exist outside of the history of the settler colonial project on which it was founded, nor can it divorce itself from the inherent and explicit racism created to justify such settlement in the face of indigenous presence.

In contrast to Curry's interpretation of the Reavers, J. Douglas Rabb and J. Michael Richardson see the Reavers as presenting the metaphorical stereotypes only in order to dismantle them. While acknowledging the problematic depictions cited by Curry and others, Rabb and Richardson argue that the text intentionally posits the specific fear of the Reavers' cannibalism, lack of philosophical rooting, and status as subhuman, only to debunk such theories late in the film *Serenity*, when we find that the Reavers are not indigenous savages, but the product of an Alliance effort to control its settlers through advanced technology.[22] In the film, the crew watches an archived recording, in which an Alliance doctor explains the Reavers' genesis. The Alliance placed some thirty million settlers on the planet of Miranda, and, in an attempt to "weed out aggression," they pumped medicines into the terraformed "atmo." Too calm to breed, work, or even breathe, most died as a result; but the Alliance medications had the opposite effect on a small portion who became hyperaggressive—the Reavers. In relation to this genesis story, Rabb and Richardson argue that "if Whedon's Reavers are Redskins, then the origin of the Reavers is Whedon's metaphor for the creation of the savage in the imagination of European settlers."[23] Similarly, other critics have offered up the origin story of the Reavers as a critique not of the savages, but the colonial presence.[24] Either interpretation highlights the paradox of the settler colonial project, which relies upon a mythology to dehumanize the savage other in order to justify their settlement of an open frontier that denies the others' existence. In this way Whedon's depiction of the Reavers as Indians interrogates the uncritical acceptance of the settler colonial experience and thus interrogates the frontier ideology upon which his show is built.

Such divergent readings of the Reavers in *Firefly* and *Serenity* reflect a problematic aspect of many post-westerns: "The term post-Western [can] be seen as 'a process of disengagement' from the system it is in tension with (the Westerns of the past)," but from which it is "probably inescapable" as it "interacts, overlaps, and interrelates in complex dialogical ways."[25] Within *Firefly*, attempts to deconstruct the frontier mythology often fall victim to reinforcement of that same mythology. Such a problem presents itself when we examine the question of indigeneity in settler colonial critiques of the Reavers. Susan Mandala states that "*Firefly* can only with difficulty be considered a post-colonial text," and equally valid readings that situate the Reavers in the context of a settler colonial or post-western paradigm struggle to address the relationship between indigenous presence and identity.[26] In defining the settler colonial project, Veracini reminds us that "while the colonies settlers build for themselves are either independent or politically subordinate to the colonising metropole, a capacity to establish a new society that replicates the original ... is inevitably premised on the possibility of controlling and dominating *indigenous peoples*. As the possibility of encountering a genuinely empty locale has been historically quite rare, building settler colonies and the exercise of colonial domination, while different, should be seen as inescapably intertwined."[27] Despite the futuristic space context that allows for that "genuinely empty locale" in which to look at larger questions of imperialism, the depiction of the border planets as western seems to insist that we look at the Reavers in light of that historical legacy of U.S. colonialism—which began with the displacement of *indigenous peoples*. Whedon's conscious avoidance of exploring the alien other within the show, despite the existence of the Reavers as metaphorical "Indians" in his space western, implies an elision of postcolonial relationships due to the absence of indigeneity.

Long before *Firefly*, *Star Trek* (1966) explored a different frontier, and, as S. Andrew Granade points out, its exploration of contact zones "viewed their universe from the powerful center."[28] This point of view assumed the benefits brought to the frontier from the federation-as-metropole, as the occupants of the ss *Enterprise* encountered various indigenous populations on that frontier. In contrast, through the *Firefly* 'verse Whedon engages this same paradigm in order to dismantle colonial assumptions, but consciously avoids the inclusion of indigenous aliens. According to Jane Espenson, the decision to not have an indigenous alien presence within the *Firefly* universe was intentional, because "Joss [Whedon] wanted to say something clear and honest about human nature, without bringing different hard-wired psychology and physiologies into it."[29] While the show interrogates the hegemon through the depiction of Reaver as a created savage on the frontier, this paradigm fails to fully address the rationale or motivations behind such mythmaking. In looking at settler colonial implications of *Firefly* and *Serenity* as they relate to the historical metaphor of the Reaver as Indian, we focus on the hypocrisy of settler colonial action, but fail to acknowledge racial justification for those actions. When we view Whedon's text as commentary on this pivotal moment in U.S. history, this commentary disrupts frontier ideologies in the parallels drawn between the Alliance and the United States as a colonizing force, but fails to interrogate the role that the othering of indigenous peoples played in those ideologies.

This failure of the show to fully address the role played by race in creating the subaltern, despite an engagement with the settler colonial problem, seems especially notable given the significant role that racial othering played in the subordination of indigenous peoples. As Nishant Upadhyay explains, "'Race' comes to be constituted in the Americas through the relation of white-European self to its racial other—the Indian. When contemporary theorizations of racial formations forget and deracialize the indigenous body, they distort the racial logics and taxonomies at play in North America. Indigeneity is intrinsic to understanding race and racism."[30] European and later U.S. claims to land in the Americas were justified through these types of assumption of the cultural and racial superiority of the Euro-American settlers, and historical policies regarding miscegenation as a tool to both disenfranchise and civilize indigenous peoples reveals these assumptions.[31] In this way, the social construction of race played a key role in the establishing of power dynamics on the frontier. As Patrick Wolfe points out, "Race is but one of various regimes of difference that have served to distinguish dominant groups from groups whom they initially encountered in colonial contexts."[32] Through his depiction of the Reavers as the savage other of the western imaginary, Whedon succeeds in his critique of the colonial United States, but his omission of race and indigeneity in this critique reenacts the historical legacy of indigenous omission that his neowestern attempts to disrupt.

Firefly's and *Serenity*'s Wild West as Metaphor

Despite such limitations, taking up a view of Whedon's space western as a critique of a settler colonial ideology opens up additional lines of inquiry when looking at the contemporary context in which the series and film were produced. Scholars note that a distinction between settler studies and postcolonial studies lies in the continuation of the dominant culture's presence and continued control within the settler colonial model, but they also note the parallels between the projects' "ultimate complementarity within imperialism."[33] In this vein, scholars of the western such as Susan Kollin have acknowledged that the frontier myth of the West and the U.S. identity forged upon that myth have in many ways enabled other imperialistic U.S. action in the global present. Furthermore, *Firefly* and *Serenity*'s blending of the western with science fiction encourages such readings. In pointing out the connection between the western and the emergence of science fiction in the United States, Steve Shaviro writes that "globalization began to appear as a subject in American science fiction in the late nineteenth century.... The official closing of the frontier in 1890 necessitated the re-imagining of imperial goals. These might be located within the Earth ... or the grand narrative of American exploration and discovery could be extended into space."[34] When looking at the contemporary context of *Firefly* and *Serenity*, it is hard to dismiss the implications the frontier may hold as a prerequisite for contemporary U.S. imperialistic actions; however, in such interpretations of *Firefly* and *Serenity* the critique of the hegemon equally fails to address racism as a rhetorical key to the elimination of the subaltern.

As Jeffrey Bussolini notes, *Firefly*, released in 2002, in many ways engaged with global concerns brought forth in a post-9/11 context.

Bussolini largely looks at Whedon's commentary on U.S. imperialism through the show's interrogation of the mission of the Alliance, specifically the way in which "the perceived threat to democratic, civilized life in the Alliance justifies virtually any measure to protect it."[35] Looking at such critiques in the context of *Firefly*'s engagement with frontier ideologies allows us to explore the relationship between the settler colonial development of the United States and twenty-first-century U.S. imperialism. Kollin writes about the ways in which depictions of east and west on the U.S. frontier engage with contemporary global perceptions of East and West: "For scholars of the American West, it is often difficult to employ 'the West' as a geographical term referring to a U.S. setting without also calling forth the other, more expansive concept. As post-colonial critics would argue, however, this may be the point. The West as a region of the United States functions in the context of European expansion, as part of an ongoing transnational history of settler colonialism, and, like the other West, it encodes a powerful geopolitical vision."[36] Within *Firefly* and *Serenity*, that "geopolitical vision" of the Alliance excuses its seizure of land, economies, and human civilizations in the name of "improvements." Like the development of the American West, the global imperialism of the United States in the contemporary Middle East relies upon an assumption of the United States as a more civilized society. These two distinct moments in history reveal a settler colonial mentality that equates colonial action with improvement, as the hegemon forces U.S. values upon those colonized peoples. In this way, Whedon's use of the western genre clarifies twenty-first-century U.S. global imperialism as a continuation of settler colonial ideology within a new context, not as a novel product of contemporary global commerce.

The parallels between the frontier of the west, the frontier of the Iraqi and Afghani deserts portrayed in contemporary media, and the frontier of the outer-rim planets in the *Firefly* 'verse are clear. The environments consist largely of desert landscapes that symbolize the barren and uncivilized nature of the land. The three frontiers present contact zones: those of the native Americans and settlers, those of the U.S.

soldiers and the Eastern other, and those of the Alliance soldiers and the varied inhabitants of the outer rims. Kollin discusses the potential of Middle Eastern "westerns" as "a useful means of critically examining how the nation has been held captive to its own fears and anxieties, with the war on terror resulting not in more freedom but in greater restrictions and fewer liberties."[37] In a parallel way, *Firefly* and *Serenity* serve as useful tools through which Whedon can critique U.S. efforts to civilize the frontier through global imperialism, which has inherited the frontier rhetoric and anxieties of settler colonial identity. Whedon draws such connections through his use of the outer rims and border planets as contact zones feared by the Alliance due to its association with savagery and the unknown.

Within such a context, the westernness of the border planets and outer rims presents an opportunity to explore the connections between the historical spatial zone of violent colonial conflict on the frontier and the contemporary Eastern frontiers of a post-9/11 global reality. Spurgeon points to the civilizing mission as part of a dichotomy between the civil and the savage that links these two periods in American history: "The nineteenth-century narrative of the Anglo duty to defeat the savages and make the West safe for white civilization now becomes the American duty to defeat the savages and make the world safe for democracy."[38] In discussing memoirs of Iraqi soldiers, Kollin discusses the ways that frontier ideology informed the occupation: "Iraq is portrayed as Indian country, a comparison that uses familiar frontier rhetoric to make sense of the new enemy in the war on terror."[39] In this way, *Firefly* and *Serenity*'s presentation of Reaver territory as Indian country presents an opportunity to explore the role of a settler colonial ideology in fostering fears and anxieties of the subaltern in the contemporary United States and in justifying U.S. actions within the contact zones.

If we examine *Firefly* and *Serenity* as products of this period of U.S. global imperialistic actions—actions facilitated by the western myth—the depictions of the Reavers and planets of the outer rim provide a clear link between the U.S. frontier ideology and the continuum of colonizing endeavors. When we look at the historical construction of the "savage Indian" of the United States, the development of the mythology relied on mass-media depictions of uncivilized peoples; the testament to the power of this media message exists as popular perceptions of Native Americans that are both homogenizing and static have changed little in a hundred years.[40] Parallel use of media depictions incited fear of the distant and uncivilized other of the Middle East. Media scholar Mojan J. Dutta-Bergman notes the importance of post-9/11 media depictions of "uncivilized" Iraqi and Afghan people and how such depictions acted to increase anxieties about the other in an already fearful post-9/11 society; he also discusses the ways in which such depictions aided in the justification leading up to the March 2003 invasion of Iraq.[41] This evidence of a frontier ideology of U.S. exceptionalism and improvement utilized to justify global invasions reveals the scope of a settler colonial ideology that exceeds the boundaries of the U.S. landscape upon which it was founded. Through depictions of the Alliance's frontier ideology of exceptionalism and improvement that facilitates, among other things, the creation of the Reavers and the suppression of the story at all costs, Whedon indirectly comments on expansion of U.S. powers as the inheritance of a settler colonial ideology.

When looking at *Firefly* and *Serenity* through that lens, the Reavers once again inhabit the polar extreme of the uncivilized opposite to the Alliance's imposed order. Like those demonized Eastern others of the war on terror, the Reavers are seen as subhuman, possessing a violent (if any) ideology, as mythical bogeymen that function to remind people of their fortunate status in their own civilized world under Alliance rule. These depictions of the Reavers, like those of the Reavers as savage indigenous other, present commentary that simultaneously critiques and reinforces ethnic and cultural stereotypes of the other within this contemporary context. In contemporary representations, Eastern otherness is marked through religious difference, but it is also marked with the assumption of incivility that accompanies that difference. For instance, the tactics utilized by the Reavers are continually referred to as "suicidal," echoing the suicidal missions of the 9/11 terrorists as well as other suicide bombers, who have become a symbol for the illogical extremes of the Eastern other. The Reavers' violent nature marks them as other, but their suicidal approach to battle marks them as uncivilized to the extreme and encourages contemporary readers to see them as the terrorists of the Alliance-controlled outer rims. Additionally, the random nature of Reaver violence and innocence of their victims echo the random violence of the terrorist act. Such parallels, at least within the series, present the other stereotypically, justifying the fear of the other through depictions that reinforce the uncivilized subaltern of frontier ideologies.

Despite such problematic depictions, Whedon's Reavers reveal a distrust in the simple binary of good and evil that inhabit both the Alliance mythology and that of contemporary global U.S. policy. If we look at the Reavers as a representation of this newly imagined savage, the creation story again disrupts an ideology of an idealized progressive civilization. Spurgeon speaks to the ways that inhabitants of the frontier can present "mythic figures, reimagined by each new generation, altered and refigured in continuing attempts to understand both a colonial past and an imperial present in which the aftereffects of conquest, far from disappearing in, continue to cast long shadows over American culture and our interactions with the rest of the world."[42] In their parallels to both the savage indigenous and the contemporary Eastern other, the Reavers reveal those long shadows: as archetypal images of the savage that are reimagined in order to justify conquest.

Bussolini uses the term "blowback" to define the "unintended consequences of [U.S.] intelligence, military and diplomatic operations" and states that the "the story of the Reavers' creation also seems to contain a meditation of precisely this same phenomenon."[43] In his analysis he speaks of the Reavers' creation story as a critique of the misguided U.S. distribution of pharmaceuticals as well as U.S. "misguided foreign policy that set up Saddam Hussein and Al-Qaeda."[44] In looking at the Reavers as blowback, in relation to their connection to the subaltern, we see Whedon's strongest critique of the U.S. civilizing mission: the savage other does not exist *until* the Alliance acts upon its own assumption of the positivist approach to progress without acknowledging the potential for collateral damage. In this choice for the genesis of the Reavers, Whedon implies that the savage other is the creation of the settler colonial ideology. The Alliance creates the Reavers through its own efforts to enforce hypercivilization, and while official record of the Alliance simply ignores the creation and existence of the Reavers, the myth of the savage other justifies its imperial mission. In this way, a postcolonial reading critiques not just U.S. contemporary imperialistic endeavors, but the frontier ideology upon which they are built. The settler colonial ideology justifies expansion through the assumption of civility, but, in order to justify expansion, the settler colonial state must create a savage other, ignore the others' existence, or, paradoxically, do both—whether through media depictions or through acts of violent occupation.

This postcolonial interpretation of the Reavers as the savage Eastern other, like that of Reavers as the savage Native American other, presents us with insight into the relationship between the subaltern and a critique of the colonizing power, but it again presents shortcomings when we look at the significance of race and indigeneity as an integral part of the system of the settler colonial ideology and the inheritance of global imperial U.S. exceptionalism. While one might argue that globalization has created a world in which the Islamic terrorist as savage other has transcended place and race (as *Firefly* and *Serenity* space seems to imply about the Reavers), the fact remains that within antiterror discourse, the other is associated with a specific Middle Eastern geography and physiognomy. In light of this, the parallels between the Reavers and post-911 terrorists create a familiar savage other, but once again the nonethnicity of that other, while seemingly progressive, ignores the important relationship between race and othering in the global imperial present. In viewing the series and the film as critique of the postcolonial continuum, *Firefly* and *Serenity* may reflect connections between a settler colonial past and a global imperial present, but they do so in a way that repeatedly fails to acknowledge the significance of racial construction as part of the historical arch of U.S. imperialistic endeavors.

The Deracialized Future of Settler Colonial Ideology

Do we just ignore this question of indigeneity and the deracialized construction of the Reavers, then, and look to the way that the show does address settler colonial history and the related U.S. imperialistic present? It is clear from his commentary in multiple contexts that Whedon himself sees this deracialized society as part of the progression of a globalized future, and thus he dismisses the race question in relation to the Reavers as insignificant within his imagined future. Other critics have viewed his failure to engage this question as further evidence of his problematic depictions of race throughout his tenure in television and film.[45] But perhaps if we focus on the implications of this imagined deracialized future, instead of merely accepting its progressive politics, this approach can provide us yet another avenue through which we can explore settler colonial assumptions of the U.S. ideology, and the assumed continuum of this ideology in the imagined future.

While the western components of *Firefly* and *Serenity* grant us a lens through which we can clearly see the settler colonial past and the global imperial present, the science fiction component of the show presents us with one more opportunity to observe this continuum: we can see the future. Jessica Langer speaks to the ability of science fiction narratives to explore not just the frontier of space, but the frontier of the future, particularly in relation to current trends of globalization: "SF narratives can track the processes of globalization, all the way to their most dreadful and apocalyptic consequences. And SF can also provide counter-narratives, visions of an alternative globalization, precisely at the time when such imagining has become so difficult for us."[46] In the case of *Firefly*'s "alternative globalization," the Reavers operate at an allegorical level to present the continuity and eventuality of the United States as a settler colonial state. Science fiction and future context allow us to imagine one potential path humankind might follow, if the progression that began with the settlement of the United States and continued into the twenty-first-century reaches its inevitable and ultimate conclusion.

Sharon Sutherland and Sarah Swan see *Firefly* and *Serenity* as demonstrating traits of the increasingly popular genre of dystopian fiction, suggesting that the world that Whedon has created reflects current anxieties about government power, social injustice, and the conflict between individual rights and a safe society.[47] Through his engagement of the settler colonial paradigm in his critique of the Alliance as hegemon, he accomplishes this warning not just about government power, but about the ideological and historical frameworks that support it. But in these depictions, the greater dystopian feat accomplished by the series and film, however unintentional, may be this ambivalent treatment of indigeneity and the denial of racial significance, even as the text clearly haunts us with reminders of the subaltern and an indigenous presence through references to past and present colonial sins.

In *Firefly* and *Serenity*, this progressive future is indicated not only through spaceships and terraforming, but through this notion of the postracial and postindigenous future. Such a postracial future does indicate progress, but, when looked at from the settler colonial and postcolonial lens that the genre of the western encourages, it may indicate a more sinister progression. While we have established the ways that *Firefly* and *Serenity* do engage in important (and admittedly problematic) critiques of settler colonial and global imperialist structures, the absence of racial difference and indigeneity in these connections implies yet another possibility. As Veracini explains, "If there is a plot in . . . settler colonial studies it is that while the structure *attempts* to eliminate indigenous peoples, it *fails* to do so."[48] Despite Whedon's engagement with settler colonial concerns, the space context and the absence of indigenous peoples has in part avoided this question of indigenous elimination, but the hybrid globalized future depicted at the time of departure to space also implies that the "Earth that was" does not account for the importance of indigeneity to place, nor to ethnic difference. We can see this in Whedon's accommodation of Chinese language, music, and names, which have not necessarily increased the Chinese presence in the show.[49] Despite his Chinese name, Simon Tam, the doctor in the show, is clearly Caucasian and played by an actor of Irish-American decent. Identity in this future space has been long divorced from notions of race and any relationship to an indigenous region on the Earth that was. These renderings imply that indigenous connection to space is outdated, and that in space no ethnic group has an original claim. Whether this goal was accomplished before or after the mythical leaving of the Earth that was is unclear, but the society spawned from this has eliminated the concept of indigenous people, or people marked as ethnic. Whedon has created a world in which the global powers seem to have accomplished that settler colonial mission of elimination.

If the destruction of the indigenous other is one eventuality of the settler colonial state, another elusive goal of that state is for the settlers themselves to become the inheritors of native claims to the frontier: "What settlers ultimately desire [is] to have the land and to have it as an Indigenous person would; that is, to indigenize."[50] On Earth, this creates what Trimble Young and Veracini refer to as the paradox of this goal: "Being indigenous is predicated on always having been indigenous."[51] However, the future space context allows us to explore that possibility of becoming indigenous: the Reavers in fact evolve into being upon Miranda. This space has become their space: while the settlers of Miranda were from elsewhere, the Reavers have always and only been in the outer rims. In this way the settlers of Miranda represent the completion of the settler colonial project; they are the indigenous peoples of the outer rims of Reaver territory.

In *Orientalism*, Edward Said claims that "ideas, cultures, and histories cannot seriously be understood or studied without their force, or more precisely their configurations of power also being studied."[52] I would argue that the opposite is also true: we cannot fully understand configurations of U.S. power without full renderings of the cultures, histories, and ideas being studied. On this new frontier, Whedon creates a recognizable savage other that recalls historical and contemporary U.S. otherings. In doing so, he critiques the endurance of the United States as a settler colonial power as well as the inexhaustible nature of the frontier mythology in serving the evolution of that settler colonial mission. Despite these successful critiques of colonial power, in the end Whedon only appropriates the struggle of the subaltern to represent a more generalized discontented U.S. identity. In the process, he fails to address indigeneity or race in critical ways beyond familiar tropes and devices of the western imaginary, and in many ways he subscribes to the very power structure that he attempts to disrupt. This failure diminishes the power, accuracy, and adequacy of his critique, and in the end he assigns indigenous othering to the settler body. In so doing, he unintentionally imagines that completion of the settler colonial project.

In what Whedon calls the "most important line" at the conclusion of *Serenity*, we see Captain Mal Reynolds share the story of the Reavers' creation with all of the 'verse. As he puts the story out for all to see, he says to an Alliance operative: "I'll show you a world without sin." Through this broadcasting of the Reavers' genesis story, Mal disrupts cultural assumptions about the Alliance's exceptionalism: he critiques its greatest sin, that of colonial arrogance. Likewise, in the historical arch of post-Columbian colonization, the most arrogant of sins have been committed in the name of salvation for less civilized societies. In regard to this message, Whedon is clear. The Reavers are evidence of the Alliance's "sin" as a colonizing state, and Whedon succeeds in this critique of the dangers of power in an ever-expanding settler colonial ideology. However, in the end, Whedon fails to address race, ethnicity, and indigeneity in his renderings of the other and U.S. colonial sins—and, consequently, he disregards the story of the subaltern on his reimagined frontier.

NOTES

1. *Firefly*'s original two-hour pilot was not aired until the end of the show's brief eleven-episode television run. According to Whedon, the hastily written, action-packed, and one-hour episode "Train Job" replaced the original two-hour pilot "Serenity" at the Fox executive's request (*Firefly*, DVD commentary).
2. Jowett, "Back to the Future," 101.
3. Johnson, *Hoo-Doo Cowboys and Bronze Buckaroos*, 226.
4. Whedon, "Train Job."

5. Whedon, "Out of Gas."
6. Johnson, *Hoo-Doo Cowboys and Bronze Buckaroos*, 225.
7. Campbell, *Postwesterns*, 3.
8. Johnson, *Hoo-Doo Cowboys and Bronze Buckaroos*, 226.
9. Lynch, "'Nothing but land'"; Veracini, "Career of a Concept."
10. Trimble-Young and Veracini, "Settler Colonial Studies," 7.
11. Spurgeon, *Exploding the Western*, 4.
12. While within the show characters often use the term "'verse" in reference to their physical universe, this other usage refers to the entirety of Whedon's created world.
13. Whedon, "Serenity."
14. Here I'm discussing the two-hour pilot "Serenity" that was aired after the show had been canceled and as a finale to the half season run.
15. Lynch, "'Nothing but land,'" 377.
16. Mamdani, "Settler Colonialism," 15.
17. Jacobs as quoted in Campbell, *Postwesterns*, 7.
18. Two of the critiques that most apply here are from Curry's "'We don't say "Indian"'" and Money's "*Firefly*'s 'Out of Gas.'"
19. Quoted in Curry, "'We don't say "Indian."'"
20. Curry, "'We don't say "Indian."'"
21. Curry, "'We don't say "Indian."'"
22. Rabb and Richardson, "Reavers and Redskins."
23. Rabb and Richardson, "Reavers and Redskins," 135.
24. Bussolini, "Geopolitical Interpretation"; Wilcox and Cochran, *Investigating Firefly and* Serenity.
25. Campbell, *Postwesterns*, 9.
26. Mandala, "Chinese Code-Switching and *Firefly*," 37.
27. Veracini, "Career of a Concept," 314.
28. Granade, "Exoticism and Identification in *Firefly*," 630.
29. Espenson, *Finding Serenity*, 1.
30. Upadhyay, "Unsettling Violence, Race, and Colonialism," 265.
31. Smithers, "Race and the Meaning of Civilization"; Wolfe, "After the Frontier."
32. Wolfe, "Land, Labor, and Difference," 867.
33. Veracini, "Understanding Colonialism," 627.
34. Shaviro, "Towards an Alternative Globalization," 384.

35. Bussolini, "Geopolitical Interpretation," 150.
36. Kollin, *Captivating Westerns*, 23–24.
37. Kollin, *Captivating Westerns*, 4.
38. Spurgeon, *Exploding the Western*, 9–10.
39. Kollin, *Captivating Westerns*, 5.
40. Leavitt et al., "Impact of Native American Media Representations."
41. Dutta-Bergman, "Operation Iraqi Freedom."
42. Spurgeon, *Exploding the Western*, 12.
43. Bussolini, "A Geopolitical Interpretation," 135, 147.
44. Bussolini, "A Geopolitical Interpretation," 147.
45. Curry, "'We don't say "Indian"'"; Granade, "Exoticism and Identification in *Firefly*."
46. Langer, "Global Science Fiction as Cosmopolitan Mutant."
47. Sutherland and Swan, "Dystopia in Joss Whedon's *Firefly/Serenity*."
48. Veracini, "Defending Settler Colonial Studies," 311.
49. Granade, "Exoticism and Identification in *Firefly*."
50. Trimble-Young and Veracini, "Settler Colonial Studies," 11.
51. Trimble-Young and Veracini, "Settler Colonial Studies," 11.
52. Said, *Orientalism*, 5.

BIBLIOGRAPHY

Bussolini, Jeffrey. "A Geopolitical Interpretation of *Serenity*." In Wilcox and Cochran, eds., *Investigating* Firefly *and* Serenity, 139–53.

Campbell, Neil. *Post-Westerns: Cinema, Region, West*. Lincoln: University of Nebraska Press, 2013.

Curry, Agnes B. "'We don't say "Indian"': On the Paradoxical Construction of the Reavers." *Slayage* 7, no. 1, 2008: http://www.whedonstudies.tv/uploads/2/6/2/8/26288593/curry_slayage_7.1.pdf (accessed November 18, 2019).

Dutta-Bergman, Mohan J. "Operation Iraqi Freedom: Mediated Public Sphere as a Public Relations Tool." *Atlantic Journal of Communication* 13, no. 4 (2005): 220–41.

Espenson, Jane. *Finding Serenity: Anti-heroes, Lost Shepherds, and Space Hookers in Joss Whedon's* Firefly. Dallas: Benbella, 2004.

Granade, S. Andrew. "'So Here's Us, On the Raggedy Edge': Exoticism and Identification in Joss Whedon's *Firefly*." *Popular Music & Society* 34, no. 5 (2011): 621–37.

Johnson, Michael K. *Hoo-Doo Cowboys and Bronze Buckaroos: Conceptions of the African American West.* Jackson: University Press of Mississippi, 2014.

Jowett, Lorna. "Back to the Future: Retrofuturism, Cyberpunk, and Humanity in *Firefly* and *Serenity*." In Wilcox and Cochran, eds., *Investigating* Firefly *and* Serenity, 101–13.

Kollin, Susan. *Captivating Westerns: The Middle East in the American West.* Lincoln: University of Nebraska Press, 2015.

Langer, Jessica. "Global Science Fiction as Cosmopolitan Mutant." In "Proceedings from the Symposium on Science Fiction," special issue, *Science Fiction Studies* 39, no. 1 (November 2012): 374–84.

Leavitt, Peter A., Rebecca Covarrubias, Yvonne A. Perez, and Stephanie A. Fryberg. "'Frozen in Time': The Impact of Native American Media Representations on Identity and Self-Understanding." *Journal of Social Issues* 71, no. 1 (2015): 39–53.

Lynch, Tom. "'Nothing but land': Women's Narratives, Gardens, and the Settler-Colonial Imaginary in the U.S. West and Australian Outback." *Western American Literature* 48, no. 4 (Winter 2014): 375–99.

Mamdani, Mahmood. "Settler Colonialism: Then and Now." *Critical Inquiry* 41, no. 3 (Spring 2015): 596–614.

Mandala, Susan. "Representing the Future: Chinese and Codeswitching in *Firefly*." In Wilcox and Cochran, eds., *Investigating* Firefly *and* Serenity, 31–40.

Money, Mary Alice. "'Firefly's Out of Gas': Genre Echoes and the Hero's Journey." In Wilcox and Cochran, eds., *Investigating* Firefly *and* Serenity, 114–25.

Rabb, J. Douglas, and J. Michael Richardson. "Reavers and Redskins: Creating the Frontier Savage." In Wilcox and Cochran, eds., *Investigating* Firefly *and* Serenity: *Science Fiction on the Frontier*, 127–38.

Said, Edward, W. *Orientalism.* New York: Vintage, 1979.

Shaviro, Steve. *Towards an Alternative Globalization.* In "Proceedings from the Symposium on Science Fiction," special issue, *Science Fiction Studies* 39, no. 1 (November 2012): 374–84.

Smithers, Gregory D. "'The Pursuits of the Civilized Man': Race and the Meaning of Civilization in the United States and Australia, 1790s–1850s." *Journal of World History* 20, no. 2 (2009): 245–72.

Spurgeon, Sara. *Exploding the Western: Myths of Empire on the Postmodern Frontier.* College Station: Texas A&M University Press, 2005.

Sutherland, Sharon, and Sarah Swan. "'The Alliance Isn't Some Evil Empire': Dystopia in Joss Whedon's *Firefly/Serenity*." In Wilcox and Cochran, *Investigating* Firefly *and* Serenity, 89–100.

Trimble-Young, Alex, and Lorenzo Veracini. "'*If* I am native to anything': Settler Colonial Studies and Western American Literature." *Western American Literature* 52, no. 1 (Spring 2017): 1–23.

Upadhyay, Nishant. "Pernicious Continuities: Unsettling Violence, Race, and Colonialism." *Sikh Formations: Religion, Culture, Theory* 9, no. 2 (August 2013): 263–68.

Veracini, Lorenzo. "Defending Settler Colonial Studies." *Australian Historical Studies* 45, no. 3 (September 2014): 311–16.

———. "'Settler Colonialism': Career of a Concept." *Journal of Imperial & Commonwealth History* 41, no. 2 (June 2013): 313–33.

———. "Understanding Colonialism and Settler Colonialism as Distinct Formations." *Interventions* 16, no. 5 (2014): 615–33.

Whedon, Joss, creator. *Firefly*. Mutant Enemy in Association with Twentieth Century Fox Television, 2002.

———. *Firefly*. Season 1, episode 5, "Out of Gas." Aired October 25, 2002, on Fox.

———. *Firefly*. Season 1, episode 1, "The Train Job," Aired September 20, 2002, on Fox.

———. *Firefly*. Season 1, episode 11, "Serenity," Aired December 20, 2002, on Fox.

———. *Firefly*. Season 1, episode 6, "Serenity," Aired November 1, 2002, on Fox.

———. *Serenity*. Universal Studios Home Entertainment, 2005.

Wilcox, Rhonda V., and Tanya R. Cochran, eds. *Investigating* Firefly *and* Serenity: *Science Fiction on the Frontier*. New York: I. B. Taurus, 2008.

Wolfe, Patrick. "After the Frontier: Separation and Absorption in U.S. Indian Policy." *Settler Colonial Studies* 1, no. 1 (January 2011): 13–51.

———. "Land, Labor, and Difference: Elementary Structures of Race." *American Historical Review* 106, no. 3 (June 2001): 866–905.

Racial Metaphors and Vanishing *indians* 9 in *Wynonna Earp*, *Buffy the Vampire Slayer*, and Emma Bull's *Territory*

REBECCA M. LUSH

The subgenre of the weird western reimagines one of the most mythologized genres in American literature, frequently recalling or directly rewriting legends involving historical actors in the American West. Stories about Wyatt Earp and Doc Holliday in particular have been fodder for traditional westerns, revisionist westerns, and weird westerns, but the weird western texts from the past two decades that view Earp and Holliday in a multicultural context have shifted the focus from white American masculinity to questions of female agency and roles for racial minorities. Of note, the weird western comic book series "Wynonna Earp" by Beau Smith (1996–2004, 2016–present), the SyFy network adaptation series *Wynonna Earp* (2016–present), and the fantasy western novel *Territory* by Emma Bull (2007) decenter Wyatt Earp in favor of focusing on supporting characters who have traditionally occupied the role of sidekick—including female protagonists and law officers from minority groups. All three texts (Smith's "Wynonna Earp," SyFy's adaptation of the same text, and Bull's *Territory*) bring supernatural conflict to the forefront, and the inherently fantastic elements of the supernatural help to emphasize the western genre's role in American cultural mythmaking.

Despite overt western aesthetics and narrative conventions, all three contemporary weird westerns have a striking lack of specific and individuated American Indian characters. The closest the texts come is in

Bull's *Territory*, where vague reference is made to the Apache but usually in the context of the past and with no Apache characters present in the narrative action or described, outside being part of the backdrop of the Arizona Territory. Thus far, the closest the "Wynonna Earp" franchise has explicitly come is in the rebooted comic books that now include a thousand-year-old Mayan warrior woman, Valdez, who arguably represents Chicana inclusion, which the comics handle differently from their metaphorically designated American Indian characters of the older comic runs and the television series. Although no specific characters are identified as American Indian in the fantastical Earp texts explored in this chapter, each text deploys a metaphoric or even surrogate *indian* character that replicates frontier and western narrative conventions long reliant on a binary of Indian versus settler or cowboy or cavalry while reproducing indigenous erasure, since white-coded characters take up the function and mantle of "Indian."[1]

The fantastical Earp texts I will discuss establish multicultural and diverse western spaces that excel at redefining gender and sexuality and have many elements that can be read as feminist and inclusive. However, when considered from an intersectional point of view, all of the texts continue the settler colonialist racial dynamics seen in many westerns. Although these texts reproduce settler colonialist racial dynamics, it is open to interpretation whether their approach tacitly endorses settler colonialism, is naïve to its structure or presence in the narratives, reveals its limits, or some complex combination thereof. What is clear, however, is how otherwise socially progressive retellings of nineteenth-century American western folklore cannot yet envision a decolonized setting that centers ongoing indigenous presence—even with the introduction of Valdez, the Maya warrior woman in the IDW Earp comics, since she is a relic of the pre-Columbian past as opposed to a contemporary indigenous character.

Before embarking on a native-studies analysis of the fantastical Earp weird westerns, I will provide a theoretical and historical grounding in American traditions of metaphoric Indian-ness and current theorizing about contemporary indigenous presence and "red readings." Then I will move to providing a cursory overview and analysis of how each text explores racial, gender, and sexual diversity outside of native issues to establish the racial complexity (e.g., *Territory*'s attention to Chinese American presence in the West) and questions of agency raised in each before turning at last to a sustained analysis of the metaphoric explorations of Native American presence in each work. I also include a comparative analysis of how the weird western episode "Pangs" (4.8) from *Buffy the Vampire Slayer* shares structural approaches to the ways contemporary weird westerns attempt to critique colonialism and western expansion while also reproducing settler colonialist rhetoric.

Playing Indian in the Weird Western

The Earp-focused weird westerns I analyze in this chapter are some of the relatively recent examples of a long-standing literary and cultural reliance on what Philip J. Deloria terms "playing Indian." Deloria and Trachtenberg are just few of the scholars who have noted white Americans' penchant for performing what they consider to be Indian identities in service of expressing a uniquely U.S. American ethnic and national identity. Whether it's the racially white Natty Bumppo of James Fenimore Cooper's Leatherstocking Tales or upper-middle-class white children attending "Indian" summer camps at the turn of the previous century, white bodies wearing what they purport to be Indian fashions or participating in Indian activities have long been part of U.S. American culture, often at the expense of what Anishinaabe scholar Gerald Vizenor (White Earth Chippewa) calls the "tribal real."[2] The tradition of playing Indian even predates the formation of the United States with the Boston Tea Party performance by white colonists in 1773, which Deloria notes as a watershed moment of American identity formation. Furthermore, the performance and co-opting of native markers by white bodies even occurred in colonial metropoles, such as the racial cross-dressing imagined of young British libertines in London's the "Mohock Club."[3] Typically, white American performance of Indian-ness has been in the service of forwarding "narratives of national identity around the rejection of an older European consciousness and an almost mystical imperative to become new."⁴ Additionally, Deloria observes that playing Indian hinges on a haunted contradiction wherein white Americans want "to savor both civilized order and savage freedom at the same time."⁵

Historical literary examples of what I term "surrogate Indians" function narratively in ways analogous to what native theorists argue happens with white Americans who have historically "played Indian": they forward a mythic view of native identity that is racially based and also part of the past. Additionally, the definition of what constitutes "Indian" is often the settler or colonizer's perception or expectation of Indian-ness, where "simulations are the absence of the tribal real."⁶ The performance of Indian-ness in the weird westerns analyzed in this chapter relies on invoking a sense of the past, which is part and parcel with native representation by nonnative communities. As Joanne Barker (Lenape) has noted, "Imperialism and colonialism require indigenous people to fit within the heteronormative archetypes of an Indigeneity that was authentic in the past but is culturally and legally vacated in the present": the time travel and fantastic elements of the weird western allow for a playful approach to time and narrative that actually enhances the sense of native performance being linked to the past.⁷ Barker goes on to add that nonnative representation also typically considers indigeneity in terms of race as opposed to culture, nation, or citizenship.⁸ My analysis of these texts notes in particular the implication that native identity is largely presented as racial in these nonnative texts, a characteristic that works to further identify how these texts are nonnative in their orientation. It is my hope that paying close attention to the interplay of race, gender, and sexuality in tandem with questions that shift the focus to native-centric issues can help to "unpack the constructedness of gender and sexuality" in order to address the structure of settler colonialism while considering how "inviting and deflecting feminism" is part of this process.⁹

Grounding my analyses of Indian metaphors and displacement in the critical frameworks afforded by indigenous feminist thought and native-studies theories provides what Scott Andrews (Cherokee Nation of Oklahoma), building on a concept explored previously by James Cox in *Muting White Noise*, dubs "red readings." Andrews asserts that indigenous-centered readings of nonnative texts that do not directly feature native peoples or issues is not only possible but a worthwhile pursuit. He defines "red reading" as a practice that "is not an attempt to racialize or essentialize a particular literary response. . . . The reader does not need to be native for this practice, but the reading should be native-centric; the reading process should be grounded in issues important to native communities and/or native intellectual histories or practices. Put most simply, a red reading produces an interpretation of a nonnative text from a native perspective."[10] While James Cox's approach to red readings considers the meanings behind how native peoples are presented in nonnative texts, Andrews expands this approach to include how such analyses can destabilize "the dominant culture's confidence in representations of itself. That includes, for example, destabilizing fundamental conceptions upon which America's settler colonial nationhood has been built."[11]

Examining how the three weird westerns steeped in the mythology of Wyatt Earp and Doc Holliday invoke native-focused issues without using native characters or bodies (literally, in the sense of casting choices for the television series) leads to a "red reading" that helps resist the erasure of contemporary indigenous bodies that might otherwise occur when consuming these works. In sum, the Earp texts analyzed in the sections that follow seek to highlight native-centric issues and explore how the western genre is used to express these issues despite the absence of native bodies.

Diverse Communities in *Territory* and "Wynonna Earp"

Territory and "Wynonna Earp" present a multicultural view of the West, and outlining some of the various ways these texts address gender, sexuality, and race helps clarify the relevance of applying a red reading. These texts do not operate in a vacuum, unaware of matters of inclusion; thus, highlighting some of their progressive aspects elucidates how these texts can then be seen as utilizing metaphoric notions of

Indian-ness. Emma Bull's revisionist fantasy western novel *Territory* is set in the nineteenth-century world of Tombstone, Arizona, where Wyatt Earp and his brothers are a haunting and menacing presence, while sorcerers and magic inform political intrigue and land territory claims; Bull conveys her story in the third person with occasional moments of free indirect discourse, which allows some limited insight into how key characters view issues of race and gender. In Bull's reimagining of the historical Earps and the town of Tombstone, we see greater multicultural emphasis through a focus on Chinese American communities and traditions and through attention to female lead Mildred Benjamin, a widowed woman acutely aware of the way her Jewish identity marks her as different from the other Anglo-American residents. The male protagonist of the story, Jesse Fox, is an ambiguous drifter and sorcerer who associates with marginalized communities and is able to "pass" in a variety of cultural contexts while ultimately learning he must combat Wyatt Earp, who is a "black magician" laying claim to Tombstone and causing bloodshed.[12] Bull's narrative characterizes Jesse and his mentor, the Chinese sorcerer Chow Lung, as metaphoric Native Americans through explicit visual comparisons and subtle development of each man's negotiation of multiple racial and cultural communities.

Bull's *Territory* decenters the iconic Wyatt Earp and Doc Holliday in favor of focusing on characters typically seen at the periphery of retellings of the now-mythologized events of nineteenth-century Tombstone, Arizona: women and immigrants. Pushing Earp and Holliday to the sidelines allows Bull to instead showcase the agency and contributions of marginalized communities in the American West. Main characters Mildred Benjamin and Jesse Fox are presumably white but closely tied to racial and ethnic others; Fox has professional and personal affiliations with the Chinese American community and is also linked to "gypsy" culture.[13] The widow Mildred Benjamin works for a local newspaper and transitions from typesetter to journalist, thus becoming intimately involved with shaping the narrative and characterization of Tombstone's history. Mildred also secretly writes sensational and melodramatic serials for literary magazines under a male pseudonym, therefore also directly participating in the mythologizing of the "wild west." Interestingly, Mildred writes stories that feature exoticized characters and interracial intrigue, which subtly parallel her own anxieties and awareness of being an ethnically Jewish woman living in a town dominated by Anglo-Americans.

Mildred's fiction speaks to her desire to promote female agency. For example, when Mildred publishes her first sensation story, "Stampede at Midnight," the literary magazine advertises it with the tagline "A New Tale of the Thrilling Frontier Adventure," illustrated with an engraving of a hatless woman rider, implying that she is the main character of the story, with "her light hair, in improbable quantities, streamed behind her like the storm clouds that boiled around the printed moon."[14] Additionally, Mildred's stories seek to invert female stereotypes, as seen when she vows that her story's heroine, Regina, "wouldn't faint at all, whatever her provocation."[15] The main character in her work in progress is a character whose name means "queen" and has sovereignty over her own body. Yet Mildred's investigative reporting provides a different social advocacy from her inversion of sensational fiction motifs. Her journalism and general distrust of Wyatt Earp helps her, along with Jesse, to uncover Earp's secret but authentic identity as a malicious and self-interested sorcerer, in contrast to his public protestations of being a civil servant.

Territory also delves more deeply into the representation of historically marginalized communities by focusing on the Chinese community of the American West. The second primary character of the novel, the racially ambiguous but presumably white Jesse Fox, aligns himself closely with the Chinese community of "Hoptown" and is a relatively fluent speaker of Chinese. Fox also seeks justice for the Chinese people who were murdered, as part of one of the novel's complicated storylines linked to sorcerer intrigue and land claims. As a result of Fox's association with the Chinese communities of the west—including San Francisco, California, and Tombstone, Arizona—the race-based prejudice and ghettoization of immigrant communities in the mythic Tombstone receives direct engagement and critique. The deaths of a

Chinese prostitute and Fox's mentor, Chow Lung, are portrayed as the tragic collateral damage of Wyatt Earp's insatiable greed for wealth, land, and power, thus inviting a reflective and critical view of the taming of the American West. Bull's narrative forces the reader to confront the racial oppression nonwhite communities face and also question the function of stereotypical representation.

Bull's Chinese characters show a hyperawareness of racial stereotypes and expectations from the town's dominant culture and perform racialized identities to maintain agency. For example, when Chow Lung needs to find Jesse Fox at the local theater so the two men can continue their investigation into the death of a young Chinese woman, he speaks in over-the-top pidgin English so as not to raise the suspicion of the white inhabitants who would be curious about Fox's alliance with Lung (especially since the two men's investigation is covert). Lung enters the opera house and says, "Missa Fox, is big message for you. Gotta go, chop-chop. Velly Solly," and the narrator goes on to say that "the Chinaman folded his hands over his stomach and bowed."[16] Lung's language and actions conform to the dominant culture's stereotypes of Chinese immigrants as unable to speak standard American English and being overly deferential. Bull's use of the dated and now pejorative "Chinaman" functions as a kind of free indirect discourse to reinforce how Lung is perceived by the surrounding white characters. Readers know that this is a performance because the first introduction of Lung emphasizes his facility with the English language, when Fox's rusty Chinese makes him the less linguistically facile of the two.[17] Fox is taken aback by Lung's performance of Chinese stereotype and later asks his friend, "Do you do that often?," to which Lung astutely replies, "When it is useful. They expect it, and what they expect is invisible to them."[18] What initially appears as a degrading moment in the opera house is reaffirmed as a strategic performance.

Like *Territory*, the fantastic world of *Wynonna Earp* on the television screen features increased roles for women and provides a racially diverse view of the West through its casting, but the show often fails to explicitly acknowledge the specific experiences faced by communities of color in the West. The Wynonna Earp titles are interrelated narratives, in part, but also have distinct differences, particularly in how each iteration approaches literal and metaphoric Native American representation. Show runner Emily Andras adapted the comic series started by Beau Smith in the late 1990s for the SyFy network in 2016. The recent television series has in turn spurred a revival of the comic books, albeit from an angle closer to the characterization and aesthetics of the television program. The series *Wynonna Earp* follows a female character who is the descendant of famed lawman Wyatt Earp and who assumes her forebearer's traditionally masculine role while "seeking justice and keeping the peace." The show has garnered instant comparisons to cult television favorite *Buffy the Vampire Slayer* (1997–2003), a show with its own weird western episode, "Pangs." While there are differences in the backstory of each Wynonna iteration, the comics by Smith and the television series both participate in the subgenre of the gothic weird western with a healthy dose of camp. The titular character is haunted by specters of, and sometimes quite literally from, the Old West that continue to threaten and endanger those living in the present. Smith's first comic book version presents a mythic character whose larger-than-life personality makes her a suitable match for her equally larger-than-life supernatural foes so emblematic of the mythic American West. In the earliest comic book runs, Smith uses Native American racial metaphors to describe Wynonna and to enhance the narrative's engagement with the mythic binaries of the traditional western tale. By contrast, the television adaptation provides a more relatable, down-to-earth Wynonna (Melanie Scrofano), haunted by her demons, both metaphorically and literally; the show's representation of race demythologizes some aspects of the traditional western by placing at the forefront an African American lead character (Shamier Anderson) for the role of chief law officer in addition to making the queer west visible.

While the initial comic book series had limited representation of communities of color, the television series that launched in 2016 broke with some of the comics' initial conventions by portraying lead U.S. Marshal Xavier Dolls as an African American (a role played by Canadian actor Shamier Anderson).[19] Season 2 added supporting characters Rosita Bustillos and Jeremy Chetri, expanding the racial diversity of the show; the character of Rosita is implied to be Latina or Hispanic, but this identity is never made explicit (at least thus far) and is made even more vague due to the casting of Canadian actress Tamara Duarte.[20] The character of Jeremy (Varun Saranga) adds another visible reoccurring character of color to the show.

The show's most explicit handling of race to date is seen in the character Agent Dolls. Initially, the series addressed Doll's racial identity and ties to African American culture in subtle ways, including his name "Xavier" being the same as a prominent HBCU and his personal office mug having an "X" on it (for his initial) that recalls the imagery of Malcolm X logos. However, the show's inclusion of historical figure U.S. Marshal Bass Reeves—the American West's first African American U.S. Marshal—in season 2 provided a rare moment that explicitly linked Dolls to African American western culture instead of black culture writ large, finally allowing viewers to see the character of Agent Dolls as enmeshed in a long-standing tradition of African American presence in the western.

The episode "Everybody Knows" (2.7) includes a time travel visit from Bass Reeves and most overtly acknowledges the racial politics of the western in a show that, thus far, has been largely quiet on such matters.[21] In this episode, viewers get a glimpse of Dolls, typically portrayed as stoic and serious, breaking from his usual stern character and showing visible excitement at encountering his longtime hero. Dolls's recognition of and depth of knowledge about Reeves shows his awareness of black involvement in the American West; he even intimates that Reeves serves as his professional inspiration. Such moments of direct acknowledgment of racial difference are rare in a show that otherwise operates within a "color-blind" casting context.[22] The show's representation of racial diversity also intersects with its gender and sexuality representational choices, particularly as Dolls and Rosita are romantic foils for many of the show's other characters, and Jeremy is a gay character with a very big crush on Doc Holliday.

Despite its diverse cast, the complex representation of sexuality on SyFy's series has thus far garnered the most attention in popular discussions of the show, more so than issues pertaining to race.[23] *Wynonna Earp* has been lauded in online fora and popular analyses for spurring a sea change regarding queer representation and for being a female-driven show. Showrunner Emily Andras has been credited with creating the "Unkillable Queer" character type with lesbian character Officer Nicole Haught (Kat Barrell), at a moment when the discussion of "Bury Your Gays" and other fan concerns about the apparent disposability of lesbian characters had reached a critical mass.[24] The show has become a staple at LGBTQ pop culture conventions such as ClexaCon, and the showrunners and actors have been active in online support for LGBTQ causes, particularly in their use of Twitter. Yanders makes the case that fandom and social media interactions from the queer viewing community played a key role in fostering support for the show, noting that SyFy became "recognized as a space for progressive representations," and that "the ongoing choices that *Wynonna Earp* makes both in terms of characterization and in its social media representation indicate a sustained interest in representing the queer community."[25]

The show has also been discussed in online commentaries as offering a frank and feminist take on the weird western due to a range of narrative choices that focus on women characters that show a spectrum of possibilities for agency and empowerment, such as representing women as physically powerful (Wynonna's athletic strength and cunning) or intellectually powerful (Waverly Earp's historical research is presented as a superpower), and sometimes both (i.e., Rosita has multiple PhDs in addition to superhuman strength). Additionally, writing lead actor Melanie Scrofano's real-life pregnancy into Wynonna's own storyline in season 2 allows the series to showcase that the character's pregnancy and motherhood do not detract from her status as a badass.

In sum, the inclusion of racial minorities as well as development of female characters with agency positions *Territory* and *Wynonna Earp* as weird westerns deeply interested in shifting the focus to a wider look at community building in the West. Yet, despite very complex engagements with and questioning of the historical roles played by these communities—or, at least, how the dominant culture has long portrayed the roles for these communities—native communities are effectively ignored, a detail that stands out sharply given the western genre and setting of these narratives.

Red Dead Redemption: *Territory*

In his study of the western in *Gunfighter Nation* (1992), Richard Slotkin argues for the narrative structure of the mythic "savage war," whereby natives and settlers inevitably collide due to political and culture differences that can only end in the subjugation of one group at the expense of the other—typically, with the native subjugated and, in the process, vilified, to justify the continued emergence of the settler state.[26] The surrogate Indian characters of the Earp weird western texts replicate Slotkin's savage war, as each text shows that the native proxy exists at the social fringes and is either subjugated or always under the threat of subjugation. In Bull's *Territory* the role of surrogate Indian falls on Jesse Fox, a drifter implied to be white-coded but who reads as racially and culturally ambiguous in certain contexts, due to his association with minority communities. Fox and his colleague, the Chinese American Chow Lung, are described using Indian metaphors, lending their bodies a racial instability and creating a binary opposition between them and the real antagonists of the story: Wyatt Earp and other dark sorcerers vying for power, including John Ringo. Although Fox is arguably the lead male protagonist, he, as his last name implies, is presented as crafty and wily and operating outside the structures of the law[27]—what Cynthia Miller and A. Bowdoin Van Riper might term the "cowboy code."[28]

While Fox is a white-coded character, the men of Tombstone use his racially ambiguous appearance to racialize Wild West violence and suggest that outliers and minority communities should be blamed. The novel introduces Jesse's body as racially ambiguous and untranslatable: "The man who stood framed in the doorway could be read like a book printed in three languages. . . . His hair, probably brown under the dust, hung in a plait to his shoulder blades, the way some Indians and a few of the Mexicans wore theirs."[29] The other men of the saloon attempt to insult Fox after he makes his entrance, by again focusing on his hair, with one character explaining, "He's got his hair braided up like a squaw," and another adding, "Or a Chinaman. . . . No, on Chinamen it's longer. You're right, Billy, it's a squaw braid."[30] Fox's appearance is described using a linguistic metaphor in which issues of translation leave ambiguities; thus, this metaphor shares much in common with Robert Gunn's definition of "interracial speech acts," where "racial misrecognition turns on problems of language, on the slipperiness of translation."[31] The use of the hypothetical "probably" underscores the uncertainty regarding Fox's identity and appearance. The continued focus on Fox's hair emerges as a source of ongoing identity anxiety; while Fox has just admitted to shooting a young man, who dies from his wounds, the danger Fox poses to the other men in the saloon is redirected by their recasting of his outlaw behavior as a gendered and racial threat. The emphasis on repeating "squaw," which many native communities acknowledge as a slur used to denigrate native women, functions to emasculate Fox, an act furthered by the men in the saloon joking immediately afterward that he may be afflicted with a venereal disease.

Furthermore, the Chinese American Chow Lung, Fox's mentor and friend, is consistently described using Indian racial metaphors. This has the effect of the implicit racial violence between the Anglo-American cowboys and the Chinese Americans of the "Hoptown" district replacing the binary of Indian versus settler common in western narratives, such as what Slotkin cites in the structure of the "savage war." For example, the narrative utilizes free indirect discourse to imply that Jesse muses, "Lung looked more Indian than Chinese—almost like the Apache scouts who rode with the cavalry. But he *was* Chinese. As far as Jesse had been able to tell, that meant more to the Chinese than being German or Italian or Irish meant to other immigrants. Clothes, food, neighbors, customs, religion—if you were Chinese, everything was Chinese, and stayed that way."[32] Jesse considers this information after he recognizes that he and Lung are "playacting" and performing specific roles for the town's onlookers; therefore, the description of Lung resonates as a variation on the idea of playing Indian. This textual passage highlights that, for Jesse, Indian is a racial identity linked to outward appearance, which is distinct from how he then goes on to define Chinese identity as a set of cultural practices. This is just one of many examples that illustrates Barker's assertion about the distinction that often separates native versus nonnative perspectives; for the nonnative, Indian identity is largely figured as racial instead of political or cultural. Fox specifically uses the tribal name "Apache" instead of a generic catch-all such as "Indian," which moves away from general pan-Indianism. However, he specifies Apache who "rode with the cavalry," so those who are separated from their tribal community thus more familiar to the nonnative communities of the American West. While Fox provides a tribal name, he does so to indicate Apache men who are hired by the settler colonial state and occupy an especially complex political position; tribal specificity in this case functions as a modifier to indicate a racial other who may be seen as less threatening to the dominant white culture. Lung himself furthers the metaphoric association with Native American imagery and racial subtext when he describes himself as the "medicine man" in Hoptown.[33]

The novel's final comparison of Fox to Indians uses the image of the cigar-store Indian, which clinches the novel's reliance on the notion of the Vanishing Indian. At a plot point when Mildred and Jesse Fox are discussing a social event in Tombstone, Fox "crossed his arms over his chest and waited. Mildred was reminded of a cigar-store Indian, except that they never looked out of temper. And that made her laugh."[34] As with the previous examples, the connection between Fox (and even Lung) with Indian comparisons comes from other characters in the story, not the third-person narrator. This move emphasizes that this is how other nonnative characters view what they consider Native American. In Mildred's case, the comparison is a source of humor and allows her to see Fox's ill temper as absurd and, therefore, not threatening. This is the reverse of the men of the saloon, who recast Fox's proven propensity to violence into a more vague, racialized—

instead of physical—threat. Instead of being compared to potentially real native people, Fox is now being compared to the cigar-store Indian, a decorative and inanimate object that is a simulacrum reflecting what Robert Berkhofer dubs the "white man's Indian." At some level, this last comparison makes explicit that the metaphoric Indian-ness evoked throughout the text has never been rooted in comparisons to real native peoples, but the dominant culture's perception of what constitutes Indian-ness; it also has the effect of fully eradicating any semblance of native presence in lieu of a constructed and commercial substitute for indigeneity. Tellingly, in the sections of the novel that follow Mildred's comparison, which makes Fox less threatening, Fox emerges as a more traditional hero who restores justice and "seals" Wyatt Earp's dark magical powers.[35]

Buffy the Vampire Slayer and *Wynonna Earp*

The "Wynonna Earp" texts also utilize metaphoric Indian-ness, typically applied to otherwise white-coded characters. Since there are multiple versions of the characters and assorted storylines in the Wynonna Earp-verse, a brief overview of the publication and production history will help clarify how issues of race and gender operate within each. The initial comic series that started the character and franchise has a complex publishing history, which the creation of the television adaptation has influenced. There are arguably four existing iterations of the character Wynonna Earp and her world that are all distinct in some manner: three comic book runs and the television version. The first run was published in 1996 by Image Comics, and the second was later picked up by IDW in 2003 for further runs; IDW and comic book creator Beau Smith released yet another, third version of new "Wynonna Earp" comics in February 2016 as a tie-in to the SyFy television adaptation. In the early Image and IDW comics pre–television adaptation, Wynonna is a busty blonde (with an exaggerated and revealing figure) who fights vampires, mummies, rednecks, and more. In the SyFy series, Wynonna starts fighting what the show terms "revenants," the ghosts of outlaws originally killed by her great-great-grandfather

Wyatt Earp; each generation, these foes come back from hell as part of the "Earp Curse" that haunts her family. In the show's mythology, each generation's first-born child is the "Earp heir" who has to "put down" the revenants using Wyatt Earp's special Peacemaker weapon, whose barrel contains occult symbols and magical properties.

Cynthia Miller notes the weird western genre's seeming ambiguity: weird west tales can "complicate, reinforce, and comment on our understanding of Westerns and the West."[36] Miller and Van Riper consider the "Cowboy Code" of "courage, fair play, loyalty, respect, and honor," key to traditional westerns, as what comes most under threat by the undead.[37] If the traditional western relies on a dualism of good and evil, then for Miller and Van Riper the weird western's undead can either further reinforce that binary or undermine it. The dualism of the Cowboy Code factors prominently in Smith's comic book version, particularly with the repeated mantra of "it's about justice." The Wynonna of the earlier comic book version chases after villains who pose a threat to public safety, such as supernatural villains who deal illicit drugs that transform humans into monsters, or Russian crime families who turn to the supernatural in hopes of world domination. The early comics portray the villains via a binary vision of right and wrong; a direct good versus bad narrative that makes it easy to see why Wynonna frequently quips about her pursuit of justice. The end of the Image comic runs reinforces this dualism with Wynonna's closing words: "As long as there are sickos, psychos, aliens, and monsters without partners I'll be on the job. Just remember . . . it's not about the law—it's about justice!"[38]

By contrast, the SyFy television adaptation does not overtly address the question of the Cowboy Code or of justice; rather, issues of justice, courage, and respect are subtly implied or handled with comic exaggeration. In the show, Wynonna's work in the Black Badge division, a covert division of U.S. Marshals who have jurisdiction in both the United States and Canada and a mission to address weird threats, is motivated by a sense of personal vengeance for the crimes revenants have committed against her nuclear family, making her form of justice different in tone from that of her earlier counterpart. Likewise, the values of courage and respect are fodder for comic relief and snappy dialogue rather than representative of Wynonna's motivations; for example, in the episode "Leavin' On Your Mind" (1.3) Wynonna passionately exclaims to her boss Agent Dolls that she wants all the revenants to "tremble with fear before me," powdered sugar from a doughnut prominently smeared across her nose, making her anything but intimidating. Additionally, Wynonna does not have any respect for Agent Dolls's preference for professional workplace conduct and for following the proper chain of command and hierarchy. The show makes it clear that Wynonna is not your traditional "good" character; she has a criminal record, a parole officer, and a drinking problem, but she happens to be the only one qualified to address the town's revenant problem. In short, the show more playfully incorporates aspects of the Cowboy Code, resulting in a narrative that sees justice less as a binary where good prevails but more so as an ongoing negotiation where the seemingly good characters must make concessions.

Unlike the Wynonna of the show, the earlier iterations of Wynonna Earp from Smith's initial 1996–97 run with Image Comics present a more mythic vision of the sultry character through metaphoric racial exoticization. Unlike the television series that presents Wynonna unquestionably as a direct lineal descendant of Wyatt Earp, the earlier comic books portray the familial tie more as unverified family legend. Wynonna's descent from the famed western figure Wyatt Earp is represented as literally mythic—nothing more than family lore that cannot be definitively proven via records. Still, it is a name and an identity she chooses to embrace (her birth surname is never revealed or confirmed). Beau Smith's official website, the Flying Fist Ranch, provides a thumbnail sketch of his character Wynonna; he writes that she "lays claim to being the great granddaughter of the famous lawman, Wyatt Earp."[39]

The early comic book portrayal positions Wynonna as a surrogate Indian: she is a white-coded character who is described using a variation of blood quantum language and as wearing fashion accessories commonly associated in the dominant pop-cultural imagination with Native American communities. Smith further portrays Wynonna's identity as defined by family fable and lore when he states that a longstanding "rumor has it" that Wynonna's great-grandmother had an affair with the famed Earp, but that "no documented fact can confirm or deny this affair. The stories of Wyatt Earp were passed down from Wynonna's family. At a very early age she became fascinated with the history of her ancestor, Wyatt. . . . She dedicated her life to living up to the legendary name that she took as her own."[40] Smith further describes Wyatt as a "possible ancestor." In the comic runs from the Image years, other characters often comment on whether she has "true" Earp blood or not in ways evocative of discussions regarding blood quantum and U.S. American family lore of possible American Indian ancestry. The Image Comics version of Wynonna reinforces this metaphor by portraying her wearing a bone choker with feathers reminiscent of Plains tribal styles. Portraying Wynonna in a metaphorical racialized position allows Smith to achieve two goals: first, he makes Wynonna a more mythic character who shares in a long tradition of western characters who play Indian and share traits with white mythological constructs of the *indian* (italicized lowercase "absolute fake" as defined by Gerald Vizenor); and, second, she can occupy both sides of the otherwise dualistic construction of the western—she can be both a woman and a lawman, both a cowboy and a metaphoric Indian. The "having it both ways" aspect is a key component of what Deloria argues happens historically with white Americans' forays into playing Indian.

Wynonna's uncertain family tree contributes to the mythic construction of her character by presenting each comic book storyline as just another variant in the Wynonna Earp folkloric tradition; contradictory backstories and differing physical attributes among comic runs can be seen not as mere narrative inconsistency but as presenting Wynonna in the tradition of American mythmaking similar to stories of American western folk heroes, be it fictional (or composite) characters such as Pecos Bill or tall tales based on real historical figures such as Davy Crockett. That Wynonna is a possible descendent of an already heavily mythologized historical figure only furthers her own mythologized representation. After all, the story of Wyatt Earp and the OK Corral is more mythic than historic in popular consciousness, since it has been told and retold countless times since the late nineteenth century; of particular note is writer Walter Noble Burns's reference to the story as the "Iliad of the Southwest," further emphasizing the story's mythic and larger-than-life qualities.[41]

Wynonna occupies both sides of dualistic identities and positions, which reinforces a common perception that the weird western challenges traditional notions and identities in the genre; however, in its erasure of actual indigenous bodies, the *Wynonna* texts reinforce western genre stereotypes. In the comic runs before the 2016 IDW reboot, there are no signs of actual native peoples, with Wynonna acting as a surrogate Indian figure analogous to Hawkeye from the Leatherstocking Tales; thus, the racial politics of the early comics are complex, to say the least, as they follow the narrative structure of Slotkin's "savage war" but replace racial others with monstrous others while having a metaphoric native woman as the lead fighter. The comic run from 2016 portrays Wynonna more as a law-woman working with other law-enforcing women and not as a surrogate Indian, in part because of the recent introduction of the Maya character, Valdez, discussed at the end of this chapter. However, in the television version, season 1's reoccurring "big bad" characters, the Revenants and their leader, Bobo Del Rey (Michael Eklund), are portrayed as metaphorically racialized, as Native American, which shifts the metaphoric Indian-ness from protagonist to antagonist.

SyFy's version of the Wynonna character shares much in common with Buffy Summers, titular character of the series *Buffy the Vampire Slayer*, particularly in how each show navigates a complex relationship with monstrous others that frequently stand in for social or racial others. It's worth examining "Pangs," *Buffy*'s western episode, before exploring SyFy's *Wynonna Earp*, as it uses a similar supernatural narrative structure and clarifies how gender-progressive shows tend to be so at the expense of racial politics. The representation of Chumash ghosts in "Pangs" sets up a useful framework of comparison to better see how *Wynonna Earp*'s revenants function as surrogate Indians. The problems of the western *Buffy* episode mirror those visible in *Wynonna Earp*'s approach to native issues. Both texts seek to invert the gender roles in traditional representations of the old west, yet even they fall back into paradigms from traditional westerns that reinforce oppressive settler colonial values. *Buffy* follows the trials and tribulations of Buffy Summers, played by Sarah Michelle Gellar, an urbanite Southern California teenager whose duty it is to protect her town of Sunnydale from vampires and demons. Similarly, in SyFy's *Wynonna Earp*, the title character is on a quest to save her hometown of Purgatory from revenants. Both shows have a strong cult following and demonstrate that the western is indeed alive and well, even when the foes are the undead.

Buffy and Wynonna both assume the role traditionally occupied by the frontiersman. The traditional frontiersman was the figure who operated at the intersections between frontier and settlement, a member of the settler culture but one who had some perceived understanding of those deemed other. Richard Slotkin defines the frontiersman as "the man who knows Indians."[42] In these new westerns, Buffy is the "woman who knows vampires" and Wynonna is the "woman who knows revenants," suggesting that, even though we have two frontierswomen rather than the traditional male frontiersmen, the general narrative structure of the western still remains. These new frontierswomen are portrayed as having intimate contact and knowledge of the other: the vampires and revenants. Their knowledge of the other, however, is more complex than that held by the traditional frontiersman, as each show explores how the title characters engage in sexual relationships with their respective others, which in a sense blurs the categorical boundaries of familiar and unfamiliar through dangerous romantic entanglements. The addition of the forbidden sexual relationship may serve to tacitly discount the new frontierswoman as able to wholly replace her male counterpart.[43] Yet, for all the updates and inversions of traditional gender and sexual roles, these shows still revert to rather troubling racial paradigms, particularly regarding how each series adapts discourses and symbolism pertaining to Native Americans.

Frontier narratives frequently highlight violent encounters between culturally estranged groups to either reinforce or challenge dominant cultural paradigms of power. Buffy fighting vampires and demons transforms the traditional western frontier narrative structure into a suburban and gothic western space. While Buffy's fight against vampires in Sunnydale, California, replicates the violence of expansion established by the western, her fight usually inverts the expectations of others, since her most significant foes are vampires of European descent who can be seen as symbols of colonization. However, the show still occasionally employs the traditional western genre's binaries regarding othering, which shows that those binaries are firmly rooted in the national imagination.

"Pangs" (a.k.a. the Thanksgiving episode) merges anxieties over vampires with anxieties over classic westward expansion. It opens with Buffy and friends attending a ground-breaking ceremony for a Cultural Partnership Center and establishes an overt post-western "cowboys and indians" context. Buffy wears an uncharacteristic cowboy hat and discusses with her close friend Willow (Alyson Hannigan) the appropriateness of the upcoming Thanksgiving holiday and her excitement for the celebration, which establishes Buffy as blind to her own privilege while presenting Willow as more politically aware and outraged by the historic abuse faced by native communities. The debate between the two resumes at a later point in the episode in their college dorm room, where Buffy's cowboy hat occupies a key central space of the mise-en-scène. While Buffy eventually acknowledges Willow's point that the holiday is a sham and not about cultural diversity, she jokes that it's a "sham with yams" to assert that she still insists on celebrating the holiday and uses levity to minimize Willow's focus and concern over issues of native genocide.

The main conflict of the episode, however, is that the construction site for the Cultural Partnership Center releases the ghost of a Chumash Warrior (Tod Thawley), referred to as a "Spirit Warrior" by most of the cast. At multiple moments the episode damns the atrocities of the colonial past, but it does so at the expense of emphasizing the erasure of indigenous peoples. Despite the presence, the survivance, of the

Chumash today, the episode only describes them as fixtures of the past. The episode reinforces the Vanishing Indian figure from frontier texts by showing the Chumash Warrior as noncorporeal. He first takes shape in the form of a rising green and pestilent-looking vapor and later turns into a flock of birds, then a coyote, and, finally, a bear.

The show valiantly attempts to invert the traditional western hero and critique the colonial past but ends up reinforcing many of the tropes and themes it is criticizing when it represents the Chumash only as ghosts; at the end of the day, the episode adheres to and continues to support the structure of settler colonialism, which also shares many structural similarities with the monster slayer genre, where the slayer eventually destroys the monster, even sympathetic ones. The representation of the vampire Spike (James Marsters) as a captive figure for much of the episode—bound with rope and later shown with arrows protruding from his body—reinforces the western context. The rest of the characters urge Buffy to take action against the Chumash Warrior, which results in her stabbing him. The episode ends with the group enjoying a Thanksgiving dinner and already forgetting the psychological and physical discomfort of confronting the sins of the past.

The at-times-contradictory and at-best-ambiguous critique and repetition of the classic frontier motif in *Buffy* reflects deep-rooted national anxieties. As Renée Bergland has argued, the use of ghostly and undead characters allegorically expresses real anxieties about America's dark past, especially anxieties about Native American encounters and the institution of slavery. While *Buffy* attempts to problematize violence and colonialism, perhaps the show's most repressed anxiety is that Buffy isn't as revisionist as her creators would like to believe.

Similar to "Pangs," the television series *Wynonna Earp* also positions the surrogate Indian characters as ghostly and threatening. Unlike the comics, the SyFy series portrays Wynonna's descent from Wyatt Earp as a clearly documented fact—her sister Waverly obsessively collects historical family records—which allows the show to shift its metaphoric engagements with Indian-ness onto the revenants instead of the lead character. The series portrays Wynonna's famed ancestor not as a source of mythic pride but as a burden, both because of the Earp curse and of all the attention from tourists who seek to "drink where Wyatt Earp drank." Being an Earp is not glamorized in the series, as the Earps feel emotionally trapped in a town cleverly named Purgatory, implied to be a border town between the United States and Canada that functions as a literal and metaphoric liminal space, as its name implies. SyFy's Wynonna is positioned more clearly as a white female protagonist helping to support a multicultural and inclusive new west, which is maintained by keeping the metaphoric Indians suppressed and part of the past.

The television series symbolically racializes the white-complected revenants and raises questions as to whether or not the show reinforces binary narrative structures associated with the more traditional western. The revenants, some of whose names and appearance share similarities with the "rednecks and white corpuscles" from the early Image years of the comic, are portrayed in ways evocative of traditional nonnative literary characterization of American Indian characters. For example, the revenants refer to their community meeting as a "war party," and their leader, Bobo Del Rey, sports a mohawked coif and wears animal skin and furs. They are quite literally figures from the past, and specter-like, as they have returned from the grave. The revenants' capture of Wynonna's oldest sister, Willa, carries undertones of Indian captivity narratives such as Mary Rowlandson's, again placing the revenants in the position of the stereotypical Indian.[44] They are further positioned as surrogate Indians via the show's "Ghost River Triangle," a magical boundary line that contains all of the revenants within Purgatory and carries connotations of a reservation; since they cannot leave Purgatory but are not welcomed into the town's society, they are forced to live grouped together at the triangle's fringes. The revenants are also consistently dehumanized; for example, Agent Dolls points out that "they're not people" when Wynonna refers to revenants with humanizing language. The show's positioning of the surrogate Indians as antagonists stands in contrasts to Bull's novel, where the protagonists occupied this position, as well as the earlier Image and

IDW *Wynonna* comic runs, and this in turn changes the racial politics of each work.

The show's representation of the revenants recalls stories and anxieties related to racial passing; Dolls explains to Wynonna that revenants "can blend in. They look just like us." In the context of a multicultural town such as Purgatory, the rhetoric of Indian-ness is thus used to mark difference so that race does not get explicitly evoked but rather is alluded to symbolically through white-appearing characters who perform aspects of the absolute fake *indian* from literary stereotype. Enforcing the inhumane qualities of the revenants via the trappings of Indian stereotype has the likely unintended consequence of reinforcing the dehumanization of Native peoples.

The newly rebooted IDW comic book run combines aspects of the television series, particularly with Wynonna's appearance and new cast of characters, with the focus on the Cowboy Code from the earlier comic runs; however, the combination of these elements provides a more complicated and nuanced approach to portraying race and gender in the weird west. The new comic run has a stronger focus on female empowerment; characters make comments that critique traditional western roles for women, such as when Valdez comments on the impracticality of nineteenth-century women's fashion. The additional women U.S. Marshals in the new comic run emphasis that Wynonna is not an anomaly, that there are other women like her.

In the new comic series, native stereotypes are simultaneously critiqued and reinforced by way of the character of Valdez. Valdez, usually called "Val" by the other characters, is a Maya woman who is a one-thousand-year old princess and warrior. Her characterization challenges the Vanishing Indian stereotype through her refusal to die. While it is a commonplace to focus on the death or vanishing of native peoples in the western, in the new comic series Val's longevity is a form of agency and power. She is not a mere indigenous casualty but an active force. Likewise, her finding it humorous as an indigenous woman to wear a vest that says "cavalry" provides a clever reversal and challenge to the notion of "cowboys and Indians" as she can be both. Her humor critiques racism against native peoples in the traditional western; however, her identity as a Maya woman opens up a consideration of indigenous representation that is distinct from American Indian representation. Her mythical characterization as more than human because she cannot be killed and her identity as princess still trade in stereotypical expectations for native characters in the western.

The "Legends" run from IDW further develops the Valdez character, who first appears in the collated collection "Homecoming," and emphasizes how she is both physically different from those around her but also the character most like Wynonna. Characters frequently refer to her as "giant" and even "Magilla Gorilla" to point out her larger stature and musculature; the frequency with which the other characters note her physical presence emphasizes her otherness. Valdez even acknowledges that she feels out of place, saying to Wynonna, "I am looked at as an oddity—a relic—with fear and distrust everywhere I have ever tread. I have been locked up in places so deep, so dark, and so desolate that hell would be a welcome source of light and warmth."[45] In a storyline where Valdez saves a baby falling from a skyscraper using an American flag, the imagery of an indigenous woman's body with the prominent flag is analogous to the female personifications of the Americas from the early modern period that utilized a tribally ambiguous native woman to portray the Western hemisphere. She is even dubbed a "wonder woman," recalling the famed DC Comics superhero that can be read as compliment and as a way to distinguish her as different.[46] While there are many ways in which Valdez is portrayed as a resourceful and strong female character, the persistent emphasis on her difference reinforces her racialization.

While the SyFy series and rebooted 2016 "Wynonna" comics move away from positioning Wynonna as a surrogate Indian, the end of the "Legends" run makes explicit that Valdez and Wynonna are meant to be read as similarly developed characters. Waverly, Wynonna's sister, says to her, "I knew you needed a mentor that you wouldn't feel threatened by so ... I found you a bad-ass-lass-with-a-long-ass-past—I sent you Valdez! Because she's scary! Like you!" The new comic run positions Valdez as the sage Indian advisor meant to mentor Wynonna in the ways of the West only so that Wynonna can take center stage (not dissimilar to Chingachgook's mentorship of Natty Bumppo). Here, Wynonna still has some characterization of metaphoric Indian-ness, just from a different angle.

Additionally, in "Season Zero" of the rebooted "Wynonna Earp" comics, which in part takes a peek at the work Wynonna was completing before returning to law enforcement in Purgatory, continues to develop Valdez as an indigenous other. In "Season Zero" she is dubbed "Pocahontas" from a "demented Disney film" and is the butt of jokes that suggest "Mayan foreplay" is brutal, as a way to make her sexuality threatening and to overall exoticize her. While Valdez is a supporting character on the side of the protagonists, the way in which her race is presented reinforces the sentiment of the surrounding characters—that they do not understand the difference between the invented Indian from the tribal real. The conflation of the tribal and political distinctions and geographies, from linking the Pamunkey region of Virginia to the Mayan empire, flattens native representation.

Race and gender intersect in the various iterations of the weird western worlds of *Wynonna Earp* and *Territory*. While all the texts explored in this chapter invoke metaphors of Native Americans, usually in a racial context, it's important to note that there are weird westerns that have imagined indigenous presence more literally and in ways that seek to subvert the frontier structure of settler colonialism, like the work of Native American authors such as Rebecca Roanhorse (Ohkay Owingeh), Stephen Graham Jones (Blackfeet), as well as others discussed within this collection. While many popular weird westerns may rely on binaries and formulas that reproduce troubling racial paradigms in terms of native inclusion, approaching these texts through the lens of a red reading and recentering native concerns can help provide more visibility for the need for more far-reaching intersectional approaches.

NOTES

1. I use "Indian" throughout this chapter to refer to what Vizenor terms the *indian* (lowercase and italicized), which is his shorthand for indicating that

America's obsession with the stereotypical Hollywood Indian is a construct that has no relation to what he terms the "tribal real." I have used *indian* in a few key places but interchange this formatting with "Indian" to reflect the language choices deployed in some of the discussed primary texts. The texts explored in this chapter generally use non–American Indian characters to fulfill the frontier and western genre expectations carved out for the *indian* archetype—or, more accurately, stereotype—as imagined and reproduced in nonnative cultural expressions.

2. Vizenor, *Manifest Manners*, 4.
3. See John Gay's dramatic farce *The Mohocks* (1712). Scholars are uncertain if there truly was a Mohock Club, despite references and fears of the group in some eighteenth-century British periodicals; it was reputed to be a gang of young men who inflicted bodily harm on others (hence, behaved "savagely"). See Abrahams "Mohawks, Mohocks, Hawkubites, Whatever."
4. Deloria, *Playing Indian*, 2.
5. Deloria, *Playing Indian*, 3.
6. Vizenor, *Manifest Manners*, 4.
7. Barker, "Introduction," 3.
8. Barker, "Introduction," 10.
9. Barker, "Introduction," 14.
10. Andrews, "Red Readings," i.
11. Andrews, "Red Readings," iii.
12. Bull, *Territory*, 250.
13. Bull, *Territory*, 122.
14. Bull, *Territory*, 188.
15. Bull, *Territory*, 218.
16. Bull, *Territory*, 137.
17. Bull, *Territory*, 34.
18. Bull, *Territory*, 141.
19. The most notable character of color in the comics is Valdez, a one-thousand-year-old Maya warrior discussed later in this chapter.
20. Duarte's family is ethnically Portuguese.
21. See Michael K. Johnson's chapter in this volume for a wider discussion of time travel weird westerns and the representation of African American westerners.

22. Season 3 introduced a new African American series regular, Kate, the vampire wife of Doc Holliday, played by Chantel Riley. The show has generally presented the African American characters as interchangeable with white westerners, sometimes explicitly so, with known white historical figures, such as Riley's character, who is based on the Hungarian prostitute westerner known to history as "Big Nose Kate," thus complicating any progressive attempts at positioning minority communities in the West.
23. There may be a shift to more public consideration and discussion of race in *Wynonna Earp* as of late July 2018, due to the apparent death of Agent Dolls in the episode "When You Call My Name" (3.2). The departure of Shamier Anderson from the show ignited Twitter debates from fans of color, expressing that they feel marginalized and unable to discuss when they feel that the show's characters of color, chiefly Dolls and Rosita, are portrayed stereotypically. "When You Call My Name" positions Dolls as sacrificing himself to save the white-coded characters, particularly the female characters, due in part to his unrequited love for Wynonna. His dying word is "Wynonna," which redirects attention to the title character and clarifies who his death benefits. Also worth considering in brief here is how Dolls and new series regular Kate are African American characters who are literally not fully human. While *Wynonna Earp* is a supernatural weird western with many nonhuman characters—including demons, angels, and even human-angel hybrids—it's particularly noticeable that the only two African American characters have dangerous and nonhuman alter egos. Dolls had "dragon powers" due to a Black Badge experiment that altered his DNA, and Kate is a vampire who has killed many human characters due to her bloodlust. Since Dolls activates his "dragon powers" to save Wynonna and others, his sacrifice and subsequent death has overtones of the "magical negro" archetype; similarly, Kate is also portrayed as magical due to her day job as a fortune-teller and her constant reliance on her tarot cards.
24. The online analysis "Emily Andras, Wynonna Earp, and the Unkillable Queer" on *TheFandomentals* web page outlines the controversy over "Bury Your Gays," a trope most commonly linked to the writing choices made on CW show *The 100*.
25. Yanders, "Earpers."
26. Slotkin, *Gunfighter Nation*, 12–13.

27. For example, Mildred jokes that she could call Jesse Fox "Reynardine," invoking the folkloric figure of English and French tradition who could be an outlaw, seducer, or trickster or some combination thereof (Bull, *Territory*, 203).
28. Miller and Van Riper, "Introduction," xv.
29. Bull, *Territory*, 17.
30. Bull, *Territory*, 19.
31. Gunn, *Ethnology and Empire*, 47.
32. Bull, *Territory*, 156.
33. Bull, *Territory*, 170.
34. Bull, *Territory*, 221.
35. Bull, *Territory*, 315.
36. Miller, "Introduction," 4.
37. Miller and Van Riper, "Introduction," xiv.
38. Smith, *Strange Inheritance*, n.p.
39. Smith, *Flying Fist Ranch*. This website is now discontinued.
40. Smith, *Flying Fist Ranch*.
41. See Dworkin, *American Mythmaker*.
42. Slotkin, *Gunfighter Nation*, 16.
43. The sexualization of the frontierswoman stands in stark contrast to the implicit celibacy of the archetypal origin point in Cooper's Natty Bumppo. Likewise, white men in westerns who have sexual relationships with women of color are frequently portrayed as "tainted" as a result (i.e., 1914's *The Squaw Man*), and, if not, they are presented as living at the fringes of frontier society (i.e., 1972's *Jeremiah Johnson*). Even the women of the recent western television series *Godless* (2017) are presented in ways that highlight their sexuality, with significant attention to the lesbian relationships among the most prominent "law keeping" women characters such as Mary Agnes (Merritt Wever).
44. Mary White Rowlandson was an English colonialist taken captive in 1676 during King Philip's War. The story of her captivity, a purported autobiography, *The Sovereignty and Goodness of God* (1682), established the parameters for what would become the Indian captivity narrative genre.
45. Smith, "Legends," n.p. Comic book lettering often uses all capitalization. I have rendered the speech-bubble quotations included throughout this chapter using standard typographical conventions for the reader's ease.
46. Smith, "Legends," n.p.

Bibliography

Abrahams, Roger D. "Mohawks, Mohocks, Hawkubites, Whatever." *Common-place* 8, no. 4 (July 2008): http://common-place.org/book/mohawks-mohocks-hawkubites-whatever/ (accessed May 25, 2018).

Andrews, Scott. "Red Readings: Decolonization Through Native-Centric Responses to Non-Native Film and Literature." *Transmotion* 4, no. 1 (2018): i–vii.

Barker, Joanne. "Introduction." In *Critically Sovereign: Indigenous Gender, Sexuality, and Feminist Studies*, edited by Joanne Barker, 1–44. Durham NC: Duke University Press, 2017.

Barzman, Paolo, dir. *Wynonna Earp*. Season 2, episode 7, "Everybody Knows." Aired July 21, 2017, on SyFy.

Bergland, Renée. *The National Uncanny: Indian Ghosts and American Subjects*. Hanover NH: University Press of New England, 2000.

Berkhofer, Robert. *The White Man's Indian: Images of the American Indian from Columbus to the Present*. New York: Vintage, 1979.

Bull, Emma. *Territory*. New York: TOR, 2007.

Deloria, Philip J. *Playing Indian*. New Haven CT: Yale University Press, 1998.

Dworkin, Mark J. *American Mythmaker: Walter Noble Burns and the Legends of Billy the Kid, Wyatt Earp, and Joaquín Murrieta*. Norman: University of Oklahoma Press, 2015.

Gay, John. *The Mohocks: A Tragi-Comical Farce*. London: n.p., 1712.

Gretchen. "Emily Andras, Wynonna Earp, and the Unkillable Queer." TheFandomentals, https://www.thefandomentals.com/emily-andras-wynonna-earp-unkillable-queer/ (accessed May 25, 2018).

Gunn, Robert. *Ethnology and Empire: Languages, Literature, and the Making of the North American Borderlands*. New York: New York University Press, 2015.

Lange, Michael, dir. *Buffy the Vampire Slayer*. Season 4, episode 8, "Pangs." Aired November 23, 1999, on WB.

Miller, Cynthia. "Introduction." In *Encyclopedia of Weird Westerns*, 2nd. ed., edited by Paul Green, 4–14. Jefferson NC: McFarland, 2016.

———, and A. Bowdoin Van Riper. "Introduction." In *Undead in the West*, edited by Cynthia Miller and A. Bowdoin Van Riper, xi–xxvi. Lanham MD: Scarecrow, 2012.

Murphy, Ron, dir. *Wynonna Earp*. Season 1, episode 3, "Leavin' Your Mind." Aired April 15, 2016, on SyFy.

Rowlandson, Mary. "A True History of the Captivity and Restoration of Mrs. Mary Rowlandson." In *Women's Indian Captivity Narratives*, edited by Kathryn Zabelle Derounian-Stodola, 1–52. London: Penguin, 1998.

Slotkin, Richard. *Gunfighter Nation: The Myth of the Frontier in Twentieth-Century America*. Norman: University of Oklahoma Press, 1998.

Smith, Beau. "Wynonna Earp: Homecoming." San Diego CA: IDW, 2016.

———. "Wynonna Earp: Legends." San Diego CA: IDW, 2017.

———. "Wynonna Earp: Season Zero." San Diego CA: IDW, 2018.

———. "Wynonna Earp: Strange Inheritance." San Diego CA: IDW, 2016.

———. "*Wynonna Earp* Trade Paperback." Flying Fist Ranch, www.flyingfistranch.com/?page_id=88 (accessed June 7, 2016; site discontinued).

Trachtenberg, Alan. *Shades of Hiawatha: Staging Indians, Making Americans, 1880–1930*. New York: Hill & Wang, 2004.

Vizenor, Gerald. *Manifest Manners*. Hanover NH: University Press of New Enland,1994.

Yanders, Jacinta. "Earpers, Interactions, and Emotions: *Wynonna Earp*, 'The Best Fandom Ever.'" *Transformative Works and Cultures*, no. 26 (2018): http://dx.doi.org/10.3983/twc.2018.1129 (accessed June 13, 2019).

PART FOUR

The African American Presence
in the Weird Western

The Mad Black Woman in Stephen King's *The Dark Tower*

10

JACOB BURG

The traditional western suppresses what it cannot—and in some ways, must not—articulate. If representations of blackness exist, they do so at the narrative peripheries. So, then, how might the genre contort itself, in the words of Toni Morrison, "when it tries to imagine an Africanist other? What are the signs, the codes, the literary strategies designed to accommodate this encounter?"[1] For Stephen King's *The Dark Tower* (1982–2004), this accommodation begins with translation. The speculative series estranges the western from itself by deploying tropes from horror, science fiction, and fantasy to create a string of realities and plotlines that "rehearse the process of literary juxtaposition and suggest that characters and even monsters from different genre traditions can coexist under the umbrella of one story."[2] In essence, King relies on generic admixture to weird the western, prying open its narrative confines in order to allow for blackness to participate within its world. Yet it is ultimately the means by which the series imagines this participation that pushes it away from an investigation into complex issues of race and gender in favor of slick resolutions that promote a singular, overdetermined, and at times even racist vision of blackness and its history. And while Susannah, the African American woman at the heart of *The Dark Tower*, is not its main protagonist, she is symptomatic of its representational practices writ large.[3] Furthermore, as André M. Carrington suggests, foregrounding blackness within discussions of genre fiction helps "augment our understanding of what genre might be and what it might do."[4] Thus, even as *The Dark Tower*'s representational practices crumble under their own weight, there remains something instructive about the implicit sense of the possible embedded within the series as it attempts to imagine a black woman riding alongside the western's prototypically white and hypermasculine hero, at times even taking the narrative reins. Effectively, in its effort to allow silence to speak, King's series produces what we might consider a mad utterance.

Western Made Weird

The frontier imaginary developed within the conventional western cannot admit such an utterance. Indeed, the genre supports a nationalist project defined by stereotype and outright exclusion, most obviously captured through the self-other binary built around the "civilized" white settler's attempts to either rehabilitate or eliminate the "savage" Native American. This particular binary is burdened by its racist history, but it nonetheless generates language and narrative structures that can then be overturned in order to explore the cultural identity of a marginalized people. The same cannot be said for the presence of blackness within arguably the most foundational iterations of the western (consider almost anything written by Louis L'Amour or starring John Wayne).[5] This racial elision also extends beyond the purview of the literary and into historical accounts of the American West, for, as Michael K. Johnson notes in *Hoo-Doo Cowboys and Bronze Buckaroos* (2013), "the dominant mythologies surrounding western migration and settlement have until recently dampened investigation of the black West," and even as historical accounts have turned their eyes toward the black West, "literary history is still lagging far behind."[6] To an extent, African Americans do not exist in the western imaginary—they are a particular other made permanently absent from the genre's social order.

Upon first glance, King's world does not confront this legacy of absence. Rather, its western sensibilities are recognizably generic. The series begins with protagonist Roland Deschain chasing a man dressed in black across a desert that "was the apotheosis of all deserts, huge, standing to the sky for what looked like eternity in all directions. It was white and blinding and waterless and without feature save for the faint, cloudy haze of the mountains which sketched themselves on the horizon."[7] Aside from its quasi-mythic proportions, the landscape resonates with popularized images of the American West. But then the façade falters, and difference emerges. The frontier once envisioned in accordance with manifest destiny is not only closed, it seems to be forgotten: "An occasional tombstone sign pointed the way, for once the drifted track . . . had been a highway. Coaches and buckas had followed it. The world had moved on since then. The world had emptied."[8] As Adam Kozaczka contends, this postapocalyptic imagery is part and parcel of King's "experimental model," which "subjects the archetypes of the American frontier to supernatural pressure."[9]

There are less horrific pressures at play as well. Captivated by the epic scale of J. R. R. Tolkien's work as a younger writer, King admits that, at least for his own narrative purposes, there was still something missing from *The Lord of the Rings* (1954–55): "I liked the idea of the quest—loved it, in fact—but I had no interest in either Tolkien's sturdy peasant characters . . . or his bosky Scandinavian settings."[10] Turning to the silver screen for inspiration,[11] King realized while watching Sergio Leone's *The Good, the Bad, and the Ugly* (1966) "that what [he] wanted to write was a novel that contained Tolkien's sense of quest and magic but set against Leone's almost absurdly majestic Western backdrop."[12] It is therefore only fitting that Roland is a spiritual successor to Clint Eastwood's Man with No Name;[13] in fact, King's antihero "belongs to a mythological American archetype, the exemplars of which are 'nihilistic and unanchored,'" which is to say he is a gunfighter "governed by an ethical system that allows for violence because it considers it to be specific to the privations and opportunities of the frontier."[14] Like misaligned magnets, Tolkien's and Leone's influences push and pull *The Dark Tower*'s ethical framework. On the one hand, Tolkien creates a cosmos neatly divided into good and evil that resists moral relativism, and, on the other, Leone produces a frontier "marked by violence and brutality" in an effort to revise "the familiar mythic West of opportunity, hope, and redemption" and replace it with "the darker, nightmarish version that had always lurked in the shadows of the American Dream."[15]

Despite the social critique Leone's revisionist sensibilities might then seem to enable, and that Tolkien's quest structure may at the same time preclude, both lines of influence—nightmare and fantasy—are ultimately aligned in their need to create a permission structure for spectacular acts of violence. In other words, violence becomes an engine for plot and character development. Inevitably, *The Dark Tower*'s construction of its central African American character is influenced by its adherence to an ethos rooted in the expurgation of the other.

Given the limitations of Leone's revisionist imaginary and Tolkien's folkloric sensibility, King deforms and supplements his weird western with tropes and figures from the horror and science fiction traditions in order to construct and, to a lesser extent, centralize the subjectivity of an African American woman. However, this tactic proves a double-edged sword. For, as Robin Means Coleman points out, historically the horror tradition has cultivated two understandings of blackness: "In the first instance, Blacks have been rendered deficient—childlike, carrying taint, lower in socioeconomic standing, a metaphor and catalyst for evil, and demonized," and yet the genre also holds "the potential to shed encumbrances of African American representations rooted in, and derived from, a sort of 'fin-de-siecle minstrelsy.'"[16] This precarious tension between horror's capacity to produce either recuperative possibilities or—more often—reified and racist catastrophes is also present in science fiction. Within the realm of filmic representation in particular, Adilifu Nama reminds us that while "the horror genre has been critiqued for reanimating racist caricatures of blackness," science fiction "is also culpable for associating physical spectacle with persons of color."[17] Even in the case of heroic portrayals of black characters, "their bizarre physicality amplifies their racial difference."[18] By adopting tropes from both genres, *The Dark Tower* amplifies difference on two fronts. Its heroic other emerges through an overdetermined representational process aimed at producing a familiar origin story (e.g., a haunted hero filled with promise) that collates socially and historically recognizable attributes given to blackness by its other, rather than construct a singular subjectivity infused with possibility.

The Drawing of Madness

In the second novel, *The Drawing of the Three* (1987), Roland Deschain must recruit three companions from across different times and universes to help him on his quest to keep the Dark Tower—a structure that holds together all the various dimensions in a larger multiverse—from falling into the hands of the Crimson King, a demonic figure similar to Satan. After enlisting the help of a drug addict named Eddie Dean, Roland moves on to his second companion, an African American woman and civil rights activist named Odetta Holmes.[19] The gunslinger once again travels across dimensions, leaving behind his home, known as Mid-World, by passing through a door engraved with the words "The Lady of Shadows." Since he has no advance information about the companions that he needs to recruit, this engraving provides Roland with his first sense of what lies ahead, which is to say, darkness and uncertainty. When Eddie insists that he join Roland on this mission, the gunslinger rejects the offer, warning that there could be something unpleasant on the other side: "For all either of us know, the Lady of Shadows might have eight eyes and nine arms."[20] As such, Odetta is preemptively figured in monstrous terms, and her body, above all else, becomes central to the construction of her character.

Furthermore, her paradoxical body is defined at turns by its overabundance of materiality (eight eyes and nine arms) as well as by its immateriality (shadows). Drawn directly from the world of horror, the Lady of Shadows is what Noël Carroll refers to as a "fusion figure": "a composite that unites attributes held to be categorically distinct and/or at odds in the cultural scheme of things."[21] According to Carroll, such figures arouse fear and disgust in other characters, as well as readers, due in large part to their perceived impurity. By even provisionally constructing Odetta Holmes in this manner, King eschews the subtlety of other allegorical approaches to race in favor of rendering obvious what is often a latent connection within the history of American ideology—that is, the construction of black bodies as monstrous and impure, as ontological nightmares worthy of both fear and disgust. The western does not readily provide the language necessary for exploring and critiquing this particular side of the American racial imaginary, but horror, with its rich history of ontological exploration and uncertainty, does. With that said, unearthing and then literalizing an often submerged white supremacist ideology is not the same as wrestling with its implications.

In short order, a further contradiction is heaped upon Odetta. Once Roland steps through the interdimensional doorway, King's folksy narrator intervenes to properly introduce the African American woman: "Stripped of jargon, what Adler said was this: the perfect schizophrenic—if there was such a person—would be a man or woman not only unaware of his other persona(e), but unaware that anything at all was amiss in his or her life. Adler should have met Detta Walker and Odetta Holmes."[22] Accordingly, Odetta is not only dealing with a mental health issue; she is apparently a perfect schizophrenic.[23] By initially framing her in such terms, the text reproduces "the cultural tendency to read people experiencing mental distress purely from a diagnostic perspective."[24] Indeed, these narrow "psychiatric models classify people as either ill or not ill," and by accepting that framework, patients—and in this context, King's narrative—must then also "accept new, limited, and diminished understandings of themselves."[25]

Through this doubled introduction both Odetta's body and mind are made to signify, but this signification inevitably exceeds the use value envisioned for it by the text. Constructing Odetta as a disabled African American woman seems to helpfully gesture toward the argument made by certain disabilities scholars, including Deborah Marks and Michelle Jarman, that we must consider "racism and ableism as intersecting processes of exclusion," and yet King's series, defined as it is by a quest structure that moves its characters from lack to fulfillment, presents these intersecting exclusions as the necessary preconditions for a moment of recuperative inclusion.[26] In so doing, *The Dark Tower* flattens—if not outright ignores—the complicated historical relationship between blackness and psychiatric discourses, a history that includes "racist misappropriations of 'madness,' not only to justify social oppression, but to perpetuate the so-called rationality of slavery itself."[27]

In part, the text's superficial engagement with its own signifiers is evidenced by its portrayal of Detta Walker as more caricature than character. The angry id to Odetta's reserved ego, Detta is violent and deceptive, wreaking havoc whenever she seizes control. The inverse relationship between the women's dispositions also manifests within their respective physical qualities. Due to an accident at a subway station, Odetta is missing the bottom half of her legs, which often leaves her reliant on others. When Detta gains control, she transforms this supposedly deficient body into one that possesses unexpected, almost supernatural, strength. Rather than turn away from a deficit-oriented understanding of either blackness or disability, this horror-inspired transformation only heightens Odetta's difference, particularly when presented within the otherwise inhospitable narrative logic of the western, in which the hero's body is always a normatively abled body. Odetta-Detta deforms and supplements the genre so it can accommodate her blackness, but in so doing she is represented stereotypically as yet another frighteningly empowered and wholly deficient black female body.

That is not to say that her representation forecloses any and all possibility for producing critique. As a radical figure of difference integrated into the western, Odetta-Detta becomes the standpoint from which the text examines the genre's mythology, as well as its historical consequences on the American sociopolitical order, particularly as it stands after the assassination of John F. Kennedy, who fashioned himself more or less as a new cowboy for a new era. In 1960, upon accepting the Democratic Party's nomination, Kennedy famously framed his political approach by introducing the concept of the New Frontier. Richard Slotkin notes that this reimagined "'Frontier' was for [Kennedy and his advisors] a complexly resonant symbol, a vivid and memorable set of hero-tales—each a model of successful and morally justifying action on the stage of historical conflict."[28] If Kennedy truly opened up a new frontier, then what became of it after his assassination? *The Drawing of the Three* finds Odetta within that historical moment, mulling over that very question. When her driver mentions a newspaper article describing the recently assassinated Kennedy as the last gunslinger, Odetta initially rejects the idea: "There was something about that phrase—*America has seen the passage of the world's last gunslinger*—that rang deeply in her mind. It was ugly, it was untrue—John Kennedy had been a peacemaker, not a leather-slapping Billy the Kid type, that was more in the Goldwater line—but it had also for some reason given her goosebumps."[29] The obvious, immediate purpose of the article is to generate dramatic irony—readers know that Kennedy cannot be the last gunslinger, because Roland exists. That Odetta senses this helps establish her fateful connection to the actual last gunslinger, and by extension the western writ large. However, the moment also functions as an initial critique of American mythology, one that Odetta then continues to develop: "In a world which had become a nuclear powder keg upon which nearly a billion people now sat, it was a mistake—perhaps one of suicidal proportions—to believe there was a difference between good shooters and bad shooters. There were too many shaky hands holding lighters near too many fuses. This was no world for gunslingers."[30] Odetta defines the legacy of the western by its instantiation of global precariousness, rather than unending bounty. Its cut-and-dry moral universe is deemed not only insufficient for the new world order, but as fundamentally flawed in the first place. As such, the black-and-white hat structure at the genre's core is upended when passed through Odetta's epistemological standpoint, with little to no distinction drawn between good and bad shooters. Violence is violence, Odetta suggests, and no matter the intent, its perpetuation only pulls the world closer to destruction. The western is therefore insidious in the ways it justifies violence, tidying up the quandaries it produces through the strict enforcement of moral simplicity.

Nonetheless, King's series does not—and in fact cannot, given its own adherence to a fundamentally patriarchal quest structure—entirely disavow the western's myths and symbols. Once Odetta affirms that "if there had ever been a time for [gunslingers], it had passed," she then undercuts her own certainty in the very next sentence: "Hadn't it?" she hesitates, suggesting a willingness, or perhaps even a desire, to imagine a world through a reductive good versus evil binary.[31] The small equivocation functions as a microcosm of the series' larger attempt to open a door of possibility through which the western can be made anew. In the last instance, this investment in generic renovation also quiets any potential for a rigorous examination of blackness because it narrows the scope of its vision to fit within the confines of the type of uplift narrative that is commensurate with the moral simplicity and narrative rhythms of the chivalric quest structure that inspires King's series. By figuring Odetta as a civil rights activist, the text has always-already interpellated her as a socially "deficient" figure struggling toward a singular goal, creating a closed narrative system in which the only possible inputs are overcoded, resulting in outputs that are all but expected. Effectively, *The Dark Tower* faces a conundrum: Can a genre be deployed to solve the very problems it helped create?

The Production of (Western) Blackness

An attempt to answer that conundrum lies—at least in part—in the implementation of tropes and figures from science fiction and horror that help to introduce specific concepts of race and gender that the conventional western is not often adept at addressing. The most apparent and arguably most significant of these newly integrated concepts is W. E. B. Du Bois's double consciousness. By splitting Odetta's mind in two, the text not only lays the groundwork for its subsequent construction of Odetta-Detta as a figure from the horror tradition; it also literalizes a version of double consciousness. Du Bois describes this "peculiar sensation" felt by African Americans as the "sense of always looking at one's self through the eyes of others," such that "one ever feels his twoness—an American, a Negro; two souls, two thoughts, two unreconciled strivings; two warring ideals in one black body, whose dogged strength alone keeps it from being torn asunder."[32] In this context, Odetta's "madness" is legible as both anger and insanity, as both the inner emotion of a potentially irresolvable self and a false perception imposed upon that same self. Understood as such, it is clear why double consciousness can be thought of as analogous to certain horror-based ontological structures. To live a life of double consciousness is, in some ways, to live a life of horror. Still, while Du Bois's concept emphasizes the great uncertainty imposed upon black subjectivities by a sociopolitical structure from which they are inherently seen as the other, it also begins to identify the "dogged strength" one could mine from this position of apparent weakness. After all, to maintain a self even as it is constantly under threat of being torn asunder requires a certain steadfast resolve—a resolve that fits within the western's archetype of the lonely, wandering gunman (e.g., 1953's *Shane*).

In the case of Odetta-Detta, additional layers built into her resolve shift her beyond the self-reliant cowboy, which suggestively alters the genre's sense of self. As a physically and mentally "disabled" African American woman, she is what Patricia Hill Collins refers to as an "outsider within," both vis-à-vis the specific sociopolitical world of *The Dark Tower* and the more general ideology of the western. Developed in accordance with feminist standpoint theories, which seek to reframe or counter dominant epistemologies through an investment in the unique value of marginalized positions, Collins deploys the outsider-within label to describe the historical status of African American women, who are subjected to, and subjugated by, the intersecting binaries of race, gender, and class. Indeed, Collins argues that this manifold marginalization actually "provide[s] a special standpoint on self, family, and society for Afro-American women."[33] This special standpoint is also what bell hooks describes as the "particular way of seeing reality" that is afforded to those who look "both from the outside in and from the inside out."[34] Crucially, for hooks, that "oppositional world view" was also "a mode of seeing unknown to most of our oppressors," which "strengthened our sense of self and our solidarity."[35] In this fashion, Collins and hooks critique the patriarchal heroism undergirding Du Bois's argument, while also elaborating upon one of its contentions. That is to say, if living a life of double consciousness and marginalization on many fronts can be a horror, it can also provide the foundation for ideological revolution. By constructing an outsider within to weird the western's sense of self, King opens the possibility that the genre's racial and gender imaginary might be transformed.

As far as *The Dark Tower* is concerned, part of this potential transformation must begin with the well-worn and tragic construction of blackness as abjection. On the one hand, Odetta-Detta's manifold marginalization allows her to render visible issues of race and gender that are otherwise obscured in the western: for example, her fraught relationship to her parents and her family's history (her father "would not speak" about the past, "perhaps *could* not, had perhaps willingly afflicted himself with a selective amnesia")[36] suggests the historical ramifications of Orlando Patterson's twin concepts of social death and natal alienation.[37] Relatedly, the narrative's fixation with her marked body indexes Hortense Spillers's argument regarding slavery's calculated work to erase black subjectivities and bodies and replace them with mere flesh.[38] On the other hand, Odetta-Detta becomes a character beholden to caricature. To look at either woman is to view a person through a fun-house mirror that creates the effect of "always looking at one's self through the eyes of others."[39] Since the narrative is often focalized through Roland's perspective, that sentiment is deployed quite literally. In fact, when he travels across dimensions, his body remains behind in Mid-World while his consciousness enters Odetta's mind undetected. An array of outside perspectives is then added to that filter, further distancing the reader's experience of Odetta-Detta. While there are moments that take place within the exposed consciousness of both personalities, more often than not the text accounts for them through the looking glass of a (white) other.

In one particularly crucial moment, when the narrative describes Odetta's experience in the hospital immediately after she loses her legs, it does so through the eyes of a nervous intern. As he witnesses the shift in Odetta's personalities in real time, the intern-as-narrator categorizes her as follows: "She talked like a cartoon black woman, Butterfly McQueen gone Loony Tunes. She—or it—also seemed superhuman. This screaming, writhing thing could not have just undergone impromptu surgery by subway train half an hour ago. She bit. She clawed out at him again and again."[40] This description, veering as it does from the comic to the horrific, speaks to how gaps in perception and identity are filled in differently for different people. Despite a shared mysteriousness connected to sudden bouts of violence, a conventional gunslinger is coded by others as charming and awe-inspiring, whereas Odetta is laughable and frightening—in both cases, the object to the gunslinger's subject. The intern's account also astutely references a popular mid-century African American actress who serves as a paradigmatic example of the narrow-minded casting practices of the film industry—Thelma "Butterfly" McQueen's first major role as Prissy in *Gone with the Wind* (1939) led to her being typecast as a maid for much of her career—and then also emphasizes the cartoonish representation of African Americans that was imposed upon performers like her. Within this framework, Odetta-Detta embodies a form of precariousness brought about by the convergence of work (servant) and play (cartoon character). That these two supposedly discrete categories have lost all shape within the black female body represents nothing if not an intensification of that subjectivity's marginalization under a capitalist system dominated by a white (male) supremacist ideology: Odetta-Detta must always be working, and her labor (both material and affective) will always help to reinstate her precarious position, rather than her preeminence within that social system, as is the case for the laconic gunslinger she is destined to meet and herself become later in the series. Neither of her two personalities can ever have a firm foothold; each is constantly subject to the sudden imposition of the other, from within and without. Witnessed through the eyes of another, Odetta-Detta is both a black mammy figure and a monstrous fleshy object that possesses both less and more than a normative body. To an extent, this is the inevitable result of King's act of translation—a result that, at last, does not activate critique so much as merely establish its preconditions. Drawn from the margins, Odetta-Detta winds up following in the tradition that Morrison describes in terms of Africanist characters and presences. For Morrison, Africanism more broadly "is the vehicle by which the American self knows itself as not enslaved, but free; not repulsive, but desirable; not helpless, but licensed and powerful."[41] Odetta is the helpless other upon which the gunslinger is built; or, put differently, her repulsiveness is constructed by, and in service of, white men.

While this fraught narrative dynamic ultimately sustains a logic of abjection, it also arguably facilitates *The Dark Tower*'s strongest critique of the submerged race relations that underpin the conventional western. It is revealed that, just as she was not born without her legs, Odetta was not born with a second personality. Both disabilities, which are figured initially as her defining traits, are thrust upon her by two interactions with a superhuman sociopath named Jack Mort—or, as his last name implies, death itself. Once again, the narrative eschews subtlety in favor of both embracing the western's proclivity toward mythic figures while also contorting the genre with the injection of a horrific character: a serial killer that can manage to be both everywhere and nowhere. With that said, Mort is not actually death incarnate. He is an accountant who meticulously plans assaults to make them appear like accidents. But the mundanity of his profession only adds to the horror of his actions. Despite its fantastical trappings, in King's world death is not a spectacular figure; death is taxes. It pervades everyday existence, and it does even more so for people like Odetta who possess a black body. When Odetta is a young girl, Mort drops a brick on her head, which leads to the emergence of Detta. Years later, unaware that she is the same person he once attacked, Mort pushes Odetta in front of a subway train. By failing to recognize her, he strips her of her subjectivity, objectifying her as a target assigned for premature death. As such, through the interactions between Mort and Odetta the narrative allegorizes an American socioeconomic system constructed upon racial oppression: a white man aligned with capitalism disables the mind and body of an African American woman, twice consigning her to "accidental" death and twice failing to satisfy his desires.

Yet while mere survival may be enough to establish Odetta as a protagonist in a horror story, it is not enough for the needs of the western. Under that narrative rubric, she remains an untrained gunslinger—more a witness to, than an enactor of, spectacular (and justified) violence. Consequently, the figure of horror must transform into the heroic fighter, but this comes at a cost. The series translates Du Bois's concept of double consciousness, which is an account of a collective social condition, into an individual's dissociative identity disorder. The tension inherent in double consciousness is maintained for the sake of narrative development, but its sociopolitical content is evacuated. It seems the series cannot alter the western's imagination by rendering a black woman's subjectivity visible without overdetermining and reducing its complexity in order to best fit one of the genre's overriding thematic concerns: specifically, the colonization of the other and the restoration of civil order. Rather than remain a figure of difference that is capable of resisting this colonizing effort because she occupies a productively liminal space, Odetta eventually facilitates the western's narrative desires. She is, in that respect, no different than Eddie, who must overcome his drug addiction, or Roland himself, riddled with guilt about a past that he must expurgate before he can claim his destiny as savior.

Perhaps more important, as Odetta's relation to the text shifts, any remnants of her critical epistemological standpoint are overridden by a different understanding of reality, one that Michelle Wright refers to in *Physics of Blackness* (2015) as the "Middle Passage epistemology," which offers a linear and limiting conception of history (i.e., one continuous progress narrative) that unhelpfully "consolidate[s] a false notion of normative Blackness within the heterosexual male."[42] As Wright argues, this epistemology is compelling and has produced great insights (e.g., the work of Du Bois), but it nonetheless refines rather than expands our understanding of blackness. Its adherence to a "strict logic of cause and effect" creates a narrative pattern within which "whiteness is the actor and Blackness the reactor," which "reduces Blackness to something far simpler than what it actually is."[43] Hence, in order to claim a normative form of agency—a desire that must be satisfied within the deficit-and-recovery model created by the Middle Passage epistemology—Odetta needs to change. However, the western's architecture restricts the means by which such a transformation can occur: one gains power through (justified) violence. In addition to the racially loaded tropes—such as blackness-as-monster—that the series deploys, by associating agency with violence *The Dark Tower* further restricts blackness. Within these parameters, Odetta's personhood is translated not only by the other characters in her world, but also by the text itself into an intentionally crude blueprint for race relations in America. She exists in a sort of settled-for-now state that was always destined for resolution. The problem is that the series is ill equipped to handle the implications of its own narrative acts. Indeed, the weird genre tropes deployed to expand the western become the very same ones that install, and then quickly resolve, superficial iterations of intricate issues of race and gender.

Synthesis, Futurity, and Regression

As Odetta is being drawn from her reality into Mid-World, Roland realizes that he must reconcile her multiple personalities and thereby save her from her monstrous state if she is to become a fellow gunslinger. The complexity of this task—and the racially informed problems of double consciousness and subjectivity that it indexes—is simplified and its resolution is expedited through the strange logics of interdimensional travel. The imposition of this science fiction mechanism creates what Darko Suvin refers to as a "novum," which is an element of narrative novelty that helps estrange the reality of the text. In so doing it produces "a feedback oscillation that moves now from the author's and implied reader's norm of reality to the narratively actualized novum . . . and now back from those novelties to the author's reality, in order to see it afresh from the new perspective gained."[44] *The Drawing of the Three* relies upon the novum of interdimensional travel to alter Odetta's, the reader's, and the western's sense of the possible, but in a particularly limited fashion. As Roland, the western hero, ventures across the threshold between worlds, he forcibly synthesizes the dueling personalities by compelling the now divided Odetta and Detta to look at one another in order to gain a new perspective—namely, his: "Detta saw herself in the doorway, saw herself through her eyes, saw herself through the *gunslinger*'s eyes."[45]

When Roland crashes back into Mid-World, he hears "Odetta

shrieking in two voices," and then he "[sees] exactly what he had heard: not one woman but two. Both were legless, both dark-skinned, both women of great beauty. Nonetheless, one of them was a hag, her interior ugliness not hidden by her outer beauty but enhanced by it."[46] Roland is drawn to this paradoxical site of intermixed beauty and horror, "star[ing] with a feverish, hypnotic intensity" at the "twins who were not really twins at all but negative and positive images of the same woman."[47] In this pivotal moment of reconciliation and reconstruction, Roland reenacts the familiar rhythms of the other's experience of blackness, which is always an experience of abjection. Simultaneously repulsed and enamored, Roland witnesses the synthesis of a dialectical relationship between two limited conceptualizations of blackness, each burdened and overdetermined with characteristics and dispositions most readily aligned with stereotypes: the pacifist and the anarchist, the assimilationist and the isolationist, the prude and the sexual deviant. These are the forms through which blackness can emerge within the confines of *The Dark Tower* because it ultimately understands it as the necessary other—the deficient precondition—of heroic whiteness. In so doing, even as the series tries to thwart the proclivities of the conventional western, it reinscribes what André M. Carrington refers to as a "dynamic of alienation between speculative fiction and Blackness."[48] Odetta-Detta must leave the text in order to become a self-reliant, and therefore nonalienated, western hero.

At first, this reclamation of self takes place in surprising fashion, given the violence that precedes it. Odetta stops attacking Detta and literally embraces her other self. As a result, she momentarily rejects what Richard Slotkin identifies as the western's guiding principle, regeneration through violence: "Through this transgression of the borders, through combat with the dark elements on the other side, the heroes reveal the meaning of the frontier line (that is, the distinctions of value it symbolizes) even as they break it down. In the process they evoke the elements in themselves (or in their society) that correspond to the 'dark'; and by destroying the dark elements and colonizing the border, they purge darkness from themselves and from the world."[49] Even as Odetta transgresses the borders of self, she does not purge herself of Detta. Instead, her previously bifurcated state is reformed as a stable trinity. When Roland asks her who she is, she replies, "I am three women."[50] Odetta and Detta are not necessarily gone, but their presence is muted in the face of the emergence of a new personality named Susannah Dean. Emboldened by her new sense of self, Susannah's first act is to save Roland and Eddie, who are under attack from monstrous lobster-like creatures. In this moment, the western's imagination has expanded: an African American woman takes up arms, becoming the gunslinger and demonstrating her fierce confidence and deadly precision with "brown hands [that] were full of thunder" as she saves two white men.[51] Once freed of the monsters, Roland tries and fails to save Eddie, who is tangled in ropes. Susannah steps in, and, much to Roland's wonder, "there was a knife in her hand . . . *his* knife."[52] The symbolism is quite apparent: if only temporarily, she has taken up his mantle as savior.

In this manner Susannah shifts beyond Odetta-Detta's stereotypical angry black woman toward a hybrid, agentive subject capable of enacting justified (according to the terms of the western's ethics), rather than senseless, violence. From her first act, she begins to construct her own history and identity, one that is granted a futurity formerly unimaginable. The clearest indication of this emerges in the final novel in the series, *The Dark Tower* (2004). As Roland approaches the end of his quest, Susannah elects to leave his side. In another context this act would serve simply to elevate the typical western protagonist's romanticized solitude and fierce individuality, allowing him to confront the antagonist on his own (often in a final duel), but in this instance Susannah's decision also functions as an assertion of self and a claim to futurity. Whereas the other main characters die or remain trapped in the series' recursive prison (the end of the last novel repeats the opening of the first), Susannah elects to leave the gunslinger's side in order to find her own ending, rather than continue to act in service of his. She steps out of time, outside the linear uplift narrative within which she was locked from her time as Odetta-Detta, and outside the Middle Passage epistemology that can only know blackness as a reactor instead of an actor. In contrast, she decides to live within what Wright refers to as "epiphenomenal spacetime," in which agency "is not tied to concrete outcomes (born of concrete goals) but to the choice to notice and wonder at differences that the linear progress narrative struggles to wholly interpellate on its own."[53] For Susannah and for the readers following her journey, to wonder and to notice is to escape the western's restrictions into science fictional futurity.

When she tells Roland that she has been dreaming of another reality and wants to leave through an interdimensional doorway, the gunslinger tries to dissuade her: "Susannah, what if the dream itself is a trick and a glammer? What if the things you see even when the door's open are nothing but tricks and glammers? What if you roll right through and into todash space?"[54] Threatened with the possibility of todash space (this universe's version of oblivion), Susannah calmly replies, "Then I'll light the darkness with thoughts of those I love."[55] In a scene that recalls and inverts her predecessor's introduction, Susannah expels her former self, the Lady of Shadows. As she offers Roland a farewell kiss, "she taste[s] death": "*But not for you, gunslinger, she thought. For others, but never for you. May I escape your glammer, and may I do fine.*"[56] Susannah recognizes that she needs to escape Roland's mythological thrall and toxic masculinity. Indeed, just as Odetta called into question the moral and ethical rationalizations of violence forged within the logics of the western mythos, so, too, does Susannah strike at the genre's core. A so-called "glammer," a distracting falsehood, pervades the very essence of the white, hypermasculine hero. The silent masses that fall victim to this deception, which are required to prop it up and perpetuate it, find their voice through Susannah. She upends the dynamic that first existed between her and the gunslinger. Now he is the monster. Now he is the one whose body exudes death.

Insofar as her decision represents a remarkable act of defiance, it then begins to crumble upon further scrutiny. Considering the larger narrative context within which it occurs, it is clear that even Susannah remains burdened by a form of Morrison's Africanism. Time and again throughout the novels she is reduced to a sexual object for, and a caretaker of, white men: she becomes Eddie's lover, is frequently gazed upon by other men, and also serves as a mother figure to a young boy named Jake, the third member recruited by Roland. As such, she cannot fully escape the stereotypical trappings inhabited by her former self. Even though she is ostensibly the solution to double consciousness, Susannah returns to her predecessor's bodily and monstrous roots when she becomes possessed in the penultimate volume, *Song of Susannah* (2004). After a demon sleeps with Roland and "steals" his semen, that demon then transfers the semen to another demon that rapes and impregnates Susannah. As a result of these convoluted and horrific encounters, Susannah becomes a fusion figure once more, embodying the stereotypical fecundity and deathliness of female blackness. She is placed in what Coleman refers to as "a complicated scheme of aberrance in which [black women] are simultaneously hypersexual and available, but are not at all feminine, beautiful, or sexy (by traditional, Western standards)."[57] Part human and part demon, Susannah then gives birth to Mordred, a monstrous spider-child prophesied to help the Crimson King destroy all world order. In once again subsuming the complex problems of race instantiated by a horror trope under the narrative's overriding desire to satisfy the expected rhythms of a fantastical and romantic quest, the series figures Susannah's overdetermined rape and pregnancy as just another obstacle in a journey toward wholeness. In fact, when she does make her decision to leave Roland's side, she does so out of her strong desire to find Eddie and Jake, both of whom have died. In *The Dark Tower*'s epilogue, Susannah comes across alternate versions of the two characters, and, although they do not know Susannah, the two find comfort in her, and she in them. In the last instance, the series resolves Susannah's fragmented life—it resolves any question regarding the relation between blackness and futurity—through a return to the more or less normative nuclear family unit. The text does try to complicate this pat resolution with a final interjection ("And will I tell you that these three lived happily ever after? I will not, for no one ever does. But there was happiness. And they *did* live") but the normative sentiment remains firmly in place.[58]

Any attempt at a complex construction of blackness is set aside so that existence *itself* can be appreciated: after admitting that the three do live, the narrator tells readers, "That's all. That's enough. Say thankya."[59]

In the end, there is a tension between the text's desire to represent Susannah as a new, agentive force within the western and the forms of representation it deploys to realize this desire. Susannah and her predecessor are rendered visible and legible first and foremost through the proliferation of disability, such that blackness is figured as a pathological condition that splits the mind asunder and radically alters the body. If potential still adheres to blackness, it does so almost exclusively outside the narrative's vision. That is, Susannah must leave the text to discover a futurity that is even marginally decoupled from the heroic and normative white male. Although King's series applies pressure to the traditional western's understanding of racial hierarchy by at times adopting the epistemological standpoint of an African American woman and by injecting devices from fantasy, horror, and science fiction, these pressures can only produce an incomplete gesture, because they remain beholden to their own complex and often racist relations to blackness. Odetta, Detta, and even Susannah are each overdetermined and therefore overburdened representations, indexing issues that are quickly resolved and easily subsumed under a master narrative focused on linear progress.

NOTES

1. Morrison, *Playing in the Dark*, 16.
2. Kozaczka, "Genre Exchange," 88.
3. Susannah is the name for the character's final identity. When she is first introduced, she is a woman named Odetta Holmes.
4. Carrington, *Speculative Blackness*, 1–2.
5. Of course, as Michael K. Johnson and others have demonstrated, there is an extensive literary history of African Americans in the West. These texts are highly significant in their own right, but their explorations of race (and often gender) operate on a different register than King's contribution to the hybrid genre known as the weird western, and therefore they fall outside the purview of my more localized argument.

6. Johnson, *Hoo-Doo Cowboys*, 4.
7. King, *Gunslinger*, 3.
8. King, *Gunslinger*, 3.
9. Kozaczka, "Genre Exchange," 90.
10. King, *Gunslinger*, xiv.
11. King's relationship to film, particularly the popular B movies of the 1950s, is crucial to keep in mind when discussing his sense of genre. For example, the horror and science fiction traditions from which he draws inspiration are just as much a product of films like *The Blob* (1958), *The Fly* (1958), and *Invasion of the Body Snatchers* (1956) as they are of H. P. Lovecraft's or Isaac Asimov's stories.
12. King, *Gunslinger*, xv.
13. Descended from frontier narratives such as James Fennimore Cooper's *Leatherstocking Tales*, the western has always had deep ties to the romantic tradition, within which the quest motif is integral. This underlying commonality makes the combination of Tolkien and Leone less strange than it first appears. In fact, King himself seems to understand this deeper generic connection, given that he makes his protagonist, Roland Deschain, a direct descendent of a variation on King Arthur named Arthur Eld. Roland is both a cowboy and a knight, and therefore figured as the protector of the realm.
14. Kozaczka, "Genre Exchange," 95.
15. Aquila, *Sagebrush Trail*, 197.
16. Coleman, *Horror Noire*, 9–10.
17. Nama, *Black Space*, 72.
18. Nama, *Black Space*, 72.
19. Odetta Holmes was a singer commonly referred to as the "Voice of the Civil Rights Movement." In alluding directly to this historical figure, King has already begun the process of interpellating blackness through a particular prism—that is, blackness as locked in a perpetual uplift narrative.
20. King, *Drawing*, 177.
21. Carroll, *Philosophy of Horror*, 43.
22. King, *Drawing of the Three*, 181.
23. It should be noted that what Odetta deals with, in as much as her condition can or should be translated into actual psychological terms, is more properly understood as dissociative identity disorder than as schizophrenia.

24. Jarman, "Coming Up," 24.
25. Jarman, "Coming Up," 16.
26. Jarman, "Coming Up," 19.
27. Jarman, "Coming Up," 16.
28. Slotkin, *Gunfighter Nation*, 3.
29. King, *Drawing of the Three*, 182.
30. King, *Drawing of the Three*, 183.
31. King, *Drawing of the Three*, 183.
32. Du Bois, *Souls of Black Folk*, 7.
33. Collins, "Outsider Within," 103.
34. hooks, "Preface," xvii.
35. hooks, "Preface," xvii–xviii.
36. King, *Drawing of the Three*, 197.
37. Patterson, *Social Death*.
38. Spillers, "Mama's Baby."
39. Du Bois, *The Souls of Black Folk*, 7.
40. King, *Drawing of the Three*, 215.
41. Morrison, *Playing in the Dark*, 51.
42. Wright, *Physics of Blackness*, 44.
43. Wright, *Physics of Blackness*, 38.
44. Suvin, *Metamorphoses*, 71.
45. King, *Drawing of the Three*, 391.
46. King, *Drawing of the Three*, 391.
47. King, *Drawing of the Three*, 391.
48. Carrington, *Speculative Blackness*, 93.
49. Slotkin, *Gunfighter Nation*, 351–52.
50. King, *Drawing of the Three*, 395.
51. King, *Drawing of the Three*, 394.
52. King, *Drawing of the Three*, 395.
53. Wright, *Physics of Blackness*, 117.
54. King, *Dark Tower*, 747.
55. King, *Dark Tower*, 748.
56. King, *Dark Tower*, 748.
57. Coleman, *Horror Noire*, 39.
58. King, *Dark Tower*, 813.
59. King, *Dark Tower*, 813.

BIBLIOGRAPHY

Aquila, Richard. *The Sagebrush Trail: Western Movies and Twentieth-Century America*. Tucson: University of Arizona Press, 2015.

Carrington, André M. *Speculative Blackness: The Future of Race in Science Fiction*. Minneapolis: University of Minnesota Press, 2016.

Carroll, Noël. *The Philosophy of Horror*. New York: Routledge, 1990.

Coleman, Robin Means. *Horror Noire: Blacks in American Horror Films from the 1890s to Present*. New York: Routledge, 2011.

Collins, Patricia Hill. "Learning from the Outsider Within." In *The Feminist Standpoint Theory Reader: Intellectual and Political Controversies*, edited by Sandra Harding, 103–26. New York: Routledge, 2004.

Du Bois, W. E. B. *The Souls of Black Folk*. New York: Pocket, 2005.

hooks, bell. "Preface to the First Edition." In *Feminist Theory: From Margin to Center*, xvii–xviii. New York: Routledge, 2015.

Jarman, Michelle. "Coming Up from Underground: Dialogues at the Intersections of Race, Mental Illness, and Disabilities Studies." In *Blackness and Disability: Critical Examinations and Cultural Interventions*, edited by Christopher M. Bell, 9–30. East Lansing: Michigan State University Press, 2011.

Johnson, Michael K. *Hoo-Doo Cowboys and Bronze Buckaroos: Conceptions of the African American West*. Jackson: University Press of Mississippi, 2014.

King, Stephen. *The Dark Tower*. New York: Scribner, 2004.

———. *The Drawing of the Three*. 1987. New York: Viking, 2003.

———. *The Gunslinger*. Rev. ed. New York: Plume, 2003.

Kozaczka, Adam S. "Genre Exchange on the Supernatural Frontier in Stephen King's *The Gunslinger*: The Gunfighter Archetype Meets the Ravenous Other." In *Undead in the West II: They Just Keep Coming*, edited by Cynthia J. Miller and A. Bowdoin Van Riper, 87–105. Toronto: Scarecrow, 2013.

Morrison, Toni. *Playing in the Dark: Whiteness and the Literary Imagination*. New York: Vintage, 1993.

Nama, Adilifu. *Black Space: Imagining Race in Science Fiction Film*. Austin: University of Texas Press, 2008.

Patterson, Orlando. *Slavery and Social Death*. Cambridge MA: Harvard University Press, 1982.

Slotkin, Richard. *Gunfighter Nation: The Myth of the Frontier in Twentieth-Century America*. Norman: University of Oklahoma Press, 1998.

Spillers, Hortense. "Mama's Baby, Papa's Maybe: An American Grammar Book." *Diacritics* 17, no. 2 (1987): 65–81.

Suvin, Darko. *Metamorphoses of Science Fiction: On the Poetics and History of a Literary Genre*. New Haven CT: Yale University Press, 1979.

Wright, Michelle. *Physics of Blackness: Beyond the Middle Passage Epistemology*. Minneapolis: University of Minnesota Press, 2015.

Uncle Tom's Cabin Showdown   11

Stowe, Tarantino, and the Minstrelsy of the Weird West

JOSHUA D. SMITH

In the closing sequence of Quentin Tarantino's *Django Unchained* (2012), Django, the protagonist, squares off against Stephen, the story's highest-ranking slave and unlikely nemesis, in a literal showdown. Tarantino's intentional fusion of the tropes of the Hollywood western with the elements of a neo–slave narrative culminate in a carefully crafted symbolic moment. The symbolism of the scene is not merely in Tarantino's allusions to traditional western tropes, nor to *Gone with the Wind*-esque gestures to southern grandeur. Rather, the most powerful symbolism of the scene rests in something far more potent: the uncanny reemergence of Harriet Beecher Stowe. Her person and work haunt the film, most conspicuously in the emblem of the Uncle Tom-ish Stephen. Tarantino, with his controversial portrayals of black life, iconic storytelling, altruistic claims, and white subject position, is a kind of artistic descendent of the author of *Uncle Tom's Cabin* (1852). Loved and loathed with comparable levels of passion, Tarantino has, if nothing else, inherited Stowe's checkered criticism. The showdown itself also casts the specter of Stowe as a confrontation of two competing heroic black archetypes from her novel. In fact, both Stowe and Tarantino center their respective literary and cinematic visions in a deep desire to reframe black (male) heroism, efforts that are inherently embedded in the fantastic: Uncle Tom is a religious exceptionality whose spiritual powers eventually spook his antagonist with gothic terror, while Django is a visually incredulous black figure whose wielding of white male western subjectivity defies racist logic and renders him a kind of de facto superhuman no less terrorizing in his gothic overtones.

Both expressions of black superheroism are in one sense or another imbued with western sensibilities. Specifically, the frontier energies of *Uncle Tom's Cabin* are inherent in its protest of the Fugitive Slave Law, which Stowe understands to be a piece of legislation turning "the broad land between the Mississippi and the Pacific" into "one great market for bodies . . . souls and human property."[1] *Django Unchained* is transparently a spaghetti western, but the movie's touting of the genre's signature tropes is not its only tie to the frontier. The backdrop of Hollywood itself is significant as well, even more so because it is a western signifier also situating Stowe in its ether. Though Stephen and Django are crude caricatures of Stowe's Uncle Tom and George Harris, they nonetheless signify the journey of Stowe's abolitionist vision to Hollywood and into Tarantino's western. *Uncle Tom's Cabin* would eventually be adapted to the stage and, in turn, to early twentieth-century film. The minstrelsy tropes already present in the novel would only be exacerbated across new media. In this regard, *Uncle Tom's Cabin* has had a direct hand in Hollywood's depiction of African Americans and comes full circle to Tarantino: the racialized elements of his films are controversial precisely because of the adaption of Uncle Tom and other iconic black caricatures from the white southern imagination to the big screen over the course of the late nineteenth and early twentieth centuries. Minstrelsy is conspicuous by way of the role it plays in expanding Stowe's influence beyond a southern regionalist context to a Hollywooded west that further mainstreams black caricature. In the end, the phenomenon Stowe creates in Uncle Tom informs Tarantino's work and marks a venture into the weird western, the uncanny and otherworldly expression of one of America's most mythologized narratives.

The Natural Weirdness of the West

According to Cynthia Miller, who writes the introduction to the *Encyclopedia of Weird Westerns* (2016), the weird western genre can be traced back 150 years, in large part because of how loosely it can be defined.[2]

She characterizes it as a story "that weave[s] elements of the fantastic into traditional Western plots, characters and settings to create stories that complicate, reinforce, and comment on our understanding of Westerns and the West."[3] The "fantastic" can encompass any number of metaphysical and supernatural elements including, but not exclusive to, the gothic, the horrific, the spiritual, the technological, and the imaginary. The relevance of the genre to a discussion of race is that the racialized other has historically been the de facto horrific, incredulous, spiritual or muse-like figure in white-authored western fiction, embedding the element of the weird into many things that would not otherwise exhibit the uncanny.

For Reneé L. Bergland, ghostliness is the most persistent manifestation of the western weird. In *The National Uncanny: Indian Ghosts and American Subjects* (2000), she identifies Native Americans as representations of a kind of absence-presence in the national literature, signifiers of a ghostly manifestation, palpable in its haunting of the American psyche.[4] Not only does Bergland cite allusions in early American literature to Native Americans as ghosts, but she also sees this phenomenon as tethered to what is essentially an incomplete exorcism;[5] writing about Native Americans loops white writers back to the original scene of horror, which in sum is "the history of European relations with Native Americans . . . a history of murders, looted graves, illegal transfers, and disruptions of sovereignty."[6] However, rather than account for these original sins, composers of both literary and mythological narrative reinterpret them in performative fictions of "legitimacy and origin."[7] Literary scholars and cultural critics Richard Slotkin and Joseph Roach note how crucial "improvised narratives of authenticity and priority" come to be in a young country lacking the millennia-old traditions of Europe, Asia, Africa, and precolonial America.[8] Moreover, Slotkin takes note of the power of a literary tool to render myth as history: "The Indian Wars proved to be the most acceptable metaphor for the American experience. To all of the complexities of that experience, it offered the simplicity of dramatic contrast and direct confrontation of opposites. It became a literary means of dealing with all sorts of social tensions and controversies—between English and American Puritans, between classes and generations within American society, and between political and religious controversialists."[9] Metaphor is such an unsuspecting instrument. Through it the act and story of warfare with Native Americans become a way of validating and euphemizing genocide. The Indian warfare narrative also serves to eulogize an Indian spirit that white mythologizers can, as a result, conjure and embody. For American writers in the nineteenth century, this entire dynamic can be distilled in the simplicity of a literary device. The poetic quality of the myth of American (re)generation through Native American conquest is not only a convenient tool for the nation's formal storytellers, but also a narrative handle for the rest of the country.[10] The rebirth of the Indian subject within the emerging (white) American one figuratively extends to western expansionism all the redemptive qualities of a Christian resurrection. Certainly, distilling the American story to a simple metaphor is reductive, irreverent, and misleading. However, early colonizing mythologizers only need it to be powerful. This "dramatic contrast . . . of opposites" is the conceptual raw material for the mythology of American whiteness. According to Roach, it is, in the end, theatrical, and one of several "public enactments of forgetting" designed "to blur the obvious discontinuities, misalliances and ruptures" of the American past.[11] Among these "public enactments" is redface minstrelsy, the performative mimicry of Native Americans and a perverse form of honor and wilderness stewardship. It is also a figurative exorcism, an invocation of ghosts from the American past in a vain attempt to quell them.

In her highly acclaimed *Playing in the Dark: Whiteness and the Literary Imagination* (1992), Toni Morrison calls attention to comparable dynamics in the print form of blackface minstrelsy, as she examines "the way black people ignite critical moments of discovery or change or emphasis in literature not written by them."[12] Her project also offers a more expansive view of the cost of the frontier as a conceptual oversimplification; namely, her scholarship situates the African American persona in the identity crisis of white Americans and implicates black

Americans in the borderland between national fantasy and nightmare. Bergland affirms this move as she draws upon Morrison's fiction and scholarship to make her case about the spectral dimensions of young America's literature.[13] Ultimately, Bergland is convinced that America is as haunted by the ghosts of black slaves as it is by the ghosts of Native Americans.[14] The convoluted relationship between western optimism and ghostly horror that she notes as present in the figure of the Native American is no less present in the figure of the African American.

Morrison's scholarship validates this observation as much as her fiction, but in a move that is both unsuspecting and artful. Namely, she seizes upon the optimism and linguistic synergy fueled by classic American frontierism to offer a much more crude, frank, and precise distillation of the mythologized American self: the "new white man."[15] Whiteness is the subject of her inquiry, but it's a concept, she argues, inextricably tied to blackness. That whiteness has hinged on blackness is a well-rehearsed argument among scholars of race, but Morrison is revelatory about this claim, as her poetic tendencies inadvertently produce culturally prophetic insights. While her book merely hints at the idea that blackness and the frontier are related, the mirroring of their relationship is so pronounced that in the opening statements of her first chapter, she finds herself articulating frontier phraseology as a kind of imperative of what is available in the ether: "These chapters put forth an argument for extending the study of American literature into what I hope will be a wider landscape. I want to draw a map, so to speak, of a critical geography and use that map to open as much space for discovery, intellectual adventure, and close exploration as did the original charting of the New World—without the mandate for conquest."[16] Notably the word "frontier" is absent here, but its conceptual presence is not lost on the reader: "landscape," "geography," "map," "space," "discovery," "adventure," "charting," "New World," "mandate," and "conquest" are all cousins of the concept and trigger words that, vis-à-vis each other, retain their hegemonic connotations, even as their imperialist force is renounced. Morrison is not being contradictory, however. Rather, her language and project at large *are* mapping; specifically, they are calling out the symbolic coordinates of racial blackness (or what she calls an "Africanist presence") and showing its uncanny influence on the European immigrant reconceptualization of American land and identity.[17] On this matter, the parallels between Native American and African American ghostliness are most apparent. For Morrison, the haunting presence of the Africanist figure is pervasive in early American literature. She makes this most clear in her chapter titled "Romancing the Shadow," a sustained focus on the racialized meanings latent in the work of Edgar Allan Poe. In it, she depicts the Africanist presence as a kind of figurative shadow, a metaphorically "dark and abiding presence," one that is perpetually available to the European immigrant as "a visible and invisible mediating force."[18] The availability and mediating powers of blackness reflect the same qualities in the frontier. Slotkin distills these qualities to a "darkness" that the pioneer must absorb to overcome: "The Indian wars are, for [the pioneers], a spiritual or psychological struggle which they can win by learning to discipline or suppress the savage or 'dark' side of their own human nature."[19] If the powers of the frontier are about a transformation mediated by darkness, how could people of African descent, signifiers of a metaphoric darkness, not be implicated in its mythology? As Morrison explains, "There is no romance free of what Herman Melville called 'the power of blackness,' especially not in a country in which there was a resident population, already black, upon which the imagination could play; through which historical, moral, metaphysical, and social fears, problems, and dichotomies could be articulated."[20]

She continues by explaining that "even, and especially when American texts are not 'about' Africanist presences or characters or narrative or idiom, the shadow hovers in implication, in sign, in line of demarcation."[21] While her explicit thesis is not about the frontier, the frontier still "hovers," "signifies," and "demarcates" in a work about the social construction of whiteness in blackness. Blackness and frontier poetically echo each other in their conceptual flexibility, which is why Morrison can describe them using the same terminology. The idea of blackness *as* frontier, though never stated explicitly, sits in the text as a conceptual possibility. This is especially clear when Morrison discusses the binary opposition of white and black, as it is analogous to the "dramatic contrast . . . of opposites" noted by Slotkin: "It is no mistake that immigrant populations (and much of immigrant literature) understood their 'Americanness' as an opposition to the resident black population."[22] Among other things, black bodies in the American story have performed the function of "demarcation lines," and "in the construction of blackness and enslavement could be found not only the not-free but also, with the dramatic polarity created by skin color, the projection of the not-me."[23]

Minstrelsy as the Western Weird

"The dramatic polarity created by skin color" in people of African descent is less about the status of skin itself and more about the historic flexibility of the concept of blackness: racial blackness, spiritual darkness, moral subversiveness, human otherness, and the literal visual quality of the color black have been conflated since antiquity, making possible easy allusions to any one of the concepts by references to black people. Nothing validates this more than the *Oxford English Dictionary* entry for the word "black." As noted by historian Winthrop D. Jordan, this single entry speaks volumes about the ease with which the English conflated people of African descent with the crudest signifiers of malefaction:

> Englishmen found in the idea of blackness a way of expressing some of their most ingrained values. No other color except white conveyed so much emotional impact. As described by the *Oxford English Dictionary*, the meaning of *black* before the sixteenth century included, "Deeply stained with dirt; soiled, dirty, foul. . . . Having dark or deadly purposes, malignant; pertaining to or involving death, deadly; baneful, disastrous, sinister. . . . Indicating disgrace, censure, liability to punishment, etc." Black was an emotionally partisan color, the handmaid and symbol of baseness and evil, a sign of danger and repulsion.[24]

Such clear connotative links render blackness to be inherently weird and its quality in a figure like Uncle Tom to be even weirder. Upon him rests the angst of Stowe's signature work of fiction, which is only a reflection of the country's—and, most pointedly, Stowe's. Blackness is a concept with which she tries desperately to grapple and about which she attempts to find closure in Tom, who is arguably more her mirror than he is a subject in his own right. As Morrison remarks, "*Uncle Tom's Cabin* was [not] written for Uncle Tom to read or be persuaded by."[25] Rather, she says, "the fabrication of the Africanist persona" (in this case, Tom's) "is reflexive; an extraordinary mediation on the self; a powerful exploration of the fears and desires that reside in the writerly" (in this case, Stowe's) "consciousness."[26] As a novelist composing in the American romantic period, Stowe is as subject as any author to the implications of the romantic philosophy undergirding this principle. Morrison expounds: "[Romance] offered platforms for moralizing and fabulation, and for the imaginative entertainment of violence, sublime incredibility, and terror—and terror's most significant, overweening ingredient: darkness, with all the connotative value it awakened."[27]

The "connotative value ... awakened" by darkness, particularly in the ways racial blackness amplifies its power to signify, becomes a creative asset for the likes of Stowe and Tarantino. They are both white artists with robust storytelling abilities. Resourced with the institutional support, capital, and cultural sanctioning of the public, they are able to produce tales about race on a massive scale and with all the inventive capacities they can muster. In their respective industries and centuries, they are narrative power brokers with the skills to leverage what Morrison calls the "huge payout of sign, symbol and agency" historically afforded to whites who own black stories.[28] Hollywood, the ultimate storytelling frontier, offers, as Slotkin proposes vis-à-vis the physical wilderness, an exploitable "dark side." This figurative darkness manifests as screen versions of the blackface minstrelsy performed on stage in the nineteenth and early twentieth centuries. The mechanics of the classic frontier myth—via this darkness—expose minstrelsy and the subdual of the West to be mutual reflections of each other.

In particular, the ways in which whites imagine the conquest of darkness (as an inherent part of the frontier), Slotkin argues, are as "mediators of a double kind who can teach civilized men how to defeat savagery on its native grounds—the natural wilderness and the wilderness of the human soul."[29] The doubleness Slotkin speaks of refers to a mirroring between the darkness in "the natural wilderness" and the shadowed tendencies of the ego, which first facilitates the instruction of pioneers "learning to discipline or suppress the savage or 'dark' side of their own nature[s]." Secondarily, those same pioneers *become* instructors who are effective because their conquest of the wilderness enables them to teach others "to defeat savagery on its native grounds." Presumably becoming more "native" than the native, they teach from a place of intimacy about savage darkness, which is minstrelsy in principle. Insofar as Native Americans *are* that darkness, Brian W. Dippie in *The Vanishing American: White Attitudes and U.S. Policy* (1982) remarks, they "surrender . . . [to whites] what [is] good in their racial character and absorb . . . [from whites] what [is] bad."[30] This dramatic reversal of racial qualities is essential to the reassuring narrative of American dominance as both good and inevitable. However, the dynamics of racial reversal and frontier conquest not only pertain to Native Americans. Specifically, if darkness is the wilderness "terror's most significant, overweening ingredient," then the globally Western tradition's most prominent personifications of darkness—figures of African descent—make available too much emblematic energy to avoid entanglement in the frontier's mythological reach. Morrison's inadvertent, though intuitive, association of frontier with blackness speaks to the parallels between the two concepts as literary devices that are employed to create fiction in both print and myth.

Centered in the relationship between American western themes and racial blackness is the weird. Certainly, Jordan's highlight of the etymological history of "black" exposes the term to be linked to a kind of moral, cultural, and figurative otherworldliness. Furthermore, as has been illustrated, Slotkin exposes another dimension of the concept's spooky overtone in the idea that the mythology of frontier conquest hinges on the prospect of white people becoming "dark." If nothing else, this part of the myth is transparently reminiscent of minstrelsy, a practice Eric Lott considers to be nestled in "the haunted realm of racial fantasy."[31] If western expansionism lends itself to the racist mimicry of Indian redface, then blackface mimicry, the most physically dramatic absorption of darkness, can also echo the implications of taming the western wilderness, with all of its ties to the uncanny. Bergland's references to ghostliness are relevant here because minstrelsy itself hinges on a kind of spectral duality, and her exposition on the ghostly further tethers the practice to Slotkin's schematic of frontier conquest. Both minstrelsy and Slotkin's theory fit within the scope of her analysis of Freudian uncanniness, which would situate both the darkness of minstrelsy and the darkness of the frontier as figurative configurations designed to repress "feeling[s] of 'dread and creeping horror.'"[32] Just as Slotkin observes a doubleness in his frontier analysis, Bergland determines that the eerie feeling associated with repressed "darkness" is a function of a "dual model of haunting."[33] The duality, she continues, is that, by Sigmund Freud's estimation, "we are haunted either by the revival of what we have repressed or by the (seeming) confirmation of what we have surmounted."[34] The application of this duality to the frontier myth is that the figurative darkness of the western wilderness haunts both in spite of and because of its conquest. This is no less true with respect to the subjugation of persons of African descent who, even after they have been enslaved—and, per Bergland (and Morrison), *because* they have been enslaved—extend to their white counterparts a visual reminder of white savagery. The militaristic and sexual violence inherent in slavery and continental expansionism highlight this as much as anything. The founding and protection of white civilization has hinged on barbaric acts, a matter about which the respective genocidal carnage and slave trade of Native Americans and African Americans serve as perpetual reminders.

    The presence of colonized and enslaved people of color in the United States raises the specter of the irony of civilization: that the repression of savagery has historically called upon savagery. It is far easier for white Americans to project their savage selves onto racialized others than to face their own barbaric tendencies. This is one reason why minstrelsy becomes "the most popular entertainment form of the nineteenth century."[35] The art form is the perfect complement to the frontier narrative, which, according to Roach's theories, is itself inherently theatrical. Blackface minstrelsy is a dramatic representation of the haunting presence of the black figure in American life, a secular séance pursuing the same kind of catharsis that frontier conquest presumably achieves for the pioneer. The wilderness of the American West—in its surmounting—is supposed to purge pioneers of their soulish darkness. The savagery of the physical wilderness seemingly mirrors the savage tendencies of the human psyche, which is figuratively distilled as an internally shadowed presence. The dynamic fosters the felt sense for pioneers that they are being purged of their barbaric tendencies as they cleanse the western landscape of its savage characteristics. Blackface minstrelsy offers the same mirroring effect. The difference is that minstrel performers literally *wear* darkness—and of a kind that not even the skin of black persons can create. As even black minstrel artists are compelled to wear burnt cork to please audiences, Africanist people are only points of reference—symbolically potent, for sure, but not themselves the darkness whites seek to purge, even though whites often state their racial angst in precisely this way. Rather, white "minstrel performers . . . attempt . . . to repress through ridicule the real interest in black cultural practices they nonetheless betray."[36] Their performances are dramatic expressions of the duality Bergland describes: in their ambivalent attraction to black life—what Lott characterizes as "a nearly insupportable fascination and self-protective derision with respect to black people"—white minstrel artists perpetually revive what they conquer in acts that are supposed to confirm the permanence of the conquest.[37] They are subject to a perpetual haunting, their minstrel performances being at once its cause and its cure.

Storytelling and the Hollywooding of Blackness

The paralleling of minstrel and frontier dynamics are not only relevant in a mythical and psychoanalytical context, but also in a physical one. To be sure, the conquest of the geographic west, among other things, relies on "fictive ethnicities" and dramatizations of racial power dynamics to convert the symbolic currency of redness and blackness to the terrestrial currency of western space.[38] With respect to persons of African descent, the "land between the Mississippi and the Pacific" would not be secured apart from a sustained mediation on the status of enslaved populations, black people, and the concept of blackness itself. At no other time is this clearer than in the mid-nineteenth century, when a national boundary to the Pacific Ocean is within reach. The Compromise of 1850, a signature development of the period, signals a watershed moment that significantly contributes to Stowe's motivation for writing *Uncle Tom's Cabin*. One of the most infamous aspects of the Compromise, the Fugitive Slave Law, is the focus of Stowe's ire. Essentially, the law requires that free states cooperate with slave owners to apprehend fugitive slaves that would otherwise find safe hiding places outside the South. This makes California and other western territories prospectively entering the Union liable for escaped slaves. However, as can be surmised from Morrison's comment on "the construction of blackness and enslavement," a free person of African descent is not necessarily disassociated from slavery. Insofar as blackness becomes a sign of the institution, every black person has the potential to become subject to the suspicions of any white person in a free state; consequently, the legal status of slavery becomes less important, as it is possible for nonslaveholding whites and free blacks to become de facto masters and slaves.

This is a phenomenon that might be rightly called southern expansionism, the extension of the power dynamics of slavery beyond the South, especially to the west. In this regard, Hollywood is paramount, especially with respect to its Los Angeles incubator, which is one of several urban geographic markers for the New Jim Crow practices of the prison-industrial complex that eerily echo slavery. By and large, America's storytelling capital is also the urban frontier outpost at which the physical and figurative dimensions of the western trek of southern slave codes culminate and congeal most completely.[39] The first instances of this in the nineteenth century have to do with literal enslavement, the specific nature of which *Uncle Tom's Cabin* addresses forthrightly in a dialogue between two slave-trading business partners, Marks and Mr. Haley: Marks comments to Haley about the availability of "justices at all p[o]ints along shore" that, per his vernacular, "does up any little jobs in our line quite reasonably."[40] The justices to which Marks refers are corrupt judges who, on the basis of a bribe, are willing to corroborate false claims about the legal entitlement of a white person to a slave. Marks's comment suggests the truth of one of historical sociologist Orlando Patterson's summative statements about slavery in *Slavery and Social Death* (1982), that the institution is "a highly symbolized domain of human experience."[41] Legal minutia and physical containment measures are merely the technical apparatuses of slavery. In the end, they do not "produce" the visceral experience of the institution. The power dynamic between slave and master, to use the words of media scholar Monica Cure, only "bec[o]me visible through the discursive practices around it."[42]

The symbolic and discursive elements of slavery are easily amenable to what eventually become the tropes of minstrelsy. The often vain aspirations of white men in the lower echelons of society to enter into the slave-owning class feed into a performance of slave mastery that, though fictional, has material implications. Though without the financial means to be plantation powerhouses or even small-to-midsized estate patriarchs, Marks and Haley can each play the role of the slave owner in spurts, and boast about his mastery over black subjects. However, this game of make-believe not only extends to people with formal slavery-related occupations; because of the Fugitive Slave Law, any white person can participate in the charade. The potential for blacks to be slaves combined with a display of the symbolic markers for slavery (namely, an African phenotype) make them, in effect, slaves. They are perpetually available as the potential property of any white person. In the end, white people do not have to be legal slaveholders, nor do black people have to be legal slaves to support the ideological effects of slavery. All that is needed is a good story supported by the symbolism of the institution.

That storytelling, a movie-industry precursor, could be an avenue to virtual slave ownership is at the heart of blackface performance. Storytelling and other performative rituals of blackness figuratively ascribe slave mastery to individuals who do not actually own slaves, but, rather, *stories* about them. Not only can stories be leveraged to create real master-slave relationships, but stories themselves can be forms of ownership over black people figuratively. They are types of intellectual property scavenged from a public domain that makes available a marketable form of blackness that whites can brand and monetize. In this regard, *Uncle Tom's Cabin* is the quintessential white story about black people. Not only does Stowe draw from a public domain that minstrelsy had already populated with caricatures of black expression, but her own work, upon its publication, immediately becomes, in effect, a contribution to it. To be clear, Stowe is a poacher herself. She adapts tropes from published works (namely, slave narratives) by African Americans, consults directly with black abolitionist and escaped slave Frederick Douglass on the writing of *Uncle Tom's Cabin*, and leverages her access to unquantifiable and unceremonious adaptations of black life through the plethora of minstrel art showcases available to the nineteenth-century American consumer. Hence, in some sense, she eventually receives a taste of her own medicine: creative and business opportunists are quick to adapt Stowe's novel to the stage without her express permission, efforts that eventually lead to comparable adaptations to film. As Kendra Hamilton comments in her essay "The Strange Career of *Uncle Tom's Cabin*," "There [is] no international copyright law in 1852. Stowe own[s] only her novel; therefore, she ha[s] no rights to the characters and [cannot] control their transmission to other media."[43]

However, an argument can be made that the exploitive reworking of Stowe's novel is not merely about intellectual-property robbers capitalizing on loopholes in copyright law. Rather, what gets explained simply as idea theft camouflages a much more sophisticated reality: the proliferation of Stowe's story in its various forms transpires as if her novel were a call for the kind of media center Hollywood would become and that forward-thinking entrepreneurs see in her work, shrewdly preempting it. Unique in its leverage of minstrelsy (the most popular form of entertainment at the time), transformative in the way it synergizes American reading culture, and electric in its resonance with the historical moment, *Uncle Tom's Cabin* is far more than a book.[44] It is a cultural phenomenon that feeds into a proto-Hollywood expansion of American entertainment. Hollywood would eventually exacerbate Stowe-infused black stereotypes fostered in the colloquialisms and regionalisms of the South. This dynamic carries with it the felt sense of inevitability one might hold about the conquest of the frontier: the combination of Hollywood's physical location, the mythology tied to its land, and the intimate relationship between the entertainment industry and minstrelsy adaptation magnetizes Hollywood and black mimicry to each other. While Stowe's role in the shaping of Hollywood and its representation of racial blackness is difficult to measure, any number of black stereotypes (many of which are derivatives of characters Stowe creates and, of those, adaptions from previously existing stock blackface minstrelsy figures) are today still the cultural archetypes against which creators of black stories measure their work. Either in indulgence of them as stereotypes or in resistance to them in protest, they are at the center of contemporary artistic invention generated by or themed around black people.

Tarantino's Burden

As a result, an uncanny aura sits over Tarantino's films. *Django Unchained* appears to give definition to this mythical specter more than his other work and, in one sense, Stowe *is* this specter. While no other Tarantino film cites Stowe in an explicit way, most of them implicate the African American experience—certainly, the reason Stowe casts a shadow on countless other films and filmmakers. However, Tarantino is distinct because he fulfills a role that mirrors Stowe's in eerily precise ways. Comparable to Stowe's role in the nineteenth century, Tarantino's positionality, his status as a white male powerbroker in Hollywood, gives him privileged access to America's storytelling and cultural branding factory, one that has historically rendered black people, black imagery, and black culture as spectacles. His subject position and the power he leverages from it extends back to the origins of both minstrelsy and the Stowe phenomenon. In fact, Jason Richards's 2017 essay "Imitation Nation: Blackface Minstrelsy and the Making of African American Selfhood in *Uncle Tom's Cabin*" determines that minstrelsy and Stowe's iconic novel are "conjoined cultural twins."[45] In sum, Tarantino is tethered to a Stowe-informed storytelling matrix that harbors the slavery and frontier energies that would travel through minstrel shows and vaudeville to eventually land in Hollywood. Stowe and Tarantino are signature participants in a tradition of white writers, artists, filmmakers, and musicians whose novelty is marked—at least in part—by their capacities, within this tradition, to repackage black people and culture for public consumption.

Moreover, Stowe and Tarantino also stand out because their ownership of black stories is also a function of altruism. *Uncle Tom's Cabin* is transparently an abolitionist text, and Tarantino states on the record that the combined lore of the American West and South in *Django Unchained* calls for an otherworldly black hero whom he wants to gift to African American men.[46] In an interview, when asked why he is motivated to create a western movie with slavery as a theme, he responds, "I've always wanted to explore slavery in a film . . . but I guess the reason that actually made me put pen to paper was to give black American males a western hero, give them a cool folkloric hero that could actually be empowering and actually pay back blood for blood."[47] The intentionality of this matches Stowe's in her depiction and revision of superheroism in a black male. For Stowe, the elements of the black and the fantastic rest in Tom's Christian religious convictions, the spirituality of which eventually unnerves his primary antagonist. In fact, in Tom, whom *Uncle Tom's Cabin* explicitly names "the hero of [the] story," Stowe is looking to redefine heroism at large.[48] Knowing "heroism" as a word that has informed the global Western tradition since the *Iliad*, Stowe is on a crusade to radically reshape the term, purging it of its savagery and hypermasculine associations while also aligning it with a feminized Christianity. Tarantino's moral and political orientations create a radically different black superhero in Django, but, in spirit, he and Stowe are participating in the same project. Specifically, Stowe's engagement with western themes have already been noted. Moreover, that Tom's move from Kentucky to Louisiana through the internal slave trade is literally a western one must be given consideration. Furthermore, Tom's physical western trek is not even the detail most relevant to Django's and Tom's frontier twinning. Rather, Tom's character, the exceptionality of his patience, kindness, and faithfulness, raises suspicions in the same way a black person traveling openly across western space would. He is Stowe's version of a "nigger on a horse." This phrase, uttered routinely in *Django Unchained*, is an indicator of the suspicion with which white observers experience Django's wielding of white western male subjectivity. Along the same lines, Tom, in his uncommonness, represents the kind of person who would raise an eyebrow among whites and spur the anxieties motivating the passage and illegal exploitation of the Fugitive Slave Law.

Other parallels between *Django Unchained* and *Uncle Tom's Cabin* further delineate Tarantino's tie to Stowe and the entertainment matrix to which she gives rise: the one-to-one correlation between Stephen and Uncle Tom is transparent. Though far removed from the meek and mild Christian leader Stowe imagines, Stephen is true to the perception of Uncle Tom adopted by African Americans after the resurgence of *Uncle Tom's Cabin* in the 1950s, which views Tom as a brown-nosing traitor to the race. The Django and George Harris characters are also comparable as verbally audacious and physically violent advocates for black freedom. Moreover, Harris and Django each engage in successful rescue missions on behalf of their respective wives, Eliza Harris and Broomhilda. Finally, Stowe and Tarantino each present the sharp contrast between an "angry" and a "loyal" black male figure through juxtaposition.

That Tarantino manages to resurrect key characters and plot points from *Uncle Tom's Cabin* is intriguing, but the structural apparatus in which this happens is most compelling. Specifically, like *Uncle Tom's Cabin*, *Django Unchained* is a neo–slave narrative. A neo–slave narrative takes on some of the attributes of the slave narrative with respect to topical content, structure, and lead character, but is categorically ineligible for slave narrative status, since it is not authored by a former slave. Both Stowe and Tarantino adapt this black storytelling form as a means of improving upon what they surmise is its original intent: to advance black freedom within the context of black agency. Clearly, to Stowe, Tom's humility, honesty, selflessness, and Christian fortitude are the qualities that characterize an ideal black hero, presumably an improvement upon other models of the heroic that might have been based on Nat Turner, or even Frederick Douglass, both of whose plights are distinguished by a violent resistance to slavery. Likewise, Tarantino sees his film's hero as gift to black culture and describes Django as if no one like him had ever before existed. Tarantino imagines *Django Unchained* to be what Marvel's *Black Panther* became upon its 2018 release, when it galvanized the black community, electrified Hollywood, situated black culture as cinematically mainstream, and broke box office records.

The superhero mystique is certainly the quality at which Tarantino is aiming in his western hero. In his unbelievability, Django's juxtaposition and fusion of the signifiers of slavery and freedom invokes the fantastic, a dynamic further extended in the film as Django gets into physical altercations. Because the historical record is sparse in its documentation of violent black revolt in the antebellum era, *Django Unchained*, though pegged by its creator and cast as a marker of historical truth, reads as fantasy.[49] The elements of make-believe are hyperenunciated in the manner in which Django exacts revenge. His facility as a quick draw in the classic western shootout, a status reserved for the white male gunslinger, makes way for a refrain comparable to the film's early signifier of anomaly, "nigger on a horse": the film touts the refrain "one nigger in ten thousand" to signify the exceptionality of the character Django or any black man with the audacity and prowess to both presume his human worth and defend it. Most of the characters in the film respond to their first encounters with Django with disbelief, looking for reasons to reject what their eyes plainly tell them. Though the film contains no formal supernatural elements, the incredulity of the spectators in Django's world (both the film's other characters and its real viewers) render Django supernatural—or at least unreal—by default. Django is a kind of superhero that, if not Black Panther–like, comes across as no less metaphysically extraordinary than Marvel's Luke Cage.

Tarantino's aspiration to create the quintessential "cool [black] folkloric hero" is clearly tied to his exposure to blaxploitation film, with its superhero-like black characters who "stick it to the man." This also marks another tie to Stowe. Just as she has the minstrel show and its marketing apparatus as resources "upon which [her] imagination [can] play," Tarantino has blaxploitation film, also pervasive during his impressionable childhood.[50] Moreover, the blaxploitation brand receives momentum from the comic book industry, which features black superheroes that reflect the swag of blaxploitation protagonists. In a comment about the comic book industry's resourcing of blaxploitation for inspiration, Tarantino scholar and black pop culture critic Adilifu Nama cites the relationship between black comic book heroes and film, suggesting how organic superheroism would be in the work of someone intrigued with the blaxploitation genre: "Without a doubt, the black superheroes of DC and Marvel comics drew much from the blaxploitation film genre, but not because they were inspired by blaxploitation film characters. The unmistakable commonality between the two exists because blaxploitation film characters *were* black superheroes" (emphasis in original).[51] As Nama implies, the very existence of a black character who could wield the subjectivity conventionally reserved for whites in service of black liberation is inherently super. The fantastic does not have to be invoked outright, but black persons who possess both the capacity and agency to "pay back blood for blood" in a racist society intrinsically radiate a superhuman aura.

The parallels between Tarantino's ties to blaxploitation and Stowe's to minstrelsy warrants further examination; curiously, Tarantino's colorful account of his early exposure to the iconic black films of the seventies is reminiscent of the story of the alleged discovery of black culture and subsequent invention of minstrelsy by T. D. Rice in the early nineteenth century. When invited to expound on the blaxploitation phenomenon in an interview, he remarks:

> My first exposure to blaxploitation films [was in] downtown [Los Angeles]. At that time, that whole Broadway area with all the old theaters and everything . . . was like a black Hollywood. [In] all those big theaters up and down the street, every film, was a blaxploitation film. . . . I felt like I was in a black world. . . . So I go into this theater and everybody is talking through it and they're making fun of everybody. They're like "Oh suck my dick! Oh yeah, ah, ha, ha, ha, ha! Fuck you muthafucka!". . . . I had never been in a theater where this was going on before. How old am I? I'm in the third grade, okay. Maybe less. And I'm like, wow, this is really kinda cool.[52]

Tarantino's unanticipated encounter with what he probably considers to be black culture in the raw takes on the mythological overtones of minstrelsy's alleged beginnings. The story of T. D. Rice stealing the clothes a of black street sideshow artist and baggage carrier named Cuff to subsequently imitate him on stage and thereby send his audience into laughing fits to launch the blackface performance industry has been a common (though likely inaccurate) explanation of the "origins" of minstrelsy.[53] However, its similarity to Tarantino's anecdote about exposure to blaxploitation film is uncanny. As in the Rice story, Tarantino relates the presumed novelty, idiosyncrasy, and marketability of black culture as an unsuspecting discovery, his filmmaking success illustrating its obvious benefit to his career. In his exposition of the anecdote's details—and as has commonly been the case for sharers of Rice's story—he "calls on minstrel devices . . . to narrate the origins of [his] minstrelsy."[54] Since Tarantino communicates his remarks in a video interview, the combined effect of changes in his body language and vocal inflections to convey the nuances of black speech and behavior are visible. His quoting of profane remarks from black audience members is low-grade minstrelsy. Moreover, the specific vernacular he cites alludes to the homoerotic in a humorously deflective way and calls to mind a comparable dynamic in blackface minstrelsy in which white men also deflect through mimicry a "real interest" in black masculinity and "betray . . . minstrelsy's mixed erotic economy of celebration and exploitation."[55] Tarantino's Freudian slips speak less to his sexuality than they do to the spirit and energy of blackface minstrelsy that is just somehow in the air.

The comments Tarantino makes after relating this anecdote further link him to minstrelsy and also circle back to what Slotkin describes as the pedagogical nature of the minstrel principle in the mythology of frontier conquest. Specifically, Tarantino comments on how *Shaft* (1971), one of the most celebrated blaxploitation films, does not fully leverage the power of the riveting score composed by music legend Isaac Hayes.[56] He continues by explaining what he would have done with Hayes's score, essentially situating himself as a teacher, a kind of "native" instructor, who by his cultural baptism in the "black world," can now "teach" black people how to express blackness "on its native ground":[57] "If you're a fan of the genre, the music is great and it's fantastic. As a filmmaker, I'm semifrustrated that it wasn't utilized better. . . . If I had the theme to *Shaft* to open up my movie, I'd open up my damn movie. Kung fu films had used the score to *Shaft* better than *Shaft* has."[58] On their face, Tarantino's comments have merit. As his adaptation of blaxploitation flair in his own work has illustrated, the creative possibilities that black artistic talent from the seventies makes available is immense. Sampling from the genre's and the period's iconic elements, Tarantino seemingly maximizes much of what might appear now to be insufficiently utilized by the producers and directors of blaxploitation film. At the same time, the way in which Tarantino positions himself in relationship to blaxploitation and, more broadly, to blackness—arguably as its guide and enhancer—is a conspicuous aspect of his commentary.

To be fair, Tarantino's intentionality can be debated, and his attempt to explain his relationship to blaxploitation film, blackness, and slavery in colorful ways should not in and of itself vindicate his critics; in most cases, he is responding to direct invitations to be forthright. Whether or not his comments are inherently insensitive, racist, or otherwise unconsciously exploitative is less the point than the uncanny resonance of his comments with the overtones of Stowe's cultural call. The presumed arbitrariness of Tarantino's creative choices, or even their stylistic intentionality—namely, that his pointed focus on tabooed subject matter could be explained as an artistic commitment to avant-garde edginess—does not belie the way in which many of his aesthetic decisions land squarely on storied apprehensions and historical trajectories centered on race. His artistic judgment is eerie and, like Stowe, some combination of his talent, intuition, privilege, and positioning in the historical moment situate him to channel the collective apprehensions of the culture about racial blackness,. Ultimately, his work plays the role that minstrelsy has traditionally played, which is at once to process and repress slavery-related tragedy, guilt, and justice.

The Ghostly Residue of Blackface

What is clearly an inventive, artistically bold, civically minded, and racially inspiring film is also, arguably, a covert, perhaps unconscious, probably therapeutic rehearsal of racial "discontinuities, misalliances and ruptures." Though calling upon otherwise reassuring Hollywood tropes—*High Noon* heroism and *Gone with the Wind* pageantry—*Django Unchained* is invested in a gothic mediation on blackness, betraying the residue of minstrelsy as a reminder of the often fractured nature of white storytelling about blackness. To be sure, Nama offers an extended commentary on how much the gothic frames both the scenery and action of the movie. However, even without the numerous examples that make Nama's point, Tarantino's cinematic citations alone invoke the weird. Careful examination of Tarantino's influences reveal that *Django Unchained* is an adaptation of at least two films, the 1966 spaghetti western *Django* and the 1972 blaxploitation film *The Legend of Nigger Charlie*, the combined effect of which lends to *Django Unchained* a supernatural element.[59] Their storylines are subtle reinforcements of the weirdness of Tarantino's western: *Django* is about a white, gun-toting maverick who, oddly, drags a coffin everywhere he goes and gets caught in the throes of an argument between Mexican revolutionaries and the Ku Klux Klan. *The Legend of Nigger Charlie* is about a black American slave who heads west to elude authorities after killing a white man. The fusion of the respective protagonists from these two films to forge Tarantino's Django is an eerie annunciation of Patterson's social death thesis. According to Patterson, social death is one of the "constituent elements of slavery" and characterized by a kind of "secular excommunication."[60] For all intents and purposes, a slave is socially dead, having no "recognized existence outside of his master."[61] Tarantino's Django does not have to drag a coffin. He *is* the coffin. He is the ultimate signifier of nonpersonhood in American culture, his social deadness leaving white observers confounded as he parades on horseback uncontested.

Django's silent horse ride through the small urban frontier establishment Daughtry, Texas, is telling in this regard. Django riding alongside Dr. King Schultz's wagon, in its slowness, draws the viewers' attention to deathly gothic imagery, which symbolically expresses the angst Django stirs up in his unapologetic wielding of a distinct and iconic expression of white male subjectivity. It is the westernness of Django—or, at least, the tropes of western movie lore that Tarantino conflates with historical fact (e.g., the lone male horse rider, his commanding heroic presence, his gun-toting posture, his physical mastery of the threats of the frontier)—that make the white public question his place in the southern world, and, by extension, *its* place in it. The "nigger on a horse" refrain is shorthand for this dynamic, marking the fragility of racial whiteness every time it is uttered. Django's wielding of the western hero persona in the South is at all times a disruption of the racial imperatives delineating black from white. The jarring quality of Django's ride into the center of the community is rendered even more uncanny by the scene's ambiance and scenery, as Daughtry has all the trappings of a ghost town. Though populated, the frontier establishment presents a spooky emptiness, underscored by a shot very early in the sequence when Django rides past a noose that briefly frames his head in the middle of it, yet another symbol of the vigilante justice collapsing at once on the American West and South.

The doubling of Django's deadness—the noose imagery and his presumed associations with slavery—reinforce the gothic theme that Nama argues is the center of the movie.[62] Nama makes the case that, as soon as the film opens, there is

> a conventional Gothic motif, a man metamorphosing in the deep dark night. The staging for this transformation occurs after several shackled black male slaves are shown marching barefoot across blistering, sun-scorched terrain as two white slave traders on horseback escort them, until nightfall when they eventually reach a dark, wind-chilled woodland. . . . Schultz subsequently frees Django, who immediately flings a flimsy blanket from around his shoulders and emerges from the dark a transformed figure. . . . The scene becomes increasingly evocative of a horror film with the actions of the remaining slaves. Like zombies from George A. Romero's classic horror film *Night of the Living Dead* (1968), they trudge forward like the walking dead to kill the white slaver trapped underneath his horse.[63]

Nama's marking of these references highlights the horror film genre as yet another potential inspiration for *Django Unchained*. Robin Coleman's *Horror Noire: American Horror Films from the 1890s to Present* (2011) is worth noting here, as her reframing of horror to account for racial terror would place *Django Unchained* solidly in the genre—or at least situate it in her self-named "blacks in horror" category.[64] If nothing else, that her work locates multiple examples of race-informed horror often unsuspectingly affirms how intuitive it is to link Django to thematic overtones of death and the supernatural. The film's opening scene situates Django as a kind of dark superhero, one that in the throwing of a blanket renders him Batman-like, his gesture temporarily lending him a caped aspect reminiscent of the Dark Knight. Such an allusion would not be out of bounds for Tarantino, as he admits that all his films aim for "a comic book panache."[65] However, what is more likely is that, as Nama claims, the opening sequence is simply introducing the film's primary mode of "Gothic horror" with all of its "historical discontinuities and contemporary cultural anxieties."[66] There is no need to rehearse the entirety of Nama's observations here, but certainly his thesis confirms the significance of the Daughtry sequence, which on the heels of the movie's opening alludes to Patterson's concept of social death. Django's ride through the town is at the pace of a dirge, ironic because, in the sequence before, he casts off his blanket, a glaring sign of his enslavement, as if it were a funeral garment. He might otherwise be a man who had risen from the dead, but because he can't cast off his skin, he is closer to, as Nama notes, a "zombie," a form of "walking dead." However, given the stark contrast offered by the image of him on a horse—social nonpersonhood juxtaposed with mythic personal autonomy—a more precise term for Django might be "dead man riding." Walking would not have contrasted with his deadness, especially alongside Schultz. In fact, to have walked beside Schultz as the dentist drove his wagon would have only mirrored Django's predicament at the movie's opening. Alternatively, riding is a metonym for American western freedom and renders incredulous the specter of a "nigger on a horse."

Uncle Tom also becomes a kind of specter by the end of the novel named after him. As with the aura of suspicion that follows Django, the questions Tom raises for a white public signify the haunting of an otherwise repressed darkness. Like the burnt cork of minstrelsy and the broadly encompassing metaphor of blackness, it is a darkness that is less about the empirical reality of people of African descent and more about hostilities centered in traditions of white savagery and racial purity. To be sure, Stowe's Haley—though he eventually purchases Tom from Tom's original master, Mr. Shelby—raises suspicions about his prospective purchase as he hears, among other things, that Mr. Shelby "let[s] [Tom] come and go round the country."[67] This virtual freedom is notable because it manifests as a geographical liberty. The prospect of Tom traveling functionally masterless in the West (where the controversy over the status of slavery is most ambiguous) makes him the mysterious beneficiary of a kind of sociolegal loophole that, in its invisibility, is uncanny. Tom's faith is at the center of this eerie quality, as it is the basis for the trust Shelby extends to Tom.[68] Notably, the bulk of *Uncle Tom's Cabin* is sandwiched between misgivings by Haley about Tom's virtue and the reprimands by Simon Legree (Tom's third and final owner), who at no time extends trust to Tom. Ultimately, Simon's encounters with Tom expose how much of a haunting and terrorizing force Tom's virtue is. An argument can even be made that Legree himself is responsible for unlocking Tom's menacing capabilities. As a case in point, upon encountering Tom reading a Methodist hymnal, Legree scolds him, which unsuspectingly unlocks Tom's superpowers, as this is the first instance of Tom's defiance:

> "Well, I'll soon have *that* out of you. I have none o' yer bawling, praying, singing niggers on my place; so remember. Now, mind yourself," he said, with a stamp and a fierce glance of his gray eye, directed at Tom, "*I'm* your church now! You understand,—you've got to be as *I* say."
>
> Something within the silent black man answered *No!* and, as if repeated by an invisible voice, came the words of an old prophetic scroll, as Eva had often read them to him,—"Fear not! for I have redeemed thee. I have called thee by my name. Thou art MINE!"[69]

This exchange marks two unprecedented moments in the text: this is the first instance in which someone claims such a totalizing ownership of Tom. Whatever physical powers previous owners levy over him, they leave him to his own devices when he retreats to his spirituality as a form of refuge. When Simon attempts to take control even over that, Tom exhibits defiance. He utters "No!" but it is a verbally silent utterance that can be read as a kind of passive resistance; outside of Stowe's fictive world, this is a valid claim. However, on her terms, Tom's "No!" is the most powerful act of rebellion in the novel, even rivaling Harris's acts of violence. For Stowe, Tom is the ultimate black revolutionary because his "No!" is a supernatural no. In his silence, he speaks—or, rather, God speaks through him, resonating at a level that is beyond the scope of Simon's understanding. The irony is that this divine utterance is actually a portent of horror, as it anticipates future exchanges with Tom that expose a parallel voice in Simon's soul. Not only is Simon later spooked by a curl that is a signifier of guilt relative to his mother, but in an attempt to break Tom's will, Simon beats Tom almost to death and dares Tom to give up his faith. Tom humbly refuses in a way that unseats Simon's power:

> "Pay away, till he gives up! Give it to him!—give it to him!" shouted Legree. "I'll take every drop of blood he has, unless he confesses!"
>
> Tom opened his eyes, and looked upon his master. "Ye poor miserable critter!" he said, "there ain't no more ye can do! I forgive ye, with all my soul!" and he fainted entirely away.
>
> "I b'lieve, my soul, he's done for, finally," said Legree, stepping forward, to look at him. "Yes, he is! Well, his mouth's shut up, at last,—that's one comfort!"
>
> Yes, Legree; but who shall shut up that voice in thy soul? that soul, past repentance, past prayer, past hope, in whom the fire that never shall be quenched is already burning![70]

As Simon has Tom beaten with naked force, the nakedness of Simon's soul is exposed. He is revealed to be utterly unprepared for the metaphysical forces acting upon him and that ultimately await him.

The uncanniness of Legree's encounters with Tom, which initially seem harmless on the surface, turn out to be portents of horror that morph into a damning loss of whiteness, symbolized by the ghost ruse orchestrated by Cassy, one of Legree's mulatta slaves. The passage referencing the haunting "voice in [Legree's] soul" is only shortly before the chapter titled "An Authentic Ghost Story," which details Cassy's ghost trick and brings to a head all of the references to gothic horror in the text. This is one of Stowe's more clever chapters, as, early on, she quotes Shakespeare's *Hamlet* with a line that contains a curious allusion to ghosts: "The sheeted dead / Did squeak and gibber in the streets of Rome."[71] The brilliance of this quote is its double reference to ghostliness. On one hand, it is an excerpt of dialogue from the character Horatio, who believes his recent witnessing of ghosts to be a harbinger of evil to come, which he claims is similar to the role ghost sightings play just before the assassination of Julius Caesar, the famed Roman emperor and namesake of another Shakespearean play. Bergland implies as much in her own comment about Shakespeare and ghostliness: "Pre-Enlightenment ghosts often protest unlawful transfers of political power. Think of Shakespeare's ghosts in Hamlet, Macbeth, Richard III, and Julius Caesar. They decry their own murders to be sure, but they also decry the usurpation of sovereignty—stolen kingdoms."[72] After comparing the matter of "stolen kingdoms" with the "murders, looted graves, illegal land transfers, and disruptions of sovereignty" that characterize the relationship of Europeans with Native Americans, she continues with a more explicit statement about the spectral consequences of stolen property in America:[73] "Ownership itself—that is to say [stolen] property—is a concept that haunts the American national mythos."[74] For Bergland, this is not just a matter of stolen land, as is the case with Native Americans, but of stolen and enslaved African Americans, who are among "the source[s] of the nation's deepest guilt."[75] As a result, Bergland continues, there is a "vexed relation between the United States" and what it claims to be its property, a vexing that produces a haunting insecurity.[76] Legree illustrates this. With his physical grip on Tom insufficient to secure Tom as his property in a meaningful way, Legree becomes aware of the fragility of his subjectivity as a white person, a matter signified by the second dimension of ghostliness inferred by Stowe's *Hamlet* reference. Quoting a play that features an unsheeted ghost (as the convention of representing ghosts by white sheets is not a function of Shakespeare's world) with a line that calls attention to the "sheeted dead" creates a revelatory irony. The quote highlights the contrived nature of ghostliness by referencing a play that retains a kind of ghostly authenticity. In the end, it underscores both the farce and the power of the sheet, as it is the tool by which Cassy and Emmeline (another mulatta slave and Cassy's coconspirator), disguised as ghosts, escape. The sheet, while certainly a sign of horror for Simon, also unavoidably signifies racial whiteness. Simon's racial status is figuratively stolen from him by two black figures in white sheets, but, more powerfully, by Uncle Tom, who, in the power of his virtue, renders Simon without honor and, by extension, without whiteness. Whiteness is not skin color, but a form of social capital that hinges on a role that Tom refuses to play. Simon's whiteness is horrifically stripped from him as he is left to ponder his worth in the absence of black signifiers of dishonor.

Conclusion

Uncle Tom's relationship to gothic terror is not be lost on D.W. Griffith, who features an Uncle Tom figure in *The Birth of a Nation* (1915), a movie Coleman categorizes as a virtual horror film: "While the violence of the Civil War was terrifying, its true horror, according to the film, came after in the form of unchecked, freed Black men."[77] In the movie, an Uncle Tom figure is lynched by his black opposites, "interloping Black Union soldiers."[78] As a metaphor for Dixie itself, Griffith's Uncle Tom—in his death—also signals the threat that free black men pose to white identity, as the southern way of life *is* that identity.

Coleman's observations about another artist and film linked to the minstrelsy tradition draw attention to what might be at stake for both Stowe and Tarantino. Their altruistic intentions, efforts, and results cannot be denied. The scholarship citing the contribution of Stowe to abolitionism and the actual end of slavery in the United States is as prolific as her criticism. Tarantino, though also much maligned, is no less admired. Moreover, no one can question the quality of Tarantino's storytelling capacities and his ability to make viewers care about quirky characters that both try and calm the viewers' nerves as those same characters mirror and affirm the viewers' quirks. Nama reserves some criticism for Tarantino but is convinced that the filmmaker should mostly be lauded, writing an entire book to advance this position.[79] At the same time, Tarantino's western neo–slave narrative revenge tale must be put in brackets, as should Stowe's watershed abolitionist novel. Though there is much to affirm about both Tarantino's and Stowe's respective creative work, that they are *white* persons constructing tales about black people must be examined. Neither their skin color nor their ancestry make their depictions of black worlds inherently flawed, but with the opportunities that African Americans have had to create black heroes and superheroes for mainstream audiences in the early twenty-first century, one must consider how differently a black superhero world looks when black people are its architects. The blaxploitation films of the seventies present a version of this in how forthrightly they contest the white power structure (at least initially), but particularly as they begin to evolve into worn tropes, spoofs, and comedic gestures, the freedom which black participants have to explore creative options must be examined more carefully. The monumental success of *Black Panther* and, to a lesser extent, the Oscar-winning notoriety of Jordan Peele's 2017 *Get Out*, speak to how differently black superheroism can look when depicted in stories told largely by African Americans. Wakandan heroism is communal and one in which men and women fight side by side. Moreover, heroism and villainy in *Black Panther* are not the stark contrasts they are in Stowe's and Tarantino's fictive worlds. Jordan Peele's protagonist is a black male who escapes his torturers through physical bravery, but the film places the terrorizing overtones not on him, but on his white antagonists.

These distinctions raise questions about what stories about black people do for the white storyteller, especially in a country in which the concepts of frontier and blackness are readily available as narrative devices. Because the frontier has only ever been a metaphor, an artistic handle lending itself to the theatricality of minstrelsy, the literal performance of "how the West was won" on the big screen becomes inevitable. Tarantino situates a black cowboy in this drama who, while not the "black first" Tarantino suggests he is—Mario Van Peebles beat him to the punch nine years earlier in his 1993 film *Posse*—is encased in a cinematic world that is signature avant-garde. However, the audacity of *Django Unchained* rests squarely in its faithfulness to historically racial taboos and controversies, the metonym for which is Uncle Tom, a figure that in Stowe's world doubles as an emblem of caricature and horror. Not only is this duality distilled in the lynching of the Uncle Tom figure in *The Birth of a Nation*, but also in the presence of the same symbolism—a noose and Tom-esque Stephen—in *Django Unchained*. Lynching and Uncle Tom–informed minstrelsy are the secular sacraments of slavery, signaling a southern expansionist thrust. The migration of these practices to the West literally and figuratively speak to the ways the nation looks to both repress and process its angst about slavery. The Uncle Tom phenomenon that feeds into these dynamics sits at the cornerstone of a white fantasy about a black one. As a symbolic referent for a white dreamworld about the black political imagination, Tom never merely represents himself but also a myriad of America's apprehensions about its relationship to its racial past. In the end, Uncle Tom is a placeholder for anxieties about the fragility of whiteness. The subject of slavery's abolition—whether posited as a nineteenth-century question or a twenty-first-century reflection—calls to mind not only the loss of an institution, but also of a symbolic apparatus that suffuses whiteness with meaning. The fear of this loss creates all kinds of frontier energies in the nineteenth century whose realities must be reevaluated in the twenty-first.

NOTES

1. Stowe, *Uncle Tom's Cabin*, 65.
2. Miller, *Encyclopedia of Weird Westerns*, 4.
3. Miller, *Encyclopedia of Weird Westerns*, 4.
4. Bergland, *National Uncanny*, 1–22.
5. Bergland, *National Uncanny*, 8.
6. Bergland, *National Uncanny*, 8.
7. Roach, *Cities of the Dead*, 3.
8. Roach, *Cities of the Dead*, 3; Slotkin, *Regeneration through Violence*, 3–4.
9. Slotkin, *Regeneration through Violence*, 68.
10. See Slotkin, *Regeneration through Violence*.
11. Roach, *Cities of the Dead*, 3.
12. Morrison, *Playing in the Dark*, vii.
13. Bergland, *National Uncanny*, 18.
14. Bergland, *National Uncanny*, 7, 9, 16–18.
15. Morrison, *Playing in the Dark*, 15, 39.

16. Morrison, *Playing in the Dark*, 3.
17. Morrison, *Playing in the Dark*, 6.
18. Morrison, *Playing in the Dark*, 46.
19. Slotkin, *Gunfighter Nation*, 14.
20. Morrison, *Playing in the Dark*, 37.
21. Morrison, *Playing in the Dark*, 46–47.
22. Morrison, *Playing in the Dark*, 47.
23. Morrison, *Playing in the Dark*, 38.
24. Jordan, *White Man's Burden*, 6.
25. Morrison, *Playing in the Dark*, 17.
26. Morrison, *Playing in the Dark*, 17.
27. Morrison, *Playing in the Dark*, 37.
28. Morrison, *Playing in the Dark*, 39.
29. Slotkin, *Gunfighter Nation*, 14.
30. Dippie, *Vanishing American*, 12.
31. Lott, *Love and Theft*, 4.
32. Bergland, *National Uncanny*, 11.
33. Bergland, *National Uncanny*, 11.
34. Bergland, *National Uncanny*, 11.
35. Lott, *Love and Theft*, 4.
36. Lott, *Love and Theft*, 6.
37. Lott, *Love and Theft*, 6.
38. Bergland, *National Uncanny*, 19; Balibar, *Race, Nation and Class*, 96.
39. Alexander, *The New Jim Crow*.
40. Stowe, *Uncle Tom's Cabin*, 61.
41. Patterson, *Slavery and Social Death*, 38.
42. Cure, *Picturing the Postcard*, 3.
43. Hamilton, "The Strange Career of *Uncle Tom's Cabin*," 24.
44. Hochman, *Uncle Tom's Cabin and the Reading Revolution*, 9.
45. Richards, "Imitation Nation," 204.
46. Tarantino, "Quentin Tarantino Interview."
47. Tarantino, "Quentin Tarantino Interview."
48. Stowe, *Uncle Tom's Cabin*, 19.
49. moviemanicasDE, "*Django Unchained* | Meet the Press."
50. Isaac, *BaadAsssss Cinema*.
51. Nama, *Super Black*, 37, 39.

52. Isaac, *BaadAsssss Cinema*.
53. Lott, *Love and Theft*, 18–19.
54. Lott, *Love and Theft*, 19.
55. Lott, *Love and Theft*, 6.
56. Isaac, *BaadAsssss Cinema*.
57. Isaac, *BaadAsssss Cinema*.
58. Isaac, *BaadAsssss Cinema*.
59. Tarantino, "Tarantino *Unchained*," Part 1.
60. Patterson, *Slavery and Social Death*, 1, 5.
61. Patterson, *Slavery and Social Death*, 5.
62. Nama, *Race on the QT*, 118.
63. Nama, *Race on the QT*, 107.
64. Coleman, *Horror Noire*, 1–13.
65. moviemanicasDE, "*Django Unchained* | Meet the Press."
66. Nama, *Race on the QT*, 118.
67. Stowe, *Uncle Tom's Cabin*, 2.
68. Stowe, *Uncle Tom's Cabin*, 2.
69. Stowe, *Uncle Tom's Cabin*, 308.
70. Stowe, *Uncle Tom's Cabin*, 377.
71. Stowe, *Uncle Tom's Cabin*, 384.
72. Bergland, *National Uncanny*, 8.
73. Bergland, *National Uncanny*, 8–9.
74. Bergland, *National Uncanny*, 9.
75. Bergland, *National Uncanny*, 8.
76. Bergland, *National Uncanny*, 9.
77. Coleman, *Horror Noire*, 21.
78. Coleman, *Horror Noire*, 21.
79. Nama, *Race on the QT*.

BIBLIOGRAPHY

Alexander, Michelle. *The New Jim Crow*. New York: New Press, 2012.
Balibar, Etienne, and Immanuel Wallerstein. *Race, Nation and Class: Ambiguous Identities*. New York: Verso, 1991.
Bergland, Reneé L. *The National Uncanny: Indian Ghosts and American Subjects*. Hanover NH: New England University Press, 2000.

Coleman, Robin R. Means. *Horror Noire: Blacks in American Horror Films from the 1890s to Present.* New York: Routledge, 2011.

Cure, Monica. *Picturing the Postcard: The Invention of the Postcard Through the Lens of Turn-of-the-Century Literature, and the Fantasy of New Media.* Minneapolis: University of Minnesota Press, 2018.

Dippie, Brian W. *The Vanishing American: White Attitudes and U.S. Policy.* Lawrence: University Press of Kansas, 1982.

Hamilton, Kendra. "The Strange Career of *Uncle Tom's Cabin.*" *Black Issues in Higher Education,* 19, no. 8 (2002): 22–27.

Hochman, Barbara. Uncle Tom's Cabin *and the Reading Revolution: Race, Literacy, Childhood, and Fiction, 1851–1911.* Amherst: University of Massachusetts Press, 2011.

Isaac, Julien, dir. *BaadAsssss Cinema: A Bold Look at 70's Blaxploitation Films.* Docurama, 2002.

Lott, Eric. *Love and Theft: Blackface Minstrelsy and the American Working Class.* Oxford: Oxford University Press, 1993.

Miller, Cynthia L. "Introduction to *Encyclopedia of Weird Westerns: Supernatural and Science Fiction Elements in Novels, Pulps, Comics, Films, Television and Games,* edited by Paul Green, 4–13. 2nd ed. *Jefferson* NC: McFarland, 2016.

Morrison, Toni. *Playing in the Dark: Whiteness in the Literary Imagination.* New York: Random House, 1992.

moviemanicasDE. "*Django Unchained* | Meet the Press (2013) Quentin Tarantino," January 1, 2013, www.youtube.com/watch?v=-1QpScB-HJg. (accessed May 1, 2018).

Nama, Adilifu. *Race on the QT: Blackness and the Films of Quentin Tarantino.* Austin: Texas University Press, 2015.

Nama, Adilifu. *Super Black: American Pop Culture and Black Superheroes.* Austin: Texas University Press, 2011.

Patterson, Orlando. *Slavery and Social Death: A Comparative Study.* Cambridge MA: Harvard University Press, 1982.

Richards, Jason. "Imitation Nation: Blackface Minstrelsy and the Making of African American Selfhood in *Uncle Tom's Cabin.*" *Novel,* 39, no. 8 (2006): 204–20.

Roach, Joseph. *Cities of the Dead: Circum-Atlantic Performance.* New York: Columbia University Press, 1996.

Slotkin, Richard. *Gunfighter Nation: The Myth of the Frontier in Twentieth-Century America*. Norman: University of Oklahoma Press, 1998.

Slotkin, Richard. *Regeneration through Violence: The Mythology of the American Frontier, 1600–1860*. Norman: University of Oklahoma Press, 1973.

Stowe, Harriet Beecher. *Uncle Tom's Cabin*. Edited by Elizabeth Ammons. New York: Norton, 2010.

Tarantino, Quentin. "Quentin Tarantino Interview: 'I'm shutting your butt down!'" Channel 4 News, January 10, 2013, https://www.youtube.com/watch?v=GrsJDy8VjZk (accessed November 21, 2019).

Tarantino, Quentin. "Tarantino *Unchained* Part 1: *Django* Trilogy?" (interview with Henry Louis Gates Jr.). The Root, December 23, 2012. www.theroot.com/views/tarantino-unchained-part-1-django-trilogy. (accessed May 1, 2018).

12

Race and Gender in the Time Travel Western

MICHAEL K. JOHNSON

Although the western no longer dominates the television schedule as it did in the 1960s and 1970s, twenty-first-century television continues to find ways to bring the venerable genre to contemporary screens, perhaps most creatively through hybrid generic forms such as the weird western. In several contemporary television series, the science fiction trope of time travel provides the means of joining the science fiction and western genres. By mixing genres, the time travel western re-creates the western form to appeal to the sensibilities of a twenty-first-century audience—by bringing, for example, currently popular generic character types such as superheroes into an Old West setting. These contemporary television shows also bring a gender-balanced and multiethnic cast to a genre that in its classic form has repeatedly been critiqued for lacking those qualities.

For my primary examples, I will focus on the first seasons of two television shows: *Legends of Tomorrow* (2016–present), a time travel superhero series airing on the CW Network, and the NBC series *Timeless* (2016–18). *Legends of Tomorrow* follows the adventures of time master Rip Hunter (Arthur Darvill), who (in season 1) chases supervillain Vandal Savage (Casper Crump) through time, trying to prevent Savage from murdering his family and, by the way, preventing him from bringing about the end of the world. To aid in his quest, Rip recruits a team of superheroes (and supervillains-turned-heroes). The team is inclusive in terms of gender and race, a diversity accomplished in part by casting African American and mixed-race actors for what in the comic books were originally white characters. In the episode "The Magnificent Eight" (1.11) the group members go back in time to the fictional town of Salvation, in Dakota Territory in the 1870s, a setting to which they return several times, including in the episodes "Outlaw Country" (2.6) and "The Good, the Bad and the Cuddly" (3.18).

In *Timeless* a trio of time travelers—an African American pilot-scientist (Rufus), a white female historian (Lucy), and a white male soldier (Wyatt)—journey through time chasing a villain (Garcia Flynn) who is attempting to change history. Two episodes from the first season address western history: "The Alamo" (1.5) and "The Murder of Jesse James" (1.12). Similar to contemporary movies such as *Hidden Figures* (2016), *Timeless* is attentive to recovering the "hidden figures" of history, especially the women and people of color who have been left out of dominant narratives.[1] Thus, "The Murder of Jesse James" focuses on the highly accomplished (but largely unknown) African American Deputy U.S. Marshal Bass Reeves. Although the prime directive of the time traveler is "don't change history," the goal of *Timeless* is to change the way we *see* history by making visible some of history's hidden figures. "The Murder of Jesse James" revises both history and genre. As the episode depicts the actual historical figures Bass Reeves and Jesse James, it also evokes the character types, conventions, and iconography of the western, intervening in and commenting on the classic versions of the genre by placing an African American lawman at the center of the narrative and as the embodiment of western justice.

The Time Travel Western as Genre

There are so many literary, comic book, cinematic, and televisual narratives that involve time travel to (and from) the Old West as to constitute a genre in itself, one that has developed its own set of conventions, character types, and iconography. In television, time travel westerns feature in every era, including episodes of *The Twilight Zone* (1959–64), *Voyagers* (1982–83), *Sliders* (1995–2000), *The Adventures of Briscoe County, Jr.* (1993–94), and the current *Timeless*.[2] Many science fiction–oriented series have included an episode or episodes involving time travel—virtual or real—to the Old West, including *Star Trek* (1966–69), *Star Trek: Next Generation* (1987–94), and *Doctor Who* (1969–89, 2005–present).³

If these series often send contemporary characters back to the Old West, others do the opposite: bring a character from the past into the present. In the 1986 television series *Outlaws*, an entire gang of outlaws along with the sheriff chasing them is transported from 1886 to 1986 via a lightning strike. *A Modern Day Western: The Sanchez Saga* (1997) posits perhaps the most unique means of time travel: Outlaw Reno Sanchez escapes hanging in 1884 Texas when chewing on the worm from the bottom of a tequila bottle transports him to contemporary America. In the official video for Lil Nas X's "Old Town Road" (featuring Billy Ray Cyrus), outlaw hero Lil Nas X escapes, in 1889, from a posse on his horse and from a homesteader with a rifle by jumping through a cellar door into a long underground tunnel that somehow transports him to California in 2019. In the time travel western, the means of time travel may be virtual (*Star Trek*'s holodeck), technological (a time machine), supernatural (a shaman, or the intervention of a supernatural creature such as an angel or demon), natural if somewhat strange (a lightning strike, sleep, a blow to the head, a mysterious tunnel or portal), or other (tequila worm).

Tombstone, Arizona, features prominently in time travel westerns that take contemporary characters back to the past. In *Doctor Who*'s "A Holiday for the Doctor" (3.34–37, 1966), the Doctor visits Tombstone, seeking Doc Holliday's help with a toothache. The contemporary *Doctor Who* series has set frequent episodes in the American West (because Stetsons are cool). "A Town Called Mercy" (7.3, 2012) is not in Tombstone, but the structure of the story is a town tamer, during which the stranger in town—the time traveler—takes on the Wyatt Earp role of protecting the town from a group of outlaws or, as in "A Town Called Mercy," a single (in this case cyborg) gunfighter. *Back to the Future III* (1990) follows a similar pattern (with Hill Valley, California, as the threatened town). It also establishes the trope of the contemporary character adopting a familiar name—not of a historical western figure, but a western actor: Clint Eastwood, Marty McFly's western name.⁴

As adopting a name like "Clint Eastwood" suggests, the Old West of the time travel western is not the West of historical reality but the mythic West of the western. In this sense, time travel serves as an engine for genre mixing. Jim Collins observes that "hyperconsciousness" (such as knowing references to other films) and hybridity have been prevalent features of genre films since the 1990s. Using *Back to the Future III* as a primary example, he notes that within the Old West of the film, "we enter a narrative universe defined by impertinent connections, no longer sustainable by one set of generic conventions. We encounter, instead, different sets of generic conventions that intermingle, constituting a profoundly intertextual diegesis, nowhere more apparent than in the shot of the DeLorean time machine being pulled through the desert by a team of horses, the very co-presence of John Ford and H. G. Wells demonstrating the film's ability to access both as simultaneous narrative options." Such moments of "co-presence" or "simultaneity" in the hybrid genre text encourage us to recognize and enjoy the impertinence of the connections they make.[5]

What Collins sees as a feature of contemporary genre films in general, the time travel western foregrounds through its explicit interest in juxtaposing two time periods in a way that also draws our attention to the co-presence of the two dominant genres that inform the story being told. Time travel narratives are often Oedipal in nature; they return to the primal scene, to the place of origin. Although science fiction, fantasy, and horror narratives with western roots may conceal those roots—by replacing six guns with ray guns, outlaws with zombies—the time travel element makes that hybridity explicit in its juxtaposition of two historical moments (which also represent two different but related genres). The Oedipal return to origins is also a return to genre origins, a means of explicitly acknowledging the western roots of what on the surface seems to be primarily science fiction, fantasy, or horror.

Genre and Race

In terms of genre the Old West episodes of *Legends of Tomorrow* and *Timeless* are both western and science fiction, and, as such, participate in two genres generally regarded as being unfriendly to African American authors, characters, and stories. African Americans—as authors, as actors, as directors—have nonetheless participated in each of those genres, with Pauline Hopkins's 1901 novel *Winona* being one of the first black westerns. Additionally, African American characters have appeared in both genres, particularly in film and television, from the earliest examples onward. And, as critics Adilifu Nama and Isiah Lavender have pointed out, race has always been an important element of science fiction, even if racial issues are represented in allegorical form—with green-skinned aliens, for example, as a representation of an otherness that is coded as racial.

As André Carrington argues in *Speculative Blackness* (2016), because of the dominance of white writers and white readers in the world of science fiction there is a "presumption of Whiteness" in the genre. Even allegorical explorations of race frequently replicate contemporaneous racial hierarchies by opposing the white hero to the alien other. Science fiction is as saturated "with race thinking as any other variety of popular culture, [and it has the tendency] to reproduce conventional understandings of race."[6] The presumption of whiteness, Carrington argues, goes a long way to explaining why many black writers and black readers are alienated by the genre. Nonetheless, Carrington argues, and his argument here could just as easily be applied to the western or most any other popular genre, "Black people's significance for speculative fiction—and sometimes our alienation from it—can be the point of departure for understanding in a more profound way what genre has to do with racial identity."[7] Carrington writes, "Every cultural form invented by Black people in the diaspora, from the sorrow songs to break dancing, demonstrates complex and potentially liberatory uses of existing cultural forms."[8] Even though "the overrepresentation of Whiteness and the comparatively limited involvement of Black people in producing speculative fiction both have a significant impact on what it means for Black people to locate ourselves in the ranks of the genre's authors and its audiences," African American artists may make "exemplary interventions in speculative fiction."[9]

Although *Timeless* has at least one African American staff writer—actor and screenwriter Anslem Richardson, who is one of the credited writers for "The Murder of Jesse James" episode—television is a collaborative medium, and we cannot lay claim to any television episode (even one with a credited black writer or director) as a black-authored text in the same way we would a novel. However, a television episode may nonetheless make an "exemplary intervention" in both science fiction and the western.

Even if there is not an identifiable African American writer involved, a text is still open to racial meanings and racial readings. Drawing on Stuart Hall's theory of preferred, negotiated, and oppositional readings, Nama writes that "intentionality does not restrict the meaning of a film nor is the message of a film passively consumed by an audience." Although there may be preferred meanings that a media text authorizes, "from an audience-centered perspective, the racial meaning of any SF film is up for grabs."[10] A television show is also a collaborative work, and the presence of African American actors in that work suggests at least a degree of African American input in the creation of the text. For television in particular, performance is central to the spectator's experience of the story. An actor or actress may suggest additional readings—that is, open up possibilities of meaning making—through physical presence and performance that potentially go beyond those scripted by the writers, directors, costumers, and set decorators whose work is part of the collaborative text that a television series creates.

A central text in studies of African American presence in science fiction has been *Star Trek: Deep Space Nine* (1993–99), which featured African American actor Avery Brooks as Benjamin Cisco, Starfleet commander and head of the Deep Space Nine space station. Although not a western, the DS9 episode "Far Beyond the Stars" (6.13) is a precursor to *Timeless* and *Legends of Tomorrow* in terms of using time travel conventions as means of addressing issues of race. Carrington's analysis of the episode helps sketch out a framework for thinking about race in other popular genre texts. In "Far Beyond the Stars" (which Brooks also directed), Cisco goes back in time—through mysterious means—to

1950s New York, to live the life of Benny Russell, a science fiction staff writer for *Incredible Tales* magazine, whose race is unknown to readers. During the episode, an inspired Russell writes a speculative story about the black commander of a space station—a future that literally cannot be imagined in the 1950s, as indicated by the publisher's decision to destroy the issue rather than send it to newsstands.

The major actors from DS9 are recast in the episode as the individuals who populate Benny's world. Among the *Incredible Tales* staff writers, Nana Visitor plays Kay (pen name K. C. Hunter—the name and character a nod to writer C. L. Moore, who likewise used initials to conceal her gender). When the editor announces that the publisher wishes to print a photograph of the writers, he also observes that Benny and Kay "can sleep late" that day. As Carrington writes, "The portrait of science fiction writers that 'Far Beyond the Stars' offers contends that women and people of color have been present as a creative force through the history of science fiction, but their contributions have disappeared."[11] *Timeless* in particular employs a similar ethics of critically examining the oppressive racial and gender formations of the past, and it likewise uses the science fiction trope of time travel to make that "disappeared" history visible.

Practitioners and advocates of science fiction have pointed to the genre's utopian visions of the future as evidence of exceptionalism regarding race and ethnicity. *Star Trek*, however, espouses an egalitarian view of the future that it only rarely achieves in practice. By traveling back to the golden age of science fiction in 1950s America, "the episode would raise troubling questions about the inspirational rhetoric of science fiction—and *Star Trek* in particular—by situating the dynamics of racial conflict squarely within the history of the genre."[12] The episode shows the genre's complicity with—rather than transcendence of—white supremacy. "Far Beyond the Stars" uses one of the science fiction genre's conventions, time travel, to critique the racial assumptions of the genre itself. Both *Timeless* and *Legends of Tomorrow* similarly use genre stories to critique (implicitly or explicitly) the longstanding assumptions of the genres in which they participate.

The Magnificent Eight

As the episode's title suggests, the western roots of *Legends of Tomorrow* go directly to the western film *The Magnificent Seven* (1960), as indicated by Rip's recruitment of a team of misfits and sometimes ne'er-do-wells. Rip Hunter has his own long history in DC comics—one not connected to the western. In contrast, this version of Rip does have a backstory rooted in the western, and the episode takes us back to those origins, to a moment when science fiction hero Rip Hunter was a western hero. Rip's "magnificent" team includes Dr. Martin Stein and Jefferson Jackson (who merge together to become the superhero Firestorm), Sara Lance (a.k.a. the League of Assassins–trained Canary), Ray Palmer (the Atom, clad in a robotic suit), Kendra Saunders (Hawkgirl), Leonard Snart (whose technological superpower is a freeze ray), and Mick Rory (who is handy with a fiery blaster). The superhero team is mostly white men but is inclusive of two women, one African American man (Jefferson Jackson, played by actor Franz Drameh), and the ethnically Egyptian Kendra Saunders (played by actress Ciara Renée, who identifies as ethnically mixed: African American, European, Native American, and Indian).[13]

The character Kendra Saunders is rooted in western comics. Kendra started out as Kate Manser, who first appeared in 1978 in *Weird Western Tales*. After her father's death, she adapted the persona of Cinnamon, who was trained as a gunfighter and martial artist and sought revenge against the bank robbers who killed him. As her story plays out in the comic books, we learn that she has been incarnated in many different times in different forms: as Cinnamon, as Shiera Saunders-Hall, and as Egyptian princess Chay-Ara (her earliest incarnation). She is immortal, sort of, in that she can be killed, but she is always reincarnated, as is her paramour, Hawkman (Egyptian Prince Khufu in his original incarnation, a.k.a. Carter Hall), although they don't always recognize one another in each new life.[14]

Kendra's roots in DC's western comics are a significant part of the episode. She meets Cinnamon in the town saloon. She later visits her camp and realizes that she has, in fact, met her older self (or an older version of one of her selves). Cinnamon, a white character in the comics, is played by African American actress and writer Anna Deavere Smith, a casting choice that contributes to the episode's diversification of both the western and the superhero genres and also references the historical reality of African American pioneers. Best known as the writer and performer of her one-woman play *Twilight: Los Angeles, 1992* (1993), about the riots in the wake of the acquittal of the officers in Rodney King case, Smith brings to the episode by her presence another layer of possible meaning, an evocation of more contemporary African American western history that is suggested allusively rather than explicitly. Cinnamon also tells the story that connects *Legends of Tomorrow*'s superhero characters to their roots in the western. Not only does Kendra meet her western self (in the form of the character that was her first comic book incarnation), but Cinnamon also describes the western roots of Hawkman, whom she knew in his nineteenth-century incarnation as Hannibal Hawkes, a.k.a. Nighthawk. As Green comments on the character, "The evolution of the Western masked crimefighter known as Nighthawk into a superhero" is typical of the way many western comic book heroes were either retired or transformed "to make them relevant to a contemporary readership rooted in superheroes, science fiction and fantasy."[15] The scene with Cinnamon, and her story with Hannibal Hawkes, provides the means of acknowledging the western roots of his contemporary incarnation, Hawkman. The episode, in the guise of a time travel western, is also a lesson in comic book history.

The revelation of Rip Hunter's western origins, although different from the character's comic book origins, allegorically reflects the more general transition of comic book characters from one genre to another. Rip Hunter's belonging to the western genre is indicated by his costuming, his long brown duster, and his choice of weapon, which looks like an old-fashioned revolver. He is the one character who doesn't change into western gear to fit in with the locals when the episode takes us back to the 1870s. Rip's costume is one way that the series signals its hybridity, its status as a weird western, even before making that connection explicit in "The Magnificent Eight." Rip has been in the Old

West—and in the town of Salvation—before, and if he is not literally walking in the boots of one of the weird western's best-known characters, he is literally wearing his coat. Jonah Hex and Rip Hunter are old friends who have fallen out; when they parted, Rip took Jonah's duster along—and named his son Jonas after him in homage. The larger homage of the episode is to the weird western itself, acknowledging the hybrid genre's influence on *Legends of Tomorrow*, and thus the inclusion of Jonah Hex (Johnathan Schaech) as a character, acknowledging the most well-known comic book weird western hero as the model for this version of Rip Hunter.

After a failed raid on the outlaw's ranch (in which each side takes a captive), the heroes and outlaws decide to settle things through a showdown on the main street. Rip goes up against the outlaw leader. Whoever wins the gunfight also wins the release of the captive. This scene, from the elements of the mise-en-scène to the action, belongs to the genre of the western. The two men face each other in the middle of a muddy street, their pistols holstered, while spectators tensely watch from the sides. There are hip-level close-ups of hands poised above holstered pistols, intercut shots of spectators' faces, close-ups of the gunfighters' faces as they stare intently at one another. Both men draw, and the outlaw falls dead.

What happens next reflects the series' awareness of itself as a self-consciously hybrid generic form. Two genres require two fight scenes, so we have a second showdown. The setting remains that of the western—the muddy street of a frontier town—but the action belongs to the superhero genre. Three men in body armor march into town and start shooting laser-like bolts from their gauntleted hands. The Legends switch out their six-shooters for their own energy-powered weapons. Kendra takes off her western duster, exposing her hawk-like wings, and takes flight. Jackson and Stein combine to become the red-and-gold-costumed Firestorm, thrust into the air by columns of fire shooting out of his legs and literally returning fire by shooting it from his hands. This scene exemplifies hyperconscious hybridity. The action is simultaneously a full-scale western gunfight and a superhero action sequence, and the pleasure of the scene is the intermingling and co-presence of the two genres: some characters in western costume, some in high-tech superhero gear, guns firing, lasers blasting, all playing out on the same western street that had just provided the setting for a quick-draw gunfight.

The first showdown celebrates the traditional western, as well as the bravery and skill of the single heroic male gunfighter. The second showdown suggests a critique of the first. In the first, the African American character is tied up and held hostage, the object rather than the agent of the action—a typical scenario in westerns (or other genre works) with African American characters. In fact, Jackson is a failure as a western hero. During the raid on the outlaw camp, all he manages to do is get himself captured, making possible—even necessary—the white male heroism of Rip. In the second showdown, in the persona of Firestorm, he contributes to the action and the mayhem. Similarly, the whole team, male and female, is involved in the action rather than simply watching the cowboy hero. If Jefferson Jackson and Kendra Saunders don't quite belong in the genre western, this episode suggests, there is certainly a place for them in the weird western.

The Murder of Jesse James

More so than *Legends of Tomorrow*, *Timeless* shares some of the same qualities and areas of emphasis as African American speculative fiction, in large part because of the centrality of Rufus, the African American scientist and timeship pilot (one of three central characters rather than a member of large ensemble). Additionally, *Timeless* is consistently attentive to African American points of view, and not just the individual point of view of Rufus (Malcolm Barrett). As Carrington points out, "Interpretations of the past shaped by attention to racial oppression as a driving force in history differentiate some SF works by Black authors from those writers focusing on the present, the future, and alternate realities from other points of view."[16] *Timeless* regularly uses the character of Rufus to draw our attention to the presence of racial oppression as a driving force in the historical periods he visits (*Legends of*

Tomorrow does so as well but less frequently). Black speculative fiction, Carrington writes, can intervene in the larger generic field by "situating conventional subject matter in alternative frames of reference," by, for example, juxtaposing the conventional science fiction trope of time travel with the history of American slavery.[17] Through time travel, Rufus confronts various levels of American racial oppression, from slavery to segregation. He must dress, act, and respond differently than his white companions in certain time periods. That is, *Timeless* does not follow the strategy of some science fiction (and western) texts of creating multiracial casts but positing postracial characters. *Timeless* offers Rufus as many opportunities for heroic action as it does his white companions, but it continually makes the audience aware of how race affects his experience in different historical contexts.

Of the various science fiction conventions that have been evoked and reimagined in African American speculative fiction, the time travel trope has been particularly important. For example, Octavia Butler's novel *Kindred* (1979) and director Haile Gerima's film *Sankofa* (1993) both feature contemporary protagonists who travel back into the past of American slavery. As Womack observes, in both these narratives time travel serves to "ingrain the realities of slave life and the ensuing sense of responsibilities into their protagonists. They used time travel to encourage connections to a painful past."[18] "Travel, escape, and mourning" in Afro-Atlantic speculative narratives, Michelle Commander writes, "are taken up as forms of resistance against narratives of progress and the supposed healing properties of the passage of time, of forgetting." The history of slavery is experienced as a "felt reality" rather than an abstraction.[19]

Timeless, on more than one occasion, takes Rufus back to slaveholding times—he is at one point chained and held captive. However, the "felt reality" of slavery for Rufus also includes the reality of resistance. Prior to his time travel to the American South, Rufus knows and fears, at least intellectually, the brutal realities of chattel slavery. He is surprised, however, to find collective resistance.[20] That discovery alters his character's behavior in the present—as he becomes more assertive in his resistance to his employer's instructions, and as he begins to realize that the freedom he experiences in the present may be more limited than he originally thought. Although *Timeless* tends to posit a more harmonious racial present, it does—in keeping with black speculative fiction generally—acknowledge that there are continuities between past and present rather than simply "comparing a deficient racial past to a promising future."[21] During his trips into the past, Rufus proves adept at applying African American survival skills such as masking and exploiting his "invisibility" (no one notices a black chauffeur stealing a car, for example), suggesting, at least, that such survival techniques are a part of his present as well.

African American speculative narratives also draw on specific elements of African American culture and history. One of the most famous African American folktales involves a fantastic story of "Flying Africans." In some versions, the Africans are newly brought to America, take one look at what is going on around them, and immediately ascend into the air and fly back to Africa. Commander argues that "African descendants in the New World have extended the legacy of Flying Africans" through the lens of "Afro-Atlantic speculation: a series of imaginings, including literary texts, films, and geographic sites, that envision return flights back to Africa."[22] The desire for flight—back to Africa, to the north, to the west—has been an essential element of African American cultural forms, visible in slave narratives, folktales, spirituals, and, in twentieth- and twenty-first-century forms, in fiction, film, nonfiction, travel narratives, and the like.

By creating the character of the pilot as African American, *Timeless*—knowingly or unknowingly—participates in the extensive fantastic legacy of Flying Africans. Naming the character Rufus suggests some familiarity with African American texts, as the character name may allude to a central character in Butler's *Kindred* (the white ancestor of main character Dana, whom she travels back in time to save from death on several occasions). Coincidental or intentional, these parallels suggest the possibilities of finding new meanings in *Timeless* by juxtaposing it with African American texts such as *Kindred*.

"The Murder of Jesse James" begins with a famous western death—Jesse James (Daniel Lissing) shot in the back while dusting a picture on April 3, 1882. That killing is interrupted by series villain Garcia Flynn (Goran Visnjic), who arrives on the scene just as Jesse turns his back. Flynn shoots and kills Robert and Charles Ford, their guns in their hands, saving Jesse's life and enlisting him to guide Flynn through Indian Territory to seek out a fellow time traveler stranded in the nineteenth century. Lucy (Abigail Spencer), Wyatt (Matt Lanter), and Rufus, our intrepid historian, soldier, and pilot trio of heroes, chase after Flynn and James. Historian Lucy realizes that they will need help and suggests they call on Bass Reeves (Colman Domingo), "arguably the best lawman in the Old West," the man whom, "they say," was the inspiration for the Lone Ranger. Lucy's use of the phrase "they say," suggesting a vagueness of sourcing, may reflect the screenwriters' awareness of just how speculative and dubious attempts to connect the historical figure Reeves with the fictional creation the Lone Ranger have been.

Lucy does not mention that Reeves is African American. His first appearance on-screen is likely to be as surprising to viewers as it is to Rufus and Wyatt. In staging the introduction of Reeves as a surprise, *Timeless* evokes a television convention for introducing a black cowboy on screen that goes back at least as far as guest appearances by Sammy Davis Jr. and Woody Strode in *The Rifleman* (1958–64) and *Rawhide* (1959–65) from the early 1960s. This scene is often staged so that the white actors who are series regulars serve as audience surrogates, staring in amazement at the unexpected appearance of an African American figure in a western.[23] In the *Timeless* version of this scene, however, it is Rufus, the African American series regular, who serves as the audience surrogate, decentering the perspective of the white cowboy hero more typically at the center of television westerns. When Reeves steps on his porch to greet his visitors, the camera cuts to Rufus's reaction, which shifts from dumbfounded surprise to pleasure: "The Lone Ranger is black? That's . . . awesome!"

Rufus brings a perspective to the Old West that is contemporary—his pop culture references provide the sense of hyperconscious intertextuality—and African American, as revealed through his responses and comments throughout the episode. It is indeed awesome that an African American lawman is at the center of *Timeless*'s western episode. While the series often takes pains in terms of historical accuracy, "The Murder of Jesse James" is more about genre than history. Musical and visual cues throughout suggest that we have not so much traveled into the past as into the western's version of history as legend. In his first appearance, the camera lingers on Reeves, who is filmed from a low angle, as the music swells, suggesting a mythic rather than realistic portrayal. In other words, Reeves is presented to us as the cowboy hero of the western.

Place and time are refracted through genre traditions. Part of the western mythmaking in the episode is the claim that Bass Reeves is the inspiration for the Lone Ranger. We view the historical figure Reeves through the lens of his supposed fictional descendent.[24] When Reeve's Cree-descended friend Grant Johnson (Zahn McClarnon) arrives to guide them through Oklahoma, Rufus exclaims, "It's Tonto," to which Johnson, without any knowledge of twentieth-century popular culture, takes offense: "This guy called me foolish."

There is no evidence that any of the individuals involved with the creation of the Lone Ranger radio show had ever heard of Reeves, much less based the character on him.[25] "The Murder of Jesse James" seems to adopt the western genre's attitude toward history: "This is the West, sir," as newspaper reporter Dutton Peabody (Edmond O'Brien) famously states in *The Man Who Shot Liberty Valance* (1962): "When the legend becomes fact, print the legend." The episode chooses legend over historical fact to assert a countermythology—an origin story for the Lone Ranger, one of the most famous fictional characters of the twentieth century—that is demonstrably untrue but, in keeping with the episode's embrace of the genre western as a mode of storytelling, is undeniably an "awesome" idea. "This is the western, sir," the episode seems to say, so let's "print (or film) the legend."

Although we learn a few details of Reeves's personal life, the character is primarily defined by his relationship to the law, and he represents the very embodiment of justice itself. When Wyatt suggests they go in with guns blazing and kill both James and Garcia, Reeves responds, "This ain't the 1820s. We capture him and bring him to justice. Alive." When Wyatt argues that "shooting on sight would be easier," Reeves responds that capturing James is "what's right. . . . Who the hell ever said easy and right were the same thing?"

As Daw-Nay Evans writes in "The Duty of Reason: Kantian Ethics in *High Noon*" (2010), the sheriff in the classic western often embodies a philosophical position similar to that espoused in Immanuel Kant's moral theory, an adherence to the belief that "doing the right thing requires us to do our duty despite any intended or negative consequences that might follow."[26] Reason "commands us to abide by principles rather than consequences" (173). The "Kantian moral agent" seeks "to do what reason dictates rather than what our instincts desire."[27] That is, our instinct for self-preservation might cause us to desire to shoot on sight, but allegiance to the principle of justice enables us to transcend personal desire to do what is objectively right. Guided by "a maxim of standing against lawlessness," the lawman of the classic western will act "to achieve justice regardless of the consequences to [his] person, [his] friends, [his] family."[28] His actions will not be influenced by desires for safety, for personal revenge, or by consideration of the possible consequences of taking the right action (such as the possibility that the captured outlaw might escape prison and cause further havoc). Like Marshal Will Kane (Gary Cooper) of *High Noon* (1952), Reeves is a "Kantian moral agent," one who acts according to principle and reason and who refuses to be swayed by others who urge him to act against that principle—even if that means that by the end of the episode he walks away in disgust from his comrades, and, in a gesture that recall's Kane's famous tossing of his badge into the dirt at the end of *High Noon*, refuses to accept the bounty money for the capture of Jesse James, turning his back when Lucy tries to hand it to him.

When the travelers return to their own time, Wyatt tells Rufus that he used to watch westerns as a child and admired the clear sense of right and wrong advocated by cowboy heroes such as Gary Cooper and John Wayne, but that experience in war taught him a different lesson, about the uncertainty and ambiguity in deciding matters of right and wrong. He finds himself shaken by encountering Reeves, whose commitment to justice recalls those silver-screen cowboy heroes of his childhood. Rather than a necessarily realistic and complex rendering of the historical figure Bass Reeves, *Timeless* offers us something perhaps even rarer: an African American western hero whose commitment to the cause of justice is unwavering. That this classic western tale and hero is contained within the framework of a time travel narrative tells us much about the possibilities the weird western offers as a genre for remaking the classic western.

Other elements of the episode suggest an awareness of participating specifically in a story of the African American West. The surprising reveal of the African American cowboy hero is a repeated feature of black westerns, as is the strategy of revealing the existence of racism through the African American character's initial arrival in a town.[29] In the Blaxploitation western *Boss Nigger* (1975), for example, star Fred Williamson (who plays "Boss") and D'Urville Martin ("Amos") ride down the main street as townspeople stare at them:

> AMOS: Sure is funny the way they think we is the devil.
> BOSS: Folks always fear the things they don't know much about, Amos. I reckon people in this town ain't ever seen blacks before.

Blazing Saddles (1974) memorably riffs on the convention by showing the comically exaggerated racist reactions of the townspeople of Rock Ridge when Cleavon Little's Sheriff Bart rides into town. There's a similar moment in *Django Unchained* (2012), when King Schultz (Cristoph Waltz) and Django (Jamie Foxx) ride into town, with Shultz asking, "What's everybody staring at?" and Django responding, "They ain't never seen no nigger on no horse before." In *Timeless* we begin with a long shot of Reeves's posse riding into town, and we then observe the townspeople noticing their presence.

WYATT: Why is everybody looking at us like they want to kill us?
REEVES: Because the two of us are black and one's an Indian.
RUFUS: Huh, so it's like the scary version of *Blazing Saddles*.

Timeless references all three of the earlier movies here, with the white character Wyatt's question echoing that of the white character (Schultz) in *Django Unchained*. Significantly, "The Murder of Jesse James" alludes more directly to the versions of this scene played out in *Boss* and *Blazing Saddles* than it does to *Django Unchained*, pointing toward an affiliation with the two films that have not only African American actors but African American screenwriters (Fred Williamson not only stars in *Boss* but receives sole credit for the screenplay, and Richard Pryor is one of the several screenwriters of *Blazing Saddles*). *Blazing Saddles* receives a shout-out in the dialogue, but the staging and camera placement in the scene come directly from *Boss*. When filming the riders, the camera consistently stays to their front and to their left (as is the case with *Boss*). In both *Timeless* and *Boss* camera placement and angle suggest that we are alternating back and forth between the perspectives of the riders (the camera placed in the center of the street looking down and at an angle toward the sidewalk) and the townspeople (the camera positioned at various places on the sidewalk, angled up to view the mounted riders). Camera movement matching the speed of the horses further suggests that we are viewing the gaping townspeople from horseback. The rhythm and pattern of the editing also follows that of the *Boss* sequence (the *Timeless* sequence is shorter, however, with fewer cutaways to the staring townspeople). Although one of the white characters, Wyatt, contributes to the conversation, the camera remains centered on the two black men, Rufus and Reeves, as it does on Boss and Amos.

The climactic scene of the episode is the expected showdown with Jesse James, who has been armed by Flynn with a twenty-first-century automatic weapon. Although not as playful in its evocation of hyperconscious hybridity as *Legends of Tomorrow*, the image of James with advanced weaponry is one such moment of co-presence—an intentional break from the story's adherence to the realist conventions of establishing time and place in the western. Grant Johnson, Reeve's Cree friend, is killed by James, and thus the sole Native American character vanishes from the story, reinscribing rather than revising a trope of the classic western. The death of Johnson sets up an expectation of revenge. However, in keeping with the episode's characterization of Reeves, he sets aside revenge for the sake of justice. As a Kantian moral agent, he acts according to reason and principle rather than desire (i.e., for vengeance). He gets the drop on James and places him under arrest, but, just after James puts down his weapon and surrenders, the historian Lucy shoots James in the back. James dies on the day he is supposed to die, and in the way (more or less) that he is supposed to die (shot in the back). The moment also provides another allusion to *High Noon*. Kane's wife Amy (Grace Kelly) shoots one of the outlaws in the back—a surprising moment there as it is in *Timeless* of a female character as the agent of western violence.

An exploration of the ethics of violence, as justified or even necessary, is a central theme of the western. *Timeless* uses "The Murder of Jesse James" to bring that theme to the forefront of the series, as it's a question that the time travelers will continue to grapple with for the rest of season. Jesse James's "Murder" represents a different form of simultaneity than does the showdown in *Legend*: Lucy's killing of James, shooting in the back a man who is in the act of surrendering to the law, is morally dubious from a Kantian—and classic western—perspective. However, in terms of the science fiction genre, she acts according to principle (to preserve the timeline). That principle involves the consequentialist thinking that the classic western rejects, but it is perfectly in keeping with the exploration of the murky morality of changing (or trying to restore changes already made) the past that is the central ethical question of the time travel narrative. This is half the fun of the time travel narrative—to entangle the characters in crisscrossing timelines, to force them to consider a headache-inducing multitude of unintended consequences and an array of befuddling ethical and moral dilemmas. Lucy's killing of James belongs equally and simultaneously to both genres, the violent climax of the western resulting in the outlaw's death, the attempted preservation of history that belongs to the time travel narrative. How we judge Lucy's actions may depend on in which generic context we situate them.

That judgment is further complicated by the failure of her act to accomplish the goal of preservation. James dies on the day he is supposed to die, but credit for the capture of the outlaw Jesse James goes to Bass Reeves—despite Reeves's refusal to accept the bounty money and his attempt to refuse credit for catching him. The body of James upright in a coffin accompanied by a sign that reads "The Vile Outlaw Jesse James Brought to Justice" comments ironically on Reeves's stance on the injustice of unnecessary killing. Rufus tries to convince Reeves that taking the credit for the capture is important to the future, that people will want to know his story and will find inspiration in that story: in the heroic actions of an African American lawman. "If you don't tell your story," Rufus warns, "some white dick in a mask might end up a legend instead of you. People are going to want to know your story. Today. Tomorrow. Maybe even a hundred years from now." Reeve responds, "I'm not doing this for them," before riding out of town on his white horse—his allegiance, as it has been throughout the episode, to doing his duty as a lawman—unconcerned with the potential consequences of his actions "a hundred years from now."

As the episode closes, Lucy is reading on her tablet a historical article about the death of Jesse James that begins with a photograph captioned "U. S. Marshall Bass Reeves with lawman Grant Johnson, who gave his life bringing down the murdering outlaw Jesse James." The article states that "Reeves and his posse delivered the lifeless body of Jesse James to the St. Joseph's Sheriff's office," and it concludes with a photograph of James in his coffin and a startled-looking Lucy in the foreground at the edge of the frame. Rather than being forgotten, in this version of history Reeves becomes a central figure. The time travelers violate their prime directive to leave history unaltered, but, in so doing, they make visible a history that has been invisible, bringing an African American figure to the forefront of history and to the center of the genre western.

From the perspective of genre, the time travel trope offers a similar possibility, an opportunity to revisit the western and make visible the histories that the genre itself has obscured—the stories of black lawmen, bounty hunters, and outlaws that the western has failed to mythologize in the way it has their white counterparts; the stories of black cowboys who historically participated alongside their white fellows in nineteenth-century cattle drives; the stories of African American settlers who, like Cinnamon in "The Magnificent Eight," made lives for themselves in western towns like Salvation. *Legends of Tomorrow* and *Timeless* critique the western by participating in it, remaking the traditional genre via the hybrid form of the weird western.

NOTES

1. There is a direct nod to *Hidden Figures* in the episode "Space Race."
2. For *The Twilight Zone*, see, for example, "Execution" and "The Seventh is Made Up of Phantoms." For *Voyagers*, see "Billy and Bully." For *Sliders*, see "The Good, The Bad and the Wealthy."
3. For *Star Trek*, see "Spectre of the Gun" and "A Fistful of Datas"; for *Doctor Who*, see "A Holiday for the Doctor."
4. The *Supernatural* episode "Frontierland" follows this pattern to the letter, down to the name "Clint Eastwood," whose serape Dean dons along with his name.
5. Collins, "Genericity in the Nineties," 249.
6. Carrington, *Speculative Blackness*, 2.
7. Carrington, *Speculative Blackness*, 15.
8. Carrington, *Speculative Blackness*, 13.
9. Carrington, *Speculative Blackness*, 27.
10. Nama, *Black Space*, 124.
11. Carrington, *Speculative Blackness*, 171.
12. Carrington, *Speculative Blackness*, 159.
13. The other actors are Arthur Darvill (Rip Hunter), Victor Garber (Martin Stein), Caity Lotz (Sara Lance), Brandon Routh (Ray Palmer), Wentworth Miller (Leonard Snart), and Dominic Purcell (Mick Rory).
14. See Green, *Encyclopedia of Weird Westerns*, 55–6, 109.
15. Green, *Encyclopedia of Weird Westerns*, 150.

16. Carrington, *Speculative Blackness*, 180.
17. Carrington, *Speculative Blackness*, 26.
18. Womack, *Afrofuturism*, 158.
19. Commander, *Afro-Atlantic Flight*, 54, 33.
20. See Dale, "Stranded."
21. Carrington, *Speculative Blackness*, 190.
22. Commander, *Afro-Atlantic Flight*, 3.
23. Johnson, *Hoo-Doo Cowboys*, 154–55, 159–60.
24. Art Burton makes this claim in his biography of Reeves, *Black Gun, Silver Star*, as well as in several interviews. See, for example, McKenzie, "Was an African American Cop the Real Lone Ranger?"
25. See Grams, "Myth Debunked."
26. Evans, "Duty of Reason," 171.
27. Evans, "Duty of Reason," 173.
28. Evans, "Duty of Reason," 180.
29. See Johnson, *Hoo-Doo Cowboys*, 174.

BIBLIOGRAPHY

Arnold, Jack, dir. *Boss Nigger*. Dimension Pictures, 1975.
Bee, Guy Norman, dir. *Supernatural*. Season 6, episode 18, "Frontierland." Aired April 22, 2011, on CW.
Beeson, Charles, dir. *Timeless*. Season 2, episode 8, "Space Race." Aired November 28, 2016, on NBC.
Brooks, Avery, dir. *Star Trek: Deep Space Nine*. Season 6, episode 13, "Far Beyond the Stars." Aired February 11, 1998, on CBS.
Brooks, Mel, dir. *Blazing Saddles*. Warner Bros., 1974.
Burton, Art. *Black Gun, Silver Star: The Life and Legend of Frontier Marshal Bass Reeves*. Lincoln: University of Nebraska Press, 2006.
Butler, Octavia. *Kindred*. Garden City NY: Doubleday, 1979.
Calmatic, dir. "Old Town Road." Columbia Records, 2019.
Carrington, André. *Speculative Blackness: The Future of Race in Science Fiction*. Minneapolis: University of Minnesota Press, 2016.
Collins, Jim. "Genericity in the Nineties: Eclectic Irony and the New Sincerity." In *Film Theory Goes to the Movies*, edited by Jim Collins et al., 242–63. New York: Routledge, 1994.

Commander, Michelle. *Afro-Atlantic Flight: Speculative Returns and the Black Fantastic*. Durham NC: Duke University Press, 2017.

Corea, Nicholas J., creator. *Outlaws*. 1986–87, on CBS.

Costo, Oscar L., dir. *Sliders*. Season 2, episode 4, "The Good, the Bad, and the Wealthy." Aired March 22, 1996, on Fox.

Crosland, Alan Jr., dir. *The Twilight Zone*. Season 5, episode 10, "The 7th Is Made Up of Phantoms." Aired December 6, 1963, on CBS.

Cullen, Charles E., dir. *A Modern Day Western: The Sanchez Saga*. Cullen Studios, 1997.

Dale, Holly, dir. *Timeless*. Season 1, episode 7, "Stranded." Aired November 21, 2016, on NBC.

Evans, Daw-Nay. "The Duty of Reason: Kantian Ethics in *High Noon*." In *The Philosophy of the Western*, edited by Jennifer L. McMahon and B. Steve Csaki, 171–83. Lexington: University Press of Kentucky, 2010.

Ford, John, dir. *The Man Who Shot Liberty Valance*. Paramount, 1962.

Freudenthal, Thor, dir. *Legends of Tomorrow*. Season 1, episode 11, "The Magnificent Eight." Aired April 14, 2016, on CW.

Gerima, Haile, dir. *Sankofa*. Channel Four Films, 1993.

Grams, Martin. "Myth Debunked: Bass Reeves Was NOT the Lone Ranger." Martin Grams Blog. April 2, 2015, http://martingrams.blogspot.com/2015/04/myth-debunked-bass-reeves-was-not-lone.html (accessed October 15, 2019).

Green, Paul. *Encyclopedia of Weird Westerns*. Jefferson NC: McFarland, 2009.

Hardy, Stuart, dir. *Doctor Who*. Season 7, episode 2, "A Town Called Mercy." Aired September 15, 2012, on BBC.

Hopkins, Pauline. *Winona: A Tale of Negro Life in the South and the Southwest* (1902). In *The Magazine Novels of Pauline Hopkins*, 285–437. New York: Oxford University Press, 1988.

Johnson, Michael K. *Hoo-Doo Cowboys and Bronze Buckaroos: Conceptions of the African American West*. Jackson: University Press of Mississippi, 2014.

Lavender, Isiah, III. *Race in American Science Fiction*. Bloomington: Indiana University Press, 2011.

McDearmon, David Orrick, dir. *The Twilight Zone*. Season 1, episode 26, "Execution." Aired April 1, 1960, CBS.

McEevty, Vincent, dir. *Star Trek*. Season 3, episode 6, "Spectre of the Gun." Aired October 25, 1968, on NBC.

McKenzie, Sheena. "Was an African American Cop the Real Lone Ranger?" CNN, August 6, 2013, https://www.cnn.com/2013/08/06/sport/lone-ranger-african-american-reeves/index.html (accessed October 15, 2019).

Nadel, Arthur H., dir. *The Rifleman*. Season 5, episode 9, "The Most Amazing Man." Aired November 26, 1962, on ABC.

Nama, Adilfu. *Black Space: Imagining Race in Science Fiction Film*. Austin: University of Texas Press, 2008.

Nowlan, Cherie, dir. *Legends of Tomorrow*. Season 2, episode 6, "Outlaw Country." Aired November 17, 2016, on CW.

Post, Ted, dir. *Rawhide*. Season 3, episode 10, "The Incident of the Buffalo Soldier." Aired March 24, 1961, on CBS.

Showalter, John F., dir. *Timeless*. Season 1, episode 12, "The Murder of Jesse James." Aired January 23, 2017, on NBC.

Stewart, Patrick, dir. *Star Trek: The Next Generation*. Season 6, episode 8, "A Fistful of Datas." Aired November 7, 1992, syndicated.

Tarantino, Quentin, dir. *Django Unchained*. Columbia Pictures, 2012.

Terlesky, John, dir. *Timeless*. Season 1, episode 5, "The Alamo." Aired October 31, 2016, on NBC.

Tucker, Rex, dir. *Doctor Who*. Season 3, episode 34, "A Holiday for the Doctor." Aired April 30, 1966, on BBC.

Vogel, Virgil W., dir. *Voyagers*. Season 1, episode 3, "Bully and Billy." Aired October 24, 1982, on NBC.

Womack, Ytasha L. *Afrofuturism: The World of Black Science Fiction and Fantasy Culture*. Chicago: Lawrence Hill, 2013.

Zemeckis, Robert, dir. *Back to the Future III*. Universal Pictures, 1990.

Zinneman, Fred, dir. *High Noon*. Stanley Kramer Productions, 1952

PART FIVE

The Undead in the Weird Western

Go West, Old Man 13

Or, Buffalo Bill and the "Yellow Peril" in *Zeppelins West*

CYNTHIA J. MILLER AND A. BOWDOIN VAN RIPER

What becomes of the Wild West when there is no more frontier—when rails, telegraph lines, and barbed-wire fences have tamed the wilderness beyond the hundredth meridian? The conventional answer is that it fades away, preserved in sepia-tinged history and the distilled, essentialized conventions of the Wild West show, but Joe R. Lansdale's novel *Zeppelins West* (2001) offers another possibility: it just keeps moving westward. Lansdale has Buffalo Bill—temporarily reduced to a disembodied head joined to a steam-powered robot body—loading Annie Oakley, Wild Bill Hickok, Sitting Bull, and other iconic figures onto an airship bound for Japan, where he intends to perform his version of the Wild West for the Emperor. The transpacific West proves, however, to be just as perilous as the one he left behind, and the Japanese prove to be adversaries just as formidable as the Indian warriors and Mexican bandits whose conquest by white civilization he replays nightly in the arena. The road show becomes a rescue mission in which Cody and his troupe attempt to rescue Frankenstein's monster from the clutches of a shogun who intends to consume him, one body part at a time, for his supposed medicinal benefits.

Set in a fantastic, alternate version of the late nineteenth century where biplanes defend the home islands against western airships and samurai warriors fight at Little Big Horn, Lansdale's novel adds the Japanese to the racial mix of the traditional western. Taking advantage of a fantasy milieu in which fictional and historical figures mingle freely, it simultaneously dramatizes and satirizes the era's standard Orientalist fantasies of Japan. The Emperor is a cruel, calculating warlord cast from the same mold as Sax Rohmer's Fu Manchu, but he is also a decadent hedonist whose repulsive Otherness is made manifest by his consumption of the helpless and decidedly sympathetic Monster. Buffalo Bill and his crew—representatives, in a dual sense, of "the West"—thus find themselves, once again, in conflict with the barbarous inhabitants of an untamed land who view themselves (and it) as nothing of the sort.

In this bizarre history, representations of race—both real and symbolic—are complicated by geography, time, and imagination. "Western" (in both territorial and ideological senses) constructions of racialized Others intermingle and shift and, in so doing, critique "real" historical practices and attitudes toward both Native Americans and the Japanese. The former, framed as icons of the West, are situated both in and out of place on the zeppelin, while the latter, re-placed in their own nation, are framed both as exotic Others and dangerous threats to Western ways of life. This essay, then, will unpack these overlapping constructions of race and explore the ways in which Lansdale, by orchestrating a collision between fantasy versions of the Wild West and Japan, simultaneously replicates and upends the racial conventions of the traditional western—a process further complicated by the presence of such debatably human characters as the Monster, the Tin Man, and, indeed, the steam-powered cyborg that is Buffalo Bill himself.

The Gonzo Frontier

Lansdale's mingling of characters from history and multiple fictional universes, along with the extravagantly anachronistic technology, marks *Zeppelins West* as a kind of "gonzo-historical" fantasy. The anachronistic elements—including references to dime novel character Frank Reade, creator of the Steam Man of the Plains—bring a significant steampunk element to the tale. This disconnect among characters, places, and times allows Lansdale to craft his critique of nineteenth-century racist national policy, even as it is being unreflexively perpetuated on an individual (micro)level by his characters.[1]

The premise of *Zeppelins West* sounds deceptively standard. In an unspecified year in the late nineteenth century, Buffalo Bill Cody is crossing the Pacific with eight hundred members of his Wild West show troupe, bound for Japan, on a diplomatic mission to perform for Sokaku Takeda, the Asian nation's most powerful shogun and its future ruler. Lansdale quickly makes it clear, however, that the characters' nineteenth century is not the audience's nineteenth century, but something wilder and stranger.

The imperial adventure story, like its cousin the western, coalesced as a genre while the events it purported to depict were still underway. It was, from the outset, rendered fantastic—in the sense of the antithesis of realistic—by its relentless simplification and stylization of those events, and its systematic erasure of moral ambiguity.[2] Attempts to move it into the realm of the overtly fantastic by blending it with science fiction, alternate history, parallel universes, mad-genius stories, or future-war narratives have generally left such simplifications intact.[3] The unexamined persistence of imperialist sociopolitical frameworks in tales framed by the vigorous disruption of other norms, including the laws of nature, has met with growing criticism, particularly by scholars from non-Western backgrounds.[4] "Come on, people," Monique Poirier rhetorically inquires of steampunk audiences and authors. "We can have clockwork robots, but not POC civilizations?"[5]

Constructing such civilizations demands more than transforming unruly Others who reject the colonial enterprise from villains into heroes.[6] It requires jettisoning familiar assumptions about what is natural or "inevitable" and envisioning a world where Tecumseh's Rebellion created a continent-spanning confederation that expanded its influence into Mexico and the Central Pacific, or where the ports of Malaysia and Indonesia were sites of cultural exchange rivaling eighth-century Baghdad or medieval Paris.[7] In Asian-Pacific contexts, particularly, it means reframing the rules of (fantastic) geopolitics, so that the expansionist ambitions of a still-potent imperial China or rapidly modernizing Japan—traditionally viewed as mortal threats to the West—are as valid as those of Britain, Germany, or Russia.[8]

Zeppelins West unfolds in such a world, where the Japanese settled North America from the west even as Europeans settled it from the east. Between them, the two civilizations crushed native resistance, sometimes collaborating, as at the Little Big Horn, where samurai warriors fought under Custer. The Civil War resulted in the "founding of Texas as a Negro state" and was quickly followed by the U.S. annexation of Canada.[9] *Zeppelins West* is not, however, an alt-history story in the conventional sense. Lansdale makes no effort to explain the differences between the novel's timeline and the reader's, or to trace those differences to a single point of divergence.[10] The cast of historical characters further subverts the unstated rules of the alt-history subgenre by making an exuberant hash of chronology. Buffalo Bill enjoys worldwide fame thanks to his Wild West (which was, in both our timeline and Lansdale's, founded in 1883), but Ulysses S. Grant (who, in historical fact, left office in March 1877) is still in the White House. Annie Oakley's husband, Frank Butler (whom she married in 1877, and who outlived her, in our world), is dead, and she has taken Wild Bill Hickok (killed, in our world, in August 1876) as a lover.

Lansdale's nineteenth century is, likewise, filled with "technology out of time." The members of Buffalo Bill's troupe cross the Pacific in a fleet of airships: "A dozen brightly colored cigars" that "hung in the sky, floated on, and from time to time, as if smoked by invisible lips . . . puffed steam."[11] Steam-driven robots (invented and marketed by technological genius Frank Reade) are familiar parts of the characters' world.[12] When Buffalo Bill, at the climax of each Wild West performance, rides to the rescue of a settler family under attack by hostile Indians, he does so on a steam-driven steel horse. Cody himself is a nineteenth-century cyborg, his disembodied head kept alive in a Mason jar—filled with a mixture of pig urine, whiskey, and a mysterious chemical compound—that an assistant attaches each morning to a robot body controlled, from inside, by a dwarf named Goober. He receives messages transmitted by "telewire," beamed across the Pacific by a communication satellite inspired (or perhaps designed) by Jules Verne.[13]

Cody's existence as a disembodied head (the result of his wife's nearly decapitating him with a fire axe after finding him in bed with paramour Lily Langtry) is made possible by a loose alliance of not-quite-mad scientists obsessed with creating life in the laboratory. They include real historical figures such as Charles Darwin and Samuel F. B. Morse, as well as fictional ones operating under their own names (Dr. Frankenstein) or tissue-thin aliases (Dr. Momo, a barely disguised version of H. G. Wells's Dr. Moreau).

Frankenstein's famous monster is the novel's pivotal figure: both character and MacGuffin. Lost in the Arctic, as in Mary Shelley's original tale, but retrieved by a Russian ship and sold to the Japanese, the Monster is coveted both by Takeda (who consumes the Monster's flesh to enhance his sexual potency), and Cody (who believes he holds the secret to making his body and head permanently whole again). The ostensible purpose of Cody's visit to Japan is diplomatic. Intended to flatter ruler-to-be Takeda, the Wild West performance has the overt purpose of building cordial relations between the countries and the covert one of providing a pretext for a gift of modern firearms that the Grant administration believes will—in an echo of our world—turn Takeda into a regular customer of the nascent American military-industrial complex and ensure his emergence as the unchallenged ruler of Japan.[14] To these intertwined goals, Cody adds a third, more personal one: acquiring the Monster for use in experiments that will enable the reunion of his own head with a flesh-and-blood body. Originally meant to be accomplished by a private side deal with Takeda, the rescue of the Monster turns into a nighttime raid mounted by Cody and his most trusted friends, using his personal airship.

The rescue succeeds, barely, but biplanes in pursuit from the shogun's air force give chase and shoot the airship down. The survivors are left floating in the Pacific, Cody's head (its robot body lost) bobbing over the waves in its tightly sealed jar. Rescued by the mysterious Captain Bemo and his associate Ned the Seal (who reads and writes English fluently, although he cannot speak), they are brought aboard the submarine *Naughty Lass* and taken to the lair of Doctor Momo, which is filled with animals surgically transformed, like Ned, into (mostly) human beings.

Cody and his crew become—like Montgomery, the shipwrecked narrator of Wells's novel—both participants in and increasingly alarmed observers of Momo's bizarre world. Cody himself is tempted by the promise of a new body; Sitting Bull finds carnal satisfaction with Catherine (a beautiful, sultry woman whose nickname, Cat, betrays her origins); and the Monster, who has adopted the name Bert, finds a spiritual and sexual soul mate in Tin, a mechanical man from another dimension with metal skin that is "smooth and flowing, like silver flesh," and a face "like that of a god."[15] The castaways remain comfortable, if uneasy, residents of Momo's island world until, realizing the true nature of his ambitions, they join forces with Tin and Ned the Seal to mount an escape in the *Naughty Lass*. Their actions trigger a revolt among the man-beasts and a maelstrom of violence that leaves only a handful of the group alive.

Westward Expansion(s)

Buffalo Bill's mission to Japan—part show of force, part diplomatic stratagem, part private enterprise—is, paradoxically, among the *least* fantastic elements of *Zeppelins West*. Beneath its exotic trappings, it acknowledges a historical reality that is often ignored, for the sake of narrative simplicity, in textbooks and documentary montages: that the history of America's westward expansion is not one story, but two stories. Read against this historical background, the plot arc of *Zeppelins West* becomes fantastic, but not outright fantasy. Like the popular culture of the late nineteenth century (e.g., the "real" Buffalo Bill's Wild West show), it is an extravagantly exuberant improvement on reality, cunningly exaggerated in order to make a point.

One thread of this real historical backdrop involves the conquest—literally by force of arms and figuratively by technological ingenuity—of the continental interior.[16] The second involves the crossing of the North Pacific and the insinuation of the United States into the affairs of its island societies and of the great powers on its East Asian rim.[17] The second expansion, normally treated as if it began at Manila Bay in 1898, actually unfolded in parallel with the first: contiguous in space and coincident in time, driven by similar assumptions and yielding similar echoes in popular culture.

America's dual westward push began when the ink was barely dry on the Constitution. Signed in July 1787, the first Northwest Ordinance opened the land west of the Appalachians and north of the Ohio River to settlement. Less than three months later—bankrolled by Yankee merchants eager for a share of the Pacific Northwest fur trade and direct access to the markets of East Asia—the *Columbia* and the *Lady Washington* left Boston under the command of Captain John Kendrick, bound for the Pacific. They arrived off of Vancouver Island a year later, staking out an American presence in the Oregon Country nearly twenty years before Lewis and Clark stood (like buckskinned versions of Keats's "stout Cortez") at the mouth of the Columbia River. By the time the defeat of the Shawnee-led Western Confederacy at the Battle of Fallen Timbers (1794) ended the first of the Indian Wars, Kendrick had called at Honolulu, spent fourteen months trading with the Chinese in Macao, and (blown north by a typhoon in May 1791) become the first American to reach Japan.[18]

And so it continued. As William Harrison's troops defeated Tecumseh's at the Battle of Tippecanoe (1811), an American naval officer briefly, abortively annexed the Marquesas Islands in Polynesia.[19] As settlers poured into the upper Midwest in the first quarter of the nineteenth century, merchant vessels from Salem and Boston poured into the Pacific, trading at Canton for silks, porcelain, and opium. The Treaty of Wanghia (1844) and the Convention of Kanagawa (1854), most-favored-nation trade agreements imposed on China and Japan under the threat of armed force, bracketed the seizure of the northern third of Mexico in the Mexican-American War of 1846–48.[20] Commodore Matthew Perry, whose naval squadron "opened" Japan to American ships at cannonpoint in 1852, came to the assignment fresh from that war, in which he had overseen the conquest of Frontera, Tampico, and San Juan Bautista. The appropriation of the Hawaiian Islands by and for American interests was achieved by the exercise of softer forms of power. The threat of military force was implied, rather than displayed or exercised. The changes wrought in the Hawaiian Islands by mid-century American missionaries, whalers, and sugar barons—land transfers on unfavorable terms, loss of autonomy, and the deliberate suppression (or systematic extinction) of traditional cultures—mirrored, however, the experiences of Latinos and, particularly, Native Americans on the continent.[21]

Expansion across the continent and across the Pacific was undergirded by similar sets of beliefs. The intertwined senses of cultural superiority and unquestioned entitlement displayed by the Salem merchants at Canton, the Tyler administration's diplomats at the Wanghia negotiations, and Commodore Perry when he threatened Tokyo with naval bombardment were reflections of the same worldview that newspaper editor John O'Sullivan made famous as "manifest destiny." The casually arrogant confidence with which white settlers dismantled native Hawaiian institutions and substituted their own—no less destructive for being well-intentioned—would have been grimly familiar to any Cherokee, Sioux, or Navajo who bore witness to it.

Native Hawaiians and other Pacific islanders fit comfortably into the niche in the American imaginary long occupied by Indians: the savage, primitive Other, "half devil and half child," as Rudyard Kipling famously warned the United States in "The White Man's Burden" (1899), written after the American conquest of the Philippines. Their shell necklaces and carved coconuts, war clubs, and elaborate canoe paddles performed for the Americans who brought them home from the Pacific the same function as a Sioux headdress or Navajo pot: evidence of a journey beyond the edge of civilization, into the realm of the savage and exotic.[22] The Chinese and Japanese—civilized by comparison, yet still profoundly and undeniably Other—were a different matter. Their exoticism, embodied in and commoditized by the trade goods from which American merchants made fortunes, carried overtones not of savage vigor but of sensual decadence locked into place, for centuries, by the iron rule of despotic princes.[23] Flowing silk garments, intricately carved fans, and impossibly thin porcelain, brought home piecemeal to a Salem drawing room or Boston boudoir, delivered a complex set of cultural signals. They marked the owners as participants in the lucrative overseas trade or (as imported Asian goods had for centuries, across two continents) as possessors of wealth from other sources, sufficient to grant them access to the rare and exotic.[24] In tandem with the depth of the owners' purse, however, they also signaled breadth of experience and refinement of taste.[25]

The very word "curiosities," as Jonathan Tchen notes, had a specifically Orientalist overtone; it connoted objects desirable because of their rarity, but specifically those from East Asia. The curiosities that filled cabinets and adorned mantelpieces in America's coastal cities were valuable *because* they signaled contact with, and knowledge of, the exotic. Objects that could be "owned, collected, and taken away from" distant lands and domesticated through display, they mirrored the imperialist enterprise in miniature.[26] An entire society furnished with such objects—China and Japan as they existed in the Western imagination—would, by contrast, be as languidly debauched as an opium addict's dreams.[27] The pulp literature of the late nineteenth century framed the two Others accordingly: Indians were dangerous because of their capacity for ruthless violence and brutality, Asians because of their duplicity and guile.

The dime novel westerns that offered readers elaborately embroidered tales of stalwart (white) heroes defending civilization against bloodthirsty savages came into their own, however, as the tide of the Indian Wars decisively tipped and their outcome became inevitable. The pulp magazine "yellow peril" stories of Asian warlords bent on toppling Western civilization and "white slavers" luring vulnerable young (white) women to fates worse than death took root as a modernized, Westernized Japan—defeating first China (1894–95) and then Russia (1904–5)—became the dominant political force in East Asia. Neither pulp tradition emerged from a vacuum; both tapped into a century's worth of sustained collisions between Americans and the Others they encountered as they moved westward, exaggerating and embroidering the memories of those encounters in order to celebrate American prowess.

Authenticity, Idealization, and Entertainment

Lansdale's novel is rooted in one of the most iconic—and problematic—representations of the American West: the Wild West show. Throughout their history, these shows perpetuated spectacular notions of masculinity, national identity, and unproblematic whiteness. Audiences are promised sights never before seen: "Imagine wild buffalo, Indians and cowboys together in an arena right before your eyes! With stagecoach attacks, gunfight showdowns, shooting demonstrations, horse-riding displays . . . this will be a night to remember!"[28] From Indian wars to trick shooting, Wild West shows offered a glimpse of the American West that was a far cry from the hardships, disease, and disappointments experienced by most who were drawn to the new territories, yet the notions that they conveyed to their audiences almost immediately became part of the stories that America told about itself.

These shows offered audiences an idealized depiction of the American West, promising "action, history, and thrills," along with a celebration of courage, independence, patriotism, the domination of nature, violence, and masculinity—the building blocks of a particular form of American national identity, and ideological impulses all replicated in Lansdale's novel. Showcasing the exotic and dangerous, Wild West shows featured displays of skill, such as trick riding, roping, and fancy shooting; competitions, such as rodeo events and races; theatrical reenactments of historical moments and battles, such as Custer's Last Stand; along with celebrated and exotic figures, such as well-known western personalities, Indian chiefs (e.g., Sitting Bull), and costumed performers from all over the world. While the fantastic Wild West show featured in the novel works on a smaller scale, the impact of its larger-than-life rendition of the West is as effective in communicating frontier tropes and ideologies, which stand in sharp contrast to the ancient tradition and regimentation of the Japanese empire.

The historical figure adapted for Lansdale's zeppelin voyage was also larger than life, ideally suited to the author's multilayered engagement with the many ways in which frontier Americana intersected with race. William "Buffalo Bill" Cody founded the original, and best-known, of the Wild West shows. It premiered in the 1870s, as the Buffalo Bill Combination, and then re-formed in 1883, as Buffalo Bill's Wild West show. Images of Cody, especially those from his Wild West show, have influenced popular conceptions of the American West for well over a hundred years. It was the "gold standard" of western traveling shows, as a writer for the *Denver Post* lauded (July 13, 1913): "There never was anything like Buffalo Bill's Wild West show before; there will never be anything like it again." Through his Wild West shows, Cody attempted to produce a re-creation of border life on a scale grander than the walls of a theater could ever accommodate. With each performance, Buffalo Bill's Wild West promoted and canonized the characters and culture of frontier life, both at home and around the globe. Billed as "America's National Entertainment," the show, which boasted a cast of hundreds, toured the United States, England, and Europe for twenty years, including a landmark performance nearby the 1893 Chicago World's Fair.[29]

Authenticity was the lifeblood of Wild West shows such as Cody's, whether presenting feats of extreme skills like sharpshooting, roping, or trick riding, or portraying events and occurrences like hunts, Indian raids, or cattle roundups. A key element in making audiences feel as though they had witnessed the "real thing" was the casting of as many Indians as possible. Great chiefs whose names, thanks to the press, were household words were, as theatrical managers would say, "good box office," drawing crowds of spectators eager to see the storied savages. Sitting Bull participated in Buffalo Bill's show for four months in 1885, appearing for a brief horseback ride through the arena; Geronimo similarly lent his notoriety to Pawnee Bill's show in 1906. They, along with others such as Black Elk and Standing Bear, were showcased as dramatic foils—hyperracialized Others whose presence lent support to the telling and retelling of the tales of the frontier—exhibited as curiosities and advertised with colorful banners resembling those found in carnival sideshows.

Alongside this emphasis on authenticity, however, entrepreneurs of Wild West extravaganzas frequently thrived on the fascination created by ambiguous pasts in the "real" Old West.[30] Some, such as one reporter for the *Detroit Free Press*, called into question Buffalo Bill's heroic history and the realism of his shows: "Buffalo Bill has at last found a manager willing to take him to England, but what the public will next want to know is whether he is to be left there or not," he quipped.[31] Others, however, such as this Londoner visiting New York, reported that the Wild West show he attended was "an entertainment in which the whole of the most interesting episodes of life on the extreme frontier of civilization in America are represented with the most graphic vividness and scrupulous detail . . . no one can exaggerate the extreme excitement and 'go' of the whole performance."[32] Historian Louis S. Warren explains that Cody, a showman on par with P. T. Barnum, mingled his real-life adventures with "colorful fictions," creating for himself an image that was the embodiment of public fantasy—indistinguishable from the very myths created by his Wild West shows.[33] *Zeppelins West* seizes on that public fantasy—one of the building blocks of American national identity—and co-opts it to craft commentary about manifest destiny and exceptionalism, packaged in the iconography of frontier spectacle.

Lansdale's Buffalo Bill, like his historical counterpart (along with his show's headliners and cast, horses and buffalo, wagons and tents, weapons and banners), became such potent symbols of the Wild West that, for many, particularly audiences in eastern cities and across the Atlantic, they *were* the American West. And as the Wild West, as well as the men and women who became synonymous with it, made its way into literature and film, that legacy would persist and deepen. A product of the danger and romance of an imagined frontier, Cody became a complex icon that combined mastery over wildness with wildness itself. Adventurer, explorer, and victor over man and beast, his reputed triumphs gave form to myths of manifest destiny and cultural supremacy, and thrived on stereotypes of the frontier's exotic Others, trafficking in white fear and fascination and transforming it into commodity and spectacle.

A Collision of Others

Even amid the fantastic pastiche of *Zeppelins West*—exotic settings animated by countless literary allusions—the framework of manifest destiny remains unaltered. Buffalo Bill's Wild West show, a metaicon of the American West, transports the values, ideals, attitudes, and lifeways of the frontier halfway around an alternate globe to continue the saga of national identity that began on the frontier. As Cody and his troupe travel across the Pacific, they continue the tradition of Wild West shows begun in the late nineteenth century, moving almost seamlessly from history to fantasy in a spectacular celebration of Anglo-American conquest.

Even in his "disabled" form, Buffalo Bill represents heroic white American masculinity, perhaps even more so, because his means of locomotion—the robotic body created by inventor Frank Reade—is a symbol of American ingenuity and progress, in much the same way that Reade's Steam Man of the Plains, from the late nineteenth century, celebrated the role (and promise) of technology in conquering the frontier. Taken from this perspective, Cody is not less of a man, but *more*: a merging of frontier heroics and technological imagination. Tall, dominant, and the consummate showman, he leads the troupe's voyage of westward expansion, carrying the myth of American national identity to the far corners of the world.

Sitting Bull serves as an even more complex figure in the novel. In the context of Lansdale's fantastic adventure, he is multivalent—at once a symbol of the untamed Native American as well as of the indigenous "sellout" who performs the white man's version of his heritage. Lansdale engages with the former in an early exchange aboard the zeppelin with Captain Jack Crawford, Indian scout and poet:

> CRAWFORD: Well, I doubt I'll be doing any recitations in Japan ... They don't speak English.
> BULL: How bad of Japanese not speak English ... Like dirty Indians who speak Indian words, not English.[34]

As the Wild West meets the Far East, Lansdale continues to critique nineteenth-century racial stereotypes in ways that are transparent, but also complex. Racial stereotypes are abundant, shaping the narrative from the outset. Sitting Bull, the principal Native American character, is portrayed as the stereotypical domesticated Indian—primitive, vigorous, ascetic, and direct, a character whose potential for personal violence (a hallmark of frontier life) is high, but who, through age and acculturation, has simply become a cipher of the Native West. He, in ways similar to many of his historical counterparts, has become complicit in both exploiting and perpetuating late nineteenth-century notions of Nativeness. Throughout the real-life history of Buffalo Bill's Wild West, the shows balanced fear and fascination, thrilling their audiences with scenes of bloodthirsty warriors attacking stagecoaches or wagon trains and in dramatic battle settings (e.g., the Battle of Little Big Horn) against white cavalry and their scouts. Other performances, such as Wild Bill Hickok's "Grand Buffalo Hunt" in 1872, reduced that melodramatic tension by portraying Indian braves as collaborating with cowboys to conquer their shared prey.[35] Wild West Indians remained, however, marked as exotic Others: an image that, as Berkhofer discusses, has its origins in white Americanness and in relation to which the identity of white Americanness was, in turn, continually constructed—a discursive practice that Lansdale's novel replicates, parodies, and ultimately critiques in complex ways.[36]

At that same historical moment, however, there existed another racialized Other in the American West: the Japanese. Between 1892 and 1910, more than eighty thousand Japanese immigrants arrived from Japan.[37] As Japanese immigration to western urban centers like Spokane, Portland, Los Angeles, and San Francisco boomed and then spread to rural areas, anti-Japanese sentiment swelled. Roger Daniels points out that evidence has been found of derogatory and racist comments about the Japanese from the 1860s on, but these sentiments had exploded into violence by the 1890s, when a true anti-Japanese movement can be documented.[38] By the turn of the century, notions of the "yellow peril" had taken hold—a fear that Gina Marchetti identifies as combining "racist terror of alien cultures, sexual anxieties, and the belief that the west will be overpowered and enveloped by the irresistible, occult, dark forces of the East"[39]—and stereotypes were rampant, of the Japanese (along with the Chinese and other Asian immigrants) as disease-ridden, illiterate, and immoral hordes threatening to overrun the American Pacific West and bring about the downfall of the territories.[40]

In transporting the Wild West across the Pacific, Cody creates a fantastic and complex extension of westward expansion and exceptionalism. The zeppelins' arrival over Japan is staged to inspire awe and intimidation, in much the same way as the military push westward into the territories made a statement about American power and superiority. The shogun and his subjects are, in Lansdale's novel, not only echoes of emerging American stereotypes and prejudices against Asians in the nineteenth century, but also simultaneously obvious stand-ins for Native Americans on the frontier.

Lansdale's framing of the Japanese, then, and particularly the shogun, as highly civilized and powerful, but also pleasure-seeking, duplicitous, and inhumane, carries this nineteenth-century caricature into the alternate world of *Zeppelins West*. The Otherness of the shogun, signaled through his decadence and cruelty, as well as his mystical beliefs about virility that bring about his torturous consumption of Frankenstein's monster, makes manifest historical nineteenth-century fears and suggests that there truly was much reason for Americans to be afraid of this savage Other, justifying the troupe's conquest of Japan in much the same way that the conquest of such Others, in the near West and the exotic East, has been justified throughout American history. With Japan already positioned in the novel as a nation to be cultivated for exploitation, rather than for valued alliance, the shift in the Wild West show's mission from diplomacy to rescue is an easy one.

Through these portrayals, however, Lansdale suggests that the constellation of racial relationships in this fantastic steampunk-inflected adaptation of history is not as simple as it might appear. As readers come to understand Cody's own motivation in saving the Monster, it becomes clear that the moral divide between the two cultures is not as wide as it might have seemed. Our first reaction to the realization that he, too, seeks to exploit the Monster is one of disappointment—we are disillusioned that Buffalo Bill falls short of his role as iconic frontier hero. But, while he may fail to embody the myth, Cody does, in fact, portray the reality of the nineteenth-century scout-cowboy-showman. With one foot in the West and one in the East, the historical Buffalo Bill Cody was, just like his fictional counterpart, an agent of exploitation of Otherness. The Monster, the Japanese, and even Cody's compatriot Sitting Bull all play roles in Lansdale's commentary on identity politics and cultural hierarchy on the frontier. Alignments shift as new Others are introduced and must be located in the narrative's hierarchy. Americanness binds the Wild West troupe, mitigating (to an extent) racial difference—in much the same way as the notion of the "good Indian" on the frontier—and highlighting even further the role of origins, borders, and boundaries in the construction of national cultural identity.

Conclusion

The acquisition, by the United States, of the territories that became the American West was accomplished by the familiar mechanisms of international great-power politics: commerce (the Louisiana and Gadsden Purchases), diplomacy (the settlement of the U.S.-Canadian Border), and interstate war (the Mexican Cession). It involved the United States engaging, as a nation-state, with other nation-states centuries older and orders of magnitude more powerful. The subjugation of those territories—the process that forms the narrative backbone of traditional and revisionist westerns alike—was accomplished by the tools of imperialism, albeit turned inward rather than outward. It was a contest not between rival states (nominally equal in standing, however stark their differences in actual power and experience), but between rival cultures, each of which saw their opponent as irrevocably inferior and innately unequal. Narratives of westward expansion reflect the distinction: Americans spread their civilization westward at the expense of "Indians" and "Mexicans"—interchangeable individuals defined by their Otherness.

Americans' nineteenth-century expansion across the Pacific was shaped by the latter set of attitudes, which reduced the peoples of East Asia to generalized, abstracted "Orientals" with the stereotyped suite of qualities—hedonism, duplicity, and guile among them—that all were presumed to possess. Even after Japan's defeat of its regional rivals (moribund imperial China in 1894–95 and overextended Tsarist Russia in 1904–5) propelled it to great-power status, the taint of Otherness clung to it, shaping Japanese-American relations through the end of World War II. Homer Lea's *The Valor of Ignorance* (1905), Jack London's "The Unparalleled Invasion" (1910), and other yellow-peril fantasies reflected not just anxiety over the intentions of a rival nation-state, but fear of conquest and defilement by a savage Other.

The anything-goes version of the late nineteenth century that Lansdale constructs in *Zeppelins West* enables him tell both stories. Cody and the members of his troupe travel to Japan as agents of the Grant administration: players in a Cold War–style scheme by the United States to insert itself into the internal politics of Japan (backing Takeda in his struggle for power) and the international politics of East Asia (gaining, in Takeda, a powerful client-ally to serve their interests).[41] Once on Japanese soil and confronted with the disorienting Otherness of Japanese culture, however, they are transformed from agents of the American nation-state to agents of American civilization, rescuing the Monster from the shogun's nightmare world of tyranny, cannibalism, and bizarre sexual practices. Even in a world of steam-driven cyborgs and literate seals, Japan remains irredeemably Other.

NOTES

1. The coinage and the reference to "fantasy written in the gonzo-historical mode" are from a letter by Jeter printed in the April 1987 issue of *Locus*. The concept is usefully contextualized by Tidhar in "Steampunk" and explored in depth by the essays in Taddeo and Miller, *Steaming into a Victorian Future*.
2. Green, *Deeds of Adventure*; Taves, *Romance of Adventure*.
3. For blending with science fiction, see London, "Unparalleled Invasion"; for alternate history, Stirling, *Peshawar Lancers*; for parallel universes, Moorcock, *Warlord of the Air*; for mad geniuses, Rohmer, *Mystery of Dr. Fu-Manchu*; and for future-war narratives, Lea, *Valor of Ignorance*, and Bywater, *Great Pacific War*.

4. Stross, "Sharp Edge of Empire"; Ho, *Neovictorianism*, 130–69; Loza, *Speculative Imperialismts*, 66–69; Goh, "Inevitability of Imperialism"; Pho and Goh, "Steampunk"; RedTurtle, "Native Steampunk."
5. Poirier, "Musing about Native Steampunk."
6. Perschon, "Finding Nemo."
7. Perschon, "Finding Nemo"; Poirier, "Overcoming the Noble Savage"; Goh, "Inevitability of Imperialism."
8. London, "Unparalleled Invasion"; Lea, *Valor of Ignorance*; Rohmer, *Mystery of Dr. Fu-Manchu*; Crichton, *Rising Sun*; Harry, *Invasion*.
9. Lansdale, *Zeppelins West*, 33.
10. On the nature of alternate history, see the works of Chamberlain, "Allohistory in Science Fiction"; Ferguson, "Virtual History"; and Helleksen, "Toward a Taxonomy."
11. Lansdale, *Zeppelins West*.
12. Reade was the hero of a series of four dime novels about an inventor who explores the West with steam-powered robots of his own design, beginning with *Frank Reade and His Steam Man of the Plains* (1892).
13. Lansdale, *Zeppelins West*, 34.
14. Scott, "Diplomats and Poets," 316–17.
15. Lansdale, *Zeppelins West*, 98.
16. Worster, *Rivers of Empire*; Limerick, *Legacy of Conquest*; Anderson and Cayton, *Dominion of War*; Cozzens, *Earth Is Weeping*.
17. MacDougall, *Let the Sea Make a Noise*; Haddad, *America's First Adventure in China*; Boot, *Savage Wars of Peace*.
18. Ridley, *Morning of Fire*.
19. Boot, *Savage Wars of Peace*, 31–38.
20. Boot, *Savage Wars of Peace*, 200–210, 269–76.
21. Daws, *Shoal of Time*; Silva, *Aloha Betrayed*.
22. Boswell, "Re-enactment and the Museum Case"; Markwyn, ""Economic Partner and Exotic Other"; Rouleau, *With Sails Whitening Every Sea*, 33–37.
23. Scott, "Diplomats and Poets," 301–10.
24. O'Connor, "Asian Art."
25. Denker, *After the Chinese Taste*; Frank, *Objectifying China*; Goldstein, "Cantonese Artifacts"; Chen, "Merchants of Asianness," 21, 25–32.
26. Tchen, *New York before Chinatown*, 99.

27. Kabbani, *Imperial Fictions*; Scott, "Diplomats and Poets," 319–21; Tchen, *New York before Chinatown*, xii, 196–224.
28. Quoted in McNenly, *Native Performers*, 3.
29. Cody, *Wild West in England*, xvi.
30. Cody was already something of a legend, thanks to the dime novels of Ned Buntline.
31. Cody, *Wild West in England*, xvi.
32. Burke, *Buffalo Bill*, 214–15.
33. Warren, *Buffalo Bill's America*.
34. Lansdale, *Zeppelins West*, 8.
35. Buffalo Bill Center, "Wild West Shows."
36. Berkhofer, *White Man's Indian*, 3.
37. Daniels, *Asian America*, 110.
38. Daniels, *Asian America*, 109.
39. Marchetti, *Romance and the "Yellow Peril,"* 2.
40. Daniels, *Asian America*, 110
41. Dower, *Embracing Defeat* recounts the early stages of a real-world version of the process.

BIBLIOGRAPHY

Anderson, Fred, and Andrew Cayton. *The Dominion of War: Empire and Liberty in North America, 1500–2000*. New York: Viking, 2004.

Berkhofer, Robert F. *The White Man's Indian: Images of the American Indian From Columbus to the Present*. New York: Random House, 1978.

Boot, Max. *The Savage Wars of Peace: Small Wars and the Rise of American Power*. New York: Basic Books, 2002.

Boswell, Anna. "Re-enactment and the Museum Case: Reading the Oceanic and Native American Displays in the Peabody Essex Museum." *New Zealand Literature* 27 (2009): 48–69.

Burke, John M. *Buffalo Bill from Prairie to Palace*. Lincoln: University of Nebraska Press, 2012.

Bywater, Hector C. *The Great Pacific War: A History of the Japanese-American Campaign of 1931–1933*. Boston: Houghton Mifflin, 1925.

Chamberlain, Gordon B. "Allohistory in Science Fiction." In *Alternative Histories*, edited by Charles G. Waugh and Martin H. Greenberg, 281–300. New York: Garland, 1986.

Chen, Constance J. S. "Merchants of Asianness: Japanese Art Dealers in the United States in the Early Twentieth Century." *Journal of American Studies* 44, no. 1 (2010): 19–46.

Cody, William F. *The Wild West in England*. Lincoln: University of Nebraska Press, 2012.

Cozzens, Peter. *The Earth Is Weeping: The Epic Story of the Indian Wars for the American West*. New York: Knopf, 2016.

Crichton, Michael. *Rising Sun*. New York: Knopf, 1992.

Daniels, Roger. *Asian America: Chinese and Japanese in the United States since 1850*. Seattle: University of Washington Press, 1988.

Daws, Gavan. *Shoal of Time: A History of the Hawaiian Islands*. Honolulu: University of Hawaii Press, 1974.

Denker, Ellen. *After the Chinese Taste*. Salem MA: Peabody Essex Museum, 1985.

Dower, John W. *Embracing Defeat: Japan in the Wake of World War II*. New York: Norton, 1999.

Fees, Paul. "Wild West Shows." Buffalo Bill Center of the West, centerofthewest .org/learn/western-essays/wild-west-shows/ (accessed January 1, 2017).

Ferguson, Niall. "Virtual History: Toward a 'Chaotic' Theory of the Past." In *Virtual History: Alternatives and Counterfactuals*, edited by Niall Ferguson, 1–90. New York: Basic Books, 1999.

Frank, Caroline. *Objectifying China, Imagining America: Chinese Commodities in Early America*. Chicago: University of Chicago Press, 2012.

Goh, Jayme. "The Inevitability of Imperialism: On Kyriarchy and How It Factors Into Steampunk." Silver Goggles, March 24, 2010, silver-goggles.blogspot .com /2010 /03 /inevitably-of-imperialism-on-kyriarchy.html (accessed October 1, 2019).

Goldstein, Jonathan. "Cantonese Artifacts, Chinoiserie, and Early American Idealization of China." In *America Views China: American Images of China Then and Now*, edited by Jonathan Goldstein et. al., 43–52. Bethlehem PA: Lehigh University Press, 1991.

———, Jerry Israel, and Hilary Conroy, eds. *America Views China: American Images of China Then and Now*. Bethlehem PA: Lehigh University Press, 2009.

Green, Martin. *Dreams of Adventure, Deeds of Empire*. London: Taylor & Francis, 1980.

Haddad, John R. *America's First Adventure in China: Trade, Treaties, Opium, and Salvation*. Philadelphia: Temple University Press, 2013.

Harry, Eric L. *Invasion*. New York: Jove, 2000.

Hellekson, Karen. "Toward a Taxonomy of the Alternate History Genre." *Extrapolation* 41, no. 3 (2000): 48–56.

Ho, Elizabeth. *Neo-Victorianism and the Memory of Empire*. London: Bloomsbury, 2012.

Jeter, K. W. "The Birth of Steampunk." Letters of Note, March 1, 2011, www.lettersofnote.com/2011/03/birth-of-steampunk.html (accessed October 1, 2019).

Kabbani, Rana. *Imperial Fictions: Europe's Myths of the Orient*. London: Saqi, 2009.

Lansdale, Joe R. *Zeppelins West*. Burton MI: Subterranean, 2001.

Lea, Homer. *The Valor of Ignorance*. New York: Harper, 1909.

Limerick, Patricia Nelson. *Legacy of Conquest: The Unbroken Past of the American West*. New York: Norton, 1987.

London, Jack. "The Unparalleled Invasion" (1910). In *The Tale of the Next Great War, 1871–1914*, edited by I. F. Clarke, 257–70. Liverpool: Liverpool University Press, 1995.

Loza, Susana. *Speculative Imperialisms: Monstrosity and Masquerade in Postracial Times*. Lanham MD: Lexington, 2018.

MacDougall, Walter A. *Let the Sea Make a Noise: The North Pacific from Magellan to MacArthur*. New York: Basic Books, 1993.

Marchetti, Gina. *Romance and the "Yellow Peril": Race, Sex, and Discursive Strategies in Hollywood Fiction*. Berkeley: University of California Press, 1993.

Markwyn, Abigail. "Economic Partner and Exotic Other: China and Japan at San Francisco's Panama-Pacific International Exposition." *Western Historical Quarterly* 39, no. 4 (2008): 439–65.

McNenly, Linda Scarangella. *Native Performers in Wild West Shows: From Buffalo Bill to Euro Disney*. Norman: University of Oklahoma Press, 2012.

Moorcock, Michael. *The Warlord of the Air*. New York: Ace, 1971.

O'Connor, Raymond G. "Asian Art." In *America Views China: American Images of China Then and Now*, edited by Jonathan Goldstein et. al., 31–42. Bethlehem PA: Lehigh University Press, 1991.

Perschon, Mike. "Finding Nemo: Verne's Antihero as Original Steampunk." *Verniana—Jules Verne Studies/Etudes Jules Verne* 2 (2009–10): 179–94.

Pho, Diana M., and Jayme Goh. "Steampunk: Stylish Subversion and Colonial Chic." *Fashion Talks: Undressing the Power of Style*, edited by Shira Tarrant and Marjorie Jolles. Albany: State University of New York Press, 2012.

Poirer, Monique. "Musing about Native Steampunk." Moniquilliloquies, December 18, 2011, https://moniquill.tumblr.com/post/14393053317/musing-about-native-steampunk (accessed January 1, 2017).

———. "Overcoming the Noble Savage and the Sexy Squaw." *Beyond Victoriana* 50 (November 21, 2010): https://beyondvictoriana.com/2010/11/21/beyond-victoriana-50-overcoming-the-noble-savage-and-the-sexy-squaw-native-steampunk-monique-poirier/ (accessed January 1, 2017).

RedTurtle, Michael. "Native Steampunk with Michael RedTurtle: A Personal Essay." *Beyond Victoriana* 22 (April 11, 2010): https://beyondvictoriana.com/2010/04/11/beyond-victoriana-22-native-steampunk-with-michael-redturtle-a-personal-essay/(accessed January 1, 2017).

Ridley, Scott. *Morning of Fire: John Kendrick's Daring American Odyssey.* New York: William Morrow, 2010.

Rohmer, Sax. *The Mystery of Dr. Fu-Manchu.* London: Methuen, 1913.

Rouleau, Brian. *With Sails Whitening Every Sea: Mariners and the Making of an American Maritime Empire.* Ithaca NY: Cornell University Press, 2014.

Scott, David. "Diplomats and Poets: 'Power and Perceptions' in American Encounters with Japan, 1860." *Journal of World History* 17, no. 3 (2006): 297–337.

Silva, Noenoe K. *Aloha Betrayed: Native Hawaiian Resistance to American Colonialism.* Durham NC: Duke University Press, 2004.

Stirling, S. M. *The Peshawar Lancers.* New York: Roc, 2002.

Stross, Charles. "The Hard Edge of Empire." Charlie's Diary, 2010, www.antipope.org/charlie/blog-static/2010/10/the-hard-edge-of-empire.html (accessed January 1, 2017).

Taddeo, Julie and Cynthia J. Miller, eds. *Steaming into a Victorian Future: The Steampunk Anthology.* Lanham MD: Rowman & Littlefield, 2012.

Taves, Brian. *The Romance of Adventure: The Genre of Historical Adventure Movies.* Jackson: University of Mississippi Press, 1993.

Tchen, John Kuo Wei. *New York Before Chinatown: Orientalism and the Shaping of American Culture, 1776–1882.* Baltimore MD: Johns Hopkins University Press, 2001.

Tidhar, Lavie. "Steampunk." Internet Review of Science Fiction, February 2005, www.irosf.com/q/zine/article/10114/Steampunk (accessed January 1, 2017).

Warren, Louis S. *Buffalo Bill's America.* New York: Knopf, 2005.

Worster, Donald. *Rivers of Empire: Water, Aridity, and the Growth of the American West.* New York: Pantheon, 1986.

14 AMC's *The Walking Dead* and the Restructuring of Gender and Race on the Neofrontier

SCOTT PEARCE

AMC's *The Walking Dead* (2010–present), through its establishment of a neofrontier in a postapocalyptic landscape, provides a faltering contribution to the ongoing critique of race and gender hierarchies commonly seen in the western genre. *The Walking Dead*, identified here as a weird western, offers a neofrontier narrative that is incrementally free from, although often troubled by, the exclusionary hierarchies of the past.

This chapter begins with a brief outline of *The Walking Dead* as a weird western. It will then, through an examination of characters Rick Grimes (Andrew Lincoln), Glenn Rhee (Steven Yuen), Carol Peletier (Melissa McBride), and Michonne (Danai Gurira), identify *The Walking Dead* as striving to promote a social constructivist position with regards to race and gender. The show demonstrates how race and gender frames have, in the past, limited full participation and agency to specific characters based on arbitrary criteria informed by biological essentialism and prejudice. Over successive seasons, many characters in *The Walking Dead* are transformed, often reluctantly, by their new context. This shedding of culturally learned performances allows for a reconfiguration of identity and power relations.

The central protagonist in *The Walking Dead*, Rick Grimes, is the unwitting, and at times unwilling, catalyst for change. Rick's gradual awareness that the past he seeks to rebuild is limiting, problematic, and damaging often comes at significant cost to those around him—a cost for which he is not always accountable. Yet, after several seasons, an inclusive space emerges in which some of those that were previously marginalized in the preapocalyptic world demonstrate capabilities equal to, if not greater than, Rick's in forging a new civilization.

Postapocalyptic Anxieties and the Weird Western

The postapocalyptic genre and its specific version of the weird western relating to *The Walking Dead* emerged in the nuclear and environmental disaster films that came in the wake of World War II. Such films ponder a future where there has been a breakdown or removal of those social institutions, such as government, that shape and regulate modern society. In such texts characters often remain in a familiar setting, such as a suburb or city, or the remnants of these. Survival, however, has become contingent on the ability to act on one's initiative, often with physical violence, rather than on the adherence to rules and laws overseen by a dominant social system.

The term "weird western" is relatively broad and includes a range of texts in "which the conventions and narrative expectations associated with different kinds of films are combined in a single context" that functions to "provide alternative ways of understanding the shifting nature of the Western."[1] *The Walking Dead* as weird western is a subgenre of the postapocalyptic genre, one that "owes much of its creation to the Cold War."[2] Films such as the influential Australian production *Mad Max* (1979) and its sequels demonstrate not only growing societal anxieties regarding the capacity of governments to navigate an increasingly complex and contradictory world, but they reimagine the frontier of the western in a future setting.[3] Katherine Sugg argues that the western frontier, the prominent fictionalized version, is paramount to understanding *The Walking Dead*, for "the 'walkers' and (the) violent and competing groups of living humans are understood through a series of tropes and plotlines that invoke the frontier West and Hollywood westerns."[4] In recontextualizing western tropes and plots *The Walking Dead* attempts to reconfigure them. However, as Gilberto Perez notes, such a process is one of continuance. The frontier is never stagnant; indeed, the "frontier, as a founding myth of the American nation, has been enlisted for diverse purposes and persuasions; if it has served the cause of American racism and imperialism, it has also served the cause of American liberty and equality."[5] This apparent need to redress the frontier in postapocalyptic texts demonstrates, to Barbara Gurr, that "the mytho-history of the American past reveals a cultural yearning for a collective identity of American-ness that has been only incompletely realized."[6] There is, it seems, a belief in the mytho-history process but a concern for what it has thus far achieved. This new frontier, and this new process of settling and civilizing, offers an opportunity to correct perceived failings relating to past examples of exclusion and oppression.

Yet *The Walking Dead* has faced a raft of criticisms for, initially, its lack of racial diversity, and for its perceived promotion of patriarchal hierarchies. However, Timothy Sandefur sees *The Walking Dead*'s "most distinctive characteristic" as "its basic belief that civilization and its virtues are not merely doomed, but fundamentally misguided. Where most post-apocalyptic stories portray civilized virtues in nostalgic terms—to show the value of cooperation, gentleness, progress, and law by imagining their absence—*The Walking Dead* is skeptical, if not downright cynical, about political society and the good life it makes possible."[7] This chapter agrees with Sandefur's position but sees *The Walking Dead* as drifting between hope and despair, both in terms of an optimistic and inclusive narrative and the show's commitment to lasting systemic change and accountability. Sugg sees that in "the show's survival plot and its nostalgic return to premodern conditions" there are "settings and plot elements that are central to both the zombie apocalypse . . . and one of its key generic forebears, the Hollywood western."[8] In merging these two genres, *The Walking Dead* as weird western begins to provide a constructivist view of race and gender, a view that is yet troubled at times by its forebears.

Rick Grimes

Police officer Rick Grimes emerges from a coma, seemingly weeks after being shot, and into a world transformed by a virus of unknown origin that reanimates the dead. These monstrous "dead" figures shuffle and gnash their teeth, determined to eat the living. A single bite from one such creature transmits a virus that is quickly terminal.

Rick, setting out to look for his wife and son in an aesthetically familiar postapocalyptic world, dons his police uniform, which had marked him as an authority figure entrusted to safeguard the community and maintain law and order. Shelley Rees states that "Rick's insistence upon maintaining his sheriff's deputy uniform in this lawless world emphasizes his function as the text's threshold between the ordered past and a (re)ordered future."[9] However, the space in which Rick formerly performed that role as a law enforcement officer, within a bureaucratized democracy, is gone, and Rick does not grasp the contextual nature of self.

Clearly Rick still sees himself as an authority, someone capable of protecting, organizing, and leading others. Yet this authority comes only in part from his role as a police officer. In putting on a badge and strapping a gun to his leg, and eventually even riding a horse into town, Rick evokes motifs common to the performance of the western hero, the type often related to American exceptionalism, or, more specifically, that version that emerges with the nineteenth century: manifest destiny. John Wilsey states that manifest destiny couples Christian nationalism and expansionism and "[takes] the figure of Christ and recast[s] him, from the orthodox pattern of Suffering Servant, Son of God, Savior of world, and eschatological Judge of all humankind to the preacher of American democracy who will ultimately bring about the Kingdom of God on earth."[10] This figure readily appears as the central protagonist in many westerns, predominately romance westerns, as a cowboy. Although his demeanor and methods significantly fluctuate, as well as his usefulness as a figure, he remains a potent reminder of the mythohistory deeply entrenched in the western genre. The cowboy, for Gurr, "has come to represent American identity against America's enemies, and these enemies have historically been raced, gendered, and sexed as 'other'—not white, not male, not heterosexual: not American."[11] That Rick seeks to channel such a figure is perhaps an attempt to control an environment in which he has little actual control. However, this position and his sense that he is indeed destined to save others does not abate after he is reunited with his family. It is soon clear that Rick is attempting to enact a performance typical of the romance western hero, and as a white heterosexual male he sees himself, initially, as the only one capable of reestablishing civilization.

Rick strives to be the hero Philip French defines as "upright, clean-living, sharp shooting, a White Anglo-Saxon Protestant who respects the law, the flag, women and children."[12] In those westerns where such figures abound, John Lenihan states that "a man could do what he had to do with an instinctive natural awareness of right and wrong. Fulfilling his personal code of honor also served society's best interests." This version of heroism "passed on to modern America something of that broader mythic quality" that endowed the hero with traits and strengths beyond the average person, making him exceptional.[13] Additionally, it reminded audiences of the necessity of such figures, in the past, in the present, and for the future. As Richard Slotkin notes, "No other genre has pre-cinematic roots of comparable depth and density" to the western.[14] Certainly, in the precinema age, stories of the frontier and the conquering white male proliferated in newspapers and dime novels. Yet, as Victoria Lamont's *Westerns: A Women's History* (2016) reveals, "women were (also) active at every turn during the period, between roughly 1880 and 1940, when the American frontier myth, after years of ghettoization in the dime novel, was supposedly 'reborn' as a dominant myth of American identity."[15] Popular novels by writers such as Caroline Kirkland were based on her own frontier experiences and provide for Edward Watts and David Rachels a style and perspective that "is an important forerunner to nineteenth-century realism."[16] Yet western films by the 1930s saw the frontier as a space mostly for and about men. Robert Ray sees in the western the clear promotion of gender hierarchies because the western was "grounded in a frontier mythology concerned almost exclusively with men," and it "minimized, or actively disparaged, women's place in American life."[17] Rather, the western was grounded in a version of frontier mythology. Attempts to subjugate women and others were met with continued resistance.

Lamont states that "in reality cowboys were a racially and ethnically mixed group that included large numbers of Mexicans and African Americans"; however, "popular westerns depicted the cowboy hero as an Anglo Saxon whose rough exterior concealed an innate nobility that is now widely identified with classic American values of masculinity and meritocracy."[18] In terms of using the frontier, real and imagined, as a rationalization for the promotion of the white male savior, western films became a powerful tool.

Much of the early critical writing on *The Walking Dead* positions the show as nostalgic for the type of white heteronormative male commonly seen in romance westerns of the pre-1950s era. Sugg sees that the "focus on Rick also reflects *The Walking Dead*'s regressive conception of gender" because "Rick is shown to be level-headed, quick-acting, and good at perceiving and planning for dangers."[19] But he is also so beholden to an idea of himself as heroic that his actions regularly place him and others in unnecessary danger. This highlights from early on Rick's incompatibility with the neofrontier.

In the episode "Tell it to the Frogs" (1.3), Rick decides he must return to the walker-infested city of Atlanta to rescue Merle (Michael Rooker), a violent and unstable member of a group that guided Rick to safety.[20] Rick had handcuffed Merle to a rooftop pipe to stop a racially motivated assault on another group member. As walkers closed in, the keys to the handcuffs were dropped by T-Dog (Irone Singleton), the target of the attack, and the group fled. However, Rick is unable to reconcile this action, and after reuniting with his family at a camp outside the city, he decides to return to free Merle. This decision is criticized by the group as unnecessarily perilous and self-sabotaging. Rick's friend Shane (Jon Bernthal) makes the point that Merle would never do such a thing for Rick. Rick's response ("What he would or wouldn't do doesn't interest me") highlights the objectivity of Rick's beliefs in right and wrong. He is willing to risk his own life and the lives of those that accompany him to allay self-doubt about his capacity to perform heroically, thus demonstrating that the welfare of the group is secondary to his need for public performance of self.

Such decisions also demonstrate, as Rees states, that Rick is an "ambassador from and to the past that underscores the text's association of the apocalyptic landscape with older western social contexts and values."[21] Still, Rick's capacity to perform this role is problematized by the absence of support from a like-minded social system and its institutions. Rick must enact the past to promote the past. He refuses, despite the circumstance, to allow what he perceives as a moral laxity to evolve. When, in "Wildfire" (1.5), it is discovered that group member Jim (Andrew Rothenberg) has been bitten by a walker, others in the group want to kill him before he turns.[22] Rick asks, "We start down that road, where do we draw the line?" He clearly understands that as the traditional hero he can only kill those that first attempt to kill him, and that the sick and injured must be cared for. He then proposes that the group seeks medical aid: "The CDC's our best choice and Jim's only chance." Jim rests in Dale's (Jeffrey DeMunn) RV, propped up against an inverted American flag—one of the few flags, or mentions of American nationalism, that appears in any of the seasons thus far. However, Rick does not seem to see it, nor understand the clear message of distress it states.

Later, in "TS-19" (1.6), Rick and the group—minus Jim, who has since died—arrive at the CDC hoping for a cure.[23] The remaining scientist, Jenner (Noah Emmerich), is critical of his former colleagues: "It was the French. They were the last ones to hold out. While our people were bolting out the doorways and committing suicide, they stayed in the labs until the end." Jenner's point is clear—at a crisis point for the entire nation, Americans acted with a type of individualism that is often promoted as a key component of democracy. Rees sees that by "conflating the traditional Western with the more modern zombie narrative, *The Walking Dead* produces a grotesque hybrid, a changeling Western, animated yet altered, infected with a strain of post ideological nihilism that disempowers its heroes."[24] This nihilism, however, is focused specifically on the past, on notions of American exceptionalism. Jenner's despair is that when exceptionalism was needed it could not be found. Yet Rick still thinks himself capable of redeeming it.

Here, *The Walking Dead* can be viewed as endorsing Judith Butler's statement from her innovative text *Gender Trouble* (1990), that "gender reality is created through sustained social performances." If Rick accepts Jenner's point that American exceptionalism is flawed, then his claim of leadership, his position as savior, is fractured and revealed as false. He would give space to Butler's idea that "the very notions of an essential sex and a true or abiding masculinity or femininity are also constituted as part of the strategy that conceals gender's performative character and the performative possibilities for proliferating gender configurations outside the restricting frames of masculinist domination and compulsory heterosexuality."[25] As *The Walking Dead* progresses, Rick's ability to enact that desired version of himself is fraught, as he increasingly fails to achieve anticipated outcomes or behaves in a way that jeopardizes those he wanted to help. Ivan Young sees that "Rick must struggle to maintain the mythic vision of America he represents, or he must change, suggesting that whatever moral view America has of itself must be adjusted in this new violent world it has engendered."[26] What this clearly articulates is that Rick's status is founded on constructs that had benefited him more than others.

As these constructs and their fraudulent hierarchies are exposed, Rick is confronted with a changing sense of self and his relationship to others. He seems to have based his personal worth and identity on the notion that these hierarchies represented a natural order; his failings and his gradual acceptance of others as equally, if not more, capable of leadership causes him significant existential angst.

Rick's angst, his adherence to the past, shifts in stages but tends to follow a specific pattern: a rejection of change and then a slow acceptance and incorporation of change. Increasingly it is Rick that needs to be directed and saved. Rees sees that with Rick's "correspondence to the Western hero, *The Walking Dead* engages the stylized familiarity of the Western genre as a narrative embodiment of stabilizing ideology," which it then "troubles it by disempowering its Western-infused protagonist and the values associated with him every time he appears to have achieved a goal through his adherence to those values."[27] Rick's values are not disempowered as much as the patriarchal gatekeeping that existed in the prewalker world is eroded. It means that characters such as Carol and Michonne can share equally in the performance of such values, not merely as Rick's subordinates or sidekicks, but, increasingly, as his equals.

Glenn Rhee

Glenn Rhee's changing position in the survivor group suggests that those formally marginalized in the preapocalypse world can transcend boundaries that once functioned to prohibit or limit performance. However, for Glenn, a character with Korean heritage, it seems that such a transition needs to follow a specific path, on which the long history of stereotyping Asian characters is transformed but not eradicated. This, then, requires a broader consideration as to whether the model minority framework apparent in early seasons of *The Walking Dead* has dissolved or has just expanded its range of acceptable behaviors and performances to include some of those that were previously only available to white males such as Rick.

Glenn is first introduced to the series in "Days Gone Bye" (1.1) as a voice on a radio that offers Rick hope when he finds himself trapped inside a tank. Rick's attempt to ride into Atlanta on a horse—a clear reference to a range of westerns in which some version of the hero emerges to tame villains or native groups, such as *7 Men from Now* (1956) or *High Plains Drifter* (1973)—is immediately subverted as Rick is overwhelmed by walkers, trapped inside a tank and on the verge of suicide. In "Guts" (1.2) Glenn provides Rick with a plan to escape the tank and then leads him to safety. However, Glenn's comment "Nice moves there, Clint Eastwood. You the new sheriff come riding in to clean up the town?" does not endorse Rick's actions but critiques a naïve and simplistic approach that has put others in danger, something Andrea also expresses moments later when she points a gun at Rick's head, stating, "We're dead because of you." This statement foreshadows for many characters what Rick's influence will be in episodes and seasons to come. At the same time, the scenario marks Glenn as someone willing to put himself in danger to help others, a characteristic that comes to define him for the remainder of his time in the series.

Despite Glenn's resourcefulness he is still subject to racial stereotyping by the group. Martina Baldwin and Mark McCarthy, writing about Glenn's position in the group, state that Glenn "is identified by his race by other characters when they refer to him as "the Asian," (and) "Short Round."[28] Such comments, although not intended as derogatory, expose the persistence of stereotyping and the ignorance of those such as Daryl (Norman Reedus) and Herschel (Scott Wilson) as to the historical marginalization faced by Asian-Americans. These "comments are either laughed off by Glenn or ignored altogether because he is incapable of drawing attention to racist discourse that surrounds him."[29] Glenn is positioned as a fringe member of the group, which makes him vulnerable. However, this is also something that Maggie (Lauren Cohan) critiques. In "Secrets" (2.6) she tells him, "You're smart. You're brave. You're a leader. But you don't know it. And your friends don't want to know it. They'd rather have you fetching peaches. There's a dead guy in the well? Send Glenn down." This is the midpoint of season 2 and the residue of the preapocalyptic world is still present, yet Maggie, as a white woman, validates Glenn's position as heroic by pursuing a sexual relationship with him. Rosalind Chou and Joe Feagin state that in the "nineteenth century Asian American men were commonly stereotyped in an omnipresent white framing as oversexed and threatening to white women, but in recent decades they have been more likely stereotyped as feminized and emasculated."[30] Maggie's burgeoning relationship with Glenn fractures the old model minority framing and offers a new space and a new frame for Glenn. Maggie encourages Glenn to see himself as transformed and unrestrained by the rigid racial hierarchies of the past. When Glenn and Maggie's relationship is revealed to the group, the racial stereotyping all but stops. Whether this is a consequence of other characters shedding their conditioning, or is dependent on Maggie's endorsement of Glenn, is not clear.

Increasingly, Glenn, from this point forward, becomes a crucial member of the group. Helen Ho's impressive work on Glenn's transition outlines how his "model minority traits are reconfigured as masculine traits, allowing him to embody characteristics typically afforded to hegemonic, white men."[31] Indeed, this stands in stark contrast to the overwhelming representations of Asian immigrants or Asian Americans in westerns or other film genres through much of the twentieth century.

American films regularly employed yellowface with Anglo actors taking on Asian characters, such as in *The Good Earth* (1937), *Inn of the Sixth Happiness* (1958), or John Wayne as Genghis Khan in the commercially successful film *The Conqueror* (1956). This practice continues, as in more recent films like *The Last Airbender* (2010). In terms of westerns, Asian males were regularly seen in submissive and stereotypical roles, such as a Shaolin monk and martial arts expert Kwai Chang Caine (David Carradine) in the television series *Kung Fu* (1972–75). Glenn's ascension to the role of hero in *The Walking Dead* endorses Ho's claims and stands in contrast to many of the historical representations of Asian and Asian American males in western films and television shows. In terms of distinguishing Glenn from the other characters in Rick's group, what becomes clear is that Glenn never wavers. He maintains a fundamental belief in what he sees is right.

Glenn becomes the hero that Rick initially desired to be. Glenn is a Christ figure, a redeemer, someone who strives to save others. Ho sees that "Glenn's transformation into a post-apocalyptic hero is made possible due to the flawed masculinity of the group's white 'cowboys.'"[32] Certainly, Glenn's desire to maintain a version of the hero belonging to the past, a past that often did not allow him access to such a position, is complex. It seemingly creates for him a positive life purpose in the chaotic events around him and this supports his emotional and psychological survival, which is something other characters struggle for. This also positions Glenn in opposition to Rick, who becomes steadily more violent and unforgiving. Ho sees Glenn as embodying "an adaptable, relational masculinity" that ultimately "reaps more rewards than Rick's stoic and traditional hegemonic masculinity."[33] Increasingly, Glenn recognizes that security is founded on compassion, forgiveness, and the allowance for reparation. But Rick does not fully embrace this, and it is Rick's actions that lead to Glenn's death.

Glenn's demise seemingly comes because he compromises—under coercion from Rick and, to a lesser degree, Maggie—his heroic identity. After Rick and Maggie bargain with the Hilltop, promising to wipe out the Saviors that are tormenting the Hilltop in return for food, Rick leads his group, including Glenn on a nighttime strike against a Savior's outpost in "Not Tomorrow Yet" (6.12).[34] Glenn is required to kill Saviors, and he reveals to Heath (Corey Hawkins) that, surprisingly, he has yet to kill a living person. A few episodes earlier, in "Heads Up" (6.7), Glenn had articulated for Enid (Katelyn Nacon) his ideological foundation: "You honor the dead by going on even when you're scared. You live because they don't get to." However, Glenn abandons this position and stabs the Saviors as they sleep, a task he performs reluctantly. The dominant characteristics of the sanctity of life, redemption, and forgiveness are replaced with a violent preemptive-strike mentality. In complying with Rick's wishes, Glenn compromises his identity and commits to a misguided plan that ultimately leads to his own death and that of Abraham (Michael Cudlitz).

The death of Glenn, his execution at the hands of Negan (Jeffrey Dean Morgan) in "The Day Will Come When You Won't Be" (7.1), was unbefitting of his personal narrative. It came about because of Rick's flawed leadership and a too-willing readiness on the part of others, including Glenn, to support him. It seems Glenn would not—could not—challenge Rick, because he felt beholden to him. Glenn could not survive, because his desire to enact a Christianized narrative of forgiveness and redemption was outmoded. Certainly, Glenn demonstrated exceptionalism, but, like the institutions that gave birth to such notions, this became dangerous and fatalistic. Perhaps, therefore, Rick was untroubled by Glenn's earlier transition: Rick had already moved out of the space Glenn came to inhabit and no longer required it. That Glenn made one transition indicates that transition is possible and that other characters also historically marginalized can build on what he established.

Carol

More so than any other character in *The Walking Dead*, Carol highlights the opportunity a destructuring of a patriarchal social system can bring to formerly maligned and marginalized characters. Carol's slow transition from devout battered housewife to action hero challenges the biological essentialism inherent in the patriarchal categories of feminine and masculine. Yet Carol's transition is complex and initially seen as dangerous by Rick. Carol must overcome past abuses from her husband, Ed (Adam Minarovich); systemic disadvantage; and the masculine gatekeeping initiated by Rick, who clearly sees Carol as a threat to his own position.

Interestingly, Rick's leadership is rarely directly challenged by anyone in the group. Yet, at several points, Rick clearly perceives he is under threat. This threat, or challenge, that Rick is affronted by and reacts to, comes predominately from the ascension of female characters, specifically Carol and Michonne. Rick's combative and adversarial relationship with Carol and Michonne begins at approximately the same time, early in season 3. At this time both Carol and Michonne, in different ways, reject former boundaries that limited or denied them access to the space and labels that would provide the type of power and recognition Rick seems to see as entirely his. Rick's eventual compromise and recognition of Carol and Michonne comes about because of their vital and life-saving performances and the widespread support they eventually garner from other group members.

Carol's willingness and ability to act challenges what John Cawelti sees as "one of the major characteristics and limitations of the Western genre"—that being "the rigidity of its gender roles. . . . Men are men and women are women."[35] This understanding is bound to dominant mytho-historical views of gender. These mytho-historical views are due to a male social dominance that is sustained by patriarchal imperatives. Male-centric cultural biases lead to male-centric sites of cultural production. Lamont makes the argument that "Western fiction gained respectability in the early twentieth century largely through its circulation in novel form, a form that was still deeply marked by its nineteenth-century feminized roots and in which both men and women participated."³⁶ Carol's rise is a promotion of the often neglected foundations of the western genre. However, as Danee Pye and Peter O'Sullivan argue, it's "not as if the characters are working from a clean slate, with no memory of their former selves. They all bring cultural baggage along with them."³⁷ Indeed, the remnants of patriarchal thinking continue to linger even after several seasons.

The transformation seen in Carol and the initial unwillingness of Rick to see her behavior as valid and reasonable is, in part, discussed in Judith Halberstam's vital work, *Female Masculinity* (1998). Halberstam sees that those females who exhibit traditional masculine characteristics and performances are commonly marginalized or othered and that "female masculinities are framed as the rejected scraps of dominant masculinity in order that male masculinity may appear to be the real thing."³⁸ Halberstam further states that the "suppression of female masculinities allows for male masculinity to stand unchallenged as the bearer of gender stability."³⁹ Therefore, female masculinity is, from the dominant male perspective, characteristic of deviance and danger. Halberstam argues that "just as we recognize distinctive types of masculinity in men," because not all men can be in the hegemonic position, "we must recognize them in women, and we must do so in place of organizing all these women in relation to a catch-all category such as lesbianism."⁴⁰ Carol's short-cropped hair at times identifies her to other characters in the show as a lesbian. In "Made to Suffer" (3.8), Axel (Lew Temple) refers to Carol as a "lesbian."⁴¹ When Carol rejects this idea, he is confused: "You got the short hair." The label of lesbian is one, for Axel, that suggests an unrelatable otherness, something corrupted, which also states that male presence is not only unwanted but unneeded. Describing Carol as a lesbian is not a compliment, but a caution and explanation that seeks to invalidate her choices.

This desire to frame female gender performance as always bound to, and needing, male affirmation or support is common in the western. The relegation of female characters to generic roles that endorse patriarchal hierarchies is rife throughout the genre. Yet writing female characters as unable to achieve a hegemonic position in the genre is a clear choice. French sees that when "women take the center stage in this most masculine of genres, the result is less likely to be a blow in favor of sexual equality than a strong whiff of erotic perversity."[42] Such a view, while at times true, also denies the genre its nuanced history. Conversely, David Lusted sees that westerns "with central female protagonists are allegories of burgeoning female independence movements."[43] There have always been female writers and directors of western films. B. M. Bower, a prolific writer of westerns, also penned several screenplays for films produced between 1914 and 1920. Lamont sees that "Bower established a tradition of satirical and humanized treatments of the masculine code that continued to resonate after her death in 1940, in films such as *True Grit* (1969) and *Unforgiven* (1991)."[44] Likewise, Dorothy M. Johnson's short stories were turned into some of the most iconic westerns of the twentieth century, such as *The Hanging Tree* (1959) and *The Man Who Shot Liberty Valance* (1962). The western has space to include complex and diverse female characters, but this requires the broader recognition that it is not history, nor does it have allegiance to the fictional past. *Godless* (2017), with its tagline "Welcome to No Man's Land" demonstrates the genre's flexibility in terms of female representation. In this limited series, with most of the men in the town of La Belle dead, women take on a variety of roles. This includes the destruction of a vicious outlaw gang in a shoot-out reminiscent of *The Wild Bunch* (1969). Through characters such as Carol, *The Walking Dead* continues to challenge the western genre as much as Carol challenges misconceptions about female gender performance. *The Walking Dead* provides a context in which female masculinity can emerge and be equal to, if not greater than, that performed by males.

In the first two seasons of *The Walking Dead*, Carol is positioned as ineffectual. She suffers from what Sandra Lee Bartky identifies as psychological oppression caused by her abusive and controlling husband and the social system that supports him: "The psychologically oppressed become their own oppressors; they come to exercise harsh dominion over their own self-esteem."[45] The capacity of characters to shed patriarchal conditioning and relations is not obvious in these early seasons, and much of the early critical writing on the show focuses on its preservation of patriarchal hierarchies even as the conditions that sustained them evaporated.

Ed tries to separate Carol from the other women in "Tell it to the Frogs" (1.3) when it seems Carol is building camaraderie with them.[46] Ed tries to physically intimidate her, saying, "You come on now, or you gonna regret it later." Eventually he strikes Carol, and former police officer Shane Walsh intervenes, brutally beating Ed and threatening him with further violence. John Greene and Michaela Meyer see that, in this scene, "Ed is displaced as the patriarch who violently domineers over his family," and now it is Shane who "assumes the role of patriarch." Further, Greene and Meyer are critical of the way in which the scene functions; while it "depicts domestic violence negatively, it also positions rescue by another man as the solution."[47] Carol survives at this point because others care for her, and despite Ed's death during a walker attack soon after, she still cannot escape the oppressive hierarchies that subjugate her. Isaac Berk sees that *The Walking Dead* "demonstrates that even when everything else has changed (her husband is dead, society as we know it has ended) sexism will continue to thrive as long as there is political inequality."[48] At this point in the series Carol is unable, or unwilling, to make a change in her perception of self.

Carol is seemingly paralyzed by the loss of bureaucratized democracy. Bartky perceives such paralysis as "institutionalized and systematic; it serves to make the work of domination easier by breaking the spirit of the dominated and by rendering them incapable of understanding the nature of those agencies responsible for their subjugation."[49] When the group is stopped on the highway and overwhelmed by walkers in "What Lies Ahead" (2.1), Sophia (Madison Lintz), Carol's daughter, flees into the woods. Rick follows, finds her, and formulates a plan to draw the walkers away while she hides, but something goes wrong and when Rick makes his way back to the group Sophia has not returned. Carol does not join the initial search for Sophia, leaving it to Daryl and Rick. Carol is quick to admonish Rick: "How could you just leave her out there to begin with?" Likewise, in "Save the Last One" (2.3), Daryl searches for Sophia as Carol sits weeping in Dale's RV, against the same inverted flag that Jim rested under. Her distress comes not only from the loss of her daughter but also her inability to recognize herself outside of socially constructed norms and regulations.

When it is discovered that Sophia is a walker and she is subsequently "killed" by Rick, in "Pretty Much Dead Already" (2.7), the death functions to strengthen the bonds between Carol and patriarchy as she turns to Christianity for support. In "Judge, Jury, Executioner" (2.11), Carol seeks to comfort Carl (Chandler Riggs) as he sits by Sophia's grave, saying, "You know, we'll see Sophia again in heaven someday. She's in a better place." Carol resolves her inability to act with belief in the divine father. When Carl responds with, "Heaven is another lie. And if you believe it, you're an idiot," Carol is outraged and complains to Rick that Carl is rude. Carol, however, is more affronted by the increasing unwillingness of those around her to endorse her passivity. Her plea to Rick is not one that asks for politeness as much as it demands he sustain the old-world hierarchies that she is so reliant on.

The new Carol emerges in "Hounded" (3.6), after—like Rick at the beginning of the series—she is thought to have been killed. Her transition is acknowledged by others. When Merle returns to the group in "This Sorrowful Life" (3.15), he comments, "You ain't like you was back in the camp," and he then describes her as "a late bloomer." Sugg sees that "the emasculation and crisis of white masculinity as well as other forms of agency" are "at the centre of the drama of Rick and the group and the conditions and challenges they face."[50] Carol's development is viewed by Rick, initially, as a threat. He is not yet reconciled to what others, like Merle, can see. Carol, someone previously kept in check by the conditions that privileged Rick, is increasingly able to demonstrate the physical and emotional strength necessary for heroism and leadership.

In season 4 Carol establishes herself as an action hero, but a variation on the traditional male version. Gladys Knight sees that a "male action hero was endowed with so-called masculine traits such as independence, physical strength, aggression, intelligence, competence, reticence, and cool headedness."[51] In the western, male action heroes proliferate, repeatedly played by actors such as John Wayne, William Holden, and Randolph Scott. Comparatively, "women were deemed to be their polar opposites."[52] Jane Tompkins states that it is "the case of women in Westerns generally . . . that there's nothing to them. They may seem strong and resilient, fiery and resourceful at first, but when push comes to shove, as it always does, they crumble."[53] Tompkins's statement, while typical, is not conclusive and needs refinement. Characters such as Vienna (Joan Crawford) in *Johnny Guitar* (1954) do not crumble. Vienna is an intimidating saloon owner who stands opposed to archrival Emma Small (Mercedes McCambridge), whom she eventually kills in a gunfight. Jennifer Peterson highlights Vienna's importance to the western in terms of resistance to prominent gender narratives: "Despite her gender—or more accurately because her gender is not static but floating, both 'feminine' and 'masculine'—Vienna is allowed to stand as a self-sufficient individualistic western hero."[54] A more recent example is *The Ballad of Little Jo* (1993), in which Jo (Suzy Amis) deliberately disguises herself as a man, so that she will be judged by her actions rather than her biological sex. Despite Jo's success, even in gunfights, when her biological sex is discovered after her death, it is met with outrage. Her body is put on public display and becomes the subject of a newspaper exposé. Women are clearly capable of being action heroes but too often are denied the opportunity unless they are disguised. Carol does not need to disguise herself. She presents as, and performs the role of, the action hero and thus forwards the challenge made by the constructivist position.

Rick is only able to reconcile Carol's transformation in what at first seems the aptly titled "Sanctuary" (5.1). Rick and his group, having reached the presumed haven of Terminus, are then captured by cannibals led by Gareth (Andrew J. West). Rick, Daryl, Glenn, and Bob (Lawrence Gilliard Jr.) are forced to kneel, hands bound and mouths gagged, in front of a draining sink where those before them are clubbed in the back of the head and then their throats are cut as they are prepared for slaughter. There is seemingly no escape. Then, Carol, despite being banished by Rick in "Indifference" (4.4), intervenes and single-handedly attacks Terminus. She covers herself in walker blood and organs, blows up a gas tank—creating a breach in the wall so that Terminus floods with walkers—then follows the walker herd inside. She recovers Rick's watch and Daryl's crossbow, kills several Terminus residents, and reunites with the group in the woods as they find their way out of Terminus. George Hagman identifies the context of *The Walking Dead* as "a landscape out of which might emerge an entirely new form of human, radically free of the assumptions, prejudices, and restraints of civilization, in direct, unmediated contact with experience."[55] This, in the immediate destruction of Terminus, is something Rick embraces when he embraces Carol and asks, "Did you do that?" His disbelief is also an act of recognition. When he then asks Carol, "Will you have us?" he acknowledges her power by requesting to join her rather than offering her readmittance to his group. The sanctuary referred to in the title of the episode is Carol, who now offers the group refuge.

Carol's strength is her cunning as much as her ability to physically act. Unlike Rick, she is also happy to assume a seemingly submissive role to gain an advantage. Whereas Rick seemingly relies on conformation of his position, Carol needs no such validation. Dan Hassler-Forest, writing on the *Walking Dead* comics, sees that the "subversive aspect of zombie narratives is frequently expressed via explicit attacks on characters and institutions associated with traditional patriarchal power."[56] These "attacks" are explicitly seen once the group reaches the walled settlement of Alexandria. Carol is able to coordinate and plan a coup by craftily using lingering patriarchal assumptions to her advantage. In "Remember" (5.12) she tells Deanna (Tovah Feldshuh), the former congressperson and town leader, "I really didn't have much to offer this group, so I just sort of became their den mother. And they've been nice enough to protect me." Carol's apparent helplessness is readily accepted by the residents of Alexandria. They see only a thin, middle-aged woman in the company of robust males. Nancy Wadsworth reads this as a demotion, stating that "Carol, a woman who has transformed from domestic violence victim to an emotional leader and one of the most effective fighters in the show, is assigned to the cooking detail, presumably as a kind of spy, but the downgrade in status is still jarring, to her and likely to audiences."[57] Rather than a downgrade, this is clearly a deliberate action on Carol's part. As she comments to Rick and Daryl, "You know what's great about this place? I get to be invisible again." The distinction is that Carol now recognizes her own capacity for agency and uses the conditioned assumptions of others to her advantage, thereby rejecting and ridiculing her former self, which relied on patriarchal relations to guide her.

When, once settled in Alexandria, Carol realizes that Pete (Corey Brill) is abusing his wife, Jessie (Alexandra Breckenridge), and potentially his son, Sam (Major Dodson), she suggests to Rick, in "Spend" (5.14), that Pete be killed. Rick, in "Try" (5.15), takes the abuse accusation to Deanna, and her response—"I hoped it would get better"—demonstrates the state's unwillingness to act against a patriarch. Deanna rationalizes this by saying, "Pete's a surgeon. He saved lives." His elevated social position provides him with influence and protection, and thus the state endorses domestic abuse through its passivity. For Carol, Alexandria is resurrecting a past. Dissatisfied with Rick and Deanna, Carol approaches Pete herself in "Conquer" (5.16). Though Pete is physically much bigger than she is, and they are alone in his house, Carol pulls a knife and states, "I could kill you right now. I could. I will." She holds the knife to his throat as he backs away in terror and she challenges him, "Come at me. No? Yeah?" and, as she leaves him, she clearly articulates his position, seemingly evoking her relationship with Ed and her inability at that time to protect herself or Sophia: "You're a small, weak nothing." This confrontation is as much about reclaiming the past as it is about not letting the emergence of a new form of society reinstate the old ways of being. Increasingly Carol becomes the antithesis of her former self, a position she has taken rather than been given.

Like Rick in season 3, however, Carol suffers an existential crisis in season 6 and finds herself not wanting to live a life of endless violence and killing. She flees Alexandria in "Twice as Far" (6.14), leaving a note that reads, in part, "I can't love anyone because I can't kill for anyone." Greene and Meyer, in an early critique of *The Walking Dead*, see that as "a result of women's need for protection, it is very uncommon for women to fight zombies in the show" and that it is the men who "mount resistance and engage in hand to hand combat with the undead while the women cower in fear, hold each other, and cry."[58] This critique is, at this point in the series, redundant. When Morgan (Lennie James) eventually tells Carol that Abraham and Glenn have been killed and that Alexandria will fight the Saviors, Carol returns to the Hilltop in "Bury Me Here" (7.13), telling Ezekiel (Khary Payton), the Hilltops' leader, "We have to fight." It is a significant character development, and it avoids positioning Carol in comparison to Rick as emotionally or psychologically broken by her experiences and unable to reconcile the consequences of her actions. Just like Rick, Carol rejoins the struggle to secure safety for her group. She is heroic and willing to do what she sees as needing to be done, and she does so as a leader and a warrior.

Michonne

Michonne emerges in the final moments of "Beside the Dying Fire" (2.13) as a hooded figure leading two armless and jawless walkers and wielding a katana. She saves Andrea (Laurie Holden) from a certain demise and establishes in those moments a character that is mysterious and enthralling. Indeed, for those unfamiliar with the *Walking Dead* comics and Michonne, the race and gender identity of the character that saves Andrea is not clear. Yet her actions and her weapon signify a capable warrior.

In the same way *The Walking Dead* faced early criticism for its adherence to traditional gender hierarchies, it also faced ongoing criticism for its lack of racial and ethnic diversity. Melissa Lavin and Brian Lowe state that early "seasons had few characters of color, and online criticism in the form of comical memes depicted the African American character (T Dog) as undeveloped, for example not given lines because of his race."[59] This criticism persisted, so Justin Moyer's headline *Washington Post* after the season 5 finale—"*The Walking Dead* Finale Recap: Black Man Survives"— expresses surprise at an apparent shift in the show's group dynamics. In his article he states that "African American men seem over-represented among those who have bitten the dust."[60] Michonne's arrival, for Rick, signals a deeply challenging otherness as she shifts into a mode of performance he covets as his own.

Michonne's characterization in the comics was also, initially, met with criticism. Kinitra Brooks sees that "[Michonne's] blackness is implicitly associated with a certain masculinity, which actively separates her from rote ideas of femininity."[61] The othering of Michonne, as something, not someone, outside of the male-female binary naturalizes the need for suspicion and concern with regards to black bodies. That in both the comics and the television series she keeps chained walkers positions her as living among the monstrous and thus is somewhat monstrous herself. When, in the comics, Michonne is tortured and raped by the Governor, she extracts a brutal revenge. For Brooks, "Michonne is raped to emphasize her femininity" that seemingly could not otherwise be established. That she takes violent revenge demonstrates her warrior persona. However, Brooks sees that, more so, Michonne's rape and revenge "lazily relies on the creative myth of the strong black woman to show Michonne is 'a machine' for whom sympathy and complexity need not exist," for she seemingly lacks capacity for the complex expression of emotion.[62]

The Michonne in the show *The Walking Dead* also comes into conflict with the Governor (David Morrissey), but the rape-revenge story does not take place. The Governor, instead, threatens to rape Maggie. Maggie is certainly a more established character than Michonne at this point in the series, someone the audience has established a relationship with. However, Sujata Moorti argues that when rape is seen or reported on television, the rape of white women and the rape of black women is framed differently. Moorti states that when "the rape coverage is concerned with nonwhite participants, the news tends to foreground race-based assumptions of sexuality," but when "the coverage is concerned with white participants, the news fore-grounds gender-based assumptions of sexuality."⁶³ For Moorti this framing is a consequence of deeply ingrained attitudes not only about race but to gender: "Patriarchal understandings present rape as anomalous behavior, and the rapist is understood to be pathologically abnormal. Feminists, on the other hand, emphasize the structural conditions that engender sexual assault, such as the institutions and structures that stratify men and women into socially defined gender roles, the dominant cultural artifacts that dehumanize and objectify women, and the educational system that effects gender role socialization."⁶⁴ *The Walking Dead* demonstrates Moorti's point. The Governor is represented as an anomaly and his actions are attributed exclusively to him. There are other incidents of rape, or attempted rape, in the show, but they are infrequent and linked to characters that are presented as villains. Perhaps the show's unwillingness to subject Michonne to sexual assault suggests a recognition that there are more complex ways in the postapocalypse to explore identity and disempowerment.

However, Samaa Abdurraqib claims that the removal of Michonne's rape does not, initially, afford her character a different position in the group from that which she has in the comics: "Michonne's character struggles against a dense history of stereotypical depictions of black womanhood that attempt to categorize her as one simplistic type: the Angry Black Woman."⁶⁵ For Abdurraqib, in Michonne's first two seasons in the show, her dominant characteristics are "defiance and recalcitrance," and that, through her "interactions with other characters, we come to see her as someone who is irreconcilably difficult."⁶⁶ The argument here is that this not the case and Michonne's position in the group is a consequence of Rick's reaction to and suspicion of her. In many of her interactions with Rick and other characters, Michonne demonstrates a desire to build relationships and integrate with the group. Michonne's position on the fringe, despite her obvious value, can be attributed more to Rick's fear of what she represents than to her own interpersonal shortcomings.

The beginning of season 3 takes place some eight months after the end of season 2. Michonne and Andrea have seemingly survived the duration of this period by themselves, moving from one derelict dwelling to another, continually scavenging for food. In "Seed" (3.1) Andrea is clearly unwell, barely able to keep moving. Michonne is still with her. Andrea sees that she could be a liability and says, "You should go . . . I'll hold you back." The situation is dire, yet Michonne remains loyal. However, in "Walk with Me" (3.3) it is clear that Michonne has divulged little about her past and that the relationship between the two, while close, was forged in present circumstances. When Andrea and Michonne are recuperating at Woodbury, Andrea asks Michonne about the walkers she kept: "Those walkers were with us all winter long, protecting us, and you took them out without any hesitation." Michonne stifles emotion, but not out of defiance; this presents as unprocessed trauma, the recognition of which could derail her survival. Andrea's questioning of Michonne seems grounded in more than not knowing who her walker protectors were. bell hooks argues that part of the divide between white feminism and black feminism is that white women do not treat black women as equals, "though they expected us to provide firsthand accounts of black experience, they felt it was their role to decide if these experiences were authentic."[67] In the proceeding months, it seems Michonne, for Andrea, served a functional purpose; she kept Andrea alive. Once back in something resembling normal society—Woodbury—Andrea returns to belief in the patriarch (the Governor) and views Michonne with misgivings. hooks writes, "They make us the 'objects' of their privileged discourse on race. As 'objects,' we remain unequals, inferiors."[68] Andrea recalls not Michonne's consideration and support during their time alone, but, back in a predominately white population, sees Michonne as distant and dangerous.

When Michonne decides to leave Woodbury in "Say the Word" (3.5), Andrea decides to remain. Andrea's trust in the Governor and their burgeoning relationship is of more importance than Michonne's feeling of trepidation. Andrea positions patriarchy as more recognizable than female blackness, thus reinforcing Michonne's otherness not only in comparison to whiteness but in comparison to femaleness.

When Michonne joins Rick's group at the prison, Rick, like Andrea and the Governor, is seemingly unable to reconcile Michonne's actions with his preapocalypse conditioning. Certainly, Michonne attempts to connect with those at the prison, despite their reluctance. In "Clear" (3.12), while on a supply run with Rick and Carl, Michonne helps Carl retrieve a photo of his parents from a walker-infested café in Rick's hometown and then saves him from a walker. This moment leads Carl to later tell Rick, "I think she might be one of us." Michonne even speaks directly to Rick about his recent behavior as he hallucinated his dead wife, Lori (Sarah Wayne Callies), telling him, "I used to talk to my dead boyfriend. It happens." These examples challenge Abdurraqih's description of Michonne as someone unknown and without motivation. However, despite Michonne seeking to bond with the group, Rick still sees her as dangerous.

When Rick and the Governor meet to try and work a truce in "Arrow on the Doorpost" (3.13), the Governor says that if Rick surrenders Michonne to him then there will be no violence between the groups. Rick talks the plan over with Hershel, who makes the point, "He'll kill her," but this is something Rick is aware of. He responds, "And then kill us anyway . . . But what if he doesn't?" In "This Sorrowful Life" (3.15) Rick has decided he will indeed sacrifice Michonne despite Hershel turning his back on the plan. Rick approaches Daryl and claims of the plan, "It's the only way. No one else knows." Daryl also feels the plan inappropriate, stating, "Just ain't us, man," but he agrees to help. Even the reemerged Merle, a brutal man whom Rick has allowed back into the group despite his recent kidnapping and torturing of Glenn—as well as his supporting role while the Governor threatened a kidnapped Maggie with sexual assault—is surprised by Rick's decision. Merle states, "You go on. Give him that girl. He ain't gonna kill her, you know. He's just gonna do things to her." It is clear to Rick, Hershel, Daryl, and Merle that the Governor will rape and brutalize Michonne, yet this is only articulated by Merle. Roxanne Donovan and Michelle Williams see that black "women's long history of sexual victimization, coupled with racial stereotypes, exacerbated their rape experiences. Overall, Black survivors may receive less empathy, consideration, and judicial support than their White counterparts."⁶⁹ The willingness of Rick to sacrifice Michonne, and of others to silently or explicitly endorse such actions, highlights the lingering power and invasiveness of racial hierarchies.

Rick is overcome, it seems, only by the power of prayer. Scenes of him searching for an appropriate tie to bind Michonne's hands is cut with Hershel and his daughters in a prayer circle. Rick later confesses his plan to the group but instead of casting him out or criticizing him, his final reluctance is seen as a strength. Rick proclaims, "I couldn't sacrifice one of us for the greater good because we are the greater good." However, Rick's decision to spare Michonne seems due to the lack of support from those around him rather than moral uneasiness with his role in her sexual assault and torture. The show, however, turns away from this troubling aspect of Rick's character. Even Michonne is not overly perturbed, telling Rick in "Welcome to the Tombs" (3.16), "The deal the Governor offered about me, you had to think about it. You had to, I get it." Michonne's relative passivity is no doubt in part because of her delicate position in the group. Yet it also makes her compliant.

Increasingly Michonne emerges as both resolute and determined, someone akin to what Lusted sees as "the cowboy gunfighter as mythic hero ... whose speed on the draw symbolises his quickness to moral action, whose mental acuity is evident in a sharp eye."⁷⁰ Rick is confronted by Michonne because he recognizes her as a version of himself, and if he acknowledges Michonne as his equal, it invalidates his assumptions about himself as the only one capable of leading the group—indeed, it positions him as in competition with Michonne. Abdurraqib sees that Michonne's introduction to Rick's group is one of tension, and that the "most salient point of tension is between Rick and Michonne, two characters who are, at this moment in their narratives, steeped in distrust and scepticism."⁷¹ Michonne demands that the narrative of the lone figure arriving to help preserve a version of civilization no longer be predominately male or white female.

When Rick and Michonne begin a sexual relationship in the aptly titled "Next World" (6.10), while establishing a new life in Alexandria, it represents the merging of the past and the future. This is foreshadowed in "Forget" (5.13) when Rick and Michonne are appointed as Alexandria's police force. Michonne, dressed in a police uniform, stands uncomfortably in front of a mirror. She resembles Rick in the first episode of the series. She is his skin, having consumed part of his identity. Interestingly, as Rick eventually embraces the idea of challenging Negan and the Saviors after the loss of Glenn and Abraham, Michonne encourages him, in "Say Yes" (7.12), to consider overseeing the world that comes after. It seems she is expressing a desire for the return of the white male patriarch, and perhaps her love for Rick is her motivation. Yet the world of *The Walking Dead* has been littered with patriarchs and their kingdoms, the Governor and Woodbury, Gareth and Terminus, Negan and the Saviors, all of whom craved power and control. Rick's arrogance as a leader has led to unnecessary loss. He declines Michonne's offer and makes a counteroffer: "But the two of us, you and me, reordering things together, I want that." Rather than a token gesture, this is perhaps recognition of the fact that he is incomplete as a leader because he lacks a diverse understanding and experience of the world.

Michonne provides a tangible example of what Butler argues in *Undoing Gender*, that to "assume that gender always and exclusively means the matrix of 'masculine' or 'feminine' is precisely to miss the critical point that production of that coherent binary is contingent, that it comes at a cost" because "those permutations of gender which do not fit the binary are as much a part of gender as its most normative instance."[72] Butler sees a danger in that the "conflation of gender with masculine/feminine, man/woman, male/female, thus performs the very naturalization that the notion of gender is meant to forestall."[73] Michonne's position in *The Walking Dead* is one in which she challenges the gendered division of the past and the limiting binary of male and female, and she does so without regard for gender or race, promising the founding of a new world.

Conclusion

The Walking Dead continues to challenge the exclusionary gender and race hierarchies that dominate the genre of the western. Through the emergence of characters such as Glenn and Carol and Michonne, the show demonstrates that it is not bound to the past, but it is not entirely free from it, either. Yet the neofrontier in *The Walking Dead* is an inclusive and promising space that reflects a diversity of experiences.

While *The Walking Dead* goes some way to promoting what might be seen as identity diversity, in that characters have seemingly begun a journey outside the gender matrix and are beginning to find some kind of personhood, it is far from a cohesive and stable narrative. Too often deeply troubling attitudes pertaining to historically marginalized groups return via protagonist Rick Grimes and are too easily dismissed by the show. However, Rick Grimes increasingly shows a willingness to recognize others, such as Carol and Maggie, as leaders. If Rick Grimes as the determined representative of traditional patriarchal power can genuinely shed his former self, then, perhaps, anyone else can, too.

There is, in *The Walking Dead*, an ongoing, but difficult, and sometimes delayed, reconfiguration of power, leadership, and heroism where seemingly the old rules are increasingly irrelevant. It is, in a sense, a performance-based context. The question as to whether this is a utopia wrapped inside a dystopia is uncertain. Certainly, the capacity for the show to revert to preapocalypse norms remains a possibility, but, strangely, the future, in a world decimated by the walking dead, is one that is hopeful.

NOTES

1. Hewitson, "Undead and Un-American," 167.
2. Glawson, "Post-Apocalyptic Cinema," 79.
3. Miller, *Mad Max*.
4. Sugg, "*Walking Dead*," 800.
5. Perez, *Material Ghost*, 244.
6. Gurr, "Masculinity, Race, and the (Re?) Imagined," 33.
7. Sandefur, "Anarchy, State, and Zombie Dystopia," 53.
8. Sugg, "*Walking Dead*," 795–96.
9. Rees, "Frontier Values Meet Big-City Zombies," 82–83.
10. Wilsey, "Our Country Is Destined," 9.

11. Gurr, "Masculinity, Race, and the (Re?) Imagined," 33.
12. French, *Westerns and Westerns Revisited*, 30.
13. Lenihan, *Showdown*, 15.
14. Slotkin, *Gunfighter Nation*, 234.
15. Lamont, *Westerns*, 1.
16. Watts and Rachels, *First West*, 603.
17. Ray, *Certain Tendency*, 75.
18. Lamont, *Westerns*, 3–4.
19. Sugg, "*Walking Dead*," 795.
20. Darabont, "Tell It to the Frogs."
21. Rees, "Frontier Values Meet Big-City Zombies," 82.
22. Darabont, "Wildfire."
23. Darabont, "TS-19."
24. Rees, "Frontier Values Meet Big-City Zombies," 81.
25. Butler, *Gender Trouble*, 192–93.
26. Young, "Walking Tall or Walking Dead?," 61.
27. Rees, "Frontier Values Meet Big-City Zombies," 87.
28. Baldwin and McCarthy, "Same as It Ever Was," 80.
29. Baldwin and McCarthy, "Same as It Ever was," 80.
30. Chou and Feagin, *Myth of the Model Minority*, 162.
31. Ho, "Model Minority," 64.
32. Ho, "Model Minority," 61.
33. Ho, "Model Minority," 70.
34. Nicotero, "Not Yet Tomorrow," *The Walking Dead*, 2015.
35. Cawelti, *Six-Gun Mystique Sequel*, 151.
36. Lamont, *Westerns*, 153.
37. Pye and O'Sullivan, "Dead Man's Party," 109.
38. Halberstam, *Female Masculinity*, 1.
39. Halberstam, *Female Masculinity*, 41.
40. Halberstam, *Female Masculinity*, 110.
41. Gearheart, "Made to Suffer," *The Walking Dead*, 2012.
42. French, *Westerns and Westerns Revisited*, 41.
43. Lusted, *Western*, 253.
44. Lamont, *Westerns*, 160.
45. Bartky, *Femininity and Domination*, 22.
46. Darabont, "Tell It to the Frogs."

47. Greene and Meyer, "Walking (Gendered) Dead," 69.
48. Berk, "*Walking Dead* as a Critique of American Democracy," 51.
49. Bartky, *Femininity and Domination*, 23.
50. Sugg, "The Walking Dead," 799.
51. Knight, *Female Action Heroes*, xiii.
52. Knight, *Female Action Heroes*, xv.
53. Tompkins, *West of Everything*, 61.
54. Peterson, "Competing Tunes of *Johnny Guitar*," 334.
55. Hagman, "Surviving the Zombie Apocalypse," 52.
56. Hassler-Forest, "Cowboys and Zombies," 345.
57. Wadsworth, "Are We *The Walking Dead?*," 576.
58. Greene and Meyer, "The Walking (Gendered) Dead," 69.
59. Lavin and Lowe, "Cops and Zombies," 120.
60. Moyer, "*Walking Dead* Finale Recap."
61. Brooks, "Importance of Neglected Intersections," 469–70.
62. Brooks, "Importance of Neglected Intersections," 471.
63. Moorti, *Color of Rape*, 73.
64. Moorti, *Color of Rape*, 75.
65. Abdurraqib, "'Just Another Monster,'" 229.
66. Abdurraqib, "'Just Another Monster,'" 230.
67. hooks, "Black Women," 141.
68. hooks, "Black Women," 142.
69. Donovan and Williams, "Living at the Intersection," 171.
70. Lusted, *Western*, 152.
71. Abdurraqib, "Just Another Monster," 243.
72. Butler, *Undoing Gender*, 42.
73. Butler, *Undoing Gender*, 43.

BIBLIOGRAPHY

Abdurraqib, Samaa. "'Just Another Monster': Michonne and the Trope of the Angry Black Woman." In *Bad Girls and Transgressive Women in Popular Television, Fiction, and Film*, edited by Julie A. Chappell and Mallory Young, 227–51. Cham: Springer International, 2017.

Abraham, Phil, dir. *The Walking Dead*. Season 2, episode 3, "Save the Last One." Aired November 4, 2011, on AMC.

Alrick, Riley, dir. *The Walking Dead*. Season 7, episode 13, "Bury Me Here." Aired March 13, 2017, on AMC.

Attias, David, dir. *The Walking Dead*. Season 3, episode 6, "Hounded." Aired November 23, 2012, on AMC.

Baldwin, Martina, and Mark McCarthy. "Same as It Ever Was: Savior Narratives and the Logics of Survival in *The Walking Dead*." In *Thinking Dead: What the Zombie Apocalypse Means*, edited by Balaji Murali, 75–87. Lanham MD: Lexington, 2013.

Bartky, Sandra Lee. *Femininity and Domination: Studies in the Phenomenology of Oppression*. New York NY: Routledge, 1990.

Berk, Isaac. "*The Walking Dead* as a Critique of American Democracy." *CineAction*, no. 95 (Winter 2015): 48–56.

Boetticher, Budd, dir. *7 Men from Now*. Warner Bros., 1956.

Boyd, David, dir. *The Walking Dead*. Season 3, episode 13, "Arrow on the Doorpost." Aired March 10, 2013, on AMC.

———. *The Walking Dead*. Season 5, episode 13, "Forget." Aired March 8, 2015, on AMC.

———. *The Walking Dead*. Season 6, episode 7, "Heads Up." Aired November 22, 2015, on AMC.

———. *The Walking Dead*. Season 2, episode 6, "Secrets." Aired November 27, 2011, on AMC.

Brock, Tricia, dir. *The Walking Dead*. Season 3, episode 12, "Clear." Aired March 3, 2013, on AMC.

———. *The Walking Dead*. Season 4, episode 4, "Indifference." Aired November 8, 2013, on AMC.

Brooks, Kinitra D. "The Importance of Neglected Intersections: Race and Gender in Contemporary Zombie Texts and Theories." *African American Review* 47, no. 4 (March 2014): 461–75.

Butler, Judith. *Gender Trouble: Feminism and the Subversion of Identity*. New York: Routledge, 1999.

———. *Undoing Gender*. New York: Routledge, 2004.

Cawelti, John G. *The Six-Gun Mystique Sequel*. Bowling Green OH: Bowling Green State University Press, 1999.

Chou, Rosalind S., and Joe R. Feagin. *Myth of the Model Minority: Asian Americans Facing Racism, Second Edition*. London: Taylor & Francis, 2015.

Darabont, Frank, dir. *The Walking Dead*. Season 1, episode 1, "Days Gone Bye." Aired November 11, 2010, on AMC.

Daves, Delmer, dir. *The Hanging Tree*. Warner Bros., 1959.

Dickerson, Ernest, dir. *The Walking Dead*. Season 2, episode 13, "Beside the Dying Fire." Aired March 23, 2012, on AMC.

———. *The Walking Dead*. Season 3, episode 12, "Seed." Aired October 19, 2012, on AMC.

———. *The Walking Dead*. Season 3, episode 16, "Welcome to the Tombs." Aired March 31, 2013, on AMC.

———. *The Walking Dead*. Season 1, episode 5, "Wildfire." Aired December 3, 2010, on AMC.

———, and Horden-Payton, Gwyneth, dir. *The Walking Dead*. Season 2, episode 1, "What Lies Ahead." Aired October 21, 2011, on AMC.

Donovan, Roxanne, and Michelle Williams. "Living at the Intersection: The Effects of Racism and Sexism on Black Rape Survivors." In *Violence in the Lives of Black Women: Battered, Black, and Blue*, edited by Caroline West, 169–85. New York: Taylor & Francis, 2014.

Eastwood, Clint, dir. *High Plains Drifter*. Universal Pictures, 1973.

Ferland, Guy, dir. *The Walking Dead*. Season 1, episode 6, "TS-19." Aired December 10, 2010, on AMC.

———. *The Walking Dead*. Season 3, episode 3, "Walk with Me." Aired November 2, 2012, on AMC.

Ford, John, dir. *The Man Who Shot Liberty Valance*. Paramount Pictures, 1962.

Frank, Scott, dir. *Godless*. Netflix, 2017.

Franklin, Sidney, dir. *The Good Earth*. Metro-Golden-Mayer, 1937.

French, Philip. *Westerns and Westerns Revisited: Aspects of a Movie Genre*. Manchester: Carcanet, 2005.

Gierhart, Billy, dir. *The Walking Dead*. Season 3, episode 8, "Made to Suffer." Aired December 2, 2012, on AMC.

Glawson, Stephen. "Post-Apocalyptic Cinema: What the Future Tells Us about Today." *Film Matters* 5, no. 2 (June 2014): 79–83.

Greene, John, and Michaela D. E. Meyer. "The Walking (Gendered) Dead: A Feminist Rhetorical Critique of Zombie Apocalypse Television Narrative." *Ohio Communication Journal* 52 (2014): 64–74.

Greenwald, Maggie, dir. *The Ballad of Little Jo*. Fine Line Pictures, 1993.

Gurr, Barbara. "Masculinity, Race, and the (Re?) Imagined American Frontier." In *Race, Gender, and Sexuality in Post-Apocalyptic TV and Film*, edited by Barbara Gurr, 31–44. New York NY: Palgrave Macmillan, 2015.

Hagman, George. "Surviving the Zombie Apocalypse: Trauma and Transformation in AMC's *The Walking Dead*." *Psychoanalytic Inquiry* 37, no. 1 (January 2017): 46–56.

Halberstam, Judith. *Female Masculinity*. Durham NC: Duke University Press, 1998.

Hassler-Forest, Dan. "Cowboys and Zombies: Destabilizing Patriarchal Discourse in *The Walking Dead*." *Studies in Comics* 2, no. 2 (January 2012): 339–55.

Hewitson, James. "Undead and Un-American: The Zombified Other in Weird Western Films." In *Undead in the West: Vampires, Zombies, Mummies, and Ghosts on the Cinematic Frontier*, edited by Cynthia J. Miller and Bowdoin Van Riper, 166–81. Lanham MD: Scarecrow, 2012.

Ho, Helen. "The Model Minority in the Zombie Apocalypse: Asian-American Manhood on AMC's *The Walking Dead*." *Journal of Popular Culture* 49, no. 1 (February 2016): 57–76.

hooks, bell. "Black Women: Shaping Feminist Theory." In *The Black Feminist Reader*, edited by Joy James and Denean Sharpley-Whiting, 131–45. Malden MA: Blackwell, 2000.

Horder-Payton, Gwyneth, dir. *The Walking Dead*. Season 1, episode 3, "Tell It to the Frogs." Aired November 19, 2010, on AMC.

Knight, Gladys L. *Female Action Heroes: A Guide to Women in Comics, Video Games, Film, and Television*. Santa Barbara CA: Greenwood, 2010.

Lamont, Victoria. *Westerns: A Women's History*. Lincoln: University of Nebraska Press, 2016.

Lavin, Melissa F., and Brian M. Lowe. "Cops and Zombies: Hierarchy and Social Location in *The Walking Dead*." In *Race, Gender, and Sexuality in Post-Apocalyptic TV and Film*, edited by Barbara Gurr, 113–24. New York: Palgrave Macmillan, 2015.

Lenihan, John H. *Showdown: Confronting Modern America in the Western Film*. Urbana: University of Illinois Press, 1980.

Lusted, David. *The Western*. Harlow: Pearson Education Limited, 2003.

Lynch, Jennifer, dir. *The Walking Dead*. Season 5, episode 14, "Spend." Aired March 15, 2015, on AMC.

MacLaren, Michelle, dir. *The Walking Dead*. Season 1, episode 2, "Guts." Aired November 12, 2010, on AMC.

———. *The Walking Dead*. Season 2, episode 7, "Pretty Much Dead Already." Aired December 2, 2011, on AMC.

Miller, George, dir. *Mad Max*. Roadshow Film Distributors, 1979.

Moorti, Sujata. *Color of Rape: Gender and Race in Television's Public Spheres*. Albany: State University of New York Press, 2002.

Moyer, Justin. "*The Walking Dead* Finale Recap: Black Man Survives." *Washington Post*, March 15, 2015, https://www.washingtonpost.com/news/morning-mix/wp/2015/03/30/walking-dead-lets-black-man-live-despite-history-of-killing-african-american-males/?utm_term=.bd0db9d078ea (accessed July 4, 2017).

Nicotero, Greg, dir. *The Walking Dead*. Season 5, episode 16, "Conquer." Aired March 29, 2015, on AMC.

———. *The Walking Dead*. Season 7, episode 1, "The Day Will Come When You Won't Be." Aired November 24, 2016, on AMC.

———. *The Walking Dead*. Season 2, episode 11, "Judge, Jury, Executioner." Aired March 4, 2012, on AMC.

———. *The Walking Dead*. Season 5, episode 1, "No Sanctuary." Aired October 12, 2014, on AMC.

———. *The Walking Dead*. Season 6, episode 12, "Not Yet Tomorrow." Aired March 7, 2016, on AMC.

———. *The Walking Dead*. Season 5, episode 12, "Remember." Aired March 1, 2015, on AMC.

———. *The Walking Dead*. Season 3, episode 5, "Say the Word." Aired November 16, 2012, on AMC.

———. *The Walking Dead*. Season 7, episode 12, "Say Yes." Aired March 6, 2017, on AMC.

———. *The Walking Dead*. Season 3, episode 15, "This Sorrowful Life." Aired March 24, 2013, on AMC.

Peckinpah, Sam, dir. *The Wild Bunch*. Warner Bros./Seven Arts, 1969.

Peterson, Jennifer. "The Competing Tunes of *Johnny Guitar*: Liberalism, Sexuality, and Masquerade." In *The Western Reader*, edited by Jim Kitses and Gregg Rickman, 321–39. New York: Limelight, 1999.

Perez, Gilberto. *The Material Ghost: Films and Their Medium*. Baltimore MD: Johns Hopkins University Press, 1998.

Powell, Dick, dir. *The Conqueror*. RKO Radio Pictures, 1956.

Pye, Danee, and Peter O'Sullivan. "Dead Man's Party." In *The Walking Dead and Philosophy*, edited by Wayne Yuen, 107–16. Chicago: Open Court, 2012.

Ray, Nicholas, dir. *Johnny Guitar*. Republic Pictures, 1954.
Ray, Robert. *A Certain Tendency of the Hollywood Cinema, 1930–1980*. Princeton NJ: Princeton University Press, 1985.
Rees, Shelley. "Frontier Values Meet Big-City Zombies: The Old West in AMC's *The Walking Dead*." In *Undead in the West: Vampires, Zombies, Mummies, and Ghosts on the Cinematic Frontier*, edited by Cynthia J. Miller and Bowdoin Van Riper, 80–94. Lanham MD: Scarecrow, 2012.
Riley, Alrick, dir. *The Walking Dead*. Season 6, episode 14, "Twice as Far." Aired March 21, 2016, on AMC.
Robson, Mark, dir. *Inn of the Sixth Happiness*. Twentieth Century Fox, 1958.
Sandefur, Timothy. "Anarchy, State, and Zombie Dystopia: Civilization and its Discontents in *The Walking Dead*." *Reason Magazine* 48, no. 2 (April 2016): 52–59.
Satrazemis, Michael, dir. *The Walking Dead*. Season 5, episode 15, "Try." Aired March 22, 2015, on AMC.
Shyamalan, M. Night, dir. *The Last Airbender*. Paramount Pictures, 2010.
Skogland, Kari, dir. *The Walking Dead*. Season 6, episode 10, "Next World." Aired February 22, 2016, on AMC.
Slotkin, Richard. *Gunfighter Nation: The Myth of the Frontier in Twentieth-Century America*. Norman: University of Oklahoma Press, 1998.
Spielman, Ed, Jerry Thorpe, and Herman Miller, dirs. *Kung Fu*. Warner Bros., 1972–75.
Sugg, Katherine. "*The Walking Dead*: Late Liberalism and Masculine Subjection in Apocalypse Fictions." *Journal of American Studies* 49, no. 4 (October 2015): 793–811.
Tompkins, Jane. *West of Everything: The Inner Life of Westerns*. Oxford: Oxford University Press, 1992.
Wadsworth, Nancy D. "Are We *The Walking Dead*? Zombie Apocalypse as Liberatory Art." *New Political Science* 38, no. 4 (December 2016): 561–81.
Watts, Edward, and David Rachels. *The First West: Writing from the American Frontier, 1776–1860*. New York: Oxford University Press, 2002.
Wilsey, John D. "'Our Country Is Destined to be the Great Nation of Futurity': John L. O'Sullivan's Manifest Destiny and Christian Nationalism, 1837–1846." *Religions* 8, no. 4 (April 2017): 68.
Young, P. Ivan. "Walking Tall or Walking Dead? The American Cowboy in the Zombie Apocalypse." In *"Were All Infected": Essays on* AMC's The Walking Dead *and the Fate of the Human*, edited by Dawn Keetley, 56–67. Jefferson NC: McFarland, 2014.

Afterword

This Is (Not) the End

STEPHEN GRAHAM JONES

There's a hundred ways to write a novel, and probably fifty more waiting behind that, but *one* of the ways, it turns out, is . . . well, it involves this book you're holding, this book you just read.

So, first, have no plans to ever actually write this novel. It's too complicated, it's too naked, it's too obtuse, it'll never work, it's just a bad idea you had in a weak moment one afternoon, it's like all the other fancy bulletproof ideas you're always sneaking into your notebook while nobody's looking. If this premise is exposed to any sort of daylight, it'll turn to smoke.

Which is to say, I had this idea to write a novel about Custer. I don't think I've messed with him since about 1998—I'd decided that even putting him on the page was giving him and the Seventh Cavalry more attention than they deserved. The real way to serve him justice would be to ignore him, to leave him buried instead of always digging him up, trotting him around like a scarecrow.

But this idea I had—*did* it have legs? Surely not.

Still, I'd come back to it every few months, turn it over with a stick to see if it could kick its legs hard enough to turn back over, crawl somewhere good.

It never did.

I wrote three other novels, waiting for this one to maybe find itself. And then I gave up.

You *can* force a book—we all know that, we've all read them—but it's a rough process and it doesn't produce the best product. It's like needing a horse so you dress up like one, run around and around the pasture kicking and neighing and trying to eat grass. The other horses kind of give you the suspicious eye you deserve, and the wolves figure out pretty fast you can't run as fast as you should be able to.

I didn't put that horse outfit on. I mean, *this* time I didn't put that horse outfit on. Instead I wrote one novel I thought adjacent enough to this idea to get me by, and when it became something altogether different, I wrote another novel that was its own complete other thing, so I wrote a *third* novel, trying to maybe think this not-a-novel through. All this in, I don't know, I'm thinking five, six months? None of them were James Michener doorstops, don't worry. Just normal-sized little novels that get in, do their thing, then tip their hat on the way out the door.

So, if you're keeping up: a novel is a turtle, a horse, and maybe a truck and a plumber. But before all that it's a ridiculous impossible unlikely idea that you have to hide and pretend you never thought of. If you don't, it'll die.

At the same time, though? If you wait too long, this turtle-horse-truck-plumber gets more and more ideas and words and books stacked in front of it, and pretty soon you forget you even thought it up at all.

That's where I was when Sara Spurgeon sent me this book to write this afterword for. Honestly, I'd forgotten I said I would, but I also know Sara *probably* wouldn't make this up just to retcon me into some obligation scenario, so I cracked in first thing. This is about . . . the very last week of December, yeah.

Five, six days later, the new year not even here yet, I'd inhaled it. Gone cover to cover, I mean, which I rarely do with a book made up of pieces. The pieces *this* time, though, they were more like parts of a single body, one that, yes, could run around the pasture like a real horse, eat grass all the day long. And, really, this is maybe the best way to come at the West, right? You don't use a monocular kind of approach, you do the karaoke thing, where the mic makes its way all around the bar, until people out on the street are stopping to hear this wonderful cacophony that's somehow rising into a single song.

The West is deep, the West is wide, the West is troubling and divisive and bloody and problematic, but it's also just so much fun to engage like these writers have been doing for all these pages, all these chapters. It's a literary landscape that changes with each rediscovery, each rearranging of the canon, each new way of considering what we thought we already knew.

This book does that. These writers do that. These editors, Kerry Fine and Michael K. Johnson and Rebecca M. Lush and Sara L. Spurgeon, they do that.

I was talking about turtles, though. About ideas dying in the safe privacy of a series of notebooks and torn-off corners of pages.

I wanted to write a novel about Custer, see. But I had no idea where to start, how to do it, why to even try.

So, the first part, like I was saying up there, it's to have given up, to have trashed this bad, broken idea, to just be sitting around thinking that maybe watching a whole lot of *Rockford Files* would be the thing to do. You've earned it, right? Three novels in half a year, with teaching and life and all the usual stuff, that'll hold you for a bit. And how many times has Jim Rockford's smile and kind of seasoned optimism saved your life already? It can save you again. And, really, you're not even in bad need of saving, are pretty happy right now to *not* be writing a novel, there's way better ways to use up your winter break.

The second part, then, is to have Sara send you a book you've already forgotten you said you'd read.

Third, man, just inhale that book, read it all through the week, steal time from yourself not out of obligation, but out of *fascination*.

Fourth, believe in . . . providence? In fate? In just plain old good luck?

What I'm saying is, the key I was looking for to write this Custer novel, it was in this book. I felt like Harry Potter in my invisibility cloak in the library after hours, paging through some forbidden tome, finding a note scribbled in the margin that was both just for me and written completely without taking me into consideration.

I held my place on the page, looked off into the other side of the room, and this novel I'd given up on, it was playing right there. Which kind of sucks, yeah, because who wants to be in the room with George Custer and John Chivington and Eugene Baker—what Indian wants to even be in the same room with a *painting* of them—but I couldn't look away, either.

So, I wrote down the first line or two of that novel, I read another chapter of *Weird Westerns: Race, Gender, Genre*, I wrote a page, I wrote another page, I had a whole scene down now, and by the end this book, I'd lucked into this novel's voice, its delivery method, its shape and its sound and its feel.

It's now the end of January when I'm writing this, and I'm, I'd guess, two-thirds through with this Custer novel, which I won't be calling a Custer novel for long. It's already an Indian novel. But a lot of the letters that make up its long string of DNA, you just read them. I'm calling the book, right now, and I think for always, *Last Stand at Saber Ridge*, which is the first time I've said that out loud, I guess.

But I can, now.

This turtle, it's up and dancing, this horse, can't nobody catch it, this truck, the plumber's at the wheel and its headlights are pointing up at the sky, and it's about to follow, I think.

Thank you, *Weird Westerns*. Thank you, Kerry and Michael and Rebecca and Sara. Thank you to too many people who wrote just the right amount of chapters. Without reading your words, your ideas, your West, I'm not writing this novel I kind of think I was meant to write. I say that about them all, yeah, but I say it especially about this one.

Sometimes the right book finds you at just the right time.

This is that book.

CONTRIBUTORS

JOSHUA T. ANDERSON is an assistant professor of American literature at the University of Saint Joseph in West Hartford, Connecticut. He completed his PhD in American Indian literatures at the Ohio State University and is the former editorial assistant at *Western American Literature, Studies in American Indian Literatures,* and *Poetics Today.* His scholarly work on Native literatures appears in *Inks: The Journal of the Comics Studies Society, Graphic Indigeneity: Comics of the Americas and Australasia, Studies in American Indian Literatures,* and *Transmotion,* and his own "weird western" creative writing appears in *Bourbon Penn* and *Sonora Review.*

JACOB BURG is a doctoral candidate in the English Department at Brandeis University. His current research focuses on how the production of space in popular genre fiction is influenced by, and reacts against, the dominant housing ideologies of postwar America.

JOHANNES FEHRLE holds a PhD in English and American literature from the Albert-Ludwigs-Univertität, Freiburg, Germany. He currently teaches at the University of Basel, Switzerland. His publications include several articles and book chapters on the western in film, literature, and comics, including the forthcoming monograph *Postmodern Gunslingers in a Transnational West: Revisions of the Western in Canadian and American Literature.* Other recent publications include a special issue of *Komparatistik Online* on "Adaptation as Translation" (coedited with Mark Schmitt, 2018) and the edited collection *Rethinking Adaptation in the*

Age of Media Convergence (coedited with Werner Schäfke, Amsterdam University Press, 2019).

KERRY FINE is an instructor in the Writing Programs at Arizona State University. She participated in the Literature, Social Justice, and Environment (LSJE) Initiative at Texas Tech University, where she completed a PhD in American literature. She has published and presented on an array of subjects and authors, including Ursula K. LeGuin, *Sons of Anarchy*, Rachel Carson, and zombies.

MEREDITH HARVEY graduated with a PhD in English and the teaching of English from Idaho State University in 2010, after which she joined the faculty at George Williams College of Aurora University, where she teaches English and interdisciplinary courses that focus on global justice as well as the environment. She's a member of the Western Literature Association, and in 2019 she published on race and African identities in Caribbean literatures in the online journal *Humanities*.

ALEX HUNT comes from a long line of frontiersmen and outdoor types. He earned his PhD from the University of Oregon and is a professor of English and western American studies at West Texas A&M University, where he is also director of the Center for the Study of the American West. He has published books and articles on many topics related to the West, including Southwestern literatures, cattle ranching history, and the atomic West.

MICHAEL K. JOHNSON is professor of American literature at the University of Maine at Farmington. He is the author of *Black Masculinity and the Frontier Myth in American Literature* (University of Oklahoma Press, 2002), *Hoo-Doo Cowboys and Bronze Buckaroos: Conceptions of the African American West* (University Press of Mississippi, 2014), and *Can't Stand Still: Taylor Gordon and the Harlem Renaissance* (University Press of Mississippi, 2019).

REBECCA M. LUSH holds a PhD in early American literature from the University of Maryland and is an associate professor and chair of the Literature and Writing Studies Department at California State University San Marcos. Her research examines contemporary Native American literature and the representation of Native peoples in American literature. She also studies horror works with an eye toward how they intersect with studies of the American West and frontier. Her past publications include articles and chapters on literary authors as wide-ranging as James Fenimore Cooper, Gerald Vizenor, Aphra Behn, Lady Gaga, and Stephen Graham Jones.

ERIC MELJAC earned his PhD from Indiana University of Pennsylvania and is currently an assistant professor of English at West Texas A&M University, where he cosponsors Sigma Tau Delta (the International English Honor Society) and is director of creative writing. His academic interests are primarily literary modernisms, and he has published on twentieth- and twenty-first-century greats such as James Joyce and J. M. Coetzee. He resides in Amarillo, Texas.

CYNTHIA J. MILLER is a cultural anthropologist specializing in visual media. She teaches in the Institute for Liberal Arts at Emerson College and is the editor or coeditor of seventeen scholarly volumes, including the recent *Dark Forces at Work: Essays on Social Dynamics and Cinematic Horrors* (Lexington Books, 2019). She is the recipient of the Peter C. Rollins prize for a book-length work in popular culture, and the James Welsh prize for lifetime achievement in adaptation studies. She serves on the editorial boards of the *Journal of Popular Culture* and the *Journal of Popular Television*.

NICHOLAS WILLIAM MOLL lectures in an eclectic range of subjects at Federation University Australia as well as researching popular culture, history, and gamification. In addition, he is a game designer with Owlman Press. He publishes on science fiction, tabletop games, western icons, and literary tropes.

SCOTT PEARCE teaches English and literature at Alia College in Victoria, Australia, and lives in Mooroolbark, Victoria, with his partner and their children. He received his PhD from Deakin University, also in Victoria, in 2016.

TARA PENRY earned her PhD from Fordham University and teaches American literature at Boise State University, where she is a professor of English. She is a past president of the Western Literature Association and serves on the board of the journal *Studies in the American Short Story*. Her previous essays on Bret Harte appear in the journal *American Literary Realism*, mostly recently addressing Harte's response to the Oscar Wilde trials of 1895. She is working on a book-length interpretation of Harte's fiction.

DOMINO RENEE PEREZ is an associate professor in the Department of English and the Center for Mexican American Studies at the University of Texas at Austin. Her book *There Was a Woman: La Llorona from Folklore to Popular Culture* (University of Texas Press, 2008) examines one of the most famous figures in U.S.-Mexican folklore, plotting her movement from postconquest oral narratives into contemporary cultural productions. Perez coedited the book *Race and Cultural Practice in Popular Culture* (Rutgers University Press, 2018) and has published numerous book chapters and articles on topics ranging from film and Latinx literature to young adult fiction and folklore.

JOSHUA DAMU SMITH is an associate professor of English at the Torrey Honors Institute at Biola University. He received his PhD in English literature at the University of Southern California. His research is in American literature, and he specializes in the nineteenth century, the American West, and the black experience in America. He has a forthcoming publication on Nat Turner and American democracy as a contributor to a multivolume series on the cultural history of democracy.

SARA L. SPURGEON is Professor of Literatures of the American Southwest at Texas Tech University, where she directs the Literature, Social Justice, and Environment Program. Her books include *Writing the Southwest* with David K. Dunaway (University of New Mexico Press, 2003); *Exploding the Western: Myths of Empire on the Postmodern Frontier*

(Texas A&M University Press, 2005); *Ana Castillo* (Boise State Unviersity, 2004); and *Cormac McCarthy: All the Pretty Horses, No Country for Old Men, The Road* (Continuum, 2011). She has published articles in such journals as *American Quarterly*, ISLE, *Western American Literature*, *Intertexts*, and others.

A. BOWDOIN VAN RIPER is a historian who specializes in depictions of science and technology in popular culture. He is the reference librarian at the Martha's Vineyard Museum. Van Riper has most recently authored *Teaching History with Science Fiction Films* (Rowman & Littlefield, 2017) and edited or coedited twelve scholarly volumes, including *Learning From Mickey, Donald, and Walt: Essays on Disney's Edutainment Films (McFarland, 2011)*, which won the Ray & Pat Browne Award for Best Edited Collection (2012).

INDEX

African Americans. *See* black/blackness
African American west/western, 290, 308n5, 342, 352, 365, 361–62, 364–65
Africanist presence, 300, 306, 318, 320
Afrofuturism, 10, 13, 21. *See also* black/blackness; speculative literature
Agresta, Michael, 191
Akinnuoye-Agbaje, Adewale, 175
aliens, 13, 200, 201, 210, 240, 352
Allen, Chadwick, 135, 136
Allmendinger, Blake, 19
alternative histories/alt-history, 92, 101–2, 151–52, 162, 375, 378
American Indian. *See* Native Americans
American Indian Movement, 3
Anderson, Joshua T., 26
Anderson, Shamier, 263
Andras, Emily, 263, 265

Andrews, Scott, 258–59
Avatar (film), 13, 171n10
Ayer, David 174, 186

Back to the Future III (film), 96, 350–51
Badu, Erykah, 22
Baker, Eugene, 436
Barker, Joanne, 258, 268
Barrell, Kat, 265
Beach, Adam, 27, 175, 185
Behn, Aphra, 30n10
Bennett, Haley, 189
Bergland, Renée, 17, 25, 62n63, 63n80, 276, 315, 317, 322–23, 340
Berkhofer, Robert, 269, 388
Bhabha, Homi, 168
Bigelow, Kathryn, 127
The Big Lebowski (film), 11
black/blackness, 20, 319–21, 324, 331; and abjection, 299, 301, 304; and cowboys, 190, 361–62; and disability, 294–6, 298, 301, 308;

443

black/blackness (*cont.*)
and horror, 282n23, 292, 293, 307, 334–40; and speculative genres, 289, 292, 304, 352–54, 358, 359; and superheroes, 314, 329, 331, 336, 352, 356, 353; as the weird, 319–20; and westerns, 19, 21, 22, 28–29, 264, 290; in *Westworld*, 19–22. *See also* African American west/western

blackface. *See* minstrelsy

Black Panther (film), 330, 342

blaxploitation, 331–33, 342, 364–65

Blazing Saddles (film), 68, 364–65

Boethius, 75, 88n36

Bold, Christine, 203, 225n12

Bomer, Matt, 189

Book of Eli (film), 20

Brokeback Mountain (film), 6

Bronson, Charles, 180, 184

Brown, Charles Brockden, 9

brownface, 181. *See also* minstrelsy

Brynner, Yul, 14–15, 180

Buchholz, Horst, 180

Buffy the Vampire Slayer (TV series), 28, 257, 263, 273–76

Bull, Emma, 28, 255–56, 260–62, 266, 277

Burg, Jacob, 28

Burns, Walter Noble, 273

Burroughs, Edgar Rice, 13

Burton, Art, 21

Bussolini, Jeffrey, 241, 245

Butch Cassidy (character), 6

Butler, Judith, 71, 88n17, 90n62, 404, 423

Byrd, Jodi A., 139, 161, 162, 165–66

Calder, Jenni, 184

California, 39–66, 94, 102, 157, 275, 324

Cameron, James, 13

Campbell, Neil, 10–11, 219, 233

captive/captivity narrative, 17, 56–58, 78–79 121, 138, 150, 155, 156, 159, 276, 277

Carrington, André M., 289, 304, 352, 354, 358

Carroll, Noël, 131, 293

Carter, Angela, 9–10

Chaney, Lon, Jr., 125

Chanoine, Alain, 175

Child, Lydia Maria, 44

Chinese communities, 190, 257, 261

Chivington, John, 436

Cixous, Hélène, 81

Clift, Montgomery, 7

Clover, Carol, 23, 132

Coburn, James, 180

Cody, Buffalo Bill, 127, 137, 375, 377–80, 384–87, 389

Cohen brothers, 137. *See also The Big Lebowski* (film)

Coleman, Robin, 23, 292, 307, 336, 341

Collins, Jim, 351

Collins, Patricia Hill, 298

Connell, R. W., 200

Cooper, James Fenimore, 4, 44, 171, 257; and Chingachgook, 5, 280; and Hawk-eye, Natty Bumppo, and Leatherstocking, 5, 6, 45, 445, 257, 273, 280, 283n43; and *The Last of the Mohicans*, 4, 44–

45, 171n10; and Leatherstocking
 tales, 4, 5, 44, 257, 273, 309n13;
 and *The Pioneers*, 4, 45; and
 The Prairie, 44; and race, 5; and
 Uncas, 5
Coover, Robert, 26, 67–91
Cortes, Hernando, 163
Courtney, Jai, 175
Cover, Jennifer Grouling, 94
Cowboys and Aliens (film), 5
Cox, James, 259
Creed, Barbara, 59n1
Creep (film), 132
Crichton, Michael, 14, 15
Crockett, Davy, 272
Crow, Charles, 60n5
Curry, Agnes, 237, 238
Curtis, Edward, 132
Custer, George Armstrong, 164, 378, 384, 433, 435, 436

Dances with Wolves (film), 96, 171n10, 181
Darwin, Charles, 133, 145n73, 379
Davis, Robert Murray, 12
Davis, Viola, 175
"Deadlands: The Weird West" (tabletop game), 26, 92–115; and "Hell on Earth" and "Lost Colony," 94, 108; and "Deadlands: Noir," 94, 99, 108; and "Lone Stars: The Texas Rangers," 94; and role-playing games, 93–95, 100, 104, 110
Deleuze, Gilles, 219
Delevigne, Cara, 175, 177

Deloria, Philip J., 79, 226n25, 257, 258, 272
Dery, Mark, 13
Dexter, Brad, 180
Dillon, Grace, 13, 128
Dippie, Brian, 321
Django Unchained (film), 19, 28, 313–43, 364–65
D'Onofrio, Vincent, 190
double consciousness, 297–98, 302, 303, 307
Dru, Joanne, 7
duality, 322, 323. *See also* savage/civilized duality
Duarte, Tamara, 264
Dubey, Madhu, 21
Du Bois, W. E. B., 297, 302. *See also* double consciousness
Duckett, Margaret, 55, 60n25
Dutta-Bergman, Mojan J., 244

Earp, Wyatt. *See* Wyatt Earp (character)
Eastwood, Clint, 291; and *High Plains Drifter*, 106, 405; and *Unforgiven*, 78, 411
Edgar Huntly (Brown), 10
Eklund, Michael, 273
Erdrich, Louise, 120, 127, 133
Espenson, Jane, 240
Everett, Percival, 125
Eyre, Chris, 124

fate, 68–69, 74–75, 85–86
Fee, Margery, 209
Fehrle, Johannes, 27, 225n8

feminism, 8–9, 265; and intersectionality, 23; and whiteness, 23
Fiedler, Leslie, 220
Firefly (TV series), 11, 20, 27, 231–50
Flying Africans (folktale), 360
Ford, John, 5, 71, 171n14, 177, 180, 199, 206, 207, 210, 224, 351
Fortune's Wheel, 68, 74–76, 85, 88n36. *See also* fate; free will
free will, 68, 75, 84
Freud, Sigmund, 133, 208, 214, 322; and castration complex, 75
frontier, 4, 5, 8, 9, 11, 12, 15, 26, 28, 42, 79, 94, 103, 150, 317, 320, 386, 398; closing of, 1, 137, 241; and darkness/blackness, 321–22; gothic, 40, 45; and masculinity, 6, 55, 67, 71, 74, 84, 87n15, 203, 204, 221, 384, 401, 407, 409; and Turner, 69, 137, 215–16
Fugitive Slave Law, 314, 324, 325, 329
Fukuhara, Karen, 174
Fuqua, Antoine, 180, 188, 191, 192

Gallagher, Catherine, 152, 163
Garcia-Rulfo, Mañuel, 190
Gellar, Sarah Michelle, 274
gender, 69; and authority, 400; as constructed, 71; and emasculation, 76, 85; norms, 71, 75
ghosts/ghostliness, 54, 273, 315, 316, 317, 322, 334, 337, 339–41. *See also* Native Americans, and ghosts
"The Giant Wistaria" (Gilman), 8
Gilman, Charlette Perkins, 8, 9–10
Gish, Lillian, 8

Goddu, Teresa, 60n11, 61n30
Godless (TV series), 22, 32n44, 283n43, 411
Gone with the Wind (film), 300, 334
gothic, 9, 17, 40, 47, 125, 275, 313, 314, 335–41
Graham, Elaine, 216
Granade, S. Andrew, 239
Green, Paul, 3, 10, 39
Grimes, Luke, 189
Guattari, Félix, 219
Gunn, Robert, 267

Halberstam, Jack, 23, 49, 63n75, 132, 410
Handley, William, 30n15, 44, 55
Hannigan, Alyson, 275
Haraway, Donna, 122, 123
Harris, Ed, 16
Harry Potter (character), 435
Harte, Bret, 26, 39–66; and "The Ancestors of Peter Atherly," 43, 55–58; and "The Bell-Ringer of Angel's," 41; and "Maruja," 43, 51–55; and "Notes by Flood and Field," 43, 46–51
Harvey, Meredith, 27–28
Hawke, Ethan, 190
Hawk-eye (character). *See* Cooper, James Fenimore
Herland (Gilman), 9
Hernandez, Jay, 27, 175
Herthum, Louis, 22
Hewitson, James, 96
High Noon (film), 180, 334, 363, 366
Hillard, Tom, 59n5

The Hills Have Eyes (film), 126, 132
Holliday, Doc, 255, 259, 260
homoeroticism, 6–7
hooks, bell, 298, 420
Hopkins, Anthony, 18
House, James, 22
House of a 1000 Corpses (film), 126
Howe, Daniel Walker, 57
Huhndorf, Shari, 79
Hunt, Alex, 26, 67–91

Indigenous Futurism, 10, 12, 13, 26; and Native slipstream, 128

Jackson, Shirley, 199
Jarman, Michelle, 294
Jawort, Adrian L., 31n31
Jewett, Robert, 175
Johnson, Michael K., 19, 28–29, 32n43, 232, 233, 290
Jones, Stephen Graham, 26, 119–41, 280; and *The Fast Red Road*, 120; and *Last Stand at Saber Ridge*, 436; and *Mongrels*, 120–41; and *Not for Nothing*, 119; and *The Ones That Got Away*, 121
Jordan, Winthrop D., 319
Jowett, Lorna, 231
Justice, Daniel Heath, 168

Kaplan, Amy, 8
Kelly, James Patrick, 129
Kennedy, John F., 295
Kessel, John, 129
Kindred (novel), 359–60
King, Stephen, 28, 41, 135, 289–308

King, Thomas, 136
Kinnaman, Joel, 175
Koehler, Jana, 8
Kollin, Susan, 241, 242, 243
Kolodny, Annette, 5–6, 69, 155, 156, 208, 209
Kozaczka, Adam, 291
Kristeva, Julia, 76
Kurosawa, Akira, 16, 180
Kvande, Marta, 4

Lamont, Victoria, 68, 401, 402, 409
L'Amour, Louis, 121, 290
landscape, 4, 50–51, 69, 73, 81, 86, 103, 207–8, 210, 222, 223, 242, 291
Langer, Jessica, 247
Lansdale, Joe R., 29; and *Zeppelins West*, 375–96
The Last of the Mohicans (novel). *See* Cooper, James Fenimore
Latinx representation, 14, 181, 193, 264
Lawrence, John Shelton, 175
Leatherstocking. *See* Cooper, James Fenimore
Lee, Ang, 6
Lee, Byung-hun, 190
Legends of Tomorrow (TV series), 348–68
Lemire, Elise, 61n31
Lenihan, John H., 183
Lenni Lenape Indians, 9
Lennox, Charlotte, 4
Leone, Sergio, 291, 292
Lethem, Jonathan, 26, 27, 199–224

Little Big Man (film), 5, 171n10
Lonely Are the Brave (film), 11
Lone Ranger (character), 6, 135–36; and Tonto, 6, 135–36
Lopez, Barry, 129–30, 140
Lott, Eric, 322
Lugosi, Bela, 124
Lush, Rebecca M., 28, 30n10, 32n42, 61n29, 138–39

The Magnificent Seven (1960 film), 6, 16, 102, 180, 181–85, 354
The Magnificent Seven (2016 film), 19, 27, 188–92
Mahmood, Mamdani, 236
A Man Called Horse (film), 181
Mandala, Susan, 239
manifest destiny, 105–6, 155, 156, 184, 234, 236, 242, 274, 291, 316, 322, 380, 382, 387, 389, 400; and Bret Harte, 42, 46, 50–51; and *Ghost Town* (Coover), 69, 73–75, 84, 93; and Native American texts, 129, 153, 159, 166; and *Zeppelins West* (Lansdale), 29, 380, 382, 387, 389
The Man Who Shot Liberty Valance (film), 362, 411
Marion, Frances, 8
Marks, Deborah, 294
Marsden, James, 22
Marsters, James, 276
McCammon, Robert, 129
McCarthy, Cormac, 79, 84, 137; and *Blood Meridian*, 85, 87n1
McClarnon, Zahn Tokiya-ku, 18

McClintock, Anne, 156
McCullers, Carson, 199
McQueen, Steve, 180
McQueen, Thelma "Butterfly," 300
Meljac, Eric, 26, 67–91
Merchant, Carolyn, 69
Micheaux, Oscar, 19
Middle Passage, 155, 302, 305
Miller, Cynthia J., 29, 109, 266, 270, 314
minstrelsy, 292, 314, 316, 319–20, 322–23, 325–27, 328, 331–34, 337, 343
miscegenation, 46, 214
Mitchell, Lee Clark, 4–5, 6, 71–72, 176
mixed-race characters, 4, 43, 55, 184. *See also* miscegenation; Native Americans; racial purity
Moctezuma, 163
Moll, Nicholas William, 26
monsters/monstrosity, 12, 26, 29, 42, 108, 119, 125–26, 127, 128, 129; and vampires, 127–28, 161, 274, 275, 276; and werewolves, 120, 122–26, 129–30, 131, 133; and *The Wolf Man*, 124, 129; and zombies, 29, 139, 337, 351, 399, 403, 415, 417
Moos, Dan, 203
Morrison, Toni, 125, 289, 300, 316–19, 320. *See also* Africanist presence
Mulvey, Laura, 80

Nama, Adilifu, 292, 331, 353

Native Americans: and blood quantum, 133, 271; and captivity narratives, 17, 55; and ghosts, 17–18, 19, 273, 275–76, 315, 315; Hollywood stereotypes of, 15, 31n34, 124, 126, 185, 236, 281n1; and Indian princess trope, 79; mixed-blood/cross-blood, 122, 123, 125, 139; and mystic stereotype, 16, 17, 18, 98, 187, 209; and noble savage trope, 4, 27, 99, 123, 209, 216, 245; and settler binary, 99, 107, 256, 267, 316, 322–23; and terminology, 2–3, 30–31n3, 31n34; and trickster characters/hermeneutics 12, 128, 150–51, 154, 159, 160, 166, 168, 169; and "Vanishing Indian"/vanishing race, 6, 13–14, 17, 27, 28, 209, 210, 215, 268, 276, 278, 366; and *Westworld*, 15–19. *See also* Indigenous Futurism; surrogate Indians

Near Dark (film), 127–28

neo-slave narrative, 28, 313, 329, 341, 359

Newton, Thandie, 20

Nugent, Frank S., 206

outer space. *See* space (outer)

outlaws, 4, 12, 14, 93, 127, 175, 177. *See also Suicide Squad* (film)

Palmer, Lorrie, 176

Pasdar, Adrian, 127

passing narratives, 20, 260, 278

The Passion of New Eve (Carter), 9–10

Patterson, Orlando, 299

Paxton, Bill, 127

Peacock, James, 216, 222, 223

Pearce, Scott, 29

Penry, Tara, 26

Perez, Domino, 27

The Pioneers (novel), 4

Portis, Charles, 199

the postapocalyptic, 12, 291

the postracial, 20, 125, 129, 248, 359

the post-western, 10, 127, 128, 218, 233, 238, 239

Pratt, Chris, 190

Proulx, Annie, 7

queer representation 23–24, 263, 264, 265; and "bury your gays" trope, 7, 265; and gay cowboys, 6–7; and homophobia, 7; and sex reassignment, 10

Rabb, J. Douglas, 238

racial purity, 43–46, 52, 58, 214, 337

redface, 316, 322. *See also* minstrelsy

Red River (film), 7, 24

Reeves, Bass, 21, 22, 264, 348, 361–67

regeneration, through violence, 15, 74, 203, 304, 316

reproduction, and parthenogenesis, 10

Rhys, Jean, 199

Richardson, J. Michael, 238
Riders of the Purple Sage (film), 7
Rieder, John, 11–12
Rio Bravo (film), 4
Roanhorse, Rebecca, 12, 31n31, 280; and *Trail of Lightning*, 12–13, 14
Robbie, Margot, 175
Rockford Files (TV show), 435
Roddenberry, Gene, 5
Roosevelt, Theodore, 132, 203
Roth, Marty, 207
Rouse, Eddie, 16
Rowlandson, Mary, 30n9, 122, 155, 277, 283n43
Ruffin, Herbert, 19
Ruiz de Burton, Maria Amparo, 62n59

Said, Edward, 249
Saldívar, Ramón, 125
Sanders, William, 26, 27, 150–70
Sandweiss, Martha, 72
Sarsgaard, Peter, 188
savage/civilized duality, 4–5, 99, 107, 123, 154, 160, 193, 232, 233, 246, 258, 290, 322, 383. *See also* Native Americans, and settler binary
Scarborough, Dorothy, 8
Scharnhorst, 55–56, 59n4, 63n77
Scrofano, Melanie, 263, 265
The Searchers (film), 5, 27, 68, 177, 181, 199, 200, 206, 207, 210, 214, 223
Sedgwick, Eve Kosofky, 7
Sensmeier, Martin, 190
Serenity (film), 27, 231–50
settler colonialism, 212, 223, 250, 257, 259, 276, 280; and classic westerns, 8, 150, 154; in contemporary U.S., 233–34, 249; and gender, 208–9, 210, 258; and global imperialism, 242–44, 247–48; postcolonial, 241, 246; and race, 167, 211, 239–40, 256; and racialized violence, 18; and as romanticized myth, 5, 28, 208–9, 222; and space 201, 235–36, 238
Seven Samurai (film), 16, 102, 180
Shakespeare, William, 9, 339
Shane (book), 7
Shane (film), 177, 298
Shaviro, Steve, 241
Shelley, Mary, 126
Silko, Leslie Marmon, 126
Silverblatt, Michael, 219
slave narrative, 155, 326, 330, 360. *See also* neo-slave narrative
slavery, 134, 154, 158, 159–60, 161, 232–33, 276, 299, 302, 322, 324–26, 333–35, 339, 343, 359–60. *See also* Fugitive Slave Law; neo-slave narrative; slave narrative; social death
Slotkin, Richard, 15, 30n9, 74, 102, 106, 155, 266, 267, 273, 274, 295, 304, 315, 318–22, 333, 401
Smith, Beau, 263, 269, 271, 272
Smith, Joshua D., 28
Smith, Will, 175

social death, 299, 325, 335, 337
space (outer), 2, 5, 11, 26, 27, 137, 201, 231, 235, 242
space aliens. *See* aliens
speculative literature, 9
Spillers, Hortense, 299
Spurgeon, Sara, 4, 27, 234, 243, 245
Stagecoach (film), 4, 71, 87n15, 171n10, 180, 206
Star Trek (TV series), 5, 6, 239, 350
Star Trek: Deep Space Nine (TV series), 353–54
Star Wars (film), 137, 142n11
Stedman, Raymond, 98
Sterling, Bruce, 128
Stowe, Harriet Beecher, 28, 313–43
Stratton, Billy J., 29n3, 123, 124, 129
Sturges, John, 180, 185, 189
Sugg, Katherine, 398, 413
Suicide Squad (film), 27, 174–81, 185–88
Sundance Kid (character), 6
superheroes, 27, 29, 314, 328–31, 336, 342, 348, 355–58
supernatural, 8, 9, 39, 52, 99, 263, 282n23, 291, 315, 331, 334, 336, 338; and interracial relationships, 26; and monsters, 93–95, 107–9, 270; and Native Americans, 99, 107, 174, 177
surrogate Indians, 27–28, 256, 257, 258; and *Firefly*, 236–38, 240; and *Girl in Landscape*, 200, 201, 210, 217–18, 225n9; and *Territory* (Bull) 260, 267; and *Westworld*, 18; and "Wynonna Earp" (comic), 263, 271, 279; and *Wynonna Earp* (TV), 273, 276, 277
survivance, 138, 275
Sutherland, Sharon, 248
Suvin, Darko, 303
Swan, Sarah, 248

TallBear, Kim, 133
Tarantino, Quentin, 28, 313–43
television, 135, 231–50, 255–80, 349–68, 397–424
The Texas Chain Saw Massacre (film), 126, 127, 132, 135
Thawley, Tod, 275
They Die by Dawn (film), 22
Thomas, Jeffrey, 39, 59n1
Thompson, Tessa, 20
Thoreau, Henry David, 72
Timeless (TV series), 22, 348–68
time travel, 349–68
Tolkien, J. R. R., 291, 292
Tombstone (film), 6
Tompkins, Jane, 3–4, 67–68, 225, 414
Tonto (character), 6, 135–36
Trachtenberg, Alan, 257
tragic mulatta, 5
transmotion, 122, 124, 127, 131, 139, 140, 141, 167, 168
True Grit (film), 4, 411
Turner, Frederick Jackson, 69, 73, 137, 215–16
Twilight Saga (films), 123

Uncle Tom's Cabin. *See* Stowe, Harriet Beecher
Upadhyay, Nishant, 240

Van Riper, A. Bowdoin, 29, 109, 266, 270
Varner, Paul, 7
Varun, Saranga, 264
Vaughn, Robert, 180
Veracini, Lorenzo, 234, 239, 248, 249
The Virginian (novel), 7, 68
Vizenor, Gerald, 2, 13, 122, 125, 126, 128, 129, 138, 150, 154, 160, 167, 192, 257, 272

The Walking Dead (TV series), 29, 397–431
Wallach, Eli, 181
Washington, Denzel, 19, 20, 189
Wayne, John, 4, 5, 7, 27, 87, 121, 199, 200, 205, 206, 224, 290, 407, 414; and Ethan Edwards, 5, 177, 206, 225n15; and *Red River*, 7; and *The Searchers*, 5, 27, 171n10, 199, 200
Weaver, Jace, 151
weird western (defined), 2, 3, 9, 39, 68, 96, 314–15, 398
weird western comics, 255, 256, 357. *See also* Wynonna Earp (comic books)
Weiss, Margaret, 82
Welch, James, 125
Wells, H. G., 12, 351
"west cure," 15, 132

the West as feminine, 69
westerns: classic, 1, 5–8, 13, 27, 39, 107–9, 137, 150–51, 155, 159, 200, 214, 224, 330, 348, 363, 366; revisionist, 5, 107, 109, 218, 225n8, 260, 292, 390
Westworld (film), 14–15, 24
Westworld (TV series), 1, 7, 14–25, 132, 137; black/blackness in, 19–22; colorblindness in, 15, 24; depiction of Native Americans in, 15–19; and gender and sexuality, 22–24; and race, 15–22; sexual violence in, 22–23
Whedon, Joss, 27, 231–50
Whitehead, Colson, 125
whiteness, 49, 106, 159, 181, 203, 384, 386, 400–401, 420; and interracial marriage, 44–45; in relation to blackness, 302, 316–17, 335, 339, 341, 352, 420; and Wild West shows, 384, 386
The Wild Bunch (film), 6, 411
Wild West Show, 29, 137
Williams, Leah, 192
Willmore, Allison, 192
The Wind (1928 film), 8–9
The Wind (2018 film), 8
The Wind (novel), 8
Wister, Owen, 203
Wolfe, Patrick, 208, 240
women: and feminist studies of westerns, 8; and sexual role reversal, 70; and prominent roles in westerns, 8, 68, 262, 278; as narrators in westerns s, 203

Wood, Evan Rachel, 20
Wood, Natalie, 199
Wright, Jeffrey, 20
Wright, Michelle, 302, 306
Wyatt Earp (character), 103, 255, 259, 260, 263, 272, 276
Wynonna Earp (comic books), 255, 256, 263, 269–70, 271–73, 278–80

Wynonna Earp (TV series), 22, 28, 255, 256, 262–65, 269–70, 273–74, 276–78

"The Yellow Wallpaper" (Gilman), 8
Young, Alex Trimble, 234, 249

Zombie, Rob, 126

IN THE POSTWESTERN HORIZONS SERIES

Dirty Wars: Landscape, Power, and Waste in Western American Literature
John Beck

Post-Westerns: Cinema, Region, West
Neil Campbell

The Rhizomatic West: Representing the American West in a Transnational, Global, Media Age
Neil Campbell

Weird Westerns: Race, Gender, Genre
Edited by Kerry Fine, Michael K. Johnson, Rebecca M. Lush, and Sara L. Spurgeon

Positive Pollutions and Cultural Toxins: Waste and Contamination in Contemporary U.S. Ethnic Literatures
John Blair Gamber

Dirty Words in Deadwood: *Literature and the Postwestern*
Edited by Melody Graulich and Nicolas Witschi

True West: Authenticity and the American West
Edited by William R. Handley and Nathaniel Lewis

We Who Work the West: Class, Labor, and Space in Western American Literature
Kiara Kharpertian
Edited by Carlo Rotella and Christopher P. Wilson

Captivating Westerns: The Middle East in the American West
Susan Kollin

Postwestern Cultures: Literature, Theory, Space
Edited by Susan Kollin

Westerns: A Women's History
Victoria Lamont

Manifest and Other Destinies: Territorial Fictions of the Nineteenth-Century United States
Stephanie LeMenager

*Unsettling the Literary West:
Authenticity and Authorship*
Nathaniel Lewis

*Morta Las Vegas: CSI and the
Problem of the West*
Nathaniel Lewis
and Stephen Tatum

*Late Westerns:
The Persistence of a Genre*
Lee Clark Mitchell

*María Amparo Ruiz de Burton:
Critical and Pedagogical Perspectives*
Edited by
Amelia María de la Luz Montes
and Anne Elizabeth Goldman

*In the Mean Time: Temporal
Colonization and the Mexican
American Literary Tradition*
Erin Murrah-Mandril

To order or obtain more information on these or other University of Nebraska Press titles, visit nebraskapress.unl.edu.

www.ingramcontent.com/pod-product-compliance
Lightning Source LLC
Chambersburg PA
CBHW030600230426
43661CB00053B/1787